HEALTH PRO RESULTS

Using Bio-Individuality To Succeed
As A Natural Health, Fitness,
Or Nutrition Professional

By
T.C. Hale
& Two Other Guys

Cover Designed by T.C. Hale & Arthur Angelo

File Version 1.01.1

In Memory of Will Wolfgang Schmidt.

WHAT THE CELEBRITIES SAY

"Working with Tony is like jumping into the arms of your favorite aunt. Except it's not. At all. I mean, his methods work. But it's not like that at all." - **Jane Lynch (*Glee*)**

"I confess to being a full-blown 'gymophobe.' (I still have flashbacks of my mean fourth-grade gym teacher!) Tony actually makes the gym panic-attack free." - **Tom Kenny (Voice of Spongebob)**

"Wait. You mean the short skinny trainer dude with the neon sneakers who writes books about women's menstrual cramps? Did he ever get a single menstrual cramp? I don't think so. The guy who helps fat people get skinnier? Was he ever fat? I don't think so. And what's with the whole fake I don't talk thing? Is it turrets? If he did talk, would it be a string of expletives even I would be offended by? I guess he has a sense of humor. That's something good." - **Betty Thomas (Director: 28 *Days*, *The Brady Bunch Movie*, etc.)**

"You can argue with Tony, or you can do what he says and buy smaller jeans." - **Kari Wahlgren (Voice of Tigress, *Kung Fu Panda: Legends of Awesomeness*)**

"Tony took on my Jewish-Cuban hips and he won! He let me pretend the punching bag was my ex's mom. That was fun and I got in shape too. I adore him but my tush loves him more." - **Brigitte Bako (*G Spot*, *The Red Shoe Diaries*)**

"I always look forward to my weekly beatings from Tony." - **Tucker Barkley (Dance Choreographer: *The X Factor*)**

"So you know that moment when you are just finishing a hard workout with Tony and he says, 'Alright, you warmed up? We can start now?' and then he laughs... I hate that moment." - **Kayla Radomski (*So You Think You Can Dance*)**

ACKNOWLEDGEMENTS

Thank you to my co-authors and collaborators. Without your help and patience, this book would still be a big stack of ideas.

Thank you to my readers, editors and contributors: Alex and Red Donnally, Nina Florez, Elaine Alcala, and James Singleton.

Thank you to my brother, Richard, who is also an author, for his insight into how to not be a sucky author. I don't understand why you haven't checked out his books yet. He writes great thrillers.

www.RichardCHaleAuthor.com

Finally, I'd like to thank you, the reader, for allowing me to entertain myself throughout this book, instead of just getting to the point, even though you may want to be a better health pro right now. I thank you for indulging me.

Big Flippin' Disclaimer

This book is not intended as a substitute for the medical recommendations of a physician or other healthcare provider. Don't be stupid. It's just a book. This book is intended to entertain and to offer information to help the reader cooperate with physicians and health professionals in a mutual quest of improved well-being.

The identities of people described in this book have been changed to protect confidentiality. Even when I talk about John Tesh. That could be a totally different John Tesh than the one you might be thinking of.

This book is written and published as an information resource and educational guide for both professionals and non-professionals. It should not be used to replace medical advice.

The publisher and the author are not responsible for any goods and/or services offered or referred to in this book and expressly disclaim all liability in connection with the fulfillment of orders for any such goods and/or services and for any damages, loss, or expense to person or property arising out of or relating to them. You are responsible for your own health and wellness and the health and wellness of your own clients.

PLEASE VISIT THE AUTHOR'S WEBSITE AT:

www.SixFigureHealthPro.com

Our Online Courses For Health Professionals
www.HealthProCourse.com

Our Natural Health Site for Consumers
www.KickItNaturally.com

Or follow him on Twitter and Facebook:

twitter.com/KickItInTheNuts
facebook.com/KickItInTheNuts
facebook.com/SixFigureHealthPro

You can hear the author's podcasts, *Kick It Naturally*, and *Six Figure Health Pro* by searching iTunes or Stitcher.

TABLE OF CONTENTS

Important Introduction

How To Use This Book

The goal of this book is to teach you how to move yourself and others toward better health. To learn how to help others, you will first learn how to look at yourself and better understand how your unique body is operating. Your participation in this process will make it easier to help others and do some good in the world.

Through finding nutrition specific to your body, you may also learn how to get the type of amazing results that will attract more clients, higher paying clients, and more influential clients. You might not care about working with celebrities, yet every community has influential people. Once you start to work with some influential people in your community, your income can go up AND your ability to create projects that matter to you will skyrocket. If a schmuck like me can connect with some of the biggest names in the country, I can certainly teach you how to attract some influential people in your community. By the time you're done with this book, you will know that, if I can do it, you can certainly succeed in this business. I will not only share how I've attracted clients like Jane Lynch, Kayla Radomski, and even SpongeBob, I'll also share what I've learned by interviewing some of the big names in the health and fitness industry: people like Bill Phillips, Robb Wolf, Dallas & Melissa Hartwig, and many more (I don't name drop often, but when I do, I definitely go overboard. At least, that's what Oprah once told me).

If this is your first time reading one of my books, you may be pleasantly surprised by what you find in these pages. I hear from readers every day who are shocked that it took a comedian to supply them with answers to health problems they have been trying to solve for years. After bouncing from one healthcare professional to another for months, or even a lifetime, most people don't expect a book from a comic to uncover health solutions that are easy to understand. These readers are often even more shocked when those solutions actually work. Every time you are able to help a client improve an issue that they thought they were stuck with, you just might look back and say, "I sure am glad I read that Results book instead of watching more reruns of *Golden Girls*."

Or maybe you used one of my other books to turn your own health around and now you're passionate about creating a career helping others do the same. If you have read any of my other books, some content of this book (as well as some of the jokes) may sound familiar to you. For example, digestion is so important when dealing with such a variety of issues, the chapter on digestion winds up in nearly all of my books. Much of this book will teach you how to look at you and your chemistry. Knowing your own chemistry is the most important factor when dealing with any health issue. In order to learn how to help others, I'm going to show you how to look at yourself and better understand how your unique body is operating. Participating in this process will make it easier to teach others. In each of my books, I have given readers a foundation of information about chemical imbalances in the body, how to test their own chemistry, and how to view the information they find through testing. Those tools and methods reveal what is important no matter what health issue a person would like to see improve. If you already have a good understanding of those techniques from one of my other books, you'll be miles ahead; and you will be able to use this book for health professionals to better understand how specific imbalances can relate to a wide variety of issues that many of your clients may be dealing with.

This book even comes with an amazing bonus—our *Kick It Naturally* podcast. My team and I have covered a wide variety of health topics on our *Kick It Naturally* podcast. Once this book teaches you how to get a better idea of imbalances you or your clients may be dealing with, the podcast can help you better understand why specific health issues may have shown up and the steps that might bring about a good result. For example, if you deal with seasonal allergies, listening to our episode on that topic could provide a better idea of the different imbalances that can exacerbate allergies. Coupling what you learn in this book with additional information on podcast episodes may turn out to be a wealth of information for you and your clients.

If you've already taken one of my advanced health coach courses, or if you've read enough of my other work to have a full understanding of digestion, imbalances, and how the body works, you might be able to skip a lot of the content where I explain all the foundational basics to those reading these ideas for the first time. For my advanced students, I will put all foundational content (the content you may already know), in a gray box. You may choose to skip those sections if you're a veteran T.C. Hale reader.

If you're a first time reader, when you see a gray box like this one, know that the material inside the box is some of the most important in the entire book. As you'll soon learn, to see good results with any health symptom, you must first understand what is causing that symptom for you or your client. Since just about every problem can have more than one underlying cause, to figure out how to improve most health issues, you first must understand how your unique body is operating.

For these foundational sections that appear in almost all of our books, I use this "gray box" formatting to help these sections stand out more. If you decide to read more of my books, this system will help you distinguish issue-specific information from the foundational topics you will have already read in this book. I will use my personal introduction as an example of this "foundational content" formatting.

About The Author

Before we get to any science or business strategy insights, let me first explain why you're reading a natural health book from a comedian. My name is Tony Hale. I use the pen name "T.C. Hale" because if you Google "Tony Hale" you find four hundred thousand pictures of Buster Bluth from *Arrested Development*. If you're unfamiliar with the actor, one of his first big national spots was that Volkswagen commercial with the guy doing the robot in his car. I can remember studying at The Groundlings (an Improv school that churns out a lot of *SNL* players) when a girl in my class told me that her friend's name was Tony Hale too, and that he was the guy in the Volkswagen commercial. I recall thinking, "That bastard's going to call dibs on my name before I do," and that's pretty much how it worked out. I run into Tony around town from time to time and he's actually a super nice guy. The first time I met him, he was shopping at Whole Foods. I walked up to him, didn't say a word, and just handed him my driver's license. "No way!" he said after seeing my name. But, enough about my name already. What about the rest? How the hell did I get here?

I guess, like most natural health and nutrition researchers, my background comes from a professional career in stand-up comedy. I became a natural health and nutrition researcher by necessity. On Valentine's Day 2003, I took my girlfriend at the time to see The Dan Band at the club, Hollywood and Highland. Most of the night, I talked over the loud music. The next day, my voice was gone and it didn't come back. Over the next year or so, 23 doctors, specialists, and surgeons couldn't figure out what the problem was. With each doctor and each medication, my health seemed to decline a little more. After exhausting my way through doctors, speech therapists, natural practitioners, and a six-figure accumulation of expenses, I told everybody to piss off and decided I was going to figure this out myself.

And that's what I did. Over the next six years I did nothing but read books, research nutrition experts, and attend workshops and seminars across the country. As I searched for my own answers, I kept stumbling across answers to problems that my friends were dealing with. I was so amazed to find explanations that I had never heard before that I started to share them with my friends. When I emailed my buddy Greg and explained to him some of the underlying issues that can make a person have to sit on the toilet twelve times a day, he ran some measurements on himself to see what the likely causes were and his chemistry matched up perfectly with most people who have similar issues. He tried the things I showed him and he was able to poop like a normal human, once or twice a day, instead of shooting soup out the back door all day.

As one friend would tell another friend, people kept emailing me and asking if I could help them understand their health issues. But I was working as a personal trainer and didn't have time to teach all those people how to look at their own chemistry to understand why they're dealing with what they're dealing with. That is, until a guy named Jim, who was so impressed with how I taught his friend how to understand and improve his insomnia, offered me $500 to help him, too. That's when I realized, "Oh, this is a business." After all, I would have gladly paid someone $10,000 to help me correct my issue years earlier. That's a lot of money, but it still would have saved me $90,000 and reduced the six years it took for me to start getting my voice back. With this revelation, I started a career as a health coach. I've never advertised, but today I help some big stars and influential people in the entertainment industry better understand how they can use nutrition to improve their health. That is also what I'm going to do with you in these pages. You will learn how to look at your own physiology and improve imbalances by changing what you're putting in your body, so you can teach your clients how to use those principles to create better results in their health. Good results attract more clients.

Before you look at anything I have to say as gospel, I want to make sure that I am very clear on the fact that I am not a doctor and I don't claim to be any sort of doctor or licensed professional. I don't even watch *House*. I used to think M*A*S*H was funny, but that hardly makes me a doctor. What I am is a guy who became fed up with the system and decided I would find my answers elsewhere. I'm just a guy who had no choice but to keep digging until solutions were uncovered. I had no choice because it was becoming clear that I wasn't going to be able to talk again unless I found real answers. If it were anything else, I probably would have given up after two years. But since I was very determined to get my voice back, I was willing to do the work. Remember, a stand-up comic with no voice is just a mime—and who wants to get punched in the face while they're working every day? You may not know this, but it has been statistically proven that 83% of the population would rather punch a mime than watch him try to entertain a crowd. Since I was so determined not to become another "mime statistic," you now get to reap the rewards of my years of research.

So, if you're looking for credentials, buy a different book. I encountered plenty of professionals with credentials, certifications, licenses, awards, accolades, expensive offices... you name it. One guy even had a live ostrich that lived in the backyard of his office complex. (That didn't help, either.) The professionals I consulted had it all. Yet, none of them could help me. As a result of that experience, I find that I'm more interested in the truth than I am in credentials. Over the last 60 years, doctor after doctor who went outside the box to try to truly help patients (by working to correct the actual causes of their illnesses instead of just treating symptoms) have been stripped of their licenses, discredited, and basically run out of town. Sadly, this happens frequently. It seems like every time someone makes a significant splash in the mainstream market with any advances that could help people correct health issues naturally, that individual is discredited so that the masses will go back to spending billions on drugs that only mask their symptoms.

With every book I write, my co-authors and I know this information will spread fast. After all, when people finally see better results for problems they have been dealing with for decades, they talk about it. So we've set up a system where people can learn about their body without having that system discredited. It can't be discredited because I am the voice and I'm telling you right now, I HAVE NO CREDENTIALS. I'm just a schmuck comedian and personal trainer who was willing to dig for his own answers. And now I'm sharing what I've learned with you, so you can dig for your answers a little quicker. Am I a doctor? No. Do I have a license? Heck no. Do we really need one more person following the same system that isn't working? I don't even shave every day, I've filed for bankruptcy in my life, I don't understand what color shirt I'm allowed to wear with brown pants, and I'm writing this book in my boxers. Credentials won't be necessary, as this information speaks for itself. Doctors, nutritionists and health professionals (spanning more than forty countries), who have raved about our online Bio-individuality Coach Course, can attest to the fact that this information speaks for itself.

Though I am not the only author for most of my books, I have been elected to be the voice and will be the only known author for many of our titles. In this book, as well as other natural health books I have written, my co-authors and contributors are made up of doctors, medical and natural health researchers, and some well respected educators who teach nutrition to doctors from all over the world. When I traveled the country looking for answers, I found a number of individuals who have dedicated their lives to this work. I've approached many of them to help me in this effort. Though some have chosen to have their names added as co-authors to a number of our titles, many are keeping their identity anonymous.

Although I won't be sharing the names of most of my co-authors with you, I will share the pioneers from the 1930s and 1940s who first discovered these truths. That was the one constant that I found no matter who I talked to. Most of the experts had studied doctors from the 30s, 40s and 50s, back when a doctor was allowed to think. I'll talk about the work of these pioneers throughout our time together, and I'll even point you in the direction of some of their amazing books so you can dig deeper if you find this information as interesting as I do.

Odds are someone who experienced incredible results with one of our books or courses recommended this book to you. So, my suggestions for you are: (1) thank your friend; and (2) put your trust in the experience of your friend instead of the authorities that seem to be more interested in profit than results. After all, wasn't it Benjamin Franklin who once said, "Though I have welcomed the words from authorities my whole life, it might be time for them to go flog themselves," or something like that?

CHAPTER ONE

Hi

This books is designed to serve three sets of individuals: Those working professionally in the fitness, nutrition, or natural health and wellness industries; those hoping to work in this capacity in the future; and those who simply want to dig deeper into human physiology and the effect of nutrition on our health. If you don't fit into one of these categories, you may have taken the phrase, "don't judge a book by its cover" far too seriously, and maybe you're hoping to find a story about the adventures of a boy and his dog.

In any case, something made you read this book. Are you the guy in the gym who has everyone asking you fitness questions but, once you decided to become a personal trainer, found that nobody wants to pay you? Have you made your own amazing transformation that inspired you to become a nutritionist, but most of your clients don't see the same results? Or are you a health and fitness enthusiast who dreams about earning a living doing something you love?

Maybe you're one of those folks who believes you just need to burn more calories than you eat and you've now worked up to seventeen hours of cardio per week. My guess is that you'd simply like to find some better answers that might allow you to sit down for a few minutes. Perhaps the deeper you get into your research, the more you find that every expert out there contradicts the other and it doesn't seem like anyone can agree on anything. Well, you're right. Nobody can agree on anything; and by the time you finish this book, you're going to understand why.

To kickstart the first chapter of this book I've decided to provide you with a life-changing piece of information that will begin to unravel that very mystery. That golden nugget is this: There is no diet or health-related strategy that is right for every person. Period. No matter what you heard in that "Shake-Weight" infomercial you watched, there is nothing out there that will benefit everyone. Each of us has a different physiological make-up. Our bodies are all operating in a slightly different way. Those subtle differences can greatly alter the choices that are best for each of us. This truth encompasses everything from the type of exercise that might benefit each of us the most, all the way down to the amount of water each person should be drinking. The only advice that is right for every person is to explain that there is no advice that is right for every person (I think I just confused myself).

This concept may be something that you already know. What I hope to teach you in this book is what to do with that knowledge. I will teach you how to look at each person as an individual, get a better understanding of how his unique physiology is affecting how his body is operating, and what you can teach each person to help him see the results he seeks. Think for a moment what that could mean in your life. For years, my personal training clients would come to me with all sorts of crazy ailments and I didn't have a clue what to tell them. "Tony, I can't sleep and it's wrecking my entire life. What will help me sleep?" they would ask. "I don't know, now do some pushups," was just about the only thing I could come up with. Now, when clients come to me with health issues, I can almost always help them improve the problem, or can at least give them an idea of what to investigate further.

Here's a sample list of health issues that you will better understand by the time you finish this book:

Cravings & Eating Disorders
Depression
Anxiety & Panic Attacks
Elevated Blood Pressure
Acid Reflux
Constipation
Bloating
Chronic Fatigue Syndrome
Acne, Eczema & Skin Issues
Elevated Cholesterol

Migraines
Joint Pain
Insomnia
Mental & Emotional Issues
And so much more...

And I don't mean that I'm going to give you a remedy for all these problems. Most of these health issues don't have a "remedy" because most of them can have more than one underlying cause. Instead, we're going to teach you to look at the individual, not at the symptom that the individual is dealing with. When I say "better understand" these issues, I mean you're going to understand what type of physiological imbalances can create problems like those listed above, and steps you can often take to improve the underlying causes. A wide variety of problems can be helped by simply facilitating better energy production.

People all over the world are learning how they can look at their own physiology and understand their biological individuality. These people are learning about nutritional and lifestyle changes, specific to their body, that can help them improve their health and rid their lives of the issues that have been plaguing them. And they're doing it without the help of medications.

Many health professionals are working to create results with their clients without a basic understanding of how the human body works. I find that students of our Bio-individuality Coach Course are pleasantly surprised when they find answers to questions like:

How can I help the clients who eat perfectly all day long yet end up bingeing on a tub of ice cream before they go to bed?

Why did a specific diet work great for one client and make another client gain ten pounds?

Why does my client have so many digestive issues?

How can I help my clients get past their cravings?

Why does my client deal with so many workout injuries?

My co-authors and I agree that, for the most part, the common answers to these questions are all over the map. The reality is this: It's not that nobody has the right answers, it's that nobody is asking the right questions. Not that I've fully examined every diet or remedy out there—I doubt that would even be humanly possible—but it is my experience that every diet and every remedy on the planet can work... for SOMEBODY. However, no diet and no remedy will work for EVERYBODY. It's not really about finding a remedy. It's more about guiding your body into a state where it can function a little more optimally.

When it comes to health, the popular approach is to attack the symptoms. A person is branded by her symptoms. Do shoes come only in one size? How about bras or even contact lenses? No. We look at people as individuals for just about anything they need, except their health. In the world of healthcare, we're a one-trick pony. We're like a 7-11 that sells only Skittles. We look only at the symptoms instead of looking at the person who is suffering from the symptoms. And when our great, great grandkids learn about our health care system in their history classes, they will laugh at us. They will point, and they will laugh... and our only excuse will be that the characters on *Grey's Anatomy* were so dreamy, we just believed everything they said.

This book was written to help you look at your own biological identity, understand how your specific body is operating, and make the necessary changes to help your body function in a more optimal way... so you can teach your clients to do the same thing. The more you can experience this knowledge first hand, the easier it will be to teach others.

Slackers and Geniuses Unite

Everyone is invited to join in. You're going to have the chance to decide what you want to get out of this book. You'll have the opportunity to begin implementing what you learn from the very beginning. Some of you will discover life-changing information and learn how to implement that knowledge within the first few chapters. You may be able to improve health issues of your own without ever reading past chapter six.

I'd also like to welcome any geniuses and those crazy people who read about something scientific and feel like they need to learn about every single aspect. That was me (the crazy person, not the genius). I became quite the researching maniac once I realized there were real answers out there. For you folks, I've included some pretty sciency stuff and I'll provide more in-depth explanations in the appendix section of the book. If you still want to learn more, you can also look into our advanced online Bio-individuality Coach Course, at www.HealthProCourse.com. This course digs deeper into physiology and how nutrition can be used to help your clients improve their health.

Not everybody wants to understand all of the science, nor is it necessary. It wouldn't be the first time someone has said to me, "Hey Monkey Boy, just tell me what to do and I'll do it." With that in mind, know that you will have the choice of using the easy-to-follow methods in this book to test them out on yourself, or you can dig into all aspects of this book and gain a new understanding about nutrition, the human body, and why health issues are so common today.

Why Am I Reading A Natural Health Book Written By A Comedian?

While working at a seafood restaurant as a teenager, I once found a nickel inside a raw oyster. A nickel! It was as if the oyster was saving up to buy a pearl because nobody told him he was supposed to make his own. Well, in the same way that you can find something beautiful—like a pearl—in something so gross and snot-looking—like an oyster—you can also find something unexpected—like a nickel. My point is, I was surprised to find cash inside an oyster, but I was still able to use the cash on my way home that night when I stopped by the Taco Bell drive-through. So, just because you find information on natural health in a place you might not expect, that doesn't mean it can't be useful to you. My nickel helped pay for a Meximelt with no pico sauce, which was very useful to me.

I studied nutrition for twenty years before I came across the information I am sharing with you in this book. I truly thought I knew what I was talking about when it came to nutrition; but since I had my own health issues that were plaguing me, I was forced to do a tremendous amount of research on my own—and I was shocked at what I discovered. Now, you're about to benefit from my need to dig for real answers for myself. As it turns out, many of the keys to your own health are also the keys to creating amazing results with your clients.

Our Books, Shows, And Philosophy

In *Health Pro Results*, I'll be helping you look at your health, body, and nutrition in a way that is different from any other natural health book you've likely read. We're going to teach you how to look at your own physiology because doing something first-hand, and learning through self-experimentation, is the fastest way to excel at any new skill. Instead of just looking at a condition and talking about all the "natural remedies" that have been known to work for that condition, we're going to spend most of our time looking at YOU—the individual. Focusing only on the condition or symptoms is the biggest mistake in the world of health. It's like focusing on the straw that broke the camel's back instead of seeing the inordinate load that needs to be lifted off. With this book, it is my goal to teach you how to offer your clients other options.

The truth is, every symptom or condition can have three or four different underlying causes. That's why so many "remedies" or methods will work great for one person with a particular symptom, but will make another person with the same symptom much worse. Rarely is anyone looking at each individual and the actual cause of the symptom for *that* individual.

Our internationally acclaimed podcast, *Kick It Naturally*, will be a great tool for you to learn more about how to look for the underlying cause of many symptoms. Go to our website, www.KickItNaturally.com. In the right column, click on the orange box, "Previous Show Topics." There is the list of all the health topics we have covered on our show. On each episode we talk about the wide variety of underlying causes that are common for each topic, and how to look at your own physiology to get a better idea of what might likely be the underlying cause for you. This list of episodes will also turn out to be an amazing tool for you. When you have clients come to you with health issues, you can send them a link to the pertinent show and let them know you can help them sort things out once they have a better understanding of their issue.

I placed a disclaimer at the beginning of this book stating that this information should not replace any medical advice, etc. etc. Let's look a little deeper into this topic so you can have an understanding of what you might get out of this book. I don't want you to look at this book like it's going to be a tool to "beat whatever might be ailing you or your clients." It's never a good idea to focus on trying to eliminate, declare war on, cure, or obliviate a problem. But once you see the direction the knowledge in this book can take you, you will see that trying to "beat" something is very rarely successful. Instead, the goal here is to teach you about the body's operational systems and what imbalances might be pushing in the wrong direction when common symptoms show up. Then I'll show you steps that others have taken to move their bodies back to a more balanced operational state. If you understand this objective, you will see that the goal should be to move toward health instead of trying to escape from or beat down symptoms or "disease."

Look at it this way... if you're in a dark, locked closet, there is nothing but darkness. You can't destroy the darkness. You can't beat it down or even run from it. To put your effort into changing that darkness into something else would be very frustrating and time consuming and your friends would say, "Hey, you've been in that closet for a long time... what the hell are you doing in there?" But if you turn on a light, the darkness will disappear on its own. Darkness cannot exist in a place where there is light. You didn't have to do anything to convince the darkness to leave or to stop tormenting you, you just invited something else into the closet that made it impossible for the darkness to exist there. You invited in the light and the darkness went away on its own.

Take The Quiz

If you have not already taken this quiz online or had a friend email it to you, take the time to answer these ten questions now. If you answer YES to any of the following questions, you may experience a boost in your own health and well-being while you work to learn these techniques that can be used with your clients. For some of these health issues, acquiring information about your body's biological individuality could be life-transforming. If you answer YES to many or most of the following questions, you might want to carry this book with you wherever you go—at least until you can answer NO to most of them. Many of the topics covered in this quiz are experienced by a large percentage of the population and these people walk through life believing this is just the way it is. By the time you finish this book, you will know that is not the case. You will know that the issues below can see improvement in almost any individual who is willing to put forth the effort. Good luck on your quiz, I know I didn't really let you prepare in any way. I always hated the teacher who would pull stunts like that.

(1) Do you ever experience constipation or diarrhea?

YES   NO

(2) Do you crave sweet or salty foods?

YES   NO

(3) If you go more than a few hours without eating, do you experience a decrease in mental performance or mood swings?

YES   NO

(4) Do you often burp after meals or feel bloated? (Even just small burps.)

YES   NO

(5) Does your meal ever feel like it's sitting in your stomach like a rock for too long?

YES   NO

(6) Are you currently on any medications or birth control?

YES   NO

(7) Do you frequently pass gas after meals?

YES   NO

(8) Do you have trouble sleeping or is it hard to get out of bed in the morning?

YES   NO

(9) Do you experience any chronic joint or muscle pains?

YES   NO

(10) Do you commonly experience headaches or brain fog?

YES   NO

How did you do? If you can answer no to all of those questions, things appear to be going pretty well for you. But if you answered yes to one or more of those questions, you will likely have some lifelong mysteries solved for yourself by the time you get to chapter six.

A New Light On Health

Let's get started by putting down a foundation. That foundation is to answer the questions that will run through your head for the duration of this book. "Why have I never heard this stuff? Why didn't my doctor tell me this when I was dealing with that health problem? Is nothing in this book true or does my doctor hate me?"

While digging for answers, there was one topic that really changed the way I looked at my health, the choices I was making, and where I wanted to find help. Before I explain this, I just want to be clear that in no way am I saying that the entire medical world is a crapshoot, or that the entire system is more evil than that blonde guy from *The Karate Kid*. The advances and information that medical professionals and researchers have provided are truly amazing and many of them do indeed save and/or prolong lives. Even some medications that result in horrible side effects still provide you with the ability to buy some time and fight off a certain death long enough to improve your health or correct the underlying problem. The only knock on how the whole system works that I cover here is this: We are given only half the story.

With that in mind, here's the piece of information I came across again and again while I was trying to figure out why each doctor and each medication was making me worse instead of better. This is the piece of information that woke me up to the realization that it was time to put my health back into my own hands. Not that I didn't still need help from health professionals, but that I would become a player in the process of understanding what my options really were and what would be best for me. Here it is: *The vast majority of curricula that are taught in medical schools in this country were put together by organizations that were founded by, or are funded by, pharmaceutical companies.* Read that again.

So let me get this straight... The people who make the most money from our being sick are the same people who are teaching our doctors how to make us healthy? I need you to stop and think about that for just a second with the intelligent part of your brain—not the part that listens to what we're taught, to what the media touts, or to what our friends say, and simply accepts it.

How Medications Work

Before I talk about how medications work, please make sure you understand that in no way am I suggesting you stop taking any medications you are currently using. In most cases, medication is doing a job, and the person taking it needs that medication to continue doing its job; so just chucking it in the trash could be dangerous for some people. But once you begin to understand why you're likely dealing with the issues that you're dealing with, and how some people's health improved by making better choices and enabling body chemistry to move in the right direction, then you can decide for yourself if you want to work toward a similar goal. Once you improve an issue by making more ideal decisions, you can then discuss with your doctor the possibility of reducing or removing meds. But promise me you won't try to do this on your own because that's just dumb. If you're currently on any meds, chances are great that you are going to need help from a professional; and the knowledge you receive in this book will be a great starting point to help you make better choices and communicate more effectively with that professional. And you should never tell a client to stop taking any medication. If you're not a doctor, that is not your place and you can get yourself into a world of trouble.

Here's how most medications work. Nearly all pharmaceutical medications are synthetic, man-made substances; otherwise the manufacturer couldn't patent the drugs and make billions because it's not legal to patent a natural substance. However, most synthetic substances that enter the body will be filtered out by the liver and removed. That's the liver's job. So, if you put a drug in, the liver will filter it out; and the drug won't be able to stay in the body and fulfill its purpose, rendering it worthless. To correct this, manufacturers upped the dosages in drugs to overwhelm the liver so enough of the drug can stay in your system and do the job (or give a physiological reaction) as it is intended to do. Well, guess what? It works. The liver can't remove all of it and the drug often corrects the symptom it was intended to correct. Yet it does so at the cost of punching your liver in the mouth with every dose. Not only can this eventually lead to liver damage (which is why nearly every drug commercial states something along the lines of, "not to be used by those with liver disease"), but even in the first dose the drug is overwhelming the liver and restricting the liver from doing the job it was intended to do: Removing foreign and toxic substances. As the liver gets backed up and can't remove enough junk, the body will often store this junk in fat cells, or deposit it into joints and tissues.

Think of it like that episode of I Love Lucy when Lucy is working in the chocolate factory on the conveyor belt. As the chocolate starts to come in faster than she has the ability to keep up, she starts to cram the chocolate in her mouth, pockets, hat, anywhere she can find a safe place. If the body left junk in your bloodstream, it could disrupt the delicate balance and you could literally die. Since the balance of the bloodstream is so important, the body wouldn't let that extreme imbalance happen so it just stores bad stuff in fat cells or other tissues and plans on coming back later to remove it when the coast is clear. Unfortunately, with our taking medications consistently and constantly punching our liver in the mouth, along with all the junk we put in our bodies, the coast is never clear and we can begin to swell like the Stay Puft Marshmallow Man as we accumulate stored water, fat or toxicity in places where it should not be. So, when we gain weight in this manner, it is actually our body's way of saving our life. Now, weight gain does have its own health dangers when it becomes excessive, but isn't it smarter for the body to gain weight rather than dying this Thursday because of all the toxins left in the bloodstream? This is only one possible cause for weight gain. I go over many more possibilities in my book, *Kick Your Fat in the Nuts*. You can also watch video clips from my upcoming documentary, *Why Am I So Fat?*, at www.WhyAmISoFatMovie.com. This film is scheduled for release in early 2019.

Getting The Most From This Book

By becoming an active participant in the workings of this book, and learning how to run simple tests on your body chemistry, you will be your first client. As you look at the self-testing markers, you get a glimpse into your physiology. You will begin to better understand how nutrition and our lifestyle choices can directly impact our health and how our bodies function. As you put steps in motion to improve imbalances and watch your self-testing numbers improve, you will see first-hand that you have the power to improve aspects of your body that may not be performing optimally.

You'll be able to start off easy as you learn the same simple self-testing techniques you will be teaching your clients. As those procedures become second nature, you can dive into more of the science that these self-tests can indicate. If you decide to jump deeper into the rabbit hole, you can learn about more advanced testing procedures in the appendix in the back of the book. If you decide that these skills can take your business to a whole new level, you may decide to take our advanced online Bio-individuality Coach Course so you can qualify to receive client referrals from the Coalition for Health Education. We will tell you more about this nonprofit organization later.

We're all walking around in these bodies that are pretty much the most amazing mechanisms on the planet, yet we hardly know how the human body works. Pharmaceutical companies bombard us with so many ads that we all feel like we're dying before we're thirty. Ads like, "Do you have hair growing out of the top of your head? Have you ever sneezed? Click here to find out if you may be at risk for face cancer." A freaked-out public is a public that spends money in fear. Education about how your body functions can relieve fears.

Testing Tools You'll Need For This Book

In chapter seven, I dig into simple self-testing and how to look at your own chemistry and get a picture of how your body is operating. Before you get to that, I want to touch on some tools that will be helpful so you can get a hold of them before you get to that section of the book. You can find links to most of the tools and supplements I talk about in this book by clicking on the "Resources" tab at www.SixFigureHealthPro.com. The testing tools are also available at just about any drug store and/or health food store in your area. The supplements I use can be harder to access. I had such a hard time finding effective supplements that I partnered with some online retailers to create a store so I could tell them exactly what needed to be made available to the public. Yes, it can be annoying to spend money on tools to improve your health, but at least you don't have to try forty different products like I did to find the ones that do the job. Plus, as you become a skilled health coach, these are the supplements that will create the best results for your clients. As you'll learn in this book, the results your clients experience will be the difference in your business. As a bonus, we'll even teach you how you can earn a commission on supplements your clients use.

pH Testing Strips

Some drug stores carry these and most health food stores keep them in stock. Just don't let them sell you other "alkalizing" products when they see you picking up pH testing strips. There is a LOT of bad information out there about pHs, so don't waste your time on that frontier like I did. You'll learn the truth about pHs later in this book. A package or roll of pH strips will usually run between $12-18. Health store clerks also sell a lot of ketone strips to those on a ketogenic diet; so be sure they don't send you home with ketone strips when you ask for pH strips. Avoid buying the type of pH strips with two different colored boxes on the same strip. These strips will often show

36

one reading for one of the colors, and another reading for the second color. pH strips with one testing box or the pH testing tape seems to bring better results. You can see the type that I use at www.NaturalReference.com.

Blood Pressure Cuff

This is a great tool that can provide a lot of insights, and one I would recommend buying. The money you spend will be well worth having the ability to monitor your progress. You can get a good one for around $40. Many of you won't know if you're on the right track without one. I like the push-button style that does all the work for you and has a cuff that is easy to put on yourself. It usually does not matter which one you get, as long as you have a way to see if you're improving or if you need to make adjustments. You can also buy the arm wrap in different sizes if needed. The wrist types are okay too, but generally not as accurate and seem to run a little low on the reading. Many drug stores also have those big sit-down machines that allow you to check your blood pressure while you're in the store. These are suitable if a blood pressure cuff is not in your budget, but it sure is nice to be able to check your blood pressure at home when you need to.

Stopwatch

You can also use a common digital kitchen timer or anything with a second hand. Or, I am also pretty sure there is an app for that.

Glucometer

A glucometer is actually a great tool to own and every household in the country should have one. The glucometer is sold separately from the glucometer testing strips because the strips expire, whereas the glucometer does not. You can find a glucometer pretty cheap these days, and the strips vary in price from $10 to $40 for a pack of fifty. If you have friends who are diabetic, ask them if you can use their glucometer one morning before you eat anything. If you find that your blood sugar is in a good range, you might be able to go without this tool for a while if you need to budget things out.

Wha'd He Say?

So far, you've learned:

- Most health symptoms can have a variety of underlying causes.
- I'm a dork.
- The people that profit the most from us being sick are the same people teaching our doctors how to keep us healthy.
- In order to get the most from this book, you need to acquire a few simple testing tools so you can look at your own chemistry and see how your body is operating.

CHAPTER TWO

Helping Your Clients See Real Results

If you're reading this book, odds are solid that you are passionate about health, nutrition or fitness. For many readers, you might be like me and became passionate about this topic because you had to figure out how to improve your own health. Many of you will have already started your career in the health industry, while others are simply testing the waters to see if they want to turn this into a career. Maybe you love to share the things you've learned and you want to find out if it's possible for you to start earning a living doing what you love.

There are plenty of people working in this industry today, so you know it can be done. What I want to do in this book is show you how to do it well. How to not only successfully create amazing results for your clients, but also create a successful and lucrative career for yourself that you truly love. If you've never worked for yourself, it definitely has its perks when business is good. My suggestion? Let's make business good.

Coaches Needed

With the success of our natural health podcast, *Kick It Naturally*, and our books and online courses, we get requests daily from folks looking for a coach in their area. More often than not, we don't have a local coach within a hundred miles of them and their only option is to work with a coach through email. When our weight-loss documentary *Why Am I So Fat?* is released, the flood of requests will be more than overwhelming. For that reason, we're doing anything we can to spread the word and help coaches attain the skills taught in this book. We're going to need all the help we can get.

Before we get into basic principles for succeeding with your clients, let's look at how we got here.

The Argument That Changed The Course of Medicine

Modern medicine has gotten to where it is today, in part, through a scientific and philosophical debate that culminated in the 19th century. On one side of the debate was French microbiologist, Antoine Bechamp. On the other side was French microbiologist, Louis Pasteur. Bechamp and Pasteur strongly disagreed in their bacteriological theories and they argued heatedly about who was correct. It was kind of like watching Letterman and Oprah during their rivalry years.

Pasteur promoted a theory of disease that described non-changeable microbes as the primary cause of disease. This is the theory of monomorphism. This theory says that a microorganism is static and unchangeable. It is what it is. Disease is solely caused by microbes or bacteria that invade the body from the outside. (This is also known as the germ theory.)

Bechamp held the view that microorganisms can go through different stages of development and they can grow into various growth forms within their life cycle. This is the theory of pleomorphism. He discovered microbes in the blood which he called microzymas. These microbes would change shape as individuals became diseased, and for Bechamp, this was the cause of disease; hence, disease comes from inside the body.

Another scientist of the day, Claude Bernard, entered the argument and said that it was actually the milieu, or the environment, that is all important to the disease process. Microbes do change, but *how* they do so is a result of the environment (or terrain) to which they are exposed. Hence, for Bernard, microbes, being pleomorphic, will change according to the environment to which they are exposed. Think of it like picking up a geeky kid, who owns every issue of *Green Lantern* comics ever printed, and dropping him off in the streets of the ghetto to see how he fairs. If that kid wants to survive, he's going to have to adapt to his surroundings. Disease in the body, as a biological process, will develop and manifest dependent upon the state of the internal biological terrain.

Both Bechamp and Pasteur acknowledged certain aspects of each other's research. It has been said that Pasteur was a stronger, more flamboyant, more vocal opponent to the quiet Bechamp. Pasteur also came from wealth and had influential family connections. He went to great lengths to disprove Bechamp's view. Pasteur eventually managed to convince the scientific community that his view alone was correct. Bechamp felt that this diverted science down a deplorable road - a road that held only half the truth.

The story is told that, on his deathbed, Pasteur finally acknowledged Bechamp's work as having some validity and even said, "Bernard was correct: the microbe is nothing; the terrain is everything." It was a 180-degree turnaround from his previous view. With his death imminent, he as much as admitted that his germ theory had flaws. But his admission fell on deaf ears. It was far too late. The inertia of ideas that had already been accepted by mainstream science at that time could not be reversed. Allopathic (drug based) medicine was firmly entrenched on the road that was paved by Pasteur.

The result of that road is today's practice of medicine. When a body is out of balance, doctors attempt to improve the situation, first through drugs, then through surgery. The general effect is to remove the symptoms, not to deal with the ultimate cause of the ailment.

Terrain Of The Body And Biochemical Individuality

As described by Dr. Claude Bernard over one hundred years ago, the terrain of the body is the interstitial fluid that bathes and nourishes every cell in the human body. He believed that the imbalances in this cellular environment affected the entire body, including the immune system. Over time, a compromised immune system had difficulty fighting disease and maintaining health. This theory later developed into the science known as Biological Terrain. By looking at the environment in which our cells live, we can find strong indications about how the body is operating and uncover imbalances that may be causing trouble.

Information is truly the smallest element in our culture; every tangible item on this planet is filled with it. Today, they can take a single hair and tell you the height, weight, sex, and race of where that hair came from because a huge amount of data lies within that hair. Everything is crammed with information. Information is not missing. People who are willing to listen to the information are hard to come across these days. When you look at urine and saliva, you're looking at fluids that are loaded with insight into the terrain (environment) in which the cells are living.

The information you find in urine and saliva is individualized. It is like snowflakes. You will see patterns that are common, like almost every snowflake has six sides. However, within the patterns, the combination is never the same. We don't see two people the same. What you're looking for is to prioritize the information you find. What does this person need most of all? People are so undernourished today, they often need about 2/3 of whatever is in any health food store in America. They are that depleted and often in deep trouble. That being said, they can't just go in and graze on 2/3 of a health food store, that's just not reasonable. By looking at the chemistry of an individual, we are trying to assess what is going to do the most good out of all those items in that health food store.

The popular trend is for people to write about specific nutrients saying, "This nutrient is good for this condition," or "That nutrient should be used by everyone." The bio-individuality is so important because, we are told, 'magnesium is good for everybody,' but there are a lot of people out there who would get worse from a "pushing dose" of magnesium. By pushing dose, I mean an amount higher than you find in a multivitamin. On the other side of this fence, we find those folks who need magnesium desperately and the small amount found in a multivitamin wouldn't do much of anything for them. So we need to look at the individual's biological identity to determine if magnesium is needed at all; if so, which type of magnesium is best. The goal is to look at our own individuality (and our client's individuality) and ask, "What is really needed for this person, and at what dosage?" NOT, "What is the most popular thing to buy?"

Be A Part Of The Nutrition Movement

It's hard to shake a stick these days without hitting someone who has improved his health by making changes to his nutrition. There was a time, not long ago, when the general consensus was that it's not possible to improve major health issues by changing your diet. Up until the beginning of the century, doctors told us that vitamins and minerals only produced expensive urine, and changing your diet was only beneficial for diabetics. It was believed that most health problems were the result of a combination of genetics and bad luck. Since information normally takes twenty years to reach the masses, it's impossible to shake that same stick without hitting someone who still holds these beliefs from twenty years ago. Heck, if a person works in the mainstream medical industry, odds are tremendous that they still hold this belief. However, as one person after another creates one miraculous health recovery after another by changing nutrition, society is chipping away at this old belief system.

I'm not even talking about our immediate community of coaches, clients and followers. I'm talking about the entire world. People are finding answers to depression, type II diabetes, obesity, high blood pressure, and this list could go on and on. This phenomenon has exploded due to the incredible results people are seeing when they change what they put on their plates.

Here's where you come in… There's one problem that is slowing the progress of this food revolution. The problem is: There is no diet that is right for every person. So, when Hank goes on the paleo diet and eliminates his acne and high blood pressure, he tells his friend Peggy she should do the same thing. When she starts her paleo diet, she experiences nausea, bloating and her energy drops like a rock. This occurs because Peggy's body is not operating in the same manner as Hank's. If Peggy moves to a diet that she can't process very well, she will not see the same miraculous changes that Hank saw. But Peggy won't understand why. She will just think that nothing works for her, or that Hank is a lucky bastard and everything goes great for him.

Your role will be to help people look at their physiology to get a better idea of how their body is operating, and to help them understand the nutritional changes that might benefit them the most. When your clients choose to implement changes, you can help them make the correct changes and see good results.

Understand Why They're Paying You

Have you seen the Internet? It's big. There is a ton of information out there that is free for the taking. I'm not saying that all that information is good, but it's out there and it's available. A person can find a lot of her own answers by just knowing where to look. I hear from people every day who have corrected some crazy malady that has been troubling them for a decade by using information that I posted. And I'm pretty sure I'm not the only one who is putting free content out there.

So, if folks are going to pay you to help them, you better be able to help them effectively or they are going to go elsewhere. In this world, there are plenty of professions you can do poorly and still keep your clients. But when it comes to health, if people don't see results, they will move on to something else. I figure I have about ten days for a client to see something change or they're going to be gone. That doesn't mean that I need to fix all their problems in ten days. That's not going to happen. But the individual wants to see an indication that he is on the right track—some type of improvement, some change to a symptom, and/or movement in the right direction of his self-test, physiological measurements.

When you're working with diet alone, those changes will often take thirty days or more to make a difference. That is where we're going to teach you to gain your edge. By understanding physiology and how digestion works, not only will you be able to speed up results, you'll be able to teach others how to look at their physiology so they can see for themselves that the adjustments they've made are moving them toward their goals. Just remember, they're not paying you for your winning smile and clever conversation. They're paying you for results.

Moving Beyond Your Limitations

Yes, I know that getting started as a health professional can be difficult. There are a million reasons why a person might fail or have an incredibly slow start. Yet, no matter what situation you feel is holding you back, know that someone else has succeeded in a similar situation. Many have succeeded while dealing with great difficulties. Once you realize that it's not about your circumstances, it may become a little easier to push through and see better results in your business.

For more than six years, I worked as a personal trainer and nutrition specialist, creating a six figure income, without having the ability to talk… at all. When my clients came into the gym, I would put them through their workout by pointing, using a few signs that would help them understand how many reps I wanted them to do, and occasionally I needed to write something on a notepad I carried in my pocket. I know, right? Why would anyone think that would work? I sure didn't. But it did work. Not only did my clients see results, they kept coming back, and they would even send their friends. Every time I got a new referral, I thought, "You understand I can't talk, right?" Maybe it was simply that they knew for a fact that I wasn't going to yell at them. I can't say for sure. The point is: If a schmuck like me (who couldn't even talk) could create a successful business, you can too.

With my nutrition clients, I had a set of laminated cards, each with instructions or a question printed on each side. As my client explained their circumstances to me, I would simply find the card with the next question I wanted to ask them. After our appointment, I would email the client any information I wanted to share with them. It was far from ideal, but it worked. The good news is: If you have the ability to talk, this process might be a whole lot easier for you. Not only will you be armed with the tools that took me years to find, but maybe you can simply ask your clients questions instead of making them fill out a color-by-numbers treasure map.

Standing Out In The Crowd

There are literally thousands of health pros in my immediate area. I live in Los Angeles, so the competition is steep here. Personal trainers, nutritionists, health coaches, and a variety of other natural health professions abound here. You likely have a plethora of competing professionals in your area as well. The good news is: The reason there are so many health pros is that there is such a large population of people hoping to improve their health. So, how do you stand out? What makes a prospective client want to work with you over one of the many other options at their disposal? The answer is simple: Results.

To help your business thrive, my goal is to supply you with as many ways as possible to help your clients see the type of results that make them want to shout from the rooftop. "Tony helped me fix my explosive diarrhea!!!" is often heard echoing through my neighborhood. Okay, maybe they won't scream about *all* the issues you help them improve, but they sure will talk with their friends about their amazing results. Attaining great results starts with knowledge about human physiology and how nutritional changes can affect that physiology. This book will launch your journey to acquiring that knowledge. But before we get to the science, there are other nuggets that can help you stand out above and beyond other health pros.

Educate Them – The Secret Sauce

"Just tell me what to do, and I'll do it." I've certainly heard my share of this phrase from clients. I'm fine with giving a client the Cliff Notes version of my suggestions because, for some clients, that's exactly what they need. However, I find that the majority of clients who make this request end up seeing zero results. They see zero results because they're not willing to be a participant in the journey. They're not willing to put in the effort that is required to see the type of "Shut-your-face!"-amazing results that you will grow accustomed to seeing with your clients.

When I'm working to help a client improve a specific situation, I want him to understand the most likely underlying cause of that problem. When you can educate someone about his body in a way that makes sense to him, you're giving that client the tools he needs to reach his goals. You're helping him understand what to look for along the way and adjustments to make when necessary. When a client comprehends how to look at his own physiology and to understand if he is on track or not, he is on the way to winning, and winning big. Here's a fun fact: When your client wins big, you win big too.

For these reasons, when I want a client to change what he's eating, I want him to know why and in what ways that could help. When a client could benefit from the use of a supplement, I want him to understand the goal of using that supplement. If your clients know what they're looking for, the feedback they can provide you will often be enough to steer the ship in the right direction. When the ship is not being steered, you can end up with some less-than-ideal results. Less-than-ideal like, "I just screamed at my neighbor because I hate the color of his mailbox." That kind of less-than-ideal. The foods we eat and our ability to process those foods matter. The more your clients understand this, the more equipped they will be to make the required adjustments.

Stop Telling Them What They Want To Hear

I see a lot of health professionals make this critical error. Rather than telling the client what will help the most, some pros simply tell their clients what the pros think their clients want to hear. Being a health pro is not a popularity contest and you're not going to "politician" your way to success. It can be a little uncomfortable at first, but when you are honest and forthright with your clients, not only will they respect you but also they will appreciate you when your advice helps them reach their goals.

Many health pros miss the mark when a client tells them, "I'm willing to work real hard, but I'm a total choco-holic and I can't make it through the day without my Cocoa Crisps every morning." I hear a lot of health pros tell these clients, "Okay, well, we'll just work harder in other areas" or "just try your best." This client is being set up for failure with this "sweet pants" approach. Being an effective health pro is no place for sweet pants. Being an overbearing bully is rarely effective either. When you teach clients the effect that sugary cereal is having on their bodies, AND steps they can take to reduce their NEED for such a food (you'll learn how to do that in this book), then your clients have a fighting chance to succeed. And they will succeed because you were willing to be honest and put in the effort to educate them with a smile.

What About Marketing?

When I survey health pros about the topics they want the most help with, marketing invariably comes up as number one. I'm about to give you some incredible marketing resources. You're literally within a paragraph or so of receiving this gift. But before I provide you with your marketing gifts, you need to understand this: It's not the most important part. I teach a wide variety of marketing techniques, but none of them will do you any good if you don't know how to help clients see real results once they show up. If you can first create a foundation of true knowledge, not only will your client's results bring you referral after referral, but also the clients who show up from your marketing efforts can become your best billboards.

If all of your efforts go toward marketing and if the clients who show up see zero results, instead of spreading the good news about your business, they'll be spreading the news that your business is a great place for people to waste their money. It's okay to start working on your marketing plan as long as you understand where your priorities are.

While you're gaining a knowledgeable foundation with this book, you can start to learn about marketing by using this list of free tools:

Marketing Resources

Health Pro Profit Squad **Support Group** - Join our free and private Facebook support group for health pro marketing. You can post questions and hear from health pros around the world about what is working and not working in their businesses. Facebook.com/groups/healthproprofitsquad

Six Figure Health Pro Podcast - In this free podcast, you'll hear mini-trainings about the latest marketing techniques that are seeing the best results. You'll also hear from some of the big names in marketing, as well as top professionals in the health, nutrition, wellness and fitness industries. Subscribe for free on iTunes or Stitcher by searching for Six Figure Health Pro.

Free Health Pro Marketing Course - This is a free introductory marketing course that will walk you through how to set up your website (and how to skip this section if you have a site already). It will walk you through, step-by-step, how to set up a lead generation system that will turn those leads into paying customers, all on autopilot. You can find this free course at HealthProCourse.com/intro.

Website Setup - If you'd simply like to set up your health pro website, I have a free blog post that walks you through the process: Sixfigurehealthpro.com/how-to-setup-your-health-pro-website

Where To Start?

It is now time to get to the real meat of what matters: Building the knowledge base that will help you create real results with your clients. We'll start in the same place you will start with all your clients: Digestion. If digestion is not working correctly, none of the dietary changes you help them make will have the effects you're hoping for. If folks can't properly break down the food they're eating, they can't pull the nutrients out of that food. Once you understand digestion, you will be able to help more clients with a wider variety of issues than you may have thought possible.

In the following chapter, I teach digestion in a way that will make it easier to understand. There are two main sides to digestion, and it's important to understand them both. For many of you, the next two chapters will be the most important chapters in this book.

Working With A Health Coach

Many topics in this book are very simple, while some get a little advanced. Keep in mind that there are professional health coaches around the world who understand how to look at your individual body chemistry and provide you with answers that you're looking for. In chapter seventeen I discuss how to find a professional near you. For now, if at any time you feel overwhelmed, know that help is available. You may benefit both from experiencing this process from the client point of view, and from seeing how an experienced health coach, who has graduated from our online Bio-individuality Coach Course, can help you see results faster.

What To Expect

In this book, you'll find answers—answers to questions that you and your clients may have had for many years. Most people who spend their life dealing with discomforts or issues feel like 'that's just the way it is' for them and there's nothing they can do about it. Issues like:

- Cravings
- Skin Issues
- Bloating
- PMS (if you're a menstrual-cycle-type person)
- Insomnia
- Mental and Emotional Issues
- Weight Gain
- Acid Reflux

The list goes on and on. Guess what? You and your clients can do something about it—all of it.

Wha'd He Say?

In this chapter, you learned:

- We're going to need a lot more educated coaches when our weight loss documentary comes out. You can be one of those coaches.
- You can be part of the nutrition movement, helping people find real answers to their health issues.
- By helping your clients create real results, you can stand out in your local community of health professionals.
- You can access our list of free marketing resources, but learning how to create amazing results should be your priority for building a successful business.

CHAPTER THREE

Digestion

Everything Goes Back To Digestion

Digestion is a huge deal when it comes to health. It's a shame that the whole digestive process is often swept under the rug. To improve a wide variety of health issues, we really need to look under the rug and better understand how the digestive system works. When I talk about digestion, I'm talking about people's ability to properly break down the foods they are eating. We all tend to assume that if food goes in one end and poop comes out the other, everything is working as planned. That is not always the case. Digestive issues are actually much more common than you might think. To illustrate: Line up 100 high school boys. You will likely find that the percentage of guys whose pants do not fit properly coincides with the percentage of people in this country who have some type of digestive issue. I know! That's a really high percentage. (And why don't they buy pants that fit... why?)

Diet is what a person eats. Nutrition is what the cells see. Nutrition not making it to the cells is where we find the big disconnect. People think that if they focus on foods that are higher in specific nutrients, calcium for example, they're improving their calcium levels with these food choices. Little do they realize, if the body can't properly break down the food they are eating, they're just treating their toilets to calcium-rich poop.

What are we doing when we digest? We're breaking down that food into elemental parts that can be used by the body. Believe it or not, the body cannot run on a peanut butter sandwich any more than your car can run on crude oil. It just doesn't work. However, what the body *can* do is break down that peanut butter sandwich into minerals, amino acids, fats and sugars—and then use those nutrients. Your body needs those nutrients. When digestion is not working properly and you can no longer break down your food enough to pull the required nutrients out of what you have eaten, bodily systems can begin to fail, just like your car would fail if it ran out of gas.

In order for digestion to function properly, there are processes that MUST be in place for most of the nutrients to be pulled from the food you eat. With digestive issues, not only are you missing out on nutrients, but undigested food also becomes a problem that your body has to deal with. When food is not digested, it rots and ferments, which creates gases and toxins. This explains how it doesn't really matter if you're eating organic, extra-virgin, all-natural, grass-fed, hormone-free lima beans washed by the prince of New Guinea. If you can't digest it, it will rot and ferment, creating garbage in your body.

Remember, the methods I explain in this chapter are not magical health improvement secrets for everyone to implement. If any symptoms or issues you're dealing with are not directly caused by digestive malfunctions, following the suggestions in this chapter may not do very much. First, figure out if you need help with your digestion. To give you a benchmark, out of twenty clients who come to me, only one of them will appear to have a properly functioning digestive system. Some health pros reading this book won't need to follow all the guidelines in this chapter; but if you are experiencing any of the symptoms listed in the quiz below on a regular basis, odds are great that you could do something to improve your digestion.

When looking at an individual, I like to know as much about his or her individual chemistry as possible. Because this is not always an option, there are questions you can ask to get a good sense of how your body is operating. In chapter seven, I add self-tests you can run. Those, coupled with the following questions that you can ask yourself, will allow you to see a better picture of the exact nutritional changes that may benefit you the most. When you try it yourself, you will see more clearly how it works with your clients.

How's Your Digestion?

In case you failed the last quiz miserably, I'll include a few of the same questions below to give you another chance to get a better score.

(1) Do you frequently pass gas?
YES   NO
(2) Do you often burp after meals or feel bloated? (Even just small burps.)
YES   NO
(3) Does your meal ever feel like it's sitting in your stomach like a rock for too long?
YES   NO
(4) Do you crave sweet or salty foods?
YES   NO
(5) Do some foods make you nauseous?
YES   NO
(6) Is your stool sometimes lighter than the color of corrugated cardboard?
YES   NO
(7) Do you ever experience heartburn or acid reflux?
YES   NO
(8) Have you recently taken any antacids or acid reflux medications?
YES   NO
(9) Are you frequently constipated? Hello?
YES   NO
(10) Do you ever see undigested food in your stool?
YES   NO

If you answered yes for one or more of those questions, you should pay special attention to this chapter.

If you answered yes for two or more of those questions, you will likely need to take action in order to get your digestion back on track.

If you answered yes for three or more of those questions, this chapter will likely change your life. If you are able to improve digestive symptoms for yourself, that first-hand experience may magnify your ability to help clients improve similar issues.

The Digestive Summary

Digestion is such an important factor when it comes to a bevy of health issues, that I've dedicated this entire chapter to explaining the whole system. I even explain strategies you can implement right away to begin to improve your digestion. In that way, by the time you get to chapter seven and begin to figure out how whacked your chemistry is, at least you will have already taken steps to improve digestion and you'll be on your way to being a real human. Stand clear because you're going to enter biology class for just a few minutes. I promise to avoid any frog dissecting flashbacks.

When we eat, our stomachs make hydrochloric acid (HCL). This stomach acid, as it is often called, has a pH of around 0.8. The pH scale goes from zero to fourteen. Zero means acidity to the max. Fourteen means alkalinity to the max.

When contents of the stomach (what we eat and drink) are mixed with this stomach acid, that combination will ideally have a pH between 2.0 and 3.0, which is still very acidic. The acidic product created by mixing stomach acid with the food you eat then goes into the duodenum (first ten inches of the small intestine). The other half of the digestive process comes from the bile that is produced by your liver. (I say "half" loosely because there are other factors that contribute to digestion that are not important for this explanation. But for the most part, the main factors in digestion are the acid created in the stomach and the alkaline bile produced by the liver.) Between meals, bile is stored in the gallbladder where it is concentrated up to 18 times. When acid product from the stomach moves into the duodenum, bile from the gallbladder is dropped onto this acid product. In the same way that HCL is acidic, bile is alkaline (which is the opposite of acidic).

Bile meeting stomach acid is like dropping baking soda into vinegar, just like at least one sixth grader does every year when he makes his version of a volcano for his science fair project. In fact, you should try that now. You don't need to build the whole volcano, but you can put a little bowl in your kitchen sink, put a couple teaspoons of baking soda in the bowl, and then slowly pour in a little vinegar. You'll hear a sizzle and see it start to foam up. C'mon, really do it! All the cool kids are doing it. It's a great visualization of what can happen when two substances with opposite pHs meet.

This is the magic of digestion. When the body drops bile onto the contents that comes from the stomach, you get a sizzle, and this is what you're living on. This is initially what makes everything that was in the food break apart and become available for your body to use. Without this sizzle, foods you eat can't be assimilated. Nutrients and minerals can't be properly extracted and utilized by your body if this action is missing. That's why you hear so many people say, "Health is like a science fair project." Okay, I've never heard anyone say that; but if you don't have that sizzle in your digestion, you might as well be that 12-year-old holding the volcano with an "F" on it because the damn lava didn't come out. You've got to have the sizzle.

If there isn't enough stomach acid, there won't be that sizzle. If there isn't enough bile to drop down onto the food that was mixed with the stomach acid, there won't be that sizzle. In order for digestion to work properly, every step of that process has to be active. Otherwise, instead of a sizzle, you get more of a fizzle; and you may break down just a very small portion of your food, or your food will partially break down by processes of rotting and fermenting. This rotting and fermenting creates chemical reactions and gases that can cause bloating, burping, nausea, bad breath, upset stomach, and all kinds of other non-fun stuff. Have you ever been around someone who had breath that smelled like a garbage can? Most people look at bad breath as a dental hygiene issue, and it can be; but more often than not it's a situation of, "I have food rotting in my stomach and intestines and the stench it creates is coming out of my mouth." Yes, I know you've met that guy.

This repulsive rotting of last night's dinner can also be the reason you don't feel like eating the next morning. Many individuals who always skip breakfast truly have no appetite when they wake up. Some people are even nauseous because last night's dinner still hasn't fully digested and is becoming toxic. Their bodies are telling them, "Look, I haven't finished dealing with last night's food that has now turned into garbage. Please don't dump anything else on top of it." By improving digestion, a person's morning appetite can also improve.

Give Me Acid Or Give Me Death

Acid or death? A bit of a drama queen? Maybe. Maybe not. A lack of stomach acid can be a huge health concern that can result in even bigger health concerns. Here are a few of the issues that can come from a need for more stomach acid. I explain some of these further in chapter four when I cover elimination.

- Nutritional deficiency. Almost every nutritional deficiency stems from a lack of stomach acid, a lack of bile flow, or poor food selection.
- Burping or bloating. Bloating is almost always due to a lack of stomach acid.
- Frequent stomach discomfort after eating.
- Acid reflux or heartburn. Yes, reflux is usually caused by NOT ENOUGH acid, not too much acid as you see in advertisements. It's one of the biggest health mistakes being made by millions of misled people today.
- Chronic constipation. I explain the Anabolic Imbalance (that can often contribute to constipation) in detail in chapter eight; but a lack of stomach acid is often a factor, if not the main cause, for constipation.
- The door is open for bad critters to sneak into your body. Stomach acid is the barrier that blocks harmful organisms from entering into and through the digestive tract.

Warning For Health Pros

We are at the point in the book where I start to introduce supplements and adjustments to nutrition that may be helpful in specific situations. Don't get excited about this information and run out and tell all your clients to start taking supplements or making nutritional changes if you are not set up to legally do so. Regulations vary greatly from state to state and from country to country.

In chapter nineteen, I go over some of the legalities that need to be considered when working with clients. I share language and phrases that need to be avoided and ways to figure out what will work for you, according to where you work. What you're about to learn is very exciting stuff, just make sure you wait until you finish the book to start implementing any of this knowledge with your clients.

Improving Your Stomach Acid

If you need to improve your stomach acid, there are supplements you can use to boost your body's ability to correct these functions. But, before I teach you how to use Betaine HCL supplements to recover your proper stomach acid function, I need to give you a huge flippin' WARNING. READ IT! DON'T IGNORE IT!!!!

*** HCL Warning ***

If you're going to use HCL, be sure to also use Beet Flow (explained below in *You Need Good Bile Flow*) or a similar product. I never allow any of my clients to use HCL unless they are also using Beet Flow. If you don't have your bile flowing correctly and you add more acid into the stomach, you could create a duodenal ulcer or other issues. I cover all of this in more detail in chapter four. I just want to make sure you understand not to use HCL without also using Beet Flow. It is also imperative to read *How to Use HCL Supplements* below before you begin supplementing with HCL.

Why Use HCL

We all know the body makes stomach acid. But when we hear about stomach acid, it's usually how people have "too much" acid and that's why they are dealing with heartburn or acid reflux issues. There is a lot of brilliant marketing by the pharmaceutical companies when it comes to stomach acid and why it might be a good idea to turn off acid, and I believe it the same way I believe that a mime is a talented artist. In Appendix A, I explain why people really get heartburn and reflux. Let's first look at why "turning off" your stomach acid with drugs is one of the worst possible things you can do for your long-term health.

Hydrochloric acid (HCL) is the protector of the human body. Let's say you are eating at the buffet and you're taking in viruses, bacteria, and microorganisms because you scoop up the salad the kids sneezed on a few minutes earlier. While you eat from this salad bar, you are taking in all this filth and you are eating undercooked hamburger and chicken drumettes that were dropped on the floor. The truth is you don't really know what you are getting. Keep in mind that I worked at a salad bar when I was a kid, and my only rule was that being funny in front of the cute waitresses was far more important to me than delivering clean, sanitary food to all the redneck patrons that came in on coupon night. Your food doesn't even need to be dropped on the floor by a zit-faced high school kid to have bacteria or other little creatures on it. Even the food you clean and prepare at home can have some little ninja-like varmints that make it through the cleaning process. (Varmints! 500 points to me for fitting in a Yosemite Sam reference.)

That's where HCL becomes such a hero. Anything that comes into YOU through your digestive system (any microorganisms, bacteria, or other types of bad guys) is going to die in an acid bath. That stomach acid is the protector of the mechanism that is YOU. The hydrochloric acid function of the stomach is your knight in very disgusting armor. When you take a drug that turns that barrier off, you're opening the door to anybody that wants to come in and raid the pantry (you are the pantry in this scenario). That's why two people can eat the same meal and one will get food poisoning and have projectile fluids coming out of both ends, and the other person will just say, "The fish didn't taste right, did it? Oh, and sorry about your luck." One person had the proper level of stomach acid to kill whatever little bastards were still living on that fish; and the other person is praying to the porcelain god, vowing to never eat seafood again.

The point is, you want that acid function to be in the stomach because it is the gatekeeper. It's the lock that keeps all the hoodlums out. I don't want you to think that taking medication for acid reflux or heartburn is the only reason a person may lose that acid function. There are many ways a person can produce less than the proper levels of acid. There are also many reasons the acid function may not fully recover for years, or even decades.

The body needs minerals in order to generate stomach acid. However, the body needs stomach acid in order to fully break down foods and pull minerals out of those foods. Without digestion, you can't assimilate minerals, but without minerals, you can't create proper digestion. See how someone could be screwed with a capital "F" for a long time? Using HCL supplementation can allow you to manufacture proper digestion so you can pull the minerals out of the food you are eating. Once the body has enough minerals, the stomach can often begin to make an appropriate amount of HCL. At this point, the HCL supplementation can often be reduced until the body is making plenty of its own HCL—and then the supplementation can be removed altogether. Depending on your mineral reserves, food choices, and many other factors, this process can take weeks, months, or longer. However, it often doesn't take a long time to begin to feel like you're improving.

Hydrochloric Acid (HCL), also labeled as Betaine HCL, is the most widely needed digestive supplement in my opinion. It's also the one that comes with the most important instructions. This is NOT a supplement you want to take willy-nilly. (Isn't it amazing that such a ridiculous phrase like "willy-nilly" could become so widely accepted? That bugs me.) Here is a list of important guidelines to follow while using HCL supplements:

- HCL capsules should always be taken in the middle of the meal and chased by at least one bite of food. If the capsules were to get stuck in your esophagus and dissolve there, it could feel like heartburn.
- Start by taking one capsule with a meal containing no starches. This means avoid foods like potatoes, bread, pasta, cereal, rice, etc. If you don't feel any new digestive discomfort after the meal, and your stool does not become too loose, you know it's okay to move up to two capsules at your next meal. You can continue in this manner until you reach a maximum of five capsules per meal. Once you reach the full dose of five capsules per meal, most people can add a few starches back into their diet without experiencing any reflux or heartburn symptoms.
- Most people will hold at five capsules per meal for months. So, when your digestive symptoms disappear, it may be time to begin reducing your dose. The goal is to see if your body has started making more of its own HCL, reducing your need to supplement with capsules. At your next meal, you can reduce by one capsule and hold at that dose for a few days to make sure none of your digestive symptoms come back. You can continue to reduce your dose in this manner until you no longer need to take any HCL capsules. If you lower your dose to one or two capsules per meal, and symptoms return, you know you may need to use a higher dose for a while longer. The most helpful signs to watch, when determining proper stomach acidification are: burping, bloating, constipation, acid reflux, heartburn, seeing food in your stool, or discomfort after eating (especially if you feel like your food is just sitting in your stomach like a rock). Any of these symptoms are possible indications that your food is not yet being properly acidified.
- If your stomach becomes extremely uncomfortable when you begin HCL supplementation, yet you know you experience symptoms that often indicate a lack of stomach acid, you may be dealing with a bacterial infection in your stomach. If bacteria

have set up camp in your stomach (which is extremely common when the stomach is not creating enough HCL), the waste from that bacteria could be making the stomach even more alkaline. When dumping HCL into a highly alkaline environment, the reaction between the acid and alkaline substances can create a fizzy mess. That interaction can create gasses and cause pressure and make you feel very uncomfortable. If this is the case for you, you may need to take steps to wipe out a layer of that bacteria before you can begin to implement HCL. I cover how to reduce bacteria in the stomach in chapter fourteen when I talk about d-limonene and a few more supplements that can be helpful for some individuals.

- Be sure to adjust your dose according to the amount of protein in each meal. If you have a meal with very little protein, you may need to reduce the number of capsules you use with that meal. I don't suggest using HCL supplementation if you're having only a protein shake.

- If you experience any diarrhea or loose stool issues after you begin to use HCL, reduce what you are taking until you can improve your bile flow using the suggestions found below in *Improving Your Bile Flow*. If you have more acid than your bile flow can handle, that can create a loose stool issue. This may not mean that you don't need the acid, you may just need to improve your bile flow before you can handle more acid. If you experience this issue, read more about loose stool issues and the need for proper bile flow in chapter four.

- If you experience magnified acid reflux when you begin using HCL, be sure to read about Acid Reflux in Appendix A so you know what steps to take to correct this. Occasionally, an individual who has never experienced acid reflux will feel heartburn symptoms when first starting HCL. Appendix A explains how this is almost always caused by having NOT ENOUGH acid. These symptoms will normally stop once your stomach is acidic enough to trigger your LES valve to close so food can't reflux up your esophagus. I go over this in much more detail in Appendix A.

You Need Good Bile Flow

Bile is what allows us to emulsify the fats we eat so those fats can be used by the body. All food is either carbohydrate, protein or fat. To process the fats, you need bile. Bile is not only needed for proper digestion, bile is also the main exit pathway for filth and toxins from the body. Junk that can't be removed is often stored in fat cells, so this can be a huge factor for a lot of your clients.

Here are a few of the issues that can come from a need for improved bile flow.

- Nutritional deficiency. Almost every nutritional deficiency stems from a lack of stomach acid, a lack of bile flow, or both. Poor food selection is usually the third factor.
- Passing gas. It can be a big indication that bile is not flowing correctly.
- Weight gain.
- Chronic diarrhea or issues like colitis, crohns, IBS, etc.
- Duodenal ulcer.
- Chronic acne.
- Stool color that is sometimes lighter than corrugated cardboard.

Improving Your Bile Flow

In chapter eight I talk about an imbalance that can cause your bile to become too thick and sticky and encumber its ability to flow correctly. For most people, however, using a supplement made predominantly of beet greens is enough to correct the problem. Beet greens have an amazing ability to help thin the bile so it will flow properly. Unfortunately, you would likely need to eat an entire bucket of beet tops on a daily basis in order to get the effect you're looking for. A concentrated supplement is far more effective and will allow you to avoid eating meals fit for a horse.

There are many beet supplements out there, but few contain as much of the organic beet green as Beet Flow from Empirical Labs. **DO NOT use a cheap beet ROOT product. The beet root is not what helps to thin the bile and you will not see the results you're looking for.** Beet Flow is the product I use with my clients. It is absolutely the most expensive supplement I use, but it's well worth the money. If you are willing to do the work to correct digestion, this upgrade could help improve any number of ailments you are dealing with, reducing the number of remedies you may buy in an attempt to fix your woes. In this regard, investing in Beet Flow can turn out to actually save you money.

Why Use Beet Flow

If you're going to use HCL, you need to use Beet Flow as well. You really need to make sure your bile is flowing correctly if you're going to be adding more acid to your stomach. That acid needs to be neutralized by bile when it reaches the duodenum. If you want to digest your food correctly, you need both sides of digestion working properly.

How to Use Beet Flow

Most people use only two or three capsules per meal. You can take them before or during your meal.

Note: If you are on birth control medication, be sure to read about it in Appendix A. It will freak you out. Birth control medication seems to have the ability to thicken the bile, reducing its ability to flow properly.

Add Digestive Enzymes

Enzymes are another factor of the digestive process. We produce enzymes in the pancreas. Additionally, all living foods are meant to contain enzymes that actually help you digest that food better. Yet, with today's despicable farming methods, even many raw foods do not contain the needed enzymes to correctly digest those foods. On top of that, any time food is processed or heated over 118 degrees (pretty much any time you cook food), the enzymes are damaged and you will not get the full benefit from that food. In order to fully break down the food you eat, you can supplement enzymes with your food. As we age, the body's stockpile of usable enzymes diminishes. People over thirty should be supplementing enzymes with their food. If you don't supply your body with the enzymes it needs, your body steals enzymes intended for repair and metabolic processes and turns them into digestive enzymes, leaving fewer repair-enzymes for their intended use.

Enzymes facilitate the food's ability to break down and mix with water. In an effort to increase shelf-life, much of today's produce has been modified to depress enzymes contained within those foods. Using digestive enzymes can help overcome this enzyme deficiency problem.

With certain imbalances, TOO MANY enzymes can facilitate deterioration. So, you want to take just enough to help you digest your food. Many enzyme companies promote taking unlimited enzymes but that is not recommended with certain imbalances.

Most people see improvement by using only one or two capsules per meal.

Where To Get Supplements

The beginning of chapter fourteen covers the world that is consumer supplement sales. There is a reason you hear so much good and bad about supplement use. Supplements are good only if you use the right ones for the imbalances you are dealing with, and they are good only if you use high quality products that can be properly absorbed. With many supplements, only a very small percentage of what is in them can be absorbed by the person using them.

I'm not saying that the supplements I recommend are the only good supplements out there. They have simply brought the best results, in my experience. Consumers miss out sometimes since most high-quality companies sell only through practitioners. Empirical Labs is a company that sells most of their products only through qualified professionals. Having a wider variety of quality supplements available to you and your clients can be another perk of working with a professional health coach, or from graduating our online Bio-individuality Coach Course. However, a few of Empirical Lab's products are available to consumers as well, since these particular supplements are considered to be safe for people to use, no matter what their chemistry is (so long as folks take the time to learn about these products and use a little common sense). This is the brand I implement most frequently for my own use.

Most health food stores sell some form of HCL. I just don't like a lot of them because they contain pepsin and other ingredients that can bother people's stomachs when they start to use more than one capsule per meal. I have also seen a number of companies that add ingredients to their HCL capsules that can literally make the product worthless by neutralizing the acidic effect of the HCL. If you were to ask me if this drove me crazy, the answer would be an astounding yes. I try to use straight HCL. Also, the capsules I use are 515mg; so if you get something different, be sure to adjust your number of capsules accordingly. I use HCL from Empirical Labs, which can be found on www.NaturalReference.com. This is the only site approved to sell

Empirical Lab's products to the public. Beet Flow and the digestive enzyme I prefer, Digesti-zyme, can also be found on this website.

I like the enzyme Digesti-zyme because it contains cofactors, like zinc, that the body can use to make its own HCL. In this regard, Digesti-zyme can reduce how long you may need to supplement HCL. It won't replace Betaine HCL, because the dose of HCL is too low, but Digesti-zyme can reduce how long you may need to supplement HCL.

Supplements Review

www.NaturalReference.com
Brand: Empirical Labs

Betaine HCL (See the HCL warning under *Improving Your Stomach Acid* in this chapter.)
1-5 per meal (In the middle of the meal.)

Beet Flow
2-3 per meal

Digesti-zyme
1-2 per meal

In chapter fourteen I go over other supplements that can be used for other imbalances. With many of those supplements, I am not as picky about the brand I use with my clients. But when it comes to correcting digestion, I haven't seen anything else work as well as these three.

Wha'd He Say?

In this chapter, you learned:
- When trying to improve a wide variety of health issues, digestion is often a big piece of that puzzle.
- Both sides of digestion are equally important. You must have enough HCL production and you must have proper bile flow.
- Few people with digestive issues are able to truly improve digestion without the temporary aid of supplements.
- Most people will benefit from the use of digestive enzymes. You can order Beet Flow, HCL and digestive enzymes from www.NaturalReference.com.

CHAPTER FOUR

Elimination & Digestion Gone Wild

Let's Talk Poop

There are two types of people in this world. There are stargazers and there are stoolgazers, and the stoolgazers fare better. There is a lot that can be learned from poop—specifically, how our bodies are operating and, especially, how well digestion is working.

Better understanding the signs of digestive trouble can guide your efforts toward improving many issues. If you ever happen to sit on your toilet and have a minor Chernobyl incident, you'll have a better idea as to why.

We all know that we poop to eliminate waste from the body. Many don't know, however, that stool often moves at its level of acidity. Stool can move too quickly and be too loose when it is too acidic. Not only does this burn the intestines, but also, if the stool is moving too quickly, the body doesn't get the opportunity to absorb as many nutrients as it should. If stool is not acidic enough, it can move too slowly and can lead to constipation.

Diarrhea and Loose Stool Issues

You don't want nutrients screaming through your intestines without being absorbed. Loose stool or chronic diarrhea issues must be corrected if the goal is to fully benefit from the food you're eating. In most cases, a chronic loose stool can be the result of a lack of bile flow. Using Beet Flow to improve bile flow can help that issue. If this is not enough, be to read chapter eight and learn about the Catabolic ....valance. Many people experiencing a Catabolic Imbalance may need to improve their bile flow.

When you get your Beet Flow and have been using it for a day or two, you can do what is called a Beet Flow Flush. Here is an outline of this simple process.

How To Do A Beet Flow Flush

We get a lot of questions about how to do a Beet Flow flush so I created this section to answer the most frequently asked questions on the topic.

I just take four Beet Flow capsules every thirty minutes for two hours (a total of four doses). This is just an as-needed event and not a technique I use daily. This can give your bile flow a quick boost; and many see improvement faster by using this technique when they start. In chapter seven you will learn how to look at your urine and saliva pHs. When saliva pH is below 6.5, this can be an indication that a Beet Flow flush could be helpful. If your saliva pH goes up the day after doing a Beet Flow flush, that is a good indication that the flush has been beneficial.

Don't read the name "flush" and think that you'll be running to the toilet after doing a Beet Flow flush. Most people feel no effect whatsoever— yet they see their saliva pH reading rise above 6.5. Since you tested your saliva pH before you did the flush and then again the following day, you now have measurements on which to base your next step toward digestive health. If your saliva pH goes up a little or if your stool gets darker, the flush likely helped improve your bile flow. When your self-test numbers show that your saliva pH has gone down again, you can do another flush. If you feel nauseous while doing a Beet Flow flush, odds are good that your system may be considerably toxic and you might want to use only one Beet Flow capsule per meal for a couple weeks to start thinning your bile and moving out garbage at a slower pace.

In very rare cases, a client may experience a skin reaction after doing a Beet Flow flush. If a Beet Flow flush thins the bile so it can flow better, and if that bile has been backed up for a long time, a large amount of filth can start to move out as well. If the filth is more than the body can handle, the body may try to push some of that junk out through the skin, creating a reaction. Increasing water intake in the short term can often help wash out enough of this junk. I normally have these clients slow down their bile thinning efforts for a week or so and allow the body to catch up and remove some of this junk that has been backing up in the system due to the poor bile flow.

The Beet Flow Flush/Coffee Suppository Combo

For most clients, bile flow will improve by simply using Beet Flow capsules with each meal or by performing a Beet Flow flush or two. But you will very likely run into clients whose bile is so backed up that these methods won't be enough. In chapter fourteen, when we talk about supplements, I will introduce you to Xeneplex coffee suppositories. Beet Flow works to thin the bile so it can flow better, while a coffee suppository works to dilate the biliary pathway so that bile can flow with more ease. For some clients, coffee suppositories (or coffee enemas) may be necessary. For the extreme cases, nothing seems to be as effective for better bile flow than to do a Beet Flow flush one day and coffee suppository the following day. This combo seems to thin the bile and then open up the biliary pathway to allow everything to move with more ease. I talk more about coffee suppositories in chapter fourteen yet wanted to tell you about this incredibly effective combo method here.

A coffee enema can also replace the coffee suppository as a very effective therapy. A coffee enema can take quite a bit more time, effort and equipment; but if it's a matter of circumstance and preference, know that a coffee enema can also work very well.

It doesn't happen very often, but sometimes an individual may not be producing adequate bile. These people could benefit from supplementing with ox bile, as this process can encourage the body to make more bile. I normally implement this strategy only if everything else I'm talking about here hasn't worked well enough. Appendix A includes more details and the cautions.

Remember, too, we all need that combination of stomach acid and bile neutralizer for proper digestion. It's best to get a loose stool under control before you add HCL supplementation. If you still have a loose stool and start pushing more acid into the duodenum without the proper level of bile dropping, you could create a duodenal ulcer.

If you are dealing with Crohn's, Colitis, or IBS, be sure to read about these topics in Appendix A and listen to our *Kick It Naturally* episode entitled *Understanding IBS, Crohn's, & Colitis.*

Constipation

Though stool that is too loose can often lead to extreme cravings due to a lack of nutrient assimilation, constipation can create its own share of problems too. If a lack of stomach acid results in stool that is too alkaline and moving too slowly, the waste that was supposed to be removed out the back door (your butt) can get held up in the system too long. If waste is not removed properly, it can be re-absorbed through the intestinal walls and will need to be filtered out all over again. If a liver is already overwhelmed, the body can end up storing some of that waste in fat cells.

Increasing your stomach acid by supplementing HCL can be a great first step toward improving constipation. If that doesn't speed up your stool and relieve your constipation, be sure to read chapter eight. There I explain an imbalance called an Anabolic Imbalance that is commonly associated with chronic constipation issues.

Don't allow your clients to ignore constipation. Any attempted weight loss results will be greatly hampered, if not totally shut down, when an individual is not having at least one good bowel movement per day. To learn more on this topic, read my book, *Constipation: Kick It Naturally*, or listen to our *Kick It Naturally* episode titled *Understanding Constipation.* C'mon! All the cool kids are pooping.

Note on improving bile flow: Understanding that constipation can result from a stool that is too alkaline, you will be ready for the rare occasion when a client, Barnaby, experiences constipation if he improves bile flow without also improving stomach acid. This can sometimes be a temporary discomfort if a client is quick to improve bile flow and the stool becomes too alkaline due to a lack of stomach acid. Barnaby may tell you, "That Beet Flow makes me constipated." You will be able to explain to him what is going on and how to improve stomach acid so both sides of digestion are working well together. This isn't common, but it's important to understand what is happening when it occurs.

Understanding Duodenal Ulcers

In chapter three I mentioned that it's important for people to use Beet Flow when supplementing with HCL to ensure they don't create a duodenal ulcer. Some folks may read that and think, "HCL gives me stomach ulcers?" Therefore, I want to explain this topic a little further.

It is actually widely accepted now (even in the medical community) that stomach ulcers are not caused by excessive stomach acid, as we once believed. Instead, it is now believed that stomach ulcers are caused by bacteria (like h. pylori) in the stomach. A duodenal ulcer is not the same thing as a stomach ulcer, but when you say "duodenal ulcer" people often hear "stomach ulcer," because that is what they are familiar with. A duodenal ulcer occurs in the duodenum (the first few inches of the small intestine, just outside of the stomach).

Remember that the stomach is made to hold stomach acid with no problem due to its mucous lining. The lining of the duodenum and the small intestine is not. When bile is not flowing well enough (or bile production is too low, or even if the gallbladder has been removed), and the bile doesn't sufficiently drop down onto the acid product leaving the stomach, that acid product doesn't get adequately neutralized. This acid product can then begin to damage the lining of the duodenum (basically digesting the proteins that make up the lining of the intestinal tract). Over time, in severe cases, this irritation can create an open wound, or an ulcer.

With this understanding you can see how some individuals create duodenal ulcers even when they are not supplementing with HCL capsules. If a person is making plenty of stomach acid, but bile is not neutralizing that acid as it leaves the stomach, that's the perfect recipe for a duodenal ulcer. These ulcers can be very painful. Imagine pouring a little acid on an open cut on your hand every time you ate. If a person begins to supplement with HCL, yet doesn't have the bile flow to neutralize the acid leaving the stomach, the increased level of acid can now magnify the chances of creating a duodenal ulcer.

This is why it's crucial to make sure you explain to clients why it's so important to use Beet Flow if they're going to supplement with HCL. Now, I'll be honest and let you know that I've never seen a client create a duodenal ulcer by supplementing with HCL. We've never even heard of anyone in our support group doing so. But that may be because we never shut up about using Beet Flow if you're going to supplement with HCL. Still, we have heard from practitioners who have had clients report duodenal ulcers occurring when supplementing with HCL. I don't know if these clients were using Beet Flow or not, but it's important to understand how a duodenal ulcer can occur so you are aware of the possibility.

For this reason, not only is it important to make sure your clients are using Beet Flow and that bile is flowing well, but also you might even want to use techniques that allow you to be less aggressive with your HCL dosages. Remember, a dose of five HCL capsules is a "max dose." That doesn't mean that every client should be using five HCL capsules per meal. If your client, Bill, can improve the acidity of his stomach by using ascorbic acid, he may see great results with a lower dose of HCL. If Karen is experiencing a bacterial overgrowth in her stomach that is causing her stomach to be too alkaline, she may be able to take steps to reduce her bacterial load, therefore allowing her to see better results with a lower dose of HCL. In order to help the HCL pathway we use Digesti-zyme which contains zinc picolinate and can give the body tools it needs to produce HCL. We're always trying to optimize HCL production while not forgetting that HCL needs to be neutralized with sufficient bile flow as it leaves the stomach.

Burping, Bloating And Passing Gas

Keeping an eye on whether you are burping or bloating is one way to get an idea of how acidic your stomach environment is during the digestive process. To figure out if you're really bloating, here's the ultimate question. (This question works only for women because men are way too oblivious of their bodies to get this one.) Are your clothes tighter in the evening when you take them off than in the morning when you put them on? If you so much as have to think about it, you're probably not bloating, because a woman knows. She will say, "Yeah, they are tighter when I take them off." She knows; and if they are tighter, she is bloating. If the acid product in the stomach is not sufficient, then people grow bacteria in their tummies. When they grow bacteria in their tummies, they produce gas. It is the same as making beer, wine, champagne or root beer; all of these things are fermented. When you ferment, you get gas and the gas bloats. Some people may feel very bloated, while others may experience more burping.

When I say burping, I don't mean these huge belches. I'm talking about those little burps that are hardly even noticed. Those little burps are usually a good sign that the stomach is not acidic enough. I see a lot of people who don't even realize that they're burping after their meals. Once I ask them, they come back later and say, "Hey, ya know what, I am burping after my meals and I never even noticed." Now, it's your turn to pay attention and see if you're burping too. You may be burping because of the gas created by undigested food rotting and fermenting, or because of the gases created by bacteria that are living in your stomach, or because of a combination of both. Taking stock of what is going on with your body is the first step to making improvements.

People think, "Everyone passes gas, what's the big deal?" The problem is most adults don't have their digestion working correctly anymore and that is why gas is so common. If you're passing gas, it's usually because your bile isn't flowing well enough. If your bile isn't dropping into the duodenum to meet the acid product from the stomach, you're not digesting properly.

Helping Your Liver

I include some thoughts about liver function in this elimination chapter because proper bile flow is such a vital part of how effectively your liver is taking care of business. I say this a lot, and I'll probably say it three or four more times in this book: In my opinion, the two most important factors for good health are digestion and liver function. I'm not trying to say that if people have a horrific imbalance in need of attention, or an extra limb growing out of the side of their head, that they first need to correct liver function. I'm just speaking generally when I say that the liver's ability to handle its affairs is a super big deal.

I've covered a multitude of factors that can reduce a liver's performance: Almost any medication, a lack of bile flow, bringing in more junk than the liver can remove, etc. Any of these things can trouble a liver; and if the liver isn't working optimally, eventually your body won't be working optimally either. Think of your liver like a huge ventilation fan that can clear smoke out of a kitchen or out of an entire house.

Growing up as a kid, my family lived in a big yellow two-story house. In the living room, just outside of the bathroom, was a huge ventilation fan that was built into the ceiling. My Mom had a friend who would come over to the house and smoke in the living room. Even at twelve years old, I hated cigarette smoke and didn't want to smell it in my house any more than I wanted to miss an episode of *The Muppet Show*. Whenever my Mom's friend, Margaret, was over for a visit, I would turn on this huge fan and immediately it would suck all the smoke out of the house, as if it never existed.

This is similar to how your liver works. To say that your body can't handle a few toxins coming in is far from true. The liver is your body's massive ventilation fan. As junk comes in, the liver moves it out to keep the system clean and operating smoothly. I came home from school one day in a thunderstorm to find that our electricity was out. There was Margaret sitting on the couch. I could barely make out her beady little eyes through all the smoke, but I knew it was Margaret. I immediately turned around to leave the house and my Mom asked where I was going. "Out to get struck by lightning," I said. I guess I was a jackass when I was a kid too. In the same way I was too miserable to exist in that house without the fan, you might be too miserable in your life without your liver working properly.

Back when I lost my voice, after all the medical doctors had their way with me, and my liver was trashed from all the prescription drugs I was taking, it was tough to even walk by some substances, much less take them into my body. When the liver is overwhelmed and can't handle the current load that it's already dealing with, it can be arduous for people to find foods they can eat without feeling miserable. There were only three or four very clean foods I could eat without feeling horrible because my body couldn't deal with the chemicals and preservatives found in most foods. Now that I have improved my liver function, those things don't bother me because now my body can handle the trouble and my liver can remove those substances.

BIG NOTE: If you have had your gallbladder removed, this can turn into a real problem. Good bile flow is required for proper digestion, and a gallbladder is required for good bile flow. If you've had your gallbladder yanked, be sure to read about gallbladder removal in Appendix A.

Acid Reflux, GERD, & Heartburn

Acid reflux, GERD, and heartburn are all issues that normally arise from digestive issues. If you deal with any of these problems, be sure to read about them in Appendix A now. I promise chapter five will still be there waiting when you come back.

Wha'd He Say?

In this chapter, you learned:
- Become a stoolgazer to gain valuable information about how your digestion is functioning.
- Digestive symptoms are often an indication of other problems.
- Increasing bile flow can help your liver clean out more junk, so the junk doesn't get stored in fat cells.

CHAPTER FIVE

Understanding Insulin & Blood Sugar Control

More Than Weight Loss

As humans, we eat 3 categories of food – carbohydrates, fats and proteins. Each category has accompanying minerals. When digestion works properly, we are nourished and energized as carbohydrates are changed to glucose, fats are emulsified, proteins become amino acids, and minerals are released to become available to our cells. Through digestion, food becomes elemental in our systems.

The purpose of insulin is to facilitate the production of energy from glucose. Insulin "sweeps" glucose into the cells from the bloodstream. Proper function is: We eat some carbohydrate; our digestive system changes it to glucose; and the pancreas secretes an appropriate amount of insulin to enable the glucose to become energy.

When it comes to helping clients lose weight, in most cases, controlling blood sugar and keeping insulin from spiking will be a huge factor. But weight loss is not the only goal where insulin control can come into play. Beyond weight gain, chronically high insulin levels can also result in inflammation and insulin resistance, along with imbalances you will learn about in chapter eight. A wide variety of problems can result from inflammation. The body soothes inflammation with cholesterol. High cholesterol levels are often the result of the body producing more cholesterol to help deal with inflammation that is being caused by chronically high insulin levels. There are other factors that can cause or contribute to elevated cholesterol as well, but in most cases, chronically elevated insulin is the main culprit.

Most health pros today understand at least some of the implications that high insulin levels and insulin resistance can have on health. However, the information you gain in this chapter will put you way ahead of the crowd. The viewpoint from most health pros seems to be that if a person eats processed junk food, packed with sugars, the result on insulin can be detrimental. But what about the so-called healthy carbs? If a health pro has the ability to consume a lot of starches without gaining weight or creating health issues, that health pro will normally believe that his clients should be able to do the same thing. After all, the powers that educate nearly every licensed nutritionist in America are teaching us to recommend these high-starch foods to everyone.

There are also plenty of nutrition experts who are telling us that all starches should be avoided, yet we see people who eat them every day and do quite well. You may be one of those people. The key that is missing for most health pros is an understanding of the effectiveness of insulin, and how it can vary greatly from person to person. First, I want to make sure you understand how blood sugar and insulin can affect your client's weight-loss effort; and then we will come back to this topic of insulin variables that can dictate a person's ability to process carbs in an optimal manner.

High Insulin Levels

Put yourself into the shoes of the typical client coming to you for weight-loss help. If you were that client, the following scenario would likely be playing out in your life on a weekly basis: Cravings are the reason that most of us eat too many starches, carbs or sugars. To simplify this chapter, I will just say "carbs" when I am referring to starches, carbohydrates or sugars. However, when I say this, I am referring to foods that are higher in carbs. Many green vegetables contain carbs in small amounts, and that is great. When talking about the ability for carbs to spike insulin levels, I'm talking about higher-carb foods, such as bread, pasta, rice, cereal, baked goods, potatoes, fruit, desserts, etc. Carbs are converted to glucose (or sugar) in the body. Foods higher in carbs, convert to higher levels of glucose. In any case, the fact that you are consuming these carbs isn't even the major problem. The real villain in most people's weight-loss story is how eating these carbs can push insulin levels too high, too often. Anytime we eat carbs, our insulin levels spike in order to sweep the excess glucose out of the bloodstream and into the cells. The more carbs taken in, the higher the insulin spike. Liquid carbs or sugars like juice, soft drinks, and alcohol spike insulin even higher because liquid hits the bloodstream faster.

Glucose levels can come down pretty quickly, while insulin levels stay high a lot longer. The problem is: As long as your insulin levels are high, your body's ability to burn stored fat is impeded. There are more hormones involved in this total process, but viewing high insulin levels as the trigger that makes it all go to hell is a simple way to explain it. High insulin levels also send the signal to your body to store fat. It says, "We have plenty of glucose to use here so store other fuel as fat in case we don't have glucose later." Make sense? So, the sugars are burned in a couple hours, yet your body can't access stored fat for fuel while the insulin levels are still high. No glucose and no access to stored fat means you don't have a good fuel source. Now, you start to crave more carbs because your body needs fuel to function. Even though the insulin isn't going to come down for another two or three hours, you eat a snack that's filled with carbs and your insulin spikes again, never giving the previous insulin a chance to come down and allow your body to burn fat for fuel. This pattern can result in insulin spike after insulin spike, all day long. Considering the way some people eat, do you see how it can be literally impossible to burn stored fat?

Charts & Food Examples

Let's look at examples of how certain meals could affect insulin levels and, therefore, fat storage. In the meal graphs below, I use a general scale from one to ten. I'm not using actual blood glucose or insulin numbers. This is a visual to show how high each level is on a scale of one to ten.

Meal 1 - 8:00 AM (Carb Count: 73 grams)
Bowl of oatmeal, whole wheat english muffin with jam, and a glass of orange juice.

If Phyllis eats meal 1 at 8:00 AM, in the graph below, we see her glucose (the dotted line) rise to a level 8 and her insulin (the solid line) follow right behind it. The shaded zone that tops out around 2.5 is the fat burning zone. Insulin levels need to be within this zone in order for your body to access stored fat and burn it as fuel. While insulin levels are outside that zone, not only can your body not access stored fat, but also your body will likely be storing *more* fat.

Meal 1 Graph

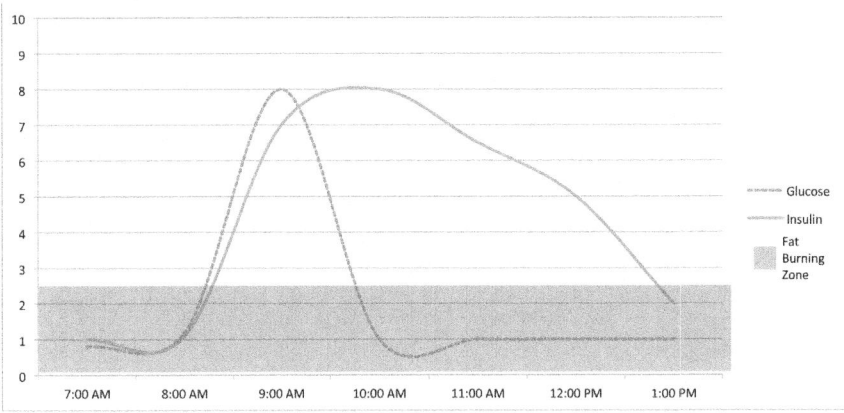

By 9:30 AM Phyllis' glucose has come down, but her insulin is still very high and will likely take a couple more hours to come down.

With glucose levels as low as they appear near 10:00 AM, the body would normally dig into fat storage and burn this fat as a fuel source. Yet, in the graph above, you can see that the high insulin levels block the body's ability to access stored fat, leaving Phyllis with no fuel.

What does Phyllis do? She eats a banana and drinks pomegranate juice because her friend saw an infomercial that stated pomegranate juice has health benefits.

Meal 2 - 10:00 AM (Carb Count: 59 grams)
Banana and a glass of pomegranate juice.

In the Meal 1 Graph you can see how insulin levels would have come down gradually, putting Phyllis back into the fat burning zone later that day. However, in the Meal 2 Graph below you can see that once she consumed Meal 2 with all those carbs (especially liquid sugars, which can spike insulin even higher than sugars in solid form) her glucose soars straight up again and another increase in insulin follows immediately. The sugar supplies her with an energy boost, but her insulin levels never have the chance to come back down before the sugars create another jump in insulin.

Meal 2 Graph

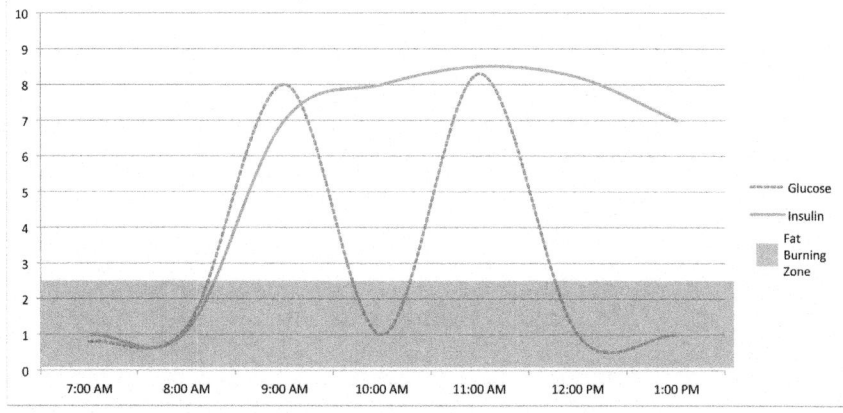

Meal 3 - 2:00 PM (Carb Count: 130 grams)
Turkey sandwich on whole grain bread with lettuce, tomato and fat-free dressing, side of brown rice and a fat-free mocha latte.

You can see that Phyllis was trying to "eat right" by selecting choices many consumers believe will lead to weight loss; yet, look at how this meal cranks up her insulin levels in the Meal 3 Graph.

Meal 3 Graph

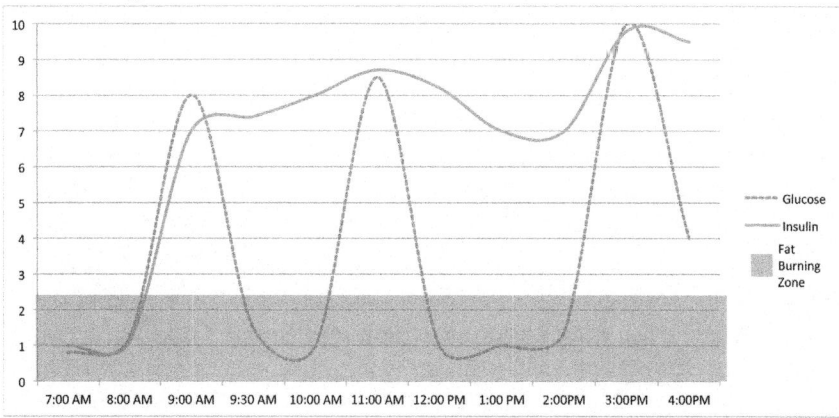

Meal 4 - 8:00 PM (Carb Count: 47 grams)
Small salad with ranch dressing and two rice cakes.

Phyllis tries not to eat too many calories late at night so she made a low-calorie meal. Too bad these low-calorie options still have high carbs. Rice cakes are one of the most nutrient-depleted, insulin-spiking foods you can eat; and many ranch dressings have more sugar than a candy bar. Graph 4 represents her glucose and insulin reaction to this meal.

Meal 4 Graph

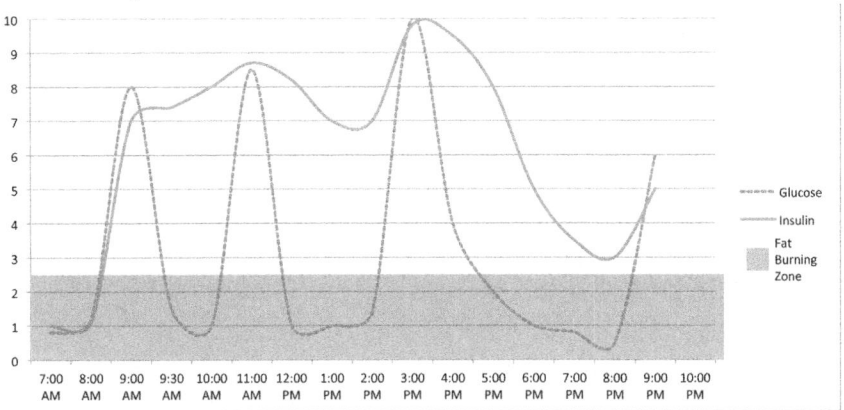

Oops - 8:20 PM (Carb Count: 64 grams)
One pint of Chubby Hubby ice cream.

An even bigger problem shows up after Phyllis eats her nighttime meal fit for a bird. Between Meals 3 and 4, she went six hours without eating, so she is now ravenous. She already lost her mind and snapped at an elderly lady in traffic earlier that afternoon. "If your hair is that blue, you're too old to be driving!" I believe were Phyllis's exact words. Now, after her tiny dinner, she thinks she'll just have a few bites of ice cream. Ten minutes later she realizes she has wiped out the whole pint of Chubby Hubby. (By the way, if the food you're eating has Chubby in the name, you might want to pick another food.)

Oops Graph

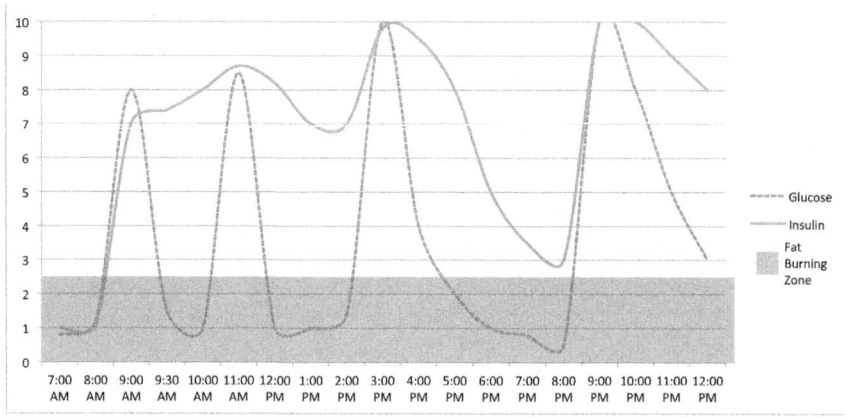

Looking at Phyllis' insulin levels over the span of the day, it's easy to see that, not only was her body unable to access stored fat for most of the day, she will likely stay out of fat burning mode for most of the night as well.

What would her insulin levels have looked like with different choices?

Meal 1 Alternative - 7:00 AM (Carb Count: 2 grams)
Spinach omelet with butter, two chicken sausages, and one cup of chamomile tea.

This meal provides a very nominal rise in insulin levels. Now, Phyllis can go right back into fat burning mode before it's time for a snack. She may be able to skip the snack altogether since her body will have the ability to access stored fat for fuel and she will have plenty of energy. But let's throw a snack in there anyway to see what happens.

Meal 2 Alternative - 10:00 AM (Carb Count: 18 grams)
Cottage cheese with berries.

This snack provides Phyllis with some needed carbs without spiking insulin levels too high.

Meal 3 Alternative - 1:00 PM (Carb Count: 4 grams)
Grilled chicken salad with balsamic vinegar.

Since Phyllis had some carbs earlier in the day, she doesn't feel the need to have many here.

Meal 4 Alternative - 4:00 PM (Carb Count: 7 grams)
Beef collagen protein shake and a handful of raw organic baby carrots.

Meal 5 Alternative - 8:00 PM (Carb Count: 5 grams)
Lamb chops with sautéed broccolini and asparagus.

Alternative Meals Graph

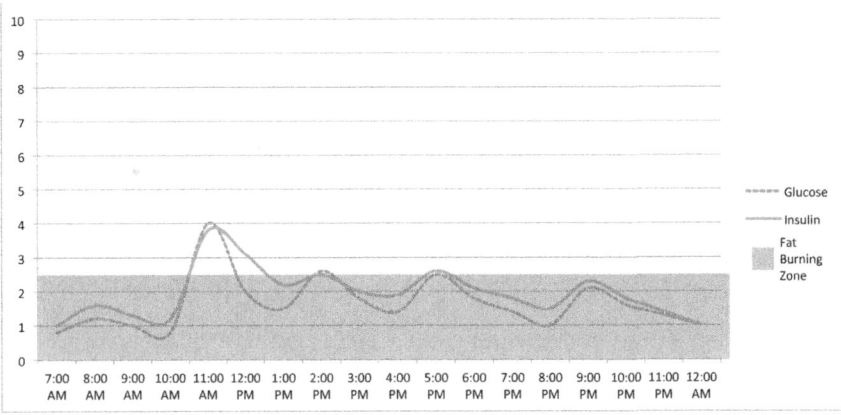

Though Phyllis had one small insulin spike mid-morning, look at the extended periods in the day where she is able to access stored fat and burn it for fuel.

When I teach you about cravings in chapter six, I show you how to help clients reduce carbs without becoming mental cases. Then, and only then, will many of your clients be able to take control of their insulin levels. This is the science behind weight loss. There is no getting around this science. If insulin levels are high, your clients will not burn much stored fat, and in most cases they will end up storing more fat. The only differences from person to person are whether or not that person's cells are still receptive to insulin and how much insulin needs to be utilized to move glucose into the cells.

Insulin Variables

This is one of the factors that allows some people to eat a high-carb diet with no weight gain. If their insulin response is effective enough, they can move a large amount of glucose into the cells with a relatively low amount of insulin; therefore, they rarely have a big insulin spike. It's not the amount of sugar that we consume that necessarily dictates the amount of body fat we store. It's the level of insulin needed to move that glucose into the cells that dictates how long the body will stay in the fat-storage mode and out of the fat-burning mode. The more carbs consumed, the more insulin is typically needed to process those carbs; but the insulin is the driving force behind fat storage. If people can keep insulin levels low, they can restrict the amount of fat their bodies store and increase the amount of stored fat their bodies burn. That's it. It's called science.

Let's use the same graphs as above to illustrate how two different people can eat the same foods and have wildly different glucose and insulin responses to those foods. We can provide Dave and Scott with identical meals throughout the day. The only difference is how each guy processes those foods. Here are the meals Dave and Scott will eat:

Meal 1 - 7:00 AM (Carb Count: 26 grams)
Mushroom omelet with butter, hash-browned yams, and one cup of chamomile tea.

Meal 2 - 10:00 AM (Carb Count: 27 grams)
Cottage cheese with a banana.

Meal 3 - 1:00 PM (Carb Count: 22 grams)
Grilled chicken caesar salad with croutons.

Meal 4 - 4:00 PM (Carb Count: 19 grams)
Protein shake and a handful of berries.

Meal 5 - 8:00 PM (Carb Count: 27 grams)
Lamb chops with a sweet potato and asparagus.

Scott's Meal Graph

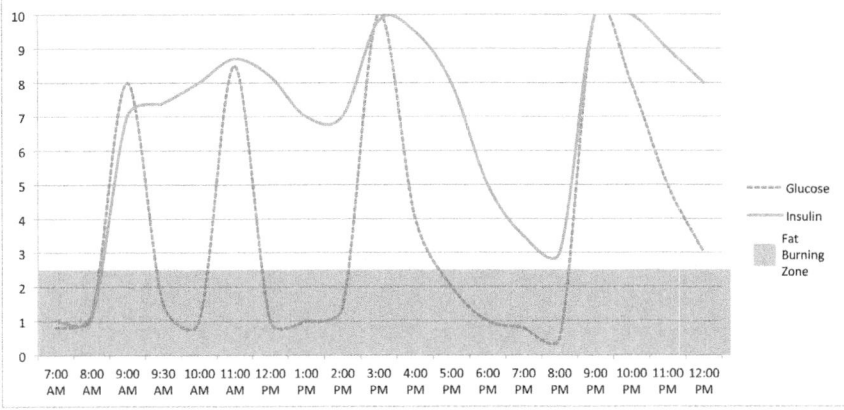

Dave's Meal Graph

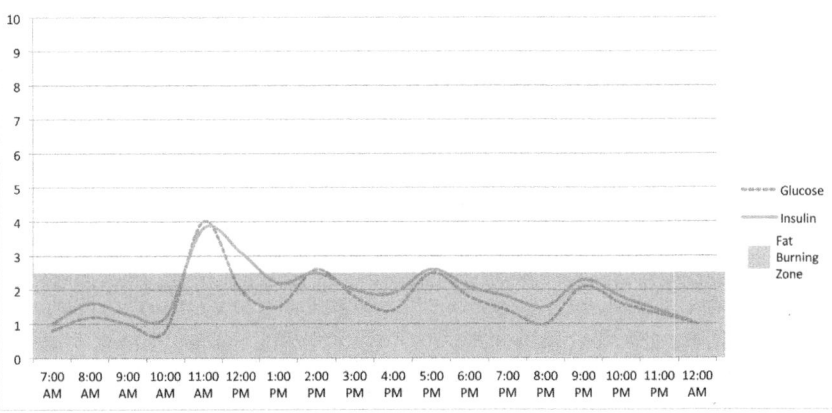

You'll notice that I used the exact same graph images as Phyllis' two graphs above to show you how two different people can have widely different insulin responses to the same foods, in the same way that one person can have a wildly different response when adjusting their food intake. Scott and Dave ate the same foods. However, because Dave's insulin response was more effective and his cells were more responsive to that insulin, Dave didn't need to produce as much insulin to get the job done.

Since Scott's insulin resistance is more pronounced and his cells have become highly resistant to insulin, his body needed to produce more insulin to accomplish the same thing that a much smaller amount of insulin was able to achieve for Dave. This is very common and can happen for a variety of reasons. If a person continues to consume a high level of starches or sugars, keeping insulin levels high most of the day, over time, the cells can stop listening to insulin.

When insulin resistance is developing, it goes like this ... Insulin is working to sweep glucose from the bloodstream into the cells. The cells say, "We'll get to that later." Because blood glucose is high, the pancreas replies, "Do it now." and sends more insulin. Over the years, insulin keeps increasing to get the job done. But eventually, while the insulin continues to scream at the cells all day, every day, the cells become more and more unresponsive, and glucose keeps on accumulating in the bloodstream. Eventually the tired pancreas slows down in its production of insulin; now the blood sugar levels go up, uncontrolled by a tired pancreas. This is the elevated blood glucose that we humans measure with the glucometer. It is said that this individual has become insulin resistant. Most of you may already know that insulin resistance can lead to a diagnosis of Type II Diabetes by a medical doctor. (As a side note, through the years of this process, polyunsaturated fatty acids seem to compound the problem by making a person more predisposed to insulin resistance.)

In any case, though Dave and Scott were eating the same foods, those meals would likely lead to weight gain and elevated inflammation for Scott, and a more balanced state for Dave—simply because Scott needed to produce a much higher amount of insulin to process those foods. This explains how one person can eat more starches without gaining weight, while another needs to reduce his carb intake when weight loss is the goal. There may be a genetic component here. Some people feel they are "mapped genetically" to fail. It helps to look at the map and see what's happening; then you can steer your way out of the situation. It all starts with learning which direction to go. That learning can start with figuring out your self-test measurements.

Am I saying that everyone should go on a low-carb diet? No, I'm not. Many people don't qualify to go on a low-carb diet because they can't process other nutrients very well. If you take away their carbs, you will take away their last source of fuel. They tend to get a little pissy when that happens. Therefore, if a guy wants to lose weight, but he doesn't qualify to reduce his carbs and lower insulin levels, the goal should be to correct those pathways that are restricting his ability to process other nutrients, like fats and protein. Once he can use fats and proteins, then he can work on reducing his carbs and bringing down his insulin levels.

A Note on Insulin Resistance

Insulin facilitates the production of energy from glucose. The pancreas puts out insulin when it senses that we have glucose in the bloodstream which needs to be moved into the cells by the insulin to produce energy. The pancreas continues to put out insulin as long as the glucose remains elevated in the bloodstream. The pancreas has the capacity to produce more than 5 times the amount of insulin that should normally be needed. In a healthy situation, the pancreas would not be called on for an extra amount of insulin. The extra amount of insulin is called for because of the cells' insulin resistance.

As an individual's insulin resistance becomes more pronounced, insulin levels continue to increase over a period of as long as a dozen years. As our cells become more resistant to insulin, the pancreas produces a more-than-normal insulin amount, which overcomes the cells' resistance to insulin. As the years pass and our cells become more and more resistant to insulin, the pancreas secretes more and more insulin. It is the high amount of insulin that becomes an issue, not just the high glucose.

For example, let's say Judy has insulin resistance that is gradually progressing. She needs three times more insulin than when her cells were not resistant. She eats some starch which causes glucose to rise explosively. Because of her insulin resistance, the blood glucose remains high until her 3X amount of insulin is released; only then does the glucose level start to go down (glucose leaving the bloodstream by going into the cells). The blood sugar (or glucose) starts to fall but insulin will continue to be produced by her pancreas as long as the blood glucose level is higher than ideal. As the blood glucose begins to approach a reasonable level, there is now a lot more insulin in the system than is optimal. This extra insulin keeps pushing down the glucose. So now, glucose is pushed too low. Judy now is desperate for a cookie (or two) or anything to lift blood glucose into a reasonable range. Because the cookie is starch, the cycle starts again.

3:00 PM Carb Cutoff

Keep in mind that some individuals burn carbs better than fats and proteins—and vice versa. Each person is different. In chapters seven and eight, I teach you how to look at your own chemistry to figure out what types of foods your body may be burning better than others. When clients appear to be processing carbs ineffectively, there is a great technique they can use to help bring insulin levels down. For some clients, if you can help them give their bodies an extended period of time where insulin is not so high, the cells can sometimes become more responsive to insulin again. Let's also assume that you would be helping clients work on digestive issues they might be dealing with. That being said, the information below is all about trying to reduce the demand for high insulin levels for at least a large part of the day so the body can be freed up to better focus on other issues such as burning stored fat as fuel.

So, here's the technique... Teach your clients to eat any carbs before 3:00 PM on every day that they can get away with it. If your clients are done with carbs by 3:00 PM, that gives their bodies fifteen or sixteen hours to focus on burning fat, removing junk (that could otherwise get stored as fat) and taking care of all the tasks that make us healthy... all the jobs that the body is meant to do but often can't because it's being slammed with high insulin levels all day long. (Keep in mind that most foods have at least a small amount of carbs in them. Proteins and low-carb vegetables are a great choice in this scenario. You just want your clients to avoid the carbs that spike insulin levels.)

Many people like this technique because it allows them to have some of the foods that they like, just earlier in the day. In that way, they're not really depriving themselves of any one thing. That doesn't mean your client should wake up and have two sandwiches, a bowl of pasta and whole box of cereal before 3:00 PM. They still have to eat healthy. They will be able to judge their success (or not) with their self-test monitoring.

Then, once a week or so, when your clients want to go out with friends and eat a bit of carbs at night or have a drink, they don't have to be so concerned about it because they just had five or six nights in a row where they allowed their bodies to do the necessities. Maybe one week they have two nights that include more carbs and one week they have none. Even if your clients just eliminate most carbs after 3:00 PM three or four times a week, it's still better than having carbs every night—and they should still see some improvement.

But please remember that any type of carbohydrate "bingeing episode" can rock a variety of systems in the body. It can take up to seventy-two hours to recover from a carb binge. So, while I am suggesting fewer carbohydrates in the evening can be beneficial for a lot of people, overindulging in carbohydrates at any point during the day can really throw the body off its kilter, ruining endocrine coordination. Some individuals have more leeway while others may need to stick to this plan on a daily basis. It's just the knowledge of how the body works that will help you teach clients how to judge for themselves how often they want to implement this plan or not. Knowledge can help your clients make better, more informed choices. The knowledge comes from the results of self-testing.

Those who have enough minerals, amino acids and emulsified fats in their systems to reduce carbs for the majority of their meals will be able to achieve much faster results. For those who need carbs because they don't have enough minerals, amino acids and emulsified fats in the system to function properly, this 3:00 PM carb cut-off plan can be a great way to still get results. Remember, a low blood pressure reading is often an indication of mineral and protein insufficiencies.

What Carbs Should I Eat?

You'll get this question from clients a lot. In chapters seven and eight, I show you how to figure out if the minerals, fats and amino acid levels in your system appear to be too low; and you'll be able to use this knowledge to help your clients figure that out as well. Since you don't want to eliminate too many carbs if you have low nutritional content, understanding which carbs are the best to eat can be helpful. We are trying to keep just enough glucose in the bloodstream to prevent cravings from manifesting themselves.

There are a variety of tools that can be used to help clients determine the effects specific foods could have on insulin levels and blood sugar stability. Since each individual is different, each person has the challenge of determining what is best for himself. Choosing what to eat can be seen as a risk-benefit decision: *Is the nutrient density of food on this plate worth the insulin requirement it will demand?* I describe a few methods for figuring the answer to that question. See what works for you then for your clients.

See, too, if your clients have better systems for optimizing blood sugar stability. The race is ON to benefit mankind with improvements in eating. Starchy foods (most carbs) are extremely hard on our systems; we could reservedly call them poisonous. Yet we have few tools for teaching the ramifications of eating processed food from food-processing factories, pasta, cereal, potatoes, rice, bread, pastries, potatoes, pasta and cereal. (Yes, some foods get double billing.)

Here are a few suggestions for when clients ask, "What should I eat?"

Glycemic Index And Glycemic Load

Glycemic Index (GI) is a measure of how quickly a food converts to glucose. Glycemic Load (GL) describes how many carbs you have ingested that your digestion must convert to glucose.

The GI explains the speed at which different carbs convert to glucose and elevate blood sugar levels. The higher the index value, the faster glucose rises in the bloodstream, resulting in higher insulin release, more inflammation, higher cholesterol and higher internal stress.

When using the GI to determine appropriate food selections, it's important to also keep an eye on the GL – how much you eat – portion sizes. Searching for "glycemic index" on the Internet will bring up a variety of charts and tables showing the GI and GL of different foods. You will notice a variety of calculations for estimating the number of carbs you are actually ingesting. Some values may surprise you. This GI/GL method of monitoring carbs may work well for you. Remember, the goal is to keep just enough glucose in the bloodstream to prevent cravings from manifesting themselves.

We all want to eat nourishing food that benefits our personal health. Your self-test monitoring will show you what happens to your system when you switch-up your food choices.

Active Carbs

I like to look at the "active carb" count of a food. While fiber does not cancel out carbs, high-fiber foods are typically digested slower. The higher the fiber and the slower the carbs, the better. To figure out the active carbs just subtract the fiber from the carbs and that will give you the active carbs (the carbs that will spike your insulin). If you can keep active carbs around 2g-20g for as many meals as possible, you'll be doing yourself a big favor in the realm of reducing insulin spikes.

For example, in the sample nutrition label image shown here, you can see the total carb count is circled and there is an arrow pointing to the fiber content. By subtracting the "Dietary Fiber" of 3g from the "Total Carbohydrates" of 13g, you have calculated that this particular food has an active carb count of 10g per serving. Be sure to keep in mind the "per serving" calculations.

Nutrition Facts

Servings Per Container 4

Amount per serving ½ cup		
Calories 90	Calories from Fat 30	
		% Daily value
Total Fat 3g		5%
Saturated Fat 0g		0%
Trans Fat 0g		0%
Cholesterol 0mg		0%
Sodium 300mg		13%
Total Carbohydrates 13g		4%
Dietary Fiber 3g		12%
Sugars 3g		12%
Protein 3g		4%
Vitamin A 80%	Vitamin C 60%	
Calcium 4%	Iron 4%	

The main thought to keep in mind is that, if some clients eliminate most carbs while their minerals, amino acids and emulsified fats content is low, they're going to have crazy cravings, end up bingeing like a madman, experience depression issues or, even worse, have a seizure. Your goal should be to have clients include carbs that won't raise their blood sugar so high. Once clients correct digestion issues and get more nutrition in the system, they can reduce carbs further, if needed. You just don't want them to drop their carbs too low in the beginning, while nutrition levels are still too low because of digestive insufficiencies. Including higher fiber carbs that have a lower active carb count, are more slowly digested, and/or are lower on the glycemic index is a great way to hold off cravings for things like sweets, and complex carbs like bread, potatoes, rice or pasta.

Avoid Liquid Sugars

Liquid sugars spike insulin levels faster and higher than most foods with a similar carb count because, of course, liquid sugars have no fiber. High fructose corn syrup is a non-food that is often in soft drinks. When you drink something like a soda, which can contain 39 grams of sugar, that liquid form of sugar could spike your insulin as high as three candy bars. Helping your clients better understand the effects of liquid sugars can improve weight loss more than just about anything else they can do.

Yes, even fruit juice is a liquid sugar. Fruit juice can be explained as fruit without the brakes (a.k.a. fiber). Fruit was designed with those brakes for a reason. Yet, we can see an interesting comparison on the glycemic index (GI): Orange Juice--50, Potatoes--90. Potatoes have 5 grams of fiber--and still are not to be preferred when compared to OJ, depending on serving size. This comparison simply emphasizes the importance of seeing the whole picture when we make choices. We want to look at the glycemic load (GL), or the active carbs, to see the ultimate effect of the sugar as it converts to glucose. Fruit juices are often made up of natural fructose (different from high fructose corn syrup) and usually have a low GI. But drinking fruit juice with no fiber allows you to very quickly have too many active carbs or a GL that is too high.

And I repeat this caution about fruit juices, vegetable juices, and other liquid sugars: It is easy to ingest a high quantity of sugar when consuming juices. Because of the lack of fiber, it's easy to glug a glassful before we even think about it!

The same goes for alcohol (which is classified as a toxin, not as a food). Drinking "clear" alcohol does not make an individual immune to weight gain. "Clear" alcohol is a toxin; it will be handled in your system as a toxin. Alcohol stops the liver from processing sugar. The one who drinks will likely continue to pack on the pounds with every glass and shot.

When Are Carbs Appropriate?

I'm not saying that carbs are the purest form of evil. There are plenty of scenarios where an individual would want to eat more carbs. If a person is trying to pack on muscle, or is working out with great intensity, there is a place for higher starches that can be beneficial for some people. However, it appears that carbs can be beneficial in these scenarios only if that individual can process carbs correctly and he is not becoming insulin resistant. Weight loss is a common topic with clients, no matter what type of health pro you are; and the US is fast approaching 50% of the population either diabetic or prediabetic. Therefore, understanding the ins and outs of insulin and how carbs might not have the same effect from client to client is necessary.

Cycling Carbs

The goal is to create a long stretch of time that a person is not consuming carbs so insulin can come down without allowing cravings to manifest themselves. Some clients may choose to change the time of day they eat their carbs.

The 3:00 PM carb cutoff technique is one of the great ways to cycle carbs. We used to believe that carbs should be eaten only during the day so we have time to burn them before we go to bed. I have been finding new evidence that the "carbs-store-as-fat-while-we-sleep" theory may not be accurate. I later explain anabolic/catabolic state and the body's natural circadian rhythms. Eating a few, slow-burning carbs at night can have a beneficial effect on this rhythm Slow-burning carbs have a low number on the glycemic index. For example, a small tangerine has a glycemic index of 35. When you have had no carbs at supper, two SECTIONS of a small tangerine before bed can provide an overnight balance … nourishment with minimal spike in insulin.

Not to mention, most of us wake up in fat-burning mode and then turn that off by eating something like oatmeal for breakfast and spiking insulin levels. In this regard, helping a client put their carbs later in the day, instead of at breakfast, while still supplying low and slow-burning carbs, could speed up fat loss. The 3:00 PM cutoff could be the simplest route for this person's schedule. My point is, you can change the time of day that clients fit their carbs in, if they like. Again, we want to create a long stretch of time that a person is not consuming too many carbs that convert to glucose quickly, so insulin can come down. For example, instead of following the 3:00 PM carb cut off, a client may try consuming carbs only at lunch or only at dinnertime and see how that works for her. Don't forget, if your client is consuming lower glycemic carbs with a lower glycemic load, it will be easier to function through the day as low and slow sugars prevent the spike in insulin that will often result from the explosion caused by high glycemic foods, like starch.

You can also achieve an even higher level of cycling by adjusting clients' intake per day. One Monday they might consume higher carbs only for lunch. Tuesday, they might stick to only low starch vegetables, and on Wednesday they might have a higher carb load than normal. This can be very effective for those who determine through self-testing that their protein and amino acid levels are low. Typically, a low-electrolyte individual will have a harder time existing on any type of low-carb diet. However, if they mix in days with higher carbs, they appear to feel and perform much better. Many refer to this as a 'cyclical low carb diet.' I find this to be effective for a lot of people.

Low And Slow Carbs

The 3:00 PM carb cutoff technique works for some people, but not for everyone. If a person has even a little insulin resistance, the resulting elevated insulin is not going to allow him to go for extended periods of time without becoming hypoglycemic. There are two important factors: (1) the amount of carbs we eat and (2) the speed the carb converts to glucose.

Remember Judy … she ate carbs that converted to glucose explosively, causing the pancreas to respond by releasing a large amount of insulin. Well, if Judy had understood the rate of a food's conversion to glucose, she would not have chosen cookies to satisfy her sweet tooth. Cookies have a GI of 85. Judy could have snacked on a small tangerine (GI 35). The whole tangerine represents 17g of sugar. (Remember 5 grams of carbohydrate equals approximately one teaspoon of sucrose, which is GI 65.) So now, because Judy understands her insulin resistance issue, she ate TWO SECTIONS of a small tangerine, which equals 3 grams of carbohydrate with a glycemic index value of 35. This "low and slow" sugar prevented the cravings that previously drove her nuts because she became so hypoglycemic. This is where an ounce of prevention is worth a pound of cure – and likely weight loss.

With "low and slow" sugars, Judy can keep her system from a hypoglycemic panic that releases stress hormones. Now her cravings are almost non-existent. Yet, when she does have a craving, she knows why it is happening and what to do about it. Judy also realized that when she had cravings, it was because something she ate earlier in the day was a fast or "explosive" carbohydrate that drove her system off balance, making her insulin go too high. With a little more vigilance, she will be back on track.

Judy chose TWO SECTIONS of tangerine. Of course, some other low-glycemic fruit or food can work as well. We are trying not to use refined carbs while being diligent about portion control. Portion control is easy with a tangerine; it comes to us all sectioned off.

Keep in mind that we are all unique. Some individual may be dealing with food sensitivities that can make a low glycemic food have the reaction of a higher glycemic food, because of that individual's response to that food.

Empty Carbs

Remember … We eat 3 categories of food – carbohydrates, fats and proteins. Each category has accompanying minerals. When digestion works properly, we are nourished and energized as carbohydrates are changed to glucose, fats are emulsified, proteins become amino acids, and minerals are released to become available to our cells. Through digestion, food becomes elemental in our systems.

Refined sugars and starch can be considered "empty" when they don't contain elements to feed our cells. Sugars and starches make our stomachs feel full; yet food value is missing. An empty starch contains many carbs that convert to glucose EXPLOSIVELY which can cause a LARGE release of insulin to attempt to push the glucose into the cells. Now you have excess insulin hanging around, with no purpose in life. You know what happens to teenagers when they don't feel they have a purpose in life … they get in trouble … they make trouble where none previously existed … they get a bad attitude … I could go on …

why don't they get pants that fit?   Anyway, an excess insulin release after we eat empty carbs (starches) wreaks havoc on our system; specifically, it can bring on hypoglycemia, which makes us go nuts.

When we eat any carbohydrate, our pancreas releases insulin to handle the glucose from that carbohydrate. In a healthy person, the insulin does its job and subsides as the sugar goes into the cells. A large portion of the population is developing insulin resistance, so the pancreas puts out extra insulin to clear the bloodstream of glucose. If we have "empty" high glycemic carbs (starch and refined sugar), the insulin levels have to become elevated to push a high quantity of glucose into our cells ... slamming our cells out of balance with too much glucose, spiking insulin, which over time results in too little glucose and a hypoglycemic incident.

A spiked amount of insulin eventually brings sugar down to where it needs to be. However, the elevated amount of insulin doesn't just stop pushing glucose into the cells. (A lesser amount of insulin would taper off when a good range is reached.) Elevated insulin keeps on pushing. The blood sugar doesn't stay in the good range very long. The elevated insulin pushes the blood sugar too low, so a person becomes hypoglycemic. The hypoglycemic incident causes stress hormones to be released. Stress hormones <u>create glucose</u> to relieve the hypoglycemic incident. Stress hormones, such as adrenaline and cortisol, keep being released, converting fat and protein into <u>more glucose</u> as long as the hypoglycemia prevails.

Having a small amount of low-glycemic fruit will provide relief from the hypoglycemic release of stress hormones. Having this same small amount of low-glycemic fruit before going to bed can protect us from this hyper / hypo-glycemic yoyo.

Intro To Cravings

The principles you learn in the next chapter about cravings will change the way you view weight loss. This really is the big kahuna. A big golden nugget was learning that it's high insulin levels that are causing your clients to store fat and restricting their bodies from burning stored fat. That's great. But that still leads you right back to trying to figure out how to limit your clients' carbs without them waking up from a zombie-like state with a half-eaten bag of M&Ms in their hands. Understanding the need to reduce carbs is one thing; learning methods to make that reduction easy for any carboholic... that will be your real pot of gold.

The good news is: Your clients are still going to be able to have a variety of carbs if they want to; plus many of your clients will be required to continue eating specific carbs because I don't want the insane asylums to be filled with nut-cases carrying my book around.

Your first job will be to follow the steps outlined in the next chapter to help reduce your clients' cravings. Saying goodbye to pizza or double fudge ice cream will seem impossible to many of your clients, but I'm here to tell you it will be a piece of cake... except without the cake. When you help your clients give their bodies what they really need due to improved digestion, it will stop that constant screaming for junk every two hours that occurs with so many people. Here's a tip for when you are 'trapped into' eating pizza: Ask for a fork; then eat the top of your piece of pizza, just don't eat the starchy, high glycemic crust.

In chapter six, I teach you how you can find foods higher in carbs that won't spike insulin levels, and how to include medium-carb foods if your clients' cravings are still hard to get past. The medium-carb and low glycemic foods will reduce any cravings and may slow weight loss a little, but should still allow your clients to continue seeing progress. And that is what they really want—progress.

Now, let's crack those cravings.

Wha'd He Say?

In this chapter, you learned:
- Consuming too many carbs can spike insulin levels. These high insulin levels block the body's ability to burn stored fat. High insulin can also send the signal to store more fuel as fat and may continue to do so for as long as those insulin levels are high. Ask: *Is the nutrient density of the food on this plate worth the insulin requirement it will demand?*
- By consuming foods lower in carbs, you can keep your insulin levels down and allow your body to access stored fat and burn it as fuel.
- Some people do not qualify to remove too many carbs from their diet. If you have a low level of minerals, amino acid, and fats in

your system, you will need to consume carbs until digestion improves.

- By eliminating most carbs after 3:00 PM, you give your body an extended period of time for insulin levels to come down so the body can access stored fat and use it as fuel.

CHAPTER SIX

Cravings

How many times have clients explained to you that they were excited to be doing so well on a diet, getting results and feeling good about themselves—only to have a craving come on that was so strong, they were certain it must have beamed into their brain by aliens? Over and over again, your clients will find ways to rationalize that eating four cupcakes will somehow help them in their weight loss long term. They tell themselves that if they just allow themselves to eat this one large pizza, they'll be perfect for the rest of the week. Your clients may even say to you, "Yes, I understand the principles of the diet that I'm on, but obviously you didn't mean to leave out chocolate. How could I function without chocolate?"

Cravings destroy more diet efforts than any other single factor. If your clients never craved bad foods, any of the thirty diets they have probably tried may have worked for them. Even when weight loss is not the goal, with what you learn in this book, you will want to help clients reduce their carb, sugar, starch, or processed junk intake when working to improve a wide variety of health issues. No matter what issue you're working to improve with clients, if they need to reduce these types of carbs, cravings could turn out to be your client's biggest obstacle. In chapters seven and eight, you'll learn how to help clients look at their physiology, have a better understanding of what is causing their cravings, and steps they can take to control impulses. But before we get to that, I want to lay down a foundation on cravings to give us a starting point. I talk about cravings throughout this book. Right now, I'll explain the issue that is usually responsible for cravings for most people; especially if they normally crave sugar, chocolate, carbs or salty foods.

Cravings can be a touchy subject for people. Some folks have dealt with this tough issue for years, or even decades. Yes, there can be emotional baggage attached to cravings that go all the way back to your client's first Easy-Bake Oven, or even earlier. But if clients have emotional issues and they are in need of finding a way past them, understanding what I'm about to explain to you can help them. The difficulty level of moving past these issues can go from a ten, all the way down to a one... once your client understands what can be done to correct this one circumstance.

As a way to clarify terminology ... When digestion is compromised, lacking or deficient, our bodies do not receive adequate nutrition. This resulting state of low nutrition can be called many things - low minerals, low salts, lack of nutrition, puny, hungry, unsatisfied, and hangry, to name a few. Optimal digestion ultimately results in the release of minerals from the food for use by our cells; this occurs after the carbohydrates are changed to glucose, fats are emulsified, and proteins become amino acids. So, when I refer to "low mineral," I include all the ramifications of inadequate digestion.

Back to cravings—here is how works. If a person's minerals are low, that person can have seizures. If a person's sugars are low, that person can have seizures. If salts and sugars are low at the same time, that person has an even greater chance of having a seizure. If blood pressure is usually low, and an individual, Julie, has additional issues that can also push her blood sugar very low, that's the perfect recipe for some crazy, crazy cravings—the type of cravings where she might literally steal candy from a baby. (I'm sure Julie rationalized it by saying that the baby was very whiny and did not deserve the candy.)

When I discuss pH levels of urine and saliva in chapter eight, I explain the circumstances that can cause blood sugars to go too low. When a person's minerals and sugars go too low at the same time, this is a compound cause for cravings. This is usually why people crave salty foods, sweet and sugary foods, or carbs like bread, pizza, potato chips, or crackers (that can be converted to sugars). Your body isn't dumb. If minerals are low, you can buffer them by raising your sugars and you'll be fine. The reverse is also true. If sugars are low, you can buffer them by raising your minerals. The cravings are your body's way of helping you to raise either your minerals or your sugars in order to keep you from pushing toward an emergency.

These cravings can cause many people to think that something is wrong with them, or they just have no willpower nor impulse control. The truth is: You can't compete with a body that demands what it needs to continue functioning properly. Does that mean that these sugars or carbs are good for you? No; but don't you think your body would be more concerned with not having seizures than it would be with gaining weight? Doesn't it make sense that if the body recognized a "looming seizure" that would shut down the whole system, it would take steps to keep that from happening? The body is reacting, and sometimes overreacting, to the immediate circumstances it is encountering. We need to "pick up the baby," so to speak, and supply what is needed before the screaming, crying, and cravings take place.

To get rid of cravings, people with low salts, low minerals, and low blood pressure can raise their mineral content by:

1. Using unrefined salt (like sea salt).
2. Using specific supplements.
3. Correcting any digestion problems that are keeping the body from properly breaking down food, so the mineral content can be assimilated by the body. If clients are not digesting correctly, they're not getting the minerals out of their food.

Many of you who have low blood pressure will be able to test these tactics on yourself before you introduce them to your clients. I go over all those steps in detail after you are able to look at your specific body chemistry and figure out which of those steps, or what combination of those steps, are appropriate for you. Remember, this book is not about doing things just because they worked for someone else. This book is about figuring out what is right for each person and his unique chemistry. Conversely, if an individual has high blood pressure, I will include steps that person can take to tackle cravings as well.

Just don't get ahead of me. I'm not saying that if a person, Angie, is craving sugar she's about to have a seizure. It just means the body is very defensive when it comes to having seizures, and it plans way ahead of time by sending out the signal for more things that can thicken the bloodstream and raise the minerals or the sugars. Your body doesn't know that you have cereal in the cupboard thirty feet away. It still operates under the assumption that you need to go out and hunt down a zebra or track down berries somewhere. Believe it or not, the body was not designed with "Special K" in mind.

The body may be feeling a little panicked about the low resources. The body may be sending a signal that you interpret as, "Hey... you... go to the store and get some double fudge ice cream and a box of those Nilla Wafers." This urge doesn't mean that a seizure is about to kick in. Even if you didn't eat anything else for another ten to twenty hours or more, you likely could still avoid a seizure. Yet, you are receiving notice that nutrition is on your TO-DO list.

Even as a health pro yourself, if you've been struggling with your "relationship" with food for most of your life, you may have just received the biggest piece of information you will see in years. If you don't struggle with cravings, this little nugget will still be one of your secret weapons that helps your clients see real results when they have failed in the past. Again, a lack of minerals is not always the cause behind cravings; it's just one of the most common. But the same goes for almost any craving. If a person, Hank, is having a craving, his body is looking for something that it needs, and that craving is merely Hank's interpretation of that need (or insufficiency). His body could be needing fats or specific amino acids or vitamins. The possibilities are countless.

The important part is learning how to figure out what each client's body needs. Then teach the client not to be so stingy. Let his body have it. That doesn't mean if a client is craving a rocky road sundae that they should let their body have it. It simply means there must be specific nutrients (or even junk that can be used in place of those nutrients) in that sundae that could help the body function better at that moment. Since simple sugars can be very easy for the body to break down and utilize, that can sometimes be what the body screams for in a pinch. The body doesn't care that the sundae is going to spike insulin levels and make it so this person can't button their pants anymore. The body is reacting only to the moment, not the long-term plan. The body is just looking for anything it can use as a resource in what is being viewed as a legitimate emergency. Giving your clients a way to provide the body with the nutrients that it truly needs will normally alleviate the craving for quick-fix junk, like sugar, that can come with its own set of problems. Much of this book will teach you how to do just that—how to give each client's body what it needs so the body will shut up and stop screaming, "Give me Sour Patch Kids!"

Correcting Cravings

If you know your blood pressure is low, I explain more steps you can take to correct cravings as you progress through the book. However, anyone with cravings can begin by adding healthy fats. Fats can be a big part of what your body is missing since so many people still live in the fictional world of the eighties that told us to reduce our fat intake. Since nutritional fats are required for so many functions, including brain function and cellular repair, cravings can be a big signal that you're not getting enough appropriate fats. The correct fats can also help you feel satiated longer after a meal and keep you from consuming more junk an hour after you finish eating.

Many of my clients are very excited to learn that foods, like butter, whole eggs or heavy cream, can actually be beneficial to their health and aid in weight loss. When it comes to fats, depending on each client's body chemistry at the cellular level, certain fats will help some individuals more than any supplement could, while other specific fats could push a person in the wrong direction. In chapter seven I teach how to look at a few simple measurements to figure out if you have any imbalances that could benefit from consuming specific fats. When you're balanced, most healthy fats can benefit you greatly.

The important factor that confuses the issue is that digestion needs to be working correctly for the body to be able to process fats correctly. Without proper bile flow, an individual can't emulsify those fats so that the body can use them. The Beet Flow supplement I talked about before will help improve that. This is why a diet that is higher in fats doesn't work for everyone. If you don't have the bile flow to process fats correctly, increasing your fat intake could lead to weight gain or digestive discomfort. But if you do have good bile flow, increasing your appropriate fats can speed up weight loss greatly; and avoiding fats can compound cravings and restrict weight loss altogether for some people.

Here is the shortlist of fats that many people avoid yet can actually aid in weight loss, and provide other health benefits, if used with the correct body chemistry:

Egg yolks

Butter or ghee

Coconut oil

Heavy cream

Olive oil (with caution)

Animal fats

Many dieters also eliminate good fats and replace them with products that boast to be healthier options, even though the replacement products create more fat storage than the version of that food that they are trying to replace. Things like:

Vegetable oils

Butter-replacement spreads

Fat-free dairy products

Fat-free baked goods

When manufacturers reduce fats in these products, they add chemicals, artificial sweeteners, and more carbohydrates in order to keep flavor. These chemicals are the things your body doesn't recognize as food; therefore the chemicals will often get stored in fat cells precipitated by the high carbohydrates. Oops.

Mineral Levels And Cravings

Remember, this is the formula:

If minerals are too low, raising sugars can help.

If sugars are too low, raising minerals can help.

Since raising sugars will also raise insulin levels and cause weight gain, or other ramifications, the solution is to look at each client's physiology to see if she is a person who needs to raise her minerals or not. If a client, Josie, has high blood pressure, this is an indication that her body is not correctly handling the minerals she currently has. So, raising mineral levels is not a good option for Josie and, in some cases, could be dangerous. However, if Pete's blood pressure is low, raising his mineral levels could give him a new lease on life, health, and especially getting past his cravings.

In chapter seven you'll learn how to test your blood pressure to get a sense of your mineral levels, whether high or low. If your mineral levels are high and you want to improve cravings, you'll likely want to focus more on hydration and excretion of electrolytes, as well as on digestion and including more good fats. But if your blood pressure is low, you'll likely want to put a lot of attention into what I'm going to explain here.

If digestion has been poor for years, the body could be very depleted when it comes to protein, fat, and mineral reserves. Increasing the minerals available to the body can make a huge difference in how every part of that body operates. It can also reduce how often the body screams for some Nutter Butters.

If you're using supplements to improve digestion, more minerals will be brought in from the food you're eating. On that same front, increasing use of unrefined salt (like unrefined sea salt) can be a life-changing step for someone with low blood pressure. Chapter eight outlines all the numbers to look for while determining if your blood pressure is high or low. Once you go through the process of determining these factors for yourself, it will give you a better understanding of how to teach your clients to do the same. If your blood pressure is low, don't be afraid of sea salt. We're taught to avoid salt because many years ago the doctor told our Uncle Phil it's going to kill him. Yes, if you have high blood pressure that is reactive to sodium chloride, you certainly may want to correct it before you start to add salt. But as a society, we have taken advice directed at those with high blood pressure and applied that advice to everyone—even to those who REALLY NEED that salt. You'll read more about salt in chapter thirteen. Just know that, more than any other suggestion I offer, I've seen more clients reduce their cravings and improve a variety of health issues from simply adding sea salt.

In chapter fourteen I talk more about supplements that can help lift minerals as well, but unrefined salt is the best place to start if you have low blood pressure.

Note: For clients on blood pressure medication, that drug will change body regulators and metabolism to keep their blood pressure low. So, don't look at those low blood pressure readings and think those clients need more mineral. If they're on blood pressure medication and now have a blood pressure reading that could be considered too low, those folks might want to talk to their doctor about lowering the dosage of their medication. Keep in mind that I'm not telling you to lower your medication, nor for you to tell your clients to lower their medication. You and your clients need to consult your doctors to make a move like that.

Soil And Minerals

It is believed that, as humans, we are hardwired for foods that are sweet. You see, when food is the way it's supposed to be, where we find sweet is also where we find a lot of minerals—like in fruit, for example. Fruit used to contain minerals to help us process the sugars in these sweet foods. The majority of fruit grown today is lacking the mineral needed to handle the sugars contained in that fruit. That is why fruit is often not as healthy a choice as it once was. The result can be people thinking that they're making a healthy selection when they're really just eating a candy bar that grew on a tree.

To make matters worse, the manufacturing industry takes a food like corn and processes the minerals out of it while producing some type of corn flake or snack food. First, they take out the germ. Next, they coat the remaining complex carbs with sugar to make it delicious and appealing to our senses. The brain is fooled into seeing this sweet product as having an abundance of mineral. This triggers the brain's happy receptors, letting the body know that nutrients are on the way. The brain says, "You need mineral badly; now eat a bucket of this stuff." An hour and a half after eating an entire bucket of sweet, nutritionally void "non-food," the person is looking for something else to eat. The body got ripped off and didn't receive the mineral content that was indicated by the food's sweetness. The brain now realizes it did not get minerals along with the sugar, so it starts to look for more sweets to bring in the mineral that it needs.

Beyond the processing of food, the real trouble with today's food source shows up when processing begins with the soil. People talk a lot about how the real problem is the American soil and how it has no mineral left in it. The Italians have been growing tomatoes for over 5,000 years, yet they still grow a good tomato. America has been farming for what, three hundred years? And we can't grow a tomato that tastes like anything anymore. You can see that it's red, but if you've ever talked to anyone who has eaten produce in other countries, they will tell you, "Over there, it actually has flavor in it."

The American soil is not the problem, it is the American farming methods. Minerals need to be in the soil in order for minerals to make it into the plant. However, it's the bacteria in the soil that allows the mineral to make that jump from the dirt to the plant, and then into the fruit of that plant. The bacteria is the life of that soil. When you fertilize with chemical and high phosphate fertilizers, you kill the bacteria and the mineral can't make the jump into the plant.

The problem is this: We now have scientists who have figured out how to engineer the seed so that it no longer requires minerals to produce an apparent crop. Why do I say 'apparent' crop? Because that's what the crops are: Produce that appears before you, even though it is void of mineral. Crops aren't even weighed anymore; they are sold by the bushel, which means they are sold by the size and not the weight. Mineral is what makes a crop weigh more, so there is no financial punishment for a farmer who sells a crop void of significant nutritional value. Are you following the path our food takes? (1) We have the farmer "processing" the very soil, (2) seed that grows food without nutrition, (3) this product is "processed" into something that doesn't resemble food at all, and then (4) we pray over it like the miracle of nature had anything to do with making it. Oops. That's why it's becoming so important to use good supplements that are appropriate for your body. This is becoming the only way to ensure that you're getting the nutrients you really need since our food supply is slowly turning into nothing more than something to chew on.

Is There Crack In These Snack Cakes?

Are you starting to understand why these processed junk foods can be so addicting? Food mad scientists have figured out how to make processed foods taste like there is nutrition inside. If your body is depleted of needed minerals and other nutrients, and you eat foods that send the brain a signal that states, "Here comes the nutrition you've been missing," of course the body will be tricked into wanting more. When artificial sweeteners are even sweeter than foods found in nature, consuming these sweet tastes can jack up your cravings even more. These chemical sweeteners should be avoided even more than sugar when trying to kill cravings.

We are also drawn to salty and fatty flavors because in nature, these flavors are attached to the nutrients we need the most. In nature, sweet, salty and fatty foods are filled with minerals, vitamins, proteins and fats that our bodies need to function. The obesity problem in this country is not often an issue of slackers who have no self control at the dinner table. These are just people who are having their innate, hard-wired system used against them by the food manufacturers. Some of these food manufacturers make the people who make cigarettes look like upstanding citizens. At least the cigarette folks tell you right on the package that their product is not good for you. There are other factors often involved in cravings and obesity, but helping people realize that the food they are eating is really more of a "non-food" and doesn't count as nutrition can be a big step in the right direction.

When the nutrients never show up, the body isn't going to change the innate functionality it has been operating on for eons. The body is not going to say, "I guess sweet taste no longer equates to a good source of minerals." Our bodies have been operating this way for thousands of years. We've only been bastardizing our food supply for a few decades. This means you should not count on evolution to correct your cravings.

You do have one option, however, and this is how I explain it to my clients: You can stop eating the crap. Just because some evil genius has discovered how to make his snack cakes more addictive than crack doesn't mean that you are required to continue supporting his new speedboat. His desire to be rich does not need to win out over your desire to be healthy.

The difficulty of eliminating these foods will come down to an individual's mineral content. If a person, Alicia, can give her body what it really needs, her body will stop screaming for this junk that mimics the nutrients her body is searching for. This can give your clients the edge over food that may have kept them captive in the past. With your knowledge of why people crave these foods and how you can help them reduce those cravings, it can be your turn to win. I wonder if you'll get a speedboat too.

Low & Medium-Carb Foods

When it comes to weight loss, or improving health issues that can be caused by spiking insulin levels too often, an important goal should be to eliminate cravings and bingeing. Once you can help a client take care of those two issues, the rest is pretty easy. You already learned that helping an individual correct digestion in order to get more nutrition into the system can reduce cravings and the need to binge.

But sometimes additional mineral isn't enough. With some people who have low blood pressure, you can add a lot more mineral and they will still have low resources because they have been depleting the body's reserves for so long. In some cases, these people seem to have a malfunction that causes them to pee out their minerals as fast as they are ingested. These individuals will often benefit from consuming more carbs, at least in the beginning, while these folks do the work to bring mineral levels up naturally.

At the same time, for those trying to lose weight or reduce their carb intake for a specific health benefit, we know that increasing carbs is going to reduce the speed at which they achieve their goal. However, if a client, Henry, doesn't have sufficient mineral reserves, I would prefer to see him achieve slow and gradual improvement. If Henry tries to lose six pounds in a week by eating very few carbs, he may end up snapping and bingeing on a box of doughnuts that makes him gain seven pounds.

This is where medium-carb foods come in. By selecting foods that can provide more carbs, without spiking insulin levels as much as high-carb choices might, a person, like Henry, with low resources can keep his cravings down and his sanity up, and still move toward his goals. The type of carbs will be important. Henry will still need to avoid all sugar and starchy carbs that will spike insulin levels too high. That means avoiding bread, rice, pasta, potatoes, etc. If Henry in this scenario consumes fruit, try to have him stick to small portions of lower glycemic fruits like berries or maybe half an apple.

Low-Carb Examples

A low-carb meal would contain between 0 and 15 active carbs.

- Spinach omelet using three whole eggs, with real butter and two turkey sausage links.
- Grilled chicken caesar salad without croutons.
- Two baked chicken legs with a side of broccoli.

Medium-Carb Examples

A medium-carb meal would contain between 16 and 25 active carbs.

- Lettuce wrap with grilled chicken, snap peas, hummus, and butternut squash.
- Greek yogurt with berries.
- Protein shake with a few berries.
- Grilled lamb with lentils and broccoli.

Turning Low-Carb Meals Into Medium-Carb Meals

Here's another great technique: For some clients, I'll suggest keeping those small cutie oranges on hand. These are small tangerines with a total of 17 g of sugar in the whole tangerine. These tangerines can be sectioned apart, with two sections eaten right after breakfast, two more sections midmorning, another two sections after lunch, and so on. I'm suggesting each person consume no more than one and half tangerines in a day. Most people use less than one of these cutie oranges per day, spread out over the day. This gives relief from cravings and can help avoid insulin spikes and hypoglycemic issues. Using this method allows the individual to simply stick with low-carb meals instead of having to figure out what is a low-carb meal and what is a medium-carb meal.

If a client is already improving digestion and adding unrefined salt or other mineral sources and cravings are still strong, the goal could be to have 16-25 active carbs (or low glycemic carbs) per meal for three meals of the day. Going higher than 25 active carbs could cause your client's insulin to spike too high and then their blood sugar will drop too low and they will crave sugar or carbs big time. So, the solution is to get in more carbs without spiking insulin levels.

Once a client, Angela, adds a few carbs and can stop the cravings and bingeing, she can begin trying to remove most of her carbs from dinner. Stopping almost all carbs after 3:00 PM will allow insulin to come down until the next day when more carbs are consumed again. If removing most carbs from dinner becomes easy, Angela can do this every day. You might want to have her try removing carbs from dinner for just one or two days in a row and then having some medium-carbs for dinner again on the third day. If that goes well, she can try to go for more days in a row. Once low-carb dinners are easy, Angela can try removing most carbs from lunch as well in the same manner. Maybe she can try that for only a day or so at a time at first to make sure cravings don't come back. Angela can then continue reducing medium-carb meals until she can do a whole day with no medium-carb meals.

When weight loss is the goal, if clients can drop the carbs on every meal other than breakfast for 3-5 days of the week, they will likely begin to lose weight. When a client, Jade, wants to be aggressive and lose weight faster, she can try reducing more carbs. If any cravings come on again or any thoughts of binges, she can eat a medium-carb food as quickly as possible and go back to more carbs in the day. (Keep in mind that Jade should still be doing the work to raise mineral levels as she learns to reduce carbs.)

Your clients will need to look at labels and watch the active carb content of what they're eating. They can try to find foods with carbs that fit the numbers they're looking for.

Don't worry about assigning a daily limit on carbs. This method can be too restrictive. Just try to teach your clients how to give themselves long periods of the day where they have no insulin spikes. Keeping insulin down is where a client's weight loss will come from. That's why no insulin spikes after 3:00 PM is so effective. It gives people the rest of the afternoon and the whole night to burn fat.

To find lists of low-carb and medium-carb foods, go to www.SixfigureHealthPro.com and click on BOOK TOOLS > LOW-CARB CHARTS or MEDIUM-CARB CHARTS

Wha'd He Say?

In this chapter, you learned:

- Cravings can be reduced or eliminated by improving digestion and finding better ways to give the body what it really needs.
- If blood pressure is low, finding ways to bring up the mineral and protein content in the system can reduce cravings. Unrefined salt and small amounts of tangerine throughout the day can be great places to start.
- Consuming appropriate fats can reduce cravings.
- Most processed foods are scientifically designed to make a person feel better by sending a false signal that nutrition is on the way—even though it's not. It will, however, trigger the happy receptors in the brain, making the individual want to eat more of this junk. Because of this, the goal should be to bring in more of the minerals and nutrients the body truly needs so the person can feel better without the junk.

- Using medium-carb foods strategically can help reduce cravings for those who have a low mineral content.

CHAPTER SEVEN

Simple Self-Testing

You're about to learn how to run simple physiological tests on your body. The information you gain from these tests will direct you to nutritional choices and lifestyle changes that could help you improve your health, and possibly even better understand why you might be dealing with specific symptoms or health issues. You could run these tests on yourself to experience them firsthand. If you discover any imbalances, you also want to experience the changes that can come about if you make changes to improve those imbalances. By using yourself as your "first client," you can gain a better understanding of how to teach these techniques to your clients. However, I'm going to share only the simple tests here. If you find that you would like to run additional tests and gain even more information, you can follow the intermediate self-testing instructions in Appendix B. With most clients, you can learn enough through the simple self-tests to help them improve a wide variety of issues. However, if you want to dig deeper, the more advanced tests in Appendix B are available to you.

This Is The Magic

You have an opportunity here to begin understanding how your specific body is operating. You may be able (through measurement) to recognize imbalances that you are experiencing and you may even find food, nutrition or lifestyle changes that could help improve those imbalances. As you read this chapter, you will likely start to ask yourself questions like, "Hey, I wonder if this is why my client was dealing with that specific issue, etc.?" Just be sure to understand that the body is very complicated and understand that each person is unique in his own special way.

In most cases, if you want to help clients better understand a severe symptom, condition, or something even more serious, you're going to need a much firmer grasp on these foundational principles. And if you happen to be dealing with your own severe issue, don't try to be a hero and figure it all out yourself. There really is no reason to show off in that way, and you will likely create added frustration for yourself. I'm going to teach you what to look at and where you can find tools to chart your progress and monitor your changes on your own. I'm also going to show you where you can find help when you need it. You will save time and effort by finding an experienced professional to help you along. Working with a professional to improve your own issues can be a good way to see how much you're going to be able to help your clients with this information.

It's important to understand that people need to take responsibility for their own health. Most people will not be able to simply take a few supplements, or remove a few foods from their diet, and correct every issue that may have been developing for the last two or three decades. We all can watch our own chemistry and see if we are moving in the right direction, even before noticing changes in how we feel. For many, improved chemistry is often enough to keep them on track long enough to reap the rewards.

This approach is much different from treating only symptoms. The medical world is not the only place where practitioners treat off of symptoms. Most natural practitioners work off of symptoms as well. They just use natural substances to improve those symptoms instead of drugs, but they are still pigeonholing a client into a "diagnosis" based on the symptoms. When working in this manner, a practitioner might as well be asking the clients to throw darts at a "diagnosis dart board." At least with this option, clients might leave the doctor's office with a stuffed animal. However, when natural practitioners do guess correctly, a natural approach often doesn't bring about an immediate "drug-like" response. Therefore, the client stops or moves on to the next big thing.

When looking to help the body correct its own issues, keep in mind that this process will take much longer than the 4-6 hours it often takes for a drug to kick in. In nature, things that happen fast are often bad things. The best things happen slowly. A flower doesn't wake up and go, "BAM!!!" open. The flower opens slowly and gradually. The sun doesn't just appear out of nowhere in full force. That would freak us out every single time. The sun rises gradually, just as it sets, just as the grass grows and the seasons change. Let your body do the same. If you're looking to "fix" a problem by Friday because you don't want it to interfere with the big square dance you hope to attend, you're going to find yourself very frustrated—not only because you really need a better social life if a square dance is your big event, but also because you're setting yourself up for failure if you believe you can change the agriculture of your body in a few days. You can't. It's also very important to explain this to clients so they understand what to expect.

Data Tracking Sheet

In this section you will find a *Data Tracking Sheet*. You can also go to the site, www.SixFigureHealthPro.com and download a free PDF to print so you won't have to mark up your pretty book. This will allow you to keep a binder of your progress so you can track your results and see patterns. You will also have that information available in case you decide to seek help from a professional. Click on the link BOOK TOOLS to download the *Data Tracking Sheet*. While you're at it, you can also download the *Basic Imbalance Guide*, as I cover that form in chapter eight.

On the top right corner of the *Data Tracking Sheet*, you will see colored boxes that are used when testing your urine with a 10- or 11-parameter strip. These strips are used as part of the intermediate testing procedures outlined in Appendix B. You won't need to use those colored boxes unless you decide you want to collect more information about your chemistry. But for some clients dealing with specific issues, these strips can be a huge help; so it would be beneficial to experience them for yourself. While you're on our website, click on the Resources Link and you'll find the link to order them on Amazon.

URINE TEST STRIP

BLOOD Hemolyzed
Non-hemolyzed
UROBILINOGEN
BILIRUBIN
PROTEIN
NITRITE
KETONES
ASCORBIC ACID
GLUCOSE
PH
SPECIFIC GRAVITY
LEUKOCYTES

Date_____ Time_____	Date_____ Time_____	Date_____ Time_____	Date_____ Time_____
Well-Being_____	**Well-Being_____**	**Well-Being_____**	**Well-Being_____**
Urine pH _____	Urine pH _____	Urine pH _____	Urine pH _____
Saliva pH _____	Saliva pH _____	Saliva pH _____	Saliva pH _____
Breath Rate _____	Breath Rate _____	Breath Rate _____	Breath Rate _____
Breat Hold _____	Breat Hold _____	Breat Hold _____	Breat Hold _____
Resting Standing	**Resting Standing**	**Resting Standing**	**Resting Standing**
Blood Pressure (Systolic) _____ _____	Blood Pressure (Systolic) _____ _____	Blood Pressure (Systolic) _____ _____	Blood Pressure (Systolic) _____ _____
Blood Pressure (Diastolic) _____ _____	Blood Pressure (Diastolic) _____ _____	Blood Pressure (Diastolic) _____ _____	Blood Pressure (Diastolic) _____ _____
Pulse _____ _____	Pulse _____ _____	Pulse _____ _____	Pulse _____ _____

Date_____ Time_____	Date_____ Time_____	Date_____ Time_____	Date_____ Time_____
Well-Being_____	**Well-Being_____**	**Well-Being_____**	**Well-Being_____**
Urine pH _____	Urine pH _____	Urine pH _____	Urine pH _____
Saliva pH _____	Saliva pH _____	Saliva pH _____	Saliva pH _____
Breath Rate _____	Breath Rate _____	Breath Rate _____	Breath Rate _____
Breat Hold _____	Breat Hold _____	Breat Hold _____	Breat Hold _____
Resting Standing	**Resting Standing**	**Resting Standing**	**Resting Standing**
Blood Pressure (Systolic) _____ _____	Blood Pressure (Systolic) _____ _____	Blood Pressure (Systolic) _____ _____	Blood Pressure (Systolic) _____ _____
Blood Pressure (Diastolic) _____ _____	Blood Pressure (Diastolic) _____ _____	Blood Pressure (Diastolic) _____ _____	Blood Pressure (Diastolic) _____ _____
Pulse _____ _____	Pulse _____ _____	Pulse _____ _____	Pulse _____ _____

Date_____ Time_____	Date_____ Time_____	Date_____ Time_____	Date_____ Time_____
Well-Being_____	**Well-Being_____**	**Well-Being_____**	**Well-Being_____**
Urine pH _____	Urine pH _____	Urine pH _____	Urine pH _____
Saliva pH _____	Saliva pH _____	Saliva pH _____	Saliva pH _____
Breath Rate _____	Breath Rate _____	Breath Rate _____	Breath Rate _____
Breat Hold _____	Breat Hold _____	Breat Hold _____	Breat Hold _____
Resting Standing	**Resting Standing**	**Resting Standing**	**Resting Standing**
Blood Pressure (Systolic) _____ _____	Blood Pressure (Systolic) _____ _____	Blood Pressure (Systolic) _____ _____	Blood Pressure (Systolic) _____ _____
Blood Pressure (Diastolic) _____ _____	Blood Pressure (Diastolic) _____ _____	Blood Pressure (Diastolic) _____ _____	Blood Pressure (Diastolic) _____ _____
Pulse _____ _____	Pulse _____ _____	Pulse _____ _____	Pulse _____ _____

The Coalition

There is an international association called *The Coalition for Health Education*. This private, nonprofit association spans the planet and consists of doctors, health coaches, nutritionists, personal trainers, a wide variety of other types of natural health professionals and members of the general public who want to learn more about natural health and how the body really works. When readers come to www.KickItNaturally.com looking for a health coach who can help them better understand the ideas that are taught in this book, we send them to *The Coalition* to find a professional in their area. If you continue to dig deeper into this work, and graduate from our online Bio-individuality Coach Course, you will then qualify to receive referrals from *The Coalition*.

We have also made arrangements with this private association to allow our readers to become members without sponsorship from a professional health coach. *The Coalition* has an advanced website that was put in place to help health coaches educate their clients and monitor the progress of their clients' chemistry. As those clients input the numbers from their self-tests into the website, the health coach can look at the client's self-test entries and help them make nutritional adjustments according to their chemistry. However, even if you are not working with a Coalition health coach, as one of my readers, you can register as a member of the site, which will grant you access to all of your own advanced monitoring and tracking tools. This will allow you to be your own Coalition health coach as you learn these techniques. I helped *the Coalition* put together many of the systems they use today so they have given my readers the hook-up. As you input the results of your self-tests into the system, you can watch the changes over time with the site's dynamic graphing systems. You can even keep a food journal to which your self-test results will transfer automatically so you can see how different foods affect your chemistry and how you feel. You will also find charts that can show you where your chemistry is now, and what foods can help offset imbalances so your metabolism moves you in the right direction if you are imbalanced.

It is an amazing tool. The best part is that $20 per year will cover your membership dues and there is no extra charge to use the tools on the website. As an added benefit, if you decide that you need the help of a professional in your area, *The Coalition* can attach your account, at your request, to a local health coach who can then see how your chemistry has been moving while you were working on your own.

The downloadable *Data Tracking Sheet* found at www.SixFigureHealthPro.com is an adequate way to keep tabs on your chemistry; but if you want to see the whole picture by using the graphs and other tools, *The Coalition* is the way to go. If you have an Internet connection and can afford $20 for the year, you'll want to take advantage of this arrangement. It has been a very helpful tool for my readers and for those who listen to our *Kick It Naturally* podcast. For the remainder of this book, it may sound like I'm assuming you are using the tools on *The Coalition* website because I feel like they can really help you see into your numbers and better understand your chemistry. Monitoring measurements can validate you are going in the right direction. This gives you the discernment that can solidify your conviction to stay on course. It's easier to keep doing the right thing when your own measurements make the process become more objective instead of subjective. Then, it's easier to help others after you have experienced it yourself.

Investing in your own health is as important as taking the time to read about it. Though improving the actual cause of a problem can take work and sometimes money, I always tell my clients that sooner or later you're going to pay for your health. You can pay now and the money you spend will go toward preventative measures and long-term improvement, or you can pay later and those funds will go toward holding you together or trying to repair something that has gone horribly wrong. We all pay, the option of *when* is up to us.

> **"If you ignore your health long enough it WILL go away."**
> **- My Pen Pal**

You can go directly to www.OurCoalition.org and click on Self-Monitoring Registration to take the tour of all the site has to offer.

Let's Get To Testing...

If you haven't acquired the necessary testing materials that I talked about at the end of chapter one, are you procrastinating, or are you just a really fast reader? Now is the time to have those tools so you can see where your chemistry is before I talk more about each imbalance. It's easy to listen to symptoms that go along with each imbalance and say, "Oh yeah, that's totally me, I must have that imbalance." But that's the wrong way to look at your individuality.

Let's say that you desperately need to go to Hallmark to pick up a card from their "I accidentally called my mother-in-law fat" section. When you get to the mall, the first thing you look for is the directory. Once you find Hallmark on the directory, what do you do next? That's right, you look for the "You Are Here" red dot. If you don't know where you are, how are you going to find where you need to go? Testing yourself is finding the red dot.

Some of your clients may not need to run all of these tests. Many of your clients will be able to run just a few procedures and the results will be so clear, it will give you an obvious path to follow. Others will need to use more tests, and some will need to seek the help of a professional who can see how multiple parameters of their chemistry fit together. Some professionals have special equipment that can supply information about physiology beyond the methods I can provide in this book.

To assist you and your clients, if any of these tests are too intimidating for you, we have an almost free 4-week digestion course at www.KickItNaturally.com that contains videos showing how to perform all of these tests. We created this course to be free for our book readers. Since we also have more advanced, paid courses, our new system requires all courses to have a fee for anyone who registers, so we made the course fifty cents, allowing anyone to cover the registration fee.

Simple Testing Procedures

It can be helpful to perform the simple self-tests on a regular basis, at least in the beginning. They are simple and can easily fit into your current daily activities once you make them a habit. I like to see people run most of these tests at least twice a week for the first few weeks so they can get an idea of where their chemistry truly is. This becomes the "You Are Here" dot on the mall directory. However, because you are in training and because I am teaching you how to look at only a few parameters, it is a good idea to run these simple tests four or five times in the first week. This gives you more of a video image of how your body is operating, instead of a snapshot.

117

Simply perform these tests and mark the results on your *Data Tracking Sheet* or input them into the Progress Charts on *The Coalition*. On the tracking sheet, there are data boxes for twelve different testings. Each time you test yourself, just add the date and time to the top of the next box and input your numbers. You see spaces for water intake, urine pH, saliva pH, breath rate and breath hold. We left a blank space below breath hold for those who may need to check their fasting glucose daily. (Some of your clients won't need to check fasting glucose every day; daily monitoring is important for those who are dealing with insulin resistance or elevated glucose levels.) In the space below breath hold you can input your blood pressure reading, which will include your systolic blood pressure (the top number), diastolic blood pressure (the number below the systolic), and your pulse (the bottom number on most automatic blood pressure cuffs).

The water intake space on the *Data Tracking Sheet* should be filled in according to how much water you have had up to the point of testing for that day. This information can be useful in helping you understand why your numbers are where they are. If your blood pressure is much lower than normal (optimal reading being 120/80), you may be able to see that you have consumed more water than normal on that day, which has washed away too many minerals and brought down your blood pressure. In any case, viewing your numbers in relation to your water intake can be helpful. Keep in mind that there are many more advanced factors that can go into how the body is using water and where that water is being sent. It's truly not a water-in, water-out formula. Still, this elementary viewpoint of looking at blood pressure in relation to water intake is important to keep in mind.

Depending on the issues you are trying to improve, you might check only your blood pressure, breath rate, or pHs on some days. That is acceptable and any information is helpful in my book. (Wait a minute; this is my book, so I guess that goes without saying.) Always put the date and time at the top of each box and fill in test results from that time only. It's okay to leave blanks when you don't run all of the tests. When you use the tracking tools on *The Coalition*, you will also have the option to input only a pH or blood pressure reading if that is all you test that day.

pH of Urine and Saliva

It is best if you don't test your urine pH right when you wake up. The first morning urine test, while being a valid test, takes greater discretion to sort out the results because you are unloading the previous day's "metabolic debt," those acids you accumulated through the previous day. Understanding the results of that first morning test is quite complicated and I don't cover it in this book. Testing your urine and saliva pH either just before lunch or just before dinner (ideally at least two hours since you have eaten any food) will be an easier test to discern what the numbers are showing.

Urine pH

Hold the test strip in your urine stream for a second and read the result against the color chart found on the packaging. If the chart reads in half-point increments, and your reading is between two colors, make an estimate for your reading. For example, if the color on your pH strip falls between 6 and 6.5, make a guess and say 6.3 or wherever you think it lands. Just pick a number and don't say "really green" or "very yellow," because that is not specific enough. Pick a number; you are simply looking for a range. If the actual reading is off by a little bit, that's okay. You won't be using NASA equipment here and you're not going to get an exact reading. You just want to be able to see, "Is it high or is it low? How high or low is it?" So, don't drive yourself nuts and think that you have to pull out the magnifying glass and read the strip under indoor lighting that mimics the sun at high noon. Just look at the pee on the strip and mark it down.

Saliva pH

Try not to drink or have anything in your mouth for 20 minutes before testing, and ideally you want to wait at least two hours after eating. Testing your saliva at the same time as your urine will keep everything simple. Don't use the same strip for both—it makes me sad that I feel like I need to explain that (however I do know one person who takes a pair of scissors and splits the strip long ways to get twice as many measurements out of a pack). Bring up a little saliva between your lips and run the test strip across your lips and through the saliva. Read against the chart right away. Timing is important. The CO_2 in your saliva will out-gas into the atmosphere. The reading will often rise the longer you wait to read it. Because of this, it is best to read the saliva as soon as you moisten the strip or you will have a less accurate reading. With urine, it is not as important to read against the chart right away.

Blood Pressure

To test your resting blood pressure, lie down and relax for two minutes or so. Perform the test on your left arm according to the directions for your blood pressure cuff. If you are using an automatic cuff, it will likely display three numbers, usually in this configuration: The top number is the systolic pressure (measure of blood pressure while the heart is beating). The middle number is the diastolic pressure (measure of blood pressure while the heart is relaxed). The bottom number is your pulse. If it is difficult for you to lie down for the reading, you can take this test in a seated, resting position.

On the Data Tracking Sheet you will see spaces for both resting and standing blood pressures. You will use the standing blood pressure slots only if you move up to the intermediate self-tests found in Appendix B.

Breath Rate

This can be difficult to test on yourself. When you're conscious of what you're doing, you might adjust your breathing, even subconsciously. Anytime you can, get someone else to count this for you so you can let your mind wander to other things and just breathe normally. Doing so will likely provide a more accurate reading. If you don't have that option, just try to count your breaths while breathing as normally as possible. Lie down and relax. Try to think of other things so that you breathe normally. Start your timer and count the number of times you inhale in 30 seconds. Double that number for the number of breaths per minute. Just be sure you don't count an inhale as one and an exhale as two. Count only the inhales. I like to continue for the entire minute to see if I get the same number the last 30 seconds as I did the first. If not, I may average the two. My preference is to use an egg timer, so you can set it for one minute and the timer will count down to zero then beep, allowing you to count your inhales without having to worry about the timer. This can be the easiest way to perform this test if you don't have someone to help you.

When you perform this test with clients, you may want to tell them that you are running a pulse test, not mentioning you are counting their breath rate. You can hold your fingers lightly on their wrist as you count their breaths. In that way, they don't start thinking, "How fast do I breathe?", and begin breathing abnormally since they are thinking about it.

Breath Hold Time

Sit comfortably. Take three full, deep breaths in and out. Near the end of the fourth inhale, start your stopwatch or timer and hold your breath as long as you can. Don't pass out or turn blue or turn this into a contest you have to win. Guys will typically try to hold their breath longer, as if this is some type of macho sign. Not once have I noticed a girl across a room, walked up to her and said, "Hey, watch how long I can hold my breath." So, guys, just know that this is not as cool as you may think it to be. That being said, do hold your breath as long as you comfortably can. It's best not to look at the stopwatch while you're holding your breath. If you do, you may be inclined to turn it into a competition and hold your breath longer than you normally would.

Bonus Test - Blood Glucose

To get your fasting glucose, test before breakfast, before you drink anything other than water, and, if possible, before you brush your teeth. When you want to check your fasting glucose, it's best to leave the glucometer out where you will see it first thing in the morning so you won't forget.

If your results fall into the normal range of 75 - 90, you probably won't need to perform this test very often. If your results are over 100, you're going to want to monitor this regularly until the reading comes into range.

It is important that you wash your hands prior to testing so residues from lotions, etc. don't affect the test results. Most glucometers come with a lancing device and a few disposable lancets. This lancing device is used to poke the skin of your finger, allowing a small amount of blood to emerge. Insert a new disposable lancet into your lancing device. (Never re-use lancets. You may also be using an all-in-one disposable lancet where you just remove the plastic safety cover from the needle, cock the lancet and push a button to set it off while holding the tip to your finger.) Prick your finger and allow the blood to make a small bead. (It's best not to squeeze your finger, if you can avoid doing so, since that may give you a lower blood sugar reading.) Depending on your glucometer, either drip the blood on top of the test strip or place the test strip up against the drop of blood and it will sip the blood into the strip, like a straw. The glucometer will normally take a few moments to calculate the measurement before it displays your blood glucose number.

Easy Peasy

That's it. Your testing is done. In chapter eight I teach you what these simple test results can indicate in regard to your body, your physiology, and your biological individuality. You're about to know a whole bunch of stuff. And when you talk about it, you'll be able to use words that are fancier than "stuff."

Wha'd He Say?

In this chapter, you learned:
- If your chemistry or health situation is complicated, get help from a professional who understands this work. You will still be a participant in your own health.
- Correcting the actual underlying cause of a problem will take longer than the four hours it takes for a drug to kick in. Be patient.
- Go to www.OurCoalition.org to register as a member and gain access to tracking tools that will help you reach your goals.
- Try to take any tests at least two hours after a meal.
- Testing yourself is the key to understanding your next move. How do you know what to do next if you don't know where you are now?
- These tests are simple, but if they appear intimidating, go to www.KickItNaturally.com and register for the 4-week digestion course for only fifty cents. The videos in the course will help you realize the simplicity of these testing procedures.

CHAPTER EIGHT

Understanding Biological Individuality

Intro To Imbalances

This will be the most sciency chapter. You can tell how complicated it will be by my use of such a technical word as "sciency." Don't let the technical aspects scare you away. I promise to talk in stories and analogies as often as possible. Learning how to look at your own biological individuality can uncover which foods, supplements or lifestyle changes could be best for you... not your neighbor or your brother or even that dreamy kid in all the vampire movies... You. Once you better understand your own biological individuality, you'll be on your way to helping your clients understand how their unique bodies are operating. This will be the edge that sets you apart from other health pros in your niche.

Beyond digestive issues that may need attention, there are ten main imbalances that can occur in the body. To simplify the process of getting started, I cover only six of these imbalances here. This is my favorite part but I tried my best not to blab on for hours. For those who want to dig in deeper, you can read Appendix C where I cover all ten imbalances. To learn about the pioneers who created the work that makes up the bulk of what I cover here, read *Those Who Paved the Way* in Appendix D. Understanding your optimal food choices is valuable enough to wade through some science. With that in mind, push through anything that is a little complicated and I promise I'll get back to the simple stuff in chapter nine. When you're ready to learn more advanced topics, go to www.HealthProCourse.com to check out our online course for health coaches.

I first want to teach you how to look at your own self-test numbers that you learned how to find and record in chapter seven. In that way, you'll know which imbalances you need to pay close attention to when I explain them in this chapter. For now, I'll give you a very brief introduction to each imbalance. Each imbalance has a polar opposite so I go over them in pairs.

Electrolyte Excess and Electrolyte Deficiency Imbalances

These imbalances can indicate the level of electrolytes in the system. An Electrolyte Excess Imbalance would show that there are likely too many minerals in the system and a possible inability for the body to remove junk, often resulting in high blood pressure. Almost 50% of Americans fall into this category. Those dealing with hypertension and cardiovascular disease are often experiencing an Electrolyte Excess Imbalance.

An Electrolyte Deficiency Imbalance would show a lack of mineral in the system, leaving the body without enough resources or electrical charge to function properly. This is a common imbalance for those with uncontrollable cravings. Depression, vertigo, menstrual or muscle cramps, or insomnia are often seen with an Electrolyte Deficiency Imbalance. PLEASE remember that these symptoms can also be caused by other imbalances for completely different reasons. Don't assume you have an imbalance because you have a symptom that often shows up with that imbalance (I will say this at least nine more times). When an individual is experiencing an Electrolyte Deficiency Imbalance and digestive insufficiencies, it's very important to look at HCL production. The body needs mineral resources to create HCL. If resources are low, the individual may not be able to make enough HCL.

Anabolic and Catabolic Imbalances

These imbalances describe cellular permeability. Whether or not the body is in the breaking down (catabolic) or building up (anabolic) phase is a major focus when it comes to these two imbalances. Knowing cellular permeability can give you system-wide information instead of the tunnel vision that symptoms normally provide.

> The body is designed to burn both fats and glucose, generally speaking. Some individuals get stuck burning more fats than glucose, or vice versa. If one of these imbalances shows as a result of your self-tests, you would likely be burning predominantly fat or glucose.

The point I drive home throughout this book is this: With just about any symptom, there can be multiple causes. Some underlying causes can be more serious than others. Some may be easier to improve. Remember that this process is about improving health and not about fighting or beating one problem. The body is a complex machine, even more complex than an Etch-a-Sketch. (I'm really good at making the stairs.) Many issues and imbalances can have layers of causes that all need to be addressed. In that same manner, one little imbalance can throw five or six systems out of whack; and, if you can improve that one imbalance, all kinds of craziness can go back to normal.

I am about to cover how symptoms can be used as a piece of data, but that DOES NOT mean that the symptoms are the data. If you and I were standing in my kitchen talking about this right now, I would shake you just to make sure you were listening to me. I also really like to shake people while I try to make a funny point just to see if I can get away with it. In any case, pretend I just shook you so that the point about symptoms and jumping to conclusions sinks in.

With chapter seven teaching you how to run simple tests, the next step is for me to help you understand how these numbers can be translated into imbalances or usable indicators. In other words, now we can look at how whacked you might be. It's always interesting to work with health pros who might be in great shape, but find that they are dealing with imbalances that are creating issues—issues they may have thought they were simply stuck with forever. Even though one of the goals of this book is to sway you from living your life through symptoms, you can still use symptoms to further understand where your body chemistry may be going awry. Symptoms become more meaningful when they are seen in a context of biological measurement. With that in mind, be certain you don't look at a symptom that is sometimes associated with an imbalance and assume you must have that imbalance. Use the self-test numbers as your main reference point.

Imbalance Guide

On the next page, you see a copy of the *Basic Imbalance Guide* (referred to as *Imbalance Guide* for the rest of the book). If you didn't download a copy when you printed off your *Data Tracking Sheet*, you can do that now. Go to our website, www.SixFigureHealthPro.com. Just click on BOOK TOOLS and BASIC IMBALANCE GUIDE.

I also include here a sample *Imbalance Guide* that has been filled out. This will give you a visual of how specific results can help to determine whether or not you should circle an imbalance that needs correction or underline an imbalance that may need a little boost in the right direction. It truly can be an amazing help to actually download and print off these forms so you can hold them in your hand. By simply taking the time to fill out your numbers, you can see that this process is not as complicated as it looks at first glance. If you run into trouble, be sure to join the private Facebook group so you can ask questions.

www.Facebook.com/groups/kickyourfatsupport/

While you're on our site, you might also want to sign up for our Free Health Pro Marketing Introductory course. In that way, you can start to set up a few marketing tools while you're learning how to create real results with your clients.

This page left blank intentionally so that your Sample Imbalance Guide and Sample Completed Imbalance Guide can appear side by side on the following pages.

You can use this space to color if you like.
Maybe you'll color a pony.

IMBALANCE GUIDE

Name: _____   Date: _____ Time: _____

Electrolyte Status

Systolic	<	92	97	102	107	112		130	135	140	145	150	>

Electrolyte Deficiency Imbalance	Balanced 112/74 - 130/87	Electrolyte Excess Imbalance

Diastolic	<	54	59	64	69	74		87	92	97	102	107	>

Circle Your Breath Rate

Less Than 10 See Appendix C	10 11 12 13 14 15 16 17 18 19 20	More Than 20 See Appendix C

Breath Hold Time = _____ Seconds

Catabolic/Anabolic Validators

Catabolic	Anabolic
•	••

__ Urine pH < 6.1	Urine pH > 6.3 __
__ Saliva pH > 6.9	Saliva pH < 6.6 __
__ Oliguria	Polyuria __
__ Soft/Loose Stool	Hard Stool / Constipation __
__ Wake Easily	Difficult to Rise __
__ High Debris in Urine	Low Debris in Urine __
__ Migraines	Anxiety __

pH Chart

	Urine	Saliva
8.0	May Push urine pH down Monitor to Validate Organ Meats Vitamin C as ascorbic acid	May Push Saliva pH down Monitor to Validate Sauerkraut Yogurt Betaine HCL Cayenne Pepper Capsules Lemon in Water
7.5		
7.0		
6.5		
6.0	5.8 – 6.3 Optimal Zone When Breath Rate is 16-20	
5.5	5.5 – 6.0 Optimal Zone When Breath Rate is 10-15	Vitamin B12 Digestive Enzymes CoQ10 Cottage Cheese Corn Meal Lima Beans
	Butter Coconut Oil	Buckwheat Squash
5.0	May Push urine pH up Monitor to Validate	May Push Saliva pH up Monitor to Validate

▇ = My Optimal Zones

Energy Validators

Fat Burner	Carb Burner
__ Breath Rate < 15bpm	Breath Rate > 16bpm __
__ Breath Hold > 50sec	Breath Hold < 50sec __
__ Systolic BP > 133	Systolic BP < 112 __
__ Glucose > 100	Glucose < 70 __
__ Urine pH < 6.1	Urine pH > 6.3 __
__ Saliva pH > 6.9	Saliva pH < 6.6 __
__ Type II Diabetes	Irritable When Hungry __

Digestive Issue Validators

__ Systolic Blood Pressure < 112
__ Diastolic Blood Pressure < 74
__ Burping and/or Bloating
__ Passing Gas
__ Reflux/Heartburn
__ Light Colored Stool
__ Constipation
__ Urgent Diarrhea
__ Nausea

Needs Improvement

Electrolyte Deficiency Electrolyte Excess	Anabolic Catabolic	Carb Burner Fat Burner	Digestive Issues

Sample Completed *Imbalance Guide*

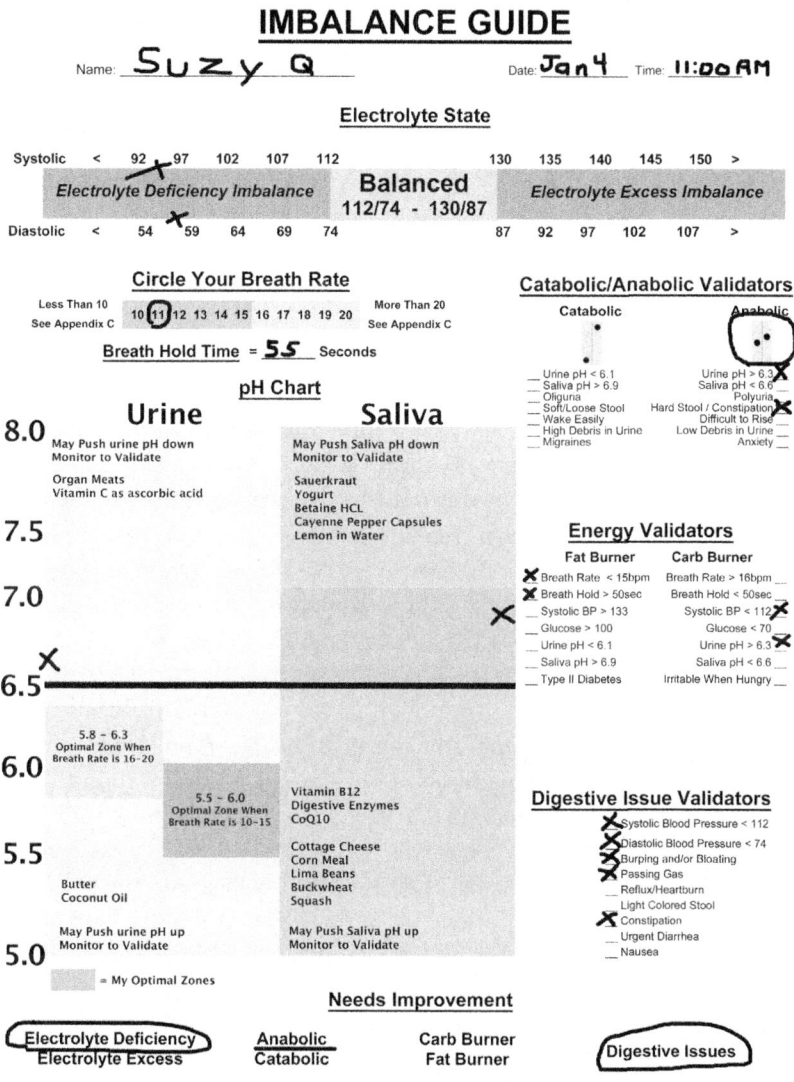

IMBALANCE GUIDE

Name: **Suzy Q**   Date: **Jan 4**   Time: **11:00 AM**

Electrolyte State

Systolic	<	92	97	102	107	112		130	135	140	145	150	>

Electrolyte Deficiency Imbalance   **Balanced** 112/74 - 130/87   **Electrolyte Excess Imbalance**

Diastolic	<	54	59	64	69	74		87	92	97	102	107	>

Circle Your Breath Rate

Less Than 10 See Appendix C   10 (11) 12 13 14 15 16 17 18 19 20   More Than 20 See Appendix C

Breath Hold Time = 55 Seconds

pH Chart

Urine	Saliva
8.0	
May Push urine pH down Monitor to Validate	May Push Saliva pH down Monitor to Validate
Organ Meats Vitamin C as ascorbic acid	Sauerkraut Yogurt Betaine HCL
7.5	Cayenne Pepper Capsules Lemon in Water
7.0	
6.5 X	
5.8 – 6.3 Optimal Zone When Breath Rate is 16-20	
6.0	5.5 – 6.0 Optimal Zone When Breath Rate is 10-15
5.5	Vitamin B12 Digestive Enzymes CoQ10 Cottage Cheese Corn Meal Lima Beans Buckwheat Squash
Butter Coconut Oil	
May Push urine pH up Monitor to Validate	May Push Saliva pH up Monitor to Validate
5.0	

= My Optimal Zones

Catabolic/Anabolic Validators

Catabolic   Anabolic

	Catabolic	Anabolic
	Urine pH < 6.1	Urine pH > 6.3 X
	Saliva pH > 6.9	Saliva pH < 6.6
	Oliguria	Polyuria
	Soft/Loose Stool	Hard Stool / Constipation X
	Wake Easily	Difficult to Rise
	High Debris in Urine	Low Debris in Urine
	Migraines	Anxiety

Energy Validators

Fat Burner	Carb Burner
X Breath Rate < 15bpm	Breath Rate > 16bpm
X Breath Hold > 50sec	Breath Hold < 50sec
Systolic BP > 133	Systolic BP < 112 X
Glucose > 100	Glucose < 70
Urine pH < 6.1	Urine pH > 6.3 X
Saliva pH > 6.9	Saliva pH < 6.6
Type II Diabetes	Irritable When Hungry

X (between columns)

Digestive Issue Validators

- X Systolic Blood Pressure < 112
- X Diastolic Blood Pressure < 74
- X Burping and/or Bloating
- X Passing Gas
- Reflux/Heartburn
- Light Colored Stool
- X Constipation
- Urgent Diarrhea
- Nausea

Needs Improvement

Electrolyte Deficiency Electrolyte Excess   **Anabolic** Catabolic   **Carb Burner** Fat Burner   **Digestive Issues**

You should already have numbers on your *Data Tracking Sheet* from your self-tests. If you don't, what's the holdup? Are you trying to hurt me? Simply take the numbers from your *Data Tracking Sheet* and fill in your *Imbalance Guide*. If any of these steps seem too complicated, there is a great video in our fifty-cent 4-Week Digestion course at www.KickItNaturally.com. Here is the easy breakdown:

Electrolyte State

On the red and green electrolyte state bar, according to your blood pressure reading, mark an "X" on the top of the bar, and another "X" on the bottom. The top "X" coincides with your systolic (top) blood pressure reading. The bottom "X" coincides with your diastolic (bottom) blood pressure reading. (Remember that "top" and "bottom" refer to systolic and diastolic, respectively. Yet, on most automatic blood pressure cuffs the very bottom number is your pulse.)

This section helps you see if your electrolyte state is balanced, electrolyte deficient or electrolyte excess. The green zone is an optimal blood pressure reading of 112/74 to 130/90. If both of your "X" marks fall in the red zone on the left, that could indicate an Electrolyte Deficiency Imbalance. If both of your "X" marks fall in the red zone on the right, this could indicate an Electrolyte Excess Imbalance. In either case, the distance from the balanced green zone counts. If your systolic blood pressure is 165, that is quite a bit higher than 130 and a person may consider this an area that could use a lot of attention. (Keep in mind that you may simply want to retest after giving yourself a chance to relax. This is why we chart the numbers on the Coalition. The visual gives us multiple measurements that can indicate how things are trending. This keeps us from overreacting to one number that might be high because you happen to be upset that day.)

If only the top number or only the bottom number pushes into the left or right red zones, you may be experiencing only a slight imbalance in that direction. For example, if your systolic pressure is 105 and your diastolic is 78, there may be only a slight Electrolyte Deficiency Imbalance.

Special note: If your systolic reading falls within the Electrolyte Deficiency Imbalance box on the left, yet your diastolic blood pressure (bottom number) is above 89, you would not be considered electrolyte deficient. However, if your diastolic blood pressure is over 90 on a regular basis, it may be time to have your doctor or health practitioner check that out.

If your systolic blood pressure is in the green zone, yet you are currently taking blood pressure lowering medications, you're really not that balanced at all, are you? If your doctor felt like you needed to be on blood pressure meds, odds are pretty great that you are experiencing an Electrolyte Excess Imbalance.

The same thing goes for the other direction. If you show a balanced blood pressure number, yet you're currently taking antidepressants, you may be dealing with an Electrolyte Deficiency Imbalance since depression medications can often restrict a person's ability to pee out salts, thereby raising blood pressure, in many cases.

Breath Rate and Breath Hold Time

Circle the number that corresponds with your breaths per minute (remember, you are counting only inhales, not inhales and exhales). You will use this information to determine your optimal urine pH zone. If your breath rate is below 10 or above 20, that's a problem. You may not need to call 911, but you do need to read *pH Balance - Acid/Alkaline Imbalances* in Appendix C. Taking steps to improve an abnormal breath rate can bring about a great deal of relief to someone who has been suffering for a long time.

Next to Breath Hold Time, simply fill in the number of seconds you were able to comfortably hold your breath.

Catabolic/Anabolic State

On your *Imbalance Guide*, notice the heading, pH Chart. For both urine and saliva you see optimal green zones. This is where most people want their pHs to fall. There are two different green zones for urine that overlap because the optimal zone for urine pH changes according to your breath rate. In this regard, if your breath rate changes due to nutritional changes you make, be sure to shoot for the optimal green zone according to your breath rate. *The Coalition* has an amazing tool called a pH Balancing Chart that changes the green zones for you automatically. I teach you how to use that later in this chapter.

Look at the urine pH and saliva pH numbers that you recorded on your *Data Tracking Sheet* and place an "X" for each of those numbers onto the pH Chart. If either of your pHs fall outside of those optimal zones, you may want to give this area some attention. If your pHs fall within both green zones, you may be balanced in this area. It's okay to be balanced; that is what you're shooting for.

You also see foods or supplements listed in each quadrant of the pH chart. The top left quadrant lists foods or supplements that may enable urine pH to come down. The bottom left are items that can enable urine pH to come up. The same idea occurs on the right side for saliva. With these guides, you can see which foods or supplements may help push you closer to a balanced state.

Under Catabolic/Anabolic Validators on your *Imbalance Guide*, below each heading you see a box that represents sample pH readings that are common for each imbalance. With an Anabolic Imbalance, urine pH is commonly higher and closer to the saliva pH reading. With a Catabolic Imbalance, the urine pH is commonly lower and further away from the saliva reading. In other words, in a Catabolic Imbalance, there is more distance between the urine pH and saliva pH numbers.

Below these sample readings are common symptoms that can accompany each imbalance. Check off any that frequently apply to you. Again, don't assume you have an imbalance just because you experience the symptoms. Use the symptoms only as validation of what the numbers are indicating as a possible imbalance.

Special Notes

1. Under "Catabolic," oliguria means that you do not urinate frequently, or maybe you urinate frequently, but in small amounts. Under "Anabolic," polyuria means you urinate frequently, with volume.
2. High or low debris in urine is asking, if you pee in a cup, do you see a lot of debris particles dispersed in your urine?
3. On the catabolic side, check off "Migraines" only if your headaches frequently originate in the back of your head or neck. If you get frontal headaches, those are not generally migraines and you should not check this box.

Energy Production

Under Energy Validators, check off the points that are appropriate for you, whether they be numbers from your self-tests or symptoms you experience. If you were unable to run some of the numbers, like glucose, leave that space blank and simply use the data that you do have.

If one side shows a predominant number of checks, you may be experiencing that imbalance. If checks are distributed fairly evenly between both sides, then you are likely balanced in your energy production and that is a good thing. Concern yourself with one of these imbalances only if you appear to sway strongly in one direction. For example, if you have five or six items checked on one side and maybe only one or two on the other.

Digestive Issues

If you can check off any of the items listed under Digestive Issues, it would be wise to focus on improving digestion.

Conclusions

Finally, draw some type of conclusion. Any conclusions you find now may change as you make adjustments to your nutrition, however, the idea is to come to a conclusion. Are you balanced in all areas? Do you need a lot of attention in the area of electrolytes but everything else looks good? Where are you? Come to a conclusion so you will know which imbalances to pay attention to while I explain them in the next chapter.

Under the Needs Improvement section, select any imbalances that you feel could use help. If you feel that the imbalance is strong (or severe) and needs a lot of work, you can circle that imbalance. If you feel that the imbalance is present, but could maybe use just a little attention, you can underline that imbalance. Keep this *Imbalance Guide* handy while you read through the rest of the book so you can remember which imbalances need attention and how much attention they deserve. This will be helpful as I go over foods and supplement choices that can be used to improve specific imbalances.

Keep in mind that the tools I have provided for you to get a glimpse of your chemistry will give you just that: A glimpse. I have placed intermediate testing procedures in Appendix B and people can learn even more in-depth information about their own body by working with a professional health coach, or by taking our online Bio-individuality Coach Course. When looking at only a few biological markers, imbalances can be disguised or misinterpreted. With this in mind, I suggest taking major steps to facilitate an imbalance moving in the optimal direction ONLY if that imbalance appears to be strong and when repeated measurements concur. After all, the goal should be to become balanced, not to create another imbalance in the opposite direction.

In chapter nine I explain how these imbalances can affect your health.

Wha'd He Say?

In this chapter, you learned:
- Interpreting your numbers on your *Imbalance Guide* is the first step toward understanding how your body may be operating.
- When deciding if you are dealing with a specific imbalance or not, the measurements are your greatest influence. Symptoms should be used only as a confirmation marker. Do not mark yourself as having an imbalance simply because you are experiencing symptoms often seen with that imbalance.
- If you appear to be experiencing a strong imbalance on your *Imbalance Guide*, go to the bottom of the page and circle that imbalance. If you appear to have a slight imbalance, you can underline that imbalance at the bottom of the *Imbalance Guide*. If you appear to be balanced in that area, don't mark that imbalance at all.
- If you understand which imbalances may need to be addressed, you will now know which information to pay more attention to for the rest of the book.
- When you see progress with your own measurements, you'll gain a clearer viewpoint of how to help your clients.

CHAPTER NINE

How Imbalances Contribute To Health Issues

This information will be your secret weapon. Beyond improving digestion, many clients won't have a lot of imbalances that need improving. But if imbalances show up on someone's *Imbalance Guide*, you may finally be able to assist her to move past any hurdles that have been sabotaging her health in a variety of ways. Time to jump into how these six imbalances can create havoc left and right.

Electrolyte State

The electrolyte state is defined by blood pressure (though as a health professional, you may end up acquiring equipment that can look at other variables in this equation, like conductivity of urine and saliva). For now, we will investigate what we learn about someone's electrolyte state from his blood pressure readings.

In the world of natural health, where the terrain of the body gives so many insights into how the body is functioning, if an imbalance can exist in one direction, there must be an opposite to that imbalance. Otherwise, there would be no middle ground, no place where the body could be considered "balanced." Seems reasonable, right? By the time you finish this book, you will likely realize how ridiculous it is that the medical world puts so much attention on high blood pressure, but totally ignores an equally debilitating imbalance in the other direction. Low blood pressure may not be as dangerous as high blood pressure, in many cases and in certain aspects. However, that doesn't mean that finding relief is less important to the person suffering from the effects of low blood pressure.

When blood pressure is low, this is often a reflection of low mineral content in the bloodstream. (Protein, amino acids and other factors can contribute to blood pressure being low, but we're focusing on the minerals here.) When the blood pressure decreases, it is a reflection of a decrease in your salts and/or protein levels lowering the viscosity of the blood, or the vascular system being too open (dilated). Our mineral content not only comes from actual salt, but from our food too. As I covered in chapter three, if your digestion is not working properly, you can't assimilate the minerals from the food you're eating; and the mineral content in the system isn't sustained. There are a few other contributing factors that could possibly result in low blood pressure and I will get back to them soon.

Very few doctors will ever talk to you about your blood pressure being low. Since there is no drug for treating low blood pressure, the ramifications of low blood pressure are not in their training. We all know that high blood pressure can contribute to heart attacks and strokes (blowouts). When they say your blood pressure is great even though it's too low, they're saying that you'll never have a blowout. But is it fun to run around on flat tires all day? An optimal blood pressure reading is said to be 120 over 80. So, if 140 over 90 is considered high blood pressure in the medical world, wouldn't having those numbers off by the same amount in the other direction be regarded as low blood pressure? Shouldn't a reading of 100 over 70 be considered low? (As this book goes to print, the AMA has announced that we should now be worried about any reading higher than 130 over 80. Can you say, "Hello, increase in sales for blood pressure lowering drugs?" Hopefully, your doctor's opinion may vary.)

The minerals or salts in the system represent the conductivity; that is, the ability for electricity to flow through the system. When the mineral content is low, there's insufficient spark or electrical current; and energy can be low. Without this energy, the brain can't function at its full potential. Some people with depression, and even other manifestations of "mental illness," are often merely cases where there is not enough mineral or protein in the system. Low mineral levels often mean there's not enough spark to give the brain what it needs to function correctly, or there is not enough mineral to control blood pH sufficiently. Of course, blood sugar is a big player in this regard also, but I get into that in a bit.

We seem to have the mindset that, if what we're eating is providing us with enough energy to stand up and walk to our car, we have all the resources we need. But every task that our bodies handle needs resources to complete it. Vitamins, minerals, amino acids, fats—they're all important. The mineral in the system is very important because, without it, there is no way for signals to travel from the body to the brain. It's like electricity in water. If you put an electrical current in water, you get shocked and it's really not that fun. You get shocked because that water contains minerals; and that current can travel through the minerals. But if you put a current in distilled water, with no mineral in it, the current doesn't travel. It's the same way with the human brain. If signals can't travel, the brain doesn't work optimally and we feel depressed, tired, lethargic or, in the worst cases, maybe we think that we're a fire truck. Many clients with depression issues come to me and my colleagues; these clients have shown a low blood pressure reading (unless they are taking an antidepressant that is artificially raising their blood pressure). There are exceptions to every rule. I mean just the other day I saw a guy with a mullet that actually looked good, so there can be a first time for everything. But generally speaking, the majority of clients I see with depression symptoms have low blood pressure.

The brain needs fuel just like anything else. If your toaster isn't working, what's the first thing you check? You look to see if it's plugged in. You don't send your toaster to therapy or soak it in medication; you just look to see if it's getting the juice it needs to function properly. I'm not saying that therapy can't be beneficial for some people; I'm just saying that, when it comes to mechanical objects, we have the sense to look for a malfunction and try to figure out what is causing that object to function at a substandard level. However, when it comes to people, we don't check to see if they have the resources for their "machine" to perform optimally. We just assume they must have daddy abandonment issues or felt inadequate as a child because their brother was always the first one to find the prize in the bottom of the cereal box. Yes, it can be very upsetting to think back on the terror of your brother having fun with all the press-on tattoos while you had none; but if your brain had the resources to function at its full potential, it would be easier to look past that and move on with your life, now that you're 36.

Don't feel like I'm downplaying depression issues just because I'm talking like a jackass. I've experienced these issues first-hand and they can be very troubling, confusing, and a huge pile of not-at-all-fun. If depression is caused by life events, it can be crucial to get help and talk to someone about how to move past it. Be sure clients understand that this is not an issue they want to try to handle on their own. But many cases of depression have a physiological component, and the person experiencing the depression has no idea why. These are the type of depression symptoms I experienced first hand, and they were especially confusing for me because I had always been a very positive person; then all of a sudden, I just wanted to ball up on the floor and cry at old episodes of *The Brady Bunch*. Once I understood how these issues can come out of nowhere, what imbalances most often contribute to them, and how to improve those imbalances, I was right back to my old self and could once again laugh at the fact that it *was* Mom's favorite vase and she *did* always say 'don't play ball in the house.' (Non-Brady fans will have no idea what I'm talking about here and may think I'm a little drunk right now.) You can learn more about why this happens and how to improve these issues by going to www.KickItNaturally.com, and searching for our depression episode in the search box. But for now, I simply want to lay down a foundation that can help you understand how the body needs adequate nourishment to do all the things it does. The body can't just show up to work every day and make it all magically happen. Resources are needed to keep your "machine" running properly.

It seems to be common for an Electrolyte Deficiency Imbalance to possibly contribute to sugar issues because a lack of minerals can create cravings. Cravings commonly lead to ingestion of sweet treats. The body uses sugars (glucose) to buffer the low minerals and the person can function and feel better. If an Electrolyte Deficiency Imbalance shows up in your numbers, you will certainly want to take steps to correct it so you can get any cravings under control. Once your body learns that junk food can thicken the blood to raise blood pressure AND trigger pleasure sensors in the brain that trick the body into thinking resources are on the way, willpower may become useless. Any wonder why people might continue to eat junk all the time if they were dealing with an Electrolyte Deficiency Imbalance? The good news is, this can be corrected.

Since sugar (glucose) is a factor when measuring blood pressure, understand what can happen if you begin to reduce your consumption of sugars, carbs or starches. As glucose levels come down, blood pressure can come down as well—unless you have implemented methods to raise your mineral and protein levels. This is why, if you are experiencing an Electrolyte Deficiency Imbalance, it is so important to raise mineral and protein levels by fixing digestion, if you want to reduce your carb intake .

Electrolyte Deficiency And Drinking Water

If an Electrolyte Deficiency Imbalance showed up on your *Imbalance Guide*, and you're a person who doesn't like drinking water, now you know you haven't been an unreasonable person. If your mineral levels are low, drinking more water will just wash away the small amount of minerals you have. You have likely subconsciously become aware that when you drink a lot of water, you feel lousy.

This doesn't mean that you may not need more water, you may. It means that you need to qualify to drink more water. By improving your Electrolyte Deficiency Imbalance you will be able to begin taking in more water, and you will even likely start to enjoy drinking it. First, do the work to bring up your mineral levels, then you can start to increase your water intake as well. This can be an excellent way to help your body wash out junk. However, this is also an excellent way to drive home the point that no recommendation is right for every person; not even drinking more water. For many clients, even if they are dealing with issues where more water may be needed (like constipation), it's always important to watch blood pressure and make sure they qualify to increase water intake before they make that move.

Imbalance - Electrolyte Excess

If an Electrolyte Deficiency Imbalance normally indicates a lack of electrolytes, the opposite would be a state where too many electrolytes are present. This is called an Electrolyte Excess Imbalance.

In general, high blood pressure can be an expression of insufficient, or lousy, kidney function. This means that, when excessive electrolytes become concentrated in the bodily fluids, it's usually a result of insufficient hydration (not drinking enough clean water) or impaired excretion of mineral salts through the kidneys. High blood pressure can also result from a constricted vascular system. In any case, electrolyte excess can lead to hypertension (high blood pressure) and other circulatory and cardiovascular problems. A vascular system that is constricted often points to an autonomic nervous system issue or a buildup on the arterial walls. (I talk more about the autonomic nervous system when I talk about Sympathetic and Parasympathetic Imbalances in Appendix C, if you're interested.)

If kidneys are not working optimally or if a person is not drinking enough water to wash the junk out, excess filth will accumulate. We poop so the body can remove waste. If that function is not working properly on a daily basis, junk can accumulate and cause any number of problems. If bile is stagnant, filth that should be going out the biliary pathway can be pushed into the bloodstream, further taxing the kidneys. You learned in chapter four that excess filth can be stored in fat cells if the body is too overwhelmed to remove that junk. Therefore, improving this imbalance can result in a cleaner, lighter you. If your *Imbalance Guide* showed an Electrolyte Excess Imbalance, have you gotten up to go get a glass of water yet? Go!

Catabolic/Anabolic States

At the cellular level, the body is always in an anabolic or a catabolic state, or in the process of switching back and forth between the two. During the day, our cells are intended to open up (much like a flower) to facilitate energy production. This "more open" state is called a catabolic state. At night, our cells are intended to become more closed (again, like a flower) so nutrients cannot get in and out as easily and so the body rebuilds as energy production slows. This "more closed" state is called an anabolic state. Cells don't actually open and close like a flower, this is just a 'basic' view that allows us to talk about the different states of our cells. Both states are appropriate, and even necessary, for a body to function optimally. Due to many possible factors, some people get stuck in one state and their body will not switch back and forth as intended.

To make the body operate correctly, we need to oscillate back and forth from the anabolic state at night, while we sleep and rebuild, to a catabolic state during the day, while we're active. Without this natural oscillation, many problems can occur.

Imbalance - Anabolic

First of all, there are many benefits that take place while a body is in an anabolic state. This is the state where the body engages in most of its repairing and rebuilding processes. You've probably heard the word anabolic in reference to steroids. Weightlifters take anabolic steroids in order to be in the tissue-building, anabolic state when they are not playing fair with muscle building. If a guy begins to add some muscle, he may think, "This is nice, but I'd really like to be so big that my neck completely disappears and I can no longer hold my arms down at my sides. I want my arms to always look like they are sticking straight out like Ralphie's little brother, Randy, from *A Christmas Story* when he was wearing his winter parka. That's what I want to look like." By using these anabolic steroids, this guy can keep his body in an anabolic, muscle-building state most of the time. It's true that he may not be thinking about the fact that these steroids are going to make everything on his body bigger except the one thing he truly wants to be bigger. If you think about it, isn't making everything else bigger just going to make that "one thing" seem smaller? C'mon guys, think it through before you make yourself look like an alien action figure.

I'm not trying to get as many Hulk-looking guys as possible to want to crush me. What I am trying to do is point out that, while an anabolic state can have its benefits, any natural state can cause problems when pushed to an unnatural extreme—even problems beyond becoming so huge that you look more like a video game character than a human. Although it is very appropriate for the cells to be in an anabolic state at night, some individuals stay in a more anabolic state most of the time. These individuals are said to be experiencing an Anabolic Imbalance.

As I mentioned in chapter four, many individuals in this overly anabolic state suffer from constipation by sending too much of the body's water to the kidneys and not enough to the bowels, making the stool harder and more difficult to move. Many of those dealing with an Anabolic Imbalance pee high volumes of urine frequently throughout the day. They will often have to get up in the middle of the night to tinkle. You will likely see a lot of clients coming to you who have been dealing with constipation issues for years. Some of those clients will likely be dealing with an Anabolic Imbalance and will be very grateful when you can show them how to improve that imbalance. Remember, an individual can still be constipated without experiencing an Anabolic Imbalance. But it is very common for an Anabolic Imbalance to be at least a contributing factor.

In this anabolic state, individuals can also have a hard time dropping weight for a number of reasons. If clients are constipated, they aren't removing junk the way the body is intended to. We don't poop to support the toilet paper industry. We poop to remove junk.

Beyond the possible constipation issues, if people are stuck in the anabolic state most of the time, they can hold on to too much stuff at the cellular level, and energy production may be subpar. The catabolic state is where tissues break down and the body gets rid of junk. If people never move into the catabolic state, that trash-removal and higher-energy- production part of the day isn't happening and folks can have a hard time dropping weight.

Imbalance - Catabolic

The catabolic state is where the body kind of "breaks down and cleans house," so to speak. In a catabolic state, the body is primed to use oxygen to create energy, so it is appropriate to be in a catabolic state during your waking hours to keep you going all day. This, along with what I just explained about the anabolic state, helps to show how both the anabolic and catabolic states are appropriate during the appropriate times of the day. However, in the same way that I talked about people who lean too anabolic, some individuals stay in a more catabolic state most of the time. These individuals are said to be experiencing a Catabolic Imbalance.

If someone is stuck in a catabolic state, it is as if the cells are too permeable and this individual will often burn up muscle and protein and even membrane fats. Breaking down tissues and muscle for rebuilding is a beneficial aspect of the catabolic state, but when a person is in that state too often and for too long, that "cleaning house" process can turn into a body that is flat out falling apart. If you bulldoze your garage to add a new wing to your house, your house could increase in value. But if you knock down your garage just because you're addicted to knocking things down, your neighbors won't like you; just like you won't like your body if you're unable to move back into that "rebuilding" state. The more muscle we lose, the lower our metabolism, and we may burn less fat. Individuals with a Catabolic Imbalance sometimes have bile that becomes too thick and sticky to flow properly, thus inhibiting digestion and restricting the body's ability to remove junk. That's not good.

Insomnia is very common with a Catabolic Imbalance because the cells function as if they are more permeable, which is a characteristic of the daytime state. These people can't sleep because their bodies are still awake and operating at full speed. Some sleeping aids knock you out in the head so you can sleep, but your body still is wide awake all night. As a result, you might either wake up exhausted or you become tired again a few hours after waking. I guess it depends on your candle, and how short it has become by burning both ends at once. The point is, I'd like to teach you how to fix the cause of the problem instead of just selling you more candles. Please keep in mind that there are other causes of insomnia beyond a Catabolic Imbalance. To learn more about insomnia, go to www.KickItNaturally.com and search for our insomnia podcast episode.

Energy Production

The next two imbalances I cover are Fat Burner Imbalance and Carb Burner Imbalance. These deal with energy production and how the body uses food for fuel. Before I explain energy production, understand that I will be leaving out complicated methods the body can use to create energy. They are not important for this explanation and I would like to finish up and leave before my cleaning lady gets here. She dresses inappropriately for a cleaning lady and it freaks me out.

To create energy, simply speaking, our bodies burn either fat or glucose. Your body is designed to burn both types of fuel for different purposes. Despite that, changes can occur in our bodies and in our lives, that will train our bodies to prefer one fuel over the other. Some may stop burning the other type of fuel almost entirely. You want to be able to burn both fats and glucose. If you have the ability to burn only one or the other, this could restrict your dietary choices and may sway you toward foods that could push another imbalance in the wrong direction.

For example, if a client, Henry, appears to have an Anabolic Imbalance, yet his body is burning more glucose than fat, that may cause him to consume more carbs and sugars. Carbohydrates can exacerbate an

Anabolic Imbalance and exacerbate any symptoms that may be common to that imbalance.

Remember, I've greatly simplified the two imbalances here. My main concern is that you understand a body can prefer to burn one type of fuel over the other and this can affect the types of foods that may be optimal for that person to consume.

Imbalance - Carb Burner

Carb Burners are people who are predisposed to burn off all their glucose and do not seem to burn fat very well. Now, it's not that they won't burn fat, but they will always prefer to burn off all their glucose first. If these individuals try to add more fat to their diet, and reduce carbs (maybe to improve an Anabolic Imbalance), they can become tired, due to the lack of fuel that their body is predisposed to function on. With these individuals, we want to facilitate burning fats.

Imbalance - Fat Burner

If you find that you show indications of having a Fat Burner Imbalance, you most likely are burning much more fat than glucose. If you also have high cholesterol, high triglycerides and a high fasting glucose, any of these markers can be another indication that you are not processing glucose effectively.

Many individuals who are overweight and have this imbalance will ask, "How is it that I'm burning mostly fat but I'm still so fat?" This is because their bodies are turning almost every carb and sugar that they eat into fat. In order to process sugar or glucose, the body is having to turn all incoming glucose into fat before "burning" it for energy.

An overarching concern with energy production is whether or not oxygen is successfully being delivered to the tissues. After all, we cannot oxidize glucose if oxygen is not being released from the bloodstream to the tissues. You'll learn more about this in Appendix C when we cover the Alkaline Imbalance.

Using The Coalition

In chapter seven I introduced you to *The Coalition for Health Education*, which can be found at www.OurCoalition.org. I recommend joining to all those who plan to monitor their own chemistry. The tools provided to members on *The Coalition* website are by far the best tracking and monitoring tools of their kind available to consumers. If you plan to use the guidelines presented in this book without monitoring your own chemistry, you might be disappointed with your results. Without watching what your numbers do, how are you going to know when to adjust the things you are implementing to balance your body? How are you going to know if you're making progress and how are you going to know when it's time to slow your efforts so you don't create an imbalance in the other direction? You have to monitor. You want to quantify your results. You have to be a participant in your own health. A monitoring device is not something one owns and ignores like the treadmill your clients hang their clothes on. A monitoring device is something you actively use. The days of telling clients to, "Take these symptom-hiding pills and come back to see me in two months" are over. You wouldn't be reading this book if you found that route worked for all of your clients. That means, to experience this process first hand, you need to monitor your progress as well. The sooner you come to the realization that you're going to have to put forth some effort, the sooner you'll improve any current health circumstances you might like to see change. Then you can reap the rewards that come with responsible ownership of your own mechanism (by mechanism, I mean YOU).

Once you have an indication of what imbalances are giving you the most trouble, you can log in to your account on *The Coalition* and begin learning more about those imbalances and different ways to improve them. You can start to input your self-test numbers into the progress charts to get a visual of how your numbers are moving and the progress you're making. There is even a graph for your "well-being" so you can monitor how the way you feel changes according to where your chemistry is. As you learn where your body seems to function optimally, you can start to understand how to keep your chemistry in the place where you feel the best. Is that like cheating or what? I just love how sneaky that is, to look inside your own body and know exactly what is needed to feel your best. Who knew we would ever be able to do that?

The Coalition also provides you with a food journal system like no other. For each day, you can input what you're eating, how you're feeling, any symptoms that have come up or improved, etc. Then, when you enter self-test results in your progress charts, those results also show up in your food journal next to the appropriate time. Now, you can look at the foods you eat and see how those foods affect your chemistry and how you feel later that day. This can really help you pinpoint the foods and choices that are working best for you. No more throwing darts blindly at the menu of life. This can give you a clear-cut visual of the optimal diet for you... and you're in charge of the menu.

The jewel of *The Coalition* is the pH Balancing Chart. This is some good stuff. As I described in chapter eight, your urine pH has an optimal zone that changes according to your breath rate. If your breath rate is above sixteen, you will normally do well with a urine pH between 5.8 and 6.3 and a saliva pH between 6.5 and 7.0. If your breath rate is below 16, you will normally do well with a urine pH between 5.5 and 6.0 and a saliva pH between 6.5 and 7.0.

The pH Balancing Chart on *The Coalition* maps all that for you. Start with entering at least one measurement for each of these: urine pH, saliva pH, breath rate and breath hold. Then the system creates your pH balancing chart and displays it within your personalized site. This chart will show you your optimal pH zones for both urine and saliva, and bring in your most recent pH entries from your progress charts so you can see if you're in your optimal zones. If you're out of your optimal zones, the chart lists foods and supplements that may help your body move closer to a balanced state. It's an amazing tool and worth ten times the price of admission all by itself. Since I assisted *The Coalition* in creating this particular gadget, if it helps you improve your health as much as I believe it will, I think you should show your appreciation by sending me a new pair of flip-flops. I have a really hard time picking out flip-flops, but when they come to me as a gift I always seem to enjoy them.

How To Look For The Underlying Cause

Understanding these imbalances can greatly improve your ability to figure out the likely underlying causes for problems your clients may be experiencing. I say likely causes because these imbalances are NOT diagnostic, and most symptoms can have a variety of underlying causes, even multiple underlying causes layered one on top of another. However, when you start to understand the imbalances that are commonly seen with different symptoms, you will begin to have a better idea of beneficial steps for you and for each of your clients.

This knowledge can give you a more educated starting place for each client. Then, by monitoring each client's changes, you can have a better idea if your client is moving in the right direction or if changes need to be made. For example; if a client, Sally, is dealing with constipation and an Anabolic Imbalance shows up on her Imbalance Guide, now the constipation makes sense, since constipation is very common with an Anabolic Imbalance. However, if Sally improves this imbalance, yet her constipation does not improve, you can consider if other issues may be causing or contributing to the constipation. Sally may be dealing with a stool that is too alkaline and moving too slowly. If other issues are present that could indicate a lack of HCL production (like burping, bloating, or maybe an Electrolyte Deficiency Imbalance), taking steps to improve this situation would allow you to monitor the results to assess if Sally's system moved in the right direction or not.

Knowledge of what steps to take in which situations will take effort to acquire. Yet you can see that by using measurements and client imbalances as your foundation, you can create better results than by simply providing remedies that often improve specific symptoms. With common remedies a practitioner is simply playing blackjack with client results. Working to address the underlying causes of an issue allows you to monitor the results of therapies implemented, and allows those results to then steer you in the right direction.

Improving Imbalances

Throughout the rest of the book I provide you with ways to improve all six of these imbalances. Be patient, the imbalances in each person were not created in a week and you will not likely correct them in a week. However, for some issues that come with these imbalances, I will be able to teach you methods that could bring improvement quickly. That will be a big key when using these techniques with clients. You don't need to fix all their problems in a week, but if you can help them see some type of improvement quickly, they will be much more likely to do the work needed to create lasting results.

Using Our Podcast As A Tool

You may have already subscribed to our *Six Figure Health Pro* podcast that focuses on marketing and business techniques that can benefit health pros. Our *Kick It Naturally* podcast can be one of your best tools in regard to creating results with your clients. By subscribing to our *Kick It Naturally* podcast, in each episode you'll hear us talk about a different health topic and the most common underlying causes that appear to create that challenge. We talk about which imbalances are often at play and how those imbalances have the ability to cause the issue we're discussing.

Not only can this give you insights into better understanding how to help your clients, you can even use the episodes to educate your clients. Educated clients see much better results, period. When a client, Linda, comes to you with a specific issue, you may be able to simply send her the link to an episode about that topic so she can listen for free. If the episode helps her better understand the likely underlying causes of that issue, she is much more likely to understand the steps that can improve her circumstances and follow any guidance you give her. Search for *Kick It Naturally* on iTunes or Stitcher and click on the Subscribe button. It's totally free and will provide you with a constant flow of new information.

Though the podcasts are geared toward consumers, we hear from health pros every week who say they learn so much by subscribing. Beyond the weekly episodes, in our Bio-individuality Coach Course, we took many of our most popular shows to the next level for health pros. We went back and added more content on each topic that could be useful for practitioners working with clients. These episodes have been a very popular feature in our coach course.

Wha'd He Say?

In this chapter, you learned:

- Don't forget about digestive issues. If a person is dealing with digestive issues, any techniques you use to improve a specific imbalance may not be as effective if the individual can't digest correctly.
- You MUST monitor your progress. If you don't monitor while trying to improve an imbalance, you won't know when it's time to reduce your efforts, and you may create an imbalance in the other direction. Measurement is the key to understanding balance.

CHAPTER TEN

Conflicting Advice Everywhere:
What The $@#* Should I Eat?

I know!!! It couldn't possibly be more confusing out in the world of nutrition and natural health, right? If the public tries to listen to a nutritionist, follow the most popular diet book on the market and read a fitness magazine at the same time, they're likely going to be pulled in three different directions. As health pros, since most of us research nutrition, it can also be easy to gravitate to one way of thinking and assume that philosophy is right for everyone. This is why almost every book on health, nutrition or weight loss seems to contradict the other. I'm hoping you're starting to realize why this occurs. I'm hoping you're starting to see the responsibility, as health pros, that we have to educate our clients about how to navigate this mess. I'm hoping you understand that there is no diet that is right for every person and this is why nobody can agree on anything. The good news is: By helping your clients learn how to look at their unique bio-individuality, all the arguments and confusion can stop. You can be the key that helps each client understand what is right for that specific individual.

In chapter thirteen I list foods that can be beneficial for improving specific imbalances. In this chapter I give you general guidelines, tell you about foods that many people may no longer need to avoid, and answer the most common questions that people ask me about food. And no, I don't want fries with that.

What About Meat?

I think I get this question more often than just about any other. Is meat healthy? So here's the breakdown:

Chemicals, Hormones And Antibiotics

If you're buying meat at your local grocery store, if you're eating at the average restaurant, or if you're eating at just about any fast food place, you're likely paying for junk meat that was mass-produced. When farmers mass-produce in this manner, they often keep the animals in small cages and feed them the cheapest type of food they can come up with so they can make a profit. Keep in mind this farmer has a competitor down the street trying to sell meat to the same large corporation cheaper, and the bean counters on Wall Street are going to tell the corporation to buy the cheaper product with no idea how it became cheaper or where the quality went. Often times, these animals are eating foods that their stomachs were not even designed to eat. The result from this upbringing is frequent illness and a lot of dying animals—animals that were supposed to have been sold to make a profit. So what does Mr. Farmer do? He pumps the animals full of antibiotics, drugs, hormones and other chemicals to keep them alive long enough to reach a size that will make them profitable.

If you pump cows or chickens full of drugs and antibiotics, they don't just poop that out at the end of the day. Those drugs go into their tissues; and guess where those tissues end up ... yes, right in your cheeseburger. That's why the antibiotic wonder drugs of 30 years ago are beginning to work less and less. We all take in a small dose of antibiotics on a daily basis through the animal protein we eat that the bad bugs (little bastards that invade our bodies and cause havoc) build up a tolerance to these drugs until the drugs are no longer effective. So, is meat bad? If this is the meat you're eating, yes it is.

Digesting Meat

Another problem with meat is that well over half of the human population doesn't have their digestion working correctly. I have seen clients correct their amazingly horrific symptoms and conditions by just correcting their digestion. More than any other issue, correct digestion is key. Like I talked about in chapter three, one of our digestive processes is the acid that is formed in our stomach to help break down protein. But if you're not making enough acid, that meat doesn't even start to get broken down. To understand how this is bad, try the following test: In the warmth of summer, take a big bag of carrots and put them in a garbage can outside your house. Take another garbage can and fill it with raw meat. Let them sit there for about a week and go back, take the lid off and stick your head in each garbage can. Let me know which one smells worse. Which one did a better job of rotting, fermenting, attracting bugs and other crazy chemical reactions? If you don't want to do this experiment, I'll let you know: It's the meat.

So, just like in the trash can, if meat doesn't get properly digested, it will rot, ferment and create nasty chemicals that can throw off your body's balance and create issues, conditions and "disease." But that doesn't mean that the real problem is the meat itself, it's just the fact that you can't break it down. Without digestion working optimally, that meat becomes something else—something else that you don't want in your body.

When Is Meat Healthy?

Does this help explain why so many authorities say that meat is bad for you? Why some vegetarians feel so much better when they stop eating meat? If their digestion isn't working well, they will feel much better "not digesting" vegetables than "not digesting" meat. Plus, if they were eating standard store- or restaurant-bought meat, they would feel better when they stopped putting all those drugs and chemicals into their systems. Nonetheless, this doesn't prove that meat is really bad for you. If you are a person who actually has your digestion working properly and you buy meat or eggs that come from organic, free-range animals, animal protein can be a very healthy, and even necessary, part of your diet. With all the "studies" they do on eating meat and diseases that come from doing so, have you ever heard of a study using organic, free-range meats? It never happens. Have you ever heard of a study using only people with their digestion working properly? Of course not. 90% of the people with bad digestion don't even know that they have bad digestion.

The truth is, a lot of people really need animal protein. Here's how it works: Everything on the planet that eats, for the most part, is doing so to bring in nutrients and minerals so their body can function correctly. Well, these nutrients and minerals actually come from the earth's soil. But as humans, we can't just pick up dirt and eat it because our bodies don't have the ability to process those nutrients. However, if we eat the plants that eat those minerals and nutrients from the soil (so to speak), we have an easier time transitioning those nutrients to something we can use in our bodies. If we take that a step further and eat the meat from the animals that ate those plants, the nutrients and minerals are even closer to a state that we can use.

Does this mean that you have to eat meat? Not necessarily. You can get a lot of the important nutrients you would get from meat by using the correct supplements. What it does mean is this: You don't have to stop eating meat to be healthy; and if you don't eat meat, you do need to supplement the important nutrients that you're missing. But as long as your digestion is working correctly, the only thing left to do is buy good, quality meats and eggs that are organic, free-range (or pastured) and hormone-free. To the person with good digestion, everything is food; to the person with poor digestion, nothing is food. To quote my own book, "Diet is what a person eats but nutrition is what the cells see."

Vegan / Vegetarian

This is a fun section because I know people become defensive when they see the heading. "Is he going to make me eat weeds?" or "Is he going to speak poorly of me and my vegan cohorts?" No matter what side of the fence some people may stand on, most simply don't want to hear about the other side. But you've figured out by now that I'm really not that nice and I'm probably going to end up bashing both sides, tear down the fence, and build a bonfire where we'll roast a pig and drink wheatgrass juice, all at the same party.

First of all, I will say that I was vegan for nearly two years; and it really is not as difficult as you may think. It's just a matter of creating new habits and learning new recipes. Everything else is just life and putting food choices into that life. (I don't know if that sentence makes any sense but I kinda like it for some reason.) If you have chosen to be a vegan or vegetarian because of your love for animals, or you hate the idea of eating anything with a face, or your religion tells you to "praise all creatures who can poop," or anything like that, then I suggest continuing that path. If that is what makes you happy, I won't argue with you. I, on the other hand, became a vegan because I thought that was the healthiest choice to make. Turns out ... not so true ... for me.

Eating Vegetarian Isn't Always Right?

When you first start eating vegetarian, you will often feel better, have better energy and you may lose weight as well. Let's look at why that happens. If you're eating the wrong kinds of meat or your digestion is not working well enough to break down the meat you were eating (as discussed under *What About Meat?* earlier in this chapter), then by eliminating that meat, you are taking away a burden that your body was dealing with while you were consuming meat. Now that your body doesn't have to deal with the chemicals, hormones and drugs that were in the meat, or your body doesn't have to try to digest a food that it doesn't have the resources to break down properly, now your body can turn its attention to removing junk. Anytime digestion is not working properly, vegetables break down much easier than meat. By making the switch to a vegetarian diet, you also free up more resources, resulting in more energy. Vegetables also contain nutrients that help bind to acids and other toxins, allowing them to be safely removed from the body, resulting in weight loss. Since you are now eating less meat, you will obviously be eating more vegetables so you will receive more of the benefits from these types of nutrients. Pretty good deal, huh? Well, that's not really the whole story.

Now pay attention because I'm about to sound smart. In the same way that vegetables contain nutrients that you need (nutrients you can't get from any other sources), so does animal protein. When you first stop eating meat, your body has a reserve of these nutrients that can be utilized for a period of time until you run out. Therefore, in the beginning, you're not overworking your digestive system by trying to eat meat that you can't digest, you're getting more good vegetable nutrients that your body needs in order to remove waste and toxins, and you still have a reserve of animal-based nutrients that your body can pull from as needed. It's all good, you feel great and you wonder why you didn't become a vegetarian a long time ago. As time passes, however, you begin to run out of the reserves of animal-based nutrients and you run into trouble. Your body will even begin to break down your own tissues to pull the nutrients required, as if you are the animal that your body is eating. As people begin to feel worse, they don't even consider the fact that they need animal protein because they felt so great in the beginning when they stopped eating it. Do you see how the confusion sets in?

Is eating vegetarian healthy for a lot of people? Sure. Especially if their digestion isn't working well enough to break down meat and the meat is just going to rot and ferment in their stomachs. But the truly optimal thing to do is to fix your digestion so you can actually break down the meat you eat, then, eat meat that is free of hormones, drugs and disease. Eating a diet that is heavier in vegetables than meat is always the best plan. But I find that most people, at least in the long run, do need some form of animal protein (even if it's just eggs) in order to be fully healthy.

If you are some type of ovo-vegetarian, or fresh-water-fish-that-begin-with-"t" vegetarian, or some new-fangled name that makes you feel more important than the rest of us, that may be a good route for you. Including some type of animal protein like fish, eggs, or chicken (even dairy can work well for many people), can be enough for a lot of people to get by on a vegetarian diet. If it isn't, you can always use supplements to try to fill in the missing pieces. That being said, just taking B12 is not enough to fill in the gaps. Animal proteins contain amino acids and nutrient cofactors that cannot be replaced with a B12 capsule. If you're not bringing in all of these cofactors, and your body starts to eat itself to source those nutrients, are you even truly a vegan? After all, you're an animal too, right? If your body is going to eat meat whether you want it to or not, you might want to consider giving your body what it needs.

Vegetarianism And Weight Gain

Here's the real problem many vegetarians face: When you're eating less meat, you're eating less protein; and the protein you are eating is most commonly some type of processed vegetarian protein. So, if you are eating an ample amount of protein, it's probably a processed non-food that you are consuming. Also, when you eat less protein, that means you are likely eating more carbohydrates. Eating more carbohydrates means that you are going to spike your insulin levels which can lead to weight gain. Yes, as a new vegetarian, you can begin to lose weight after the initial release of toxins that were building up from undigested meat and chemicals you were consuming from eating the wrong meat. However, a lot of vegetarians have a hard time losing weight in the long run because they are eating so many complex carbohydrates that they block their body's ability to burn any stored fat as fuel.

Balance is always the best route.
Correcting digestion is always the first step.
It will always be that way.

Organic vs. Conventional

I'm going to share a couple viewpoints on this topic and one of them may surprise you. As a way to recognize natural products as being the best in their field, my old company, www.ShapeYou.com, developed a program called the GearAwards. Manufacturers would send us their products in hopes of winning one of our awards. With this program, I got to see a lot of new merchandise before it hit the market and I will say this: Nothing is more popular right now than slapping the word "organic" on a label. More people than ever are realizing the importance of buying organic. Since I like to hang out with the cool kids, let me first explain why buying organic is a good thing before I share the other viewpoint.

Wikipedia (which is always correct, right?) lists the definition of Organic Food as "foods that are produced using methods that do not involve modern synthetic inputs such as synthetic pesticides and chemical fertilizers, do not contain genetically modified organisms, and are not processed using irradiation, industrial solvents, or chemical food additives." If you combine this definition with what I wrote about chemicals and hormones found in meats, you can probably guess what I'm going to say next. When we eat foods that are filled with all these chemicals, where do you think those chemicals go? They go right into us, into our machines that we count on to carry us around all day. Just like any other synthetic or toxic substance that I've covered in this book, when these materials enter the body, the alarm sounds and the question is asked, "What the hell is this stuff?" When the human body encounters something that it doesn't recognize, it wants to send it out of the system. In essence, it becomes a problem to be dealt with.

People are starting to get the idea that if you're going to make the effort to eat healthier and swap out your corn chips for broccoli, it might be a good idea to make sure the broccoli isn't loaded with harmful chemicals. Otherwise, you might as well stick with the corn chips.

Since the market is asking for organic products, organic products are showing up in places you might not expect to see them. It's fantastic that America's eyes are being opened to how harmful our despicable, almost bionic, farming methods have become. But it does freak me out a little to think about how some of the bigger corporations may take this organic foundation and start to figure out how to cut corners and save a buck. It's concerning when a plant that was not grown in dirt (hydroponics), can still have an organic label. It can have an organic label because it still fits within the government's definition of organic. But if it's not grown in dirt, it certainly isn't natural. Remember, just like the meat producers, the same economic pressures fall on the vegetable producers. These businesses are trying to produce more product for less money. It's concerning, but for now I will continue to enjoy the increased variety of organic foods available.

Fresh vs. Frozen

One thing that may surprise you is that frozen organic vegetables can sometimes be even better for you than the fresh produce. Most of the fresh produce you find in a store was picked days or even weeks ago and has been making its way through the handling process to show up on the shelf where you can buy it. During this time, the vegetable can cannibalize itself to stay alive. If you look at the bottom of a broccoli stem, you can often see where it has started to become hollow from the broccoli eating itself. Also, fresh produce is often picked before it is ripened so it can ripen during its travels. If the produce is picked early, its ability to absorb minerals was stunted by an early dismissal from the fields. Now this vegetable is not as dense with nutrients as it could have been if it matured properly.

Frozen vegetables are ripened on the vine and picked and frozen right away so all of that mineral stays intact. Plus, now you have the convenience of keeping vegetables in your freezer that are good for you.

Of course, the best way to go is to grow your own food or buy it at a trusted farmer's market where the produce was picked fresh. Not everyone has these options; but if you do, it's worth the extra effort or cost involved.

Organic Does Not Mean Healthy

I see this a lot. People adapt to some new form of eating, whether it be vegan, organic, gluten-free, etc., and then think that, as long as a food is gluten-free or organic, it must be healthy. Guess what? That's not even close to being true. If you make an organic candy bar, it's still a candy bar. Using organic ingredients doesn't change the fact that it's a pile of sugar that is going to spike your insulin levels. I will say that I do applaud the effort of some companies to remove chemicals, preservatives, artificial sweeteners and such, and make a sweet snack for kids that is sweetened by more natural things, like agave, honey or raw sugar. I applaud it, but that doesn't mean I would eat it or tell my clients to eat it. It is simply a step in the right direction. I appreciate the companies that are trying to provide an alternative to the submarine shaped non-food snack cakes that I grew up on. I have even been known to give a company an award for their attempts, even if it's a product I wouldn't eat myself. It's still something that is at least a 50% improvement over what else is out there, and I commend them on their efforts. I also appreciate the market pressures they are trying to answer.

Organic just means that it doesn't include harmful chemicals. It's not a magic wand that automatically makes any food good for you. You still need to make good choices. Yes, by eating organic you can eliminate some detrimental materials from entering your body, just do so intelligently. (I just had to use the spell corrector on the word "intelligently." Is that funny only to me?)

Organic Does Not Mean Nutritious

Here is the viewpoint that is often missed: Our food sucks. I mean, it contains a fraction of the nutrients that it did sixty years ago. Our "franken-farming" methods are making it possible for us to create beautiful looking produce that contains almost no minerals whatsoever. This is generally done by using chemicals that allow the plant to grow without the intended mineral. This concern is not restricted to conventional farming methods by any means. Organic restrictions don't impose any rules on whether or not the soil needs to be properly replenished, or even if the soil contained appropriate amounts of mineral in the first place. The earth is where the mineral in our food comes from—the plant pulls it out of the soil. If the soil has been depleted, and if proper methods have not been utilized to allow the earth to replenish itself, those organic crops are going to be missing nutrients.

You probably know that there is a variety of pests that can destroy farmers' crops. It is said that the mineral that exists within a plant is what helps the plant fight off pests that can destroy it. That is why conventional farming methods require pesticides—the lack of mineral in those crops has rendered them helpless against invaders. This is the basis of my optimism about organic farming. I like to believe that an organic crop must have at least enough mineral in it to survive without pesticides. I do not know that this is a fact, this is just an optimistic view that I hold on organic farming. However, my optimism does not mean that organic farmers are properly replenishing the soil, and it doesn't mean that organic farmers aren't figuring out ways to grow crops with fewer nutrients.

I agree that, when buying organic, we know at least that we are eliminating some poisons. It just doesn't mean that we're getting everything that is intended to be in that food. Organic food could still be lacking the nutrition that we are seeking. Studies have indicated that organic produce does contain more mineral than conventionally grown, but there is no way to show that this is true and consistent with all organic produce. The level of mineral within a food is more dependent on the soil it came from, rather than the organic label on the product itself.

You Mean I Can Eat That?

Chapter thirteen will dig further into specific foods that can benefit specific imbalances. Here I just want to give you a simple list of foods that many of your clients may be avoiding unnecessarily. Since so many health pros are misinformed by the same powers that are misinforming the public, I like to make sure we're all on the same page before we get to the good stuff. Seriously, American Heart Association? You're going to tell us that coconut oil is bad for us and expect us to listen to anything else you say without giggling?

Foods to include that many of your clients may be avoiding:

Eggs
Eat the whole egg, including the yolk. You can even have more than two a day. Just be sure to eat good eggs from hormone-free, free-range or pastured chickens.

Meat
Whenever possible, choose meat from grass-fed, free-roaming and hormone-free animals. You don't even need to eat lean cuts. Animal fats can be very beneficial when your digestion is working properly. On the other hand, if you are eating conventionally raised meats (meat from animals that are not grass-fed, hormone-free, free-roaming animals), it is important to consume lean cuts and avoid fat. Animals store their toxins in fat, like we do; so if an animal is pumped full of antibiotics and other harmful chemicals, you don't want to consume the animal's fat where much of those toxins have been stored.)

Fish
Try to find wild-caught options.

Butter
Real butter. Clarified butter and ghee are good options as well.

Extra virgin olive and coconut oils
Make sure the label says "Raw" or "Extra Virgin." Because olive oil contains a lot of fatty acids (and most fatty acids are not as beneficial as many think), and because it is difficult to find olive oil that is not rancid by the time you get it home, coconut oil is actually the far superior choice.

Eat Real Food

This heading may sound like I'm speaking a foreign language to some people. When I say real food, I mean food that grew out of the ground or fell off of a tree that grew out of the ground or came from an animal that peed on the tree while it was standing on the ground. That food doesn't include ingredients that were created in a laboratory. It's just food. Vegetables, eggs, animal proteins, fruits. These are real foods. These are the things that your body recognizes as real food. Do you really think your body recognizes squirt cheese as real food?

I know a package out of the vending machine is convenient and it's cheap. But you're going to pay for it one way or the other. Either you can spend your money on real food or you can start sending your local hospital a check every month; because sooner or later, that is where your money is going to end up. This doesn't mean that you can never eat anything processed. Our bodies are designed to remove junk safely when the body is not overwhelmed. What I am saying is this: Every meal you eat that is made of real food is giving your body nutrients it can actually use (as long as you digest well). Every meal you eat that is made from processed, chemical-ridden ingredients that you can't spell is giving your body a problem it has to deal with. Be nice to your body now and it may let you crap your pants less when you're older.

"Your body keeps an accurate journal regardless of what you write down."
- Unknown

Wha'd He Say?

In this chapter, you learned:
- Meat can be healthy if it is from hormone-free, grass-fed, free-range sources and if you can digest it properly.
- By eating vegan or vegetarian, you may be denying your body nutrients it requires.
- Organic foods are normally a better choice, but organic does not mean healthy. You still need to make good choices.
- Frozen organic produce can contain more nutrients than fresh organic produce.

CHAPTER ELEVEN

Remove The Trouble

Conquering Our Food - Food Allergies & Sensitivities

It is likely that you will eventually see a number of clients who are dealing with food sensitivities, or have even been diagnosed with food allergies. The information found in this chapter can bring about some unbelievable outcomes. Not all of your clients who could benefit from this information will be willing to do the work, but those who are may turn out to be very grateful. I find that this chapter can be so helpful, I posted the entire thing on my website so anyone can read it for free. If you happen to be dealing with any food sensitivity issues, I will be speaking directly to you in this chapter. If you aren't dealing with such issues, I will still try to leave the chapter as it is online (with a couple extra notes for health pros), so you can read it as your clients will read it when you share it with them. When you end up having clients you'd like to share the whole chapter with, you can find it here: http://kickitinthenuts.com/remove-trouble-new-chapter-nine

If you go to SixFigureHealthPro.com and click on Book Tools, you can find downloadable PDF or Word document files of the food lists found in Appendix E. You can print this off and use as handouts with your clients.

When you eat a salami sandwich (and no, I'm not recommending that you eat a salami sandwich... it's just fun to say salami sandwich), the goal is to conquer that sandwich instead of having it cause all kinds of trouble and carry you off captive. Food allergies are a very hot topic these days; and people come to me all the time and tell me about the testing they had done for food allergies. They tell me their tests showed they're allergic to nuts, dairy, wheat, gluten, soy, pork, turkey jerky, the board game Parcheesi, and Lou Diamond Phillips. Well, at what point does this person have to leave Earth in order to eat lunch? He's been told that he's allergic to just about everything on the planet. If you get to the point where you can eat only things that resemble Al Roker, it might be time to understand food allergies.

You may have already come across some of the rules or diets to help those with food sensitivities. There are gluten-free diets, blood-type diets, food-combining diets, raw-food diets—this list could keep going all the way down to the "*Saved by the Bell*, Zack & Kelly" diet. Most of these diets can actually benefit some individuals; yet many people who need to employ a diet like this in order to feel better could find long-term relief by correcting any digestive issues. Once you can fully digest what you're eating, the need to complete the "Screech-free" phase of the Zack & Kelly diet becomes less of a requirement.

So, what are all of these theories about food based on? There are so many books and diets and "gurus" out there it's enough to make you lose your appetite, even if you did know what you were supposed to eat. So, who's right? Do I eat for my blood type? Do I alkalize? Do I avoid carbs? Do I eat whatever I want as long as it starts with the letter "B"? Who's right? Well, I don't know. Whose research was everybody using as a basis for fact when they came up with these diets? Maybe most of the test subjects they used did, indeed, thrive on the ice cream sandwich diet. But, if you're interested in how the human body works, which I know I am, you first need to know how that particular human's digestion is functioning. If digestion is not so great, there is no diet that will fix all that person's woes.

Improper digestion is the reason juicing and blending have become so popular. Many fancy-pants gurus advocate buying these blenders that cost as much as a car and can liquefy your iPhone in thirty seconds. They tell us that we need to liquefy our food or we can't pull the nutrients out. And they're right, if you're a person with horrible digestion. That's why so many people feel better when they start to juice—they're actually getting some nutrients into the system. I do find that these juicing maniacs get a little upset when they learn that simply fixing their digestion can give them the same benefit. "You mean it was unnecessary for me to blend my turkey meatloaf and brussels sprouts and drink it through a straw?"

Let me get back to the point and break down these food allergies a little bit. Enzymes can play a factor in food sensitivities. If people don't have the correct enzymes to break down a specific type of food, that food can give them trouble. Take dairy for example. Many cases of lactose intolerance are just situations where people are lacking the enzyme lactase. If they supplement this enzyme, they may see improvement with their intolerance. Though the Digesti-zyme supplement I mentioned in chapter three is a broad-based enzyme that includes lactase, it may not be a suitable amount of lactase for some people. Many lactose intolerant individuals may need a product like Milk-Gest from Daily Manufacturing. Milk-Gest is available on NaturalReference.com and from health care practitioners across the country. If you find a similar product, you may find success with that as well, as long as it doesn't include cheap binders, etc.

The main cause for food allergies, however, often has more to do with improper digestion than a lack of enzymes. In chapter three, I talked about how your body can't use a peanut butter sandwich until that sandwich has been broken down into elemental nutrients. This same understanding is used when looking at food allergies. Once you break down that peanut butter sandwich, it's no longer a peanut butter sandwich. Instead, it is now minerals, fats, amino acids—the things your body needs and recognizes as nutrients that can be used to rebuild your body.

However, if you never break down that peanut butter sandwich because your digestion is not working properly, that food still has its own identity since it was never conquered. That identity says, "Hi, I'm a peanut butter sandwich." Well, there is no use for a "peanut butter sandwich" in the body. The body can use only the nutrients that are pulled out of that peanut butter sandwich once it has been broken down into its elemental parts by a functioning digestive system. If this peanut butter sandwich enters the system, is absorbed by the bloodstream, etc., and still has its own identity, it is looked upon by the body as an invader and will be attacked and removed. A peanut butter sandwich is not going to be recognized as something that can be used. For this reason, the defense system is going to run and scream and sound the alarms. As your immune system creates antibodies to deal with this invader, an imprint of those antibodies is saved in the "security files." Now, the next time you eat a peanut butter sandwich, all hell breaks loose as the system comes down hard on this "invader" and you can feel an "allergic response." And why wouldn't you? Your body just went to war against a peanut butter sandwich for cryin' out loud. You're not supposed to be trying to digest a peanut butter sandwich in your bloodstream using your immune system. **PLEASE NOTE: This is not to say that those with a peanut allergy or something as severe and life-threatening as that should not take it seriously.** They absolutely should. That is not what I'm talking about here. Most of those individuals were born with an allergy like that. I'm talking about sensitivities that people have developed in their life due to an inability to digest, or properly and completely conquer, their food.

When Can I Reintroduce Troublesome Foods?

Once digestion is fully corrected, for many people, foods that caused distress in the past will once again be well tolerated. However, there are two points to consider. One, how does anyone know when digestion is truly fully recovered? Moving up to an appropriate dose of HCL with improved bile flow is not a slam dunk for perfect digestion. Some people will be dealing with major bacterial infections in their stomachs, small intestines, or even further down the intestinal tract. Other digestive disrupters can include parasites, intestinal permeability issues, bacterial dysbiosis, along with many other possible issues we've heard of, and probably a few more we don't even know about yet. Conclusion: It's complicated. You may be able to fix digestion enough to improve some major symptoms and even speed up weight loss, but that may not mean that you're truly breaking down everything to the point to where it no longer has its own identity. Two, even if you are fully breaking down your foods, if a specific food has been sounding the alarms for your immune system for some time, doesn't it make sense that even the remote suggestion of that food could send the body into a bit of a panic? For these reasons, some of you may need to avoid your trouble-causing foods longer than others.

The first step should be to improve digestion so you can stop the full out assault. The second step is to give your body a rest from that food to see if it's possible to reintroduce it again later. How long is later for you? I don't know. A month appears to be long enough for some issues, while other individuals have reported seeing success after three to six months. In some cases, specific foods may need to be avoided for the long haul if those foods continue to cause trouble.

How I Fixed This For Myself

As I mentioned in chapter four, when I was very sick and toxic and my digestion was not working well, most things I ate made me feel lousy. I didn't understand how to correct digestion at the time, so I simply did what made sense to me. I started entirely removing any foods that did not make me feel good. First I removed gluten. (Keep in mind that my first step included going to Whole Foods to buy every processed, garbage product that said "gluten-free" on the label. That was the ignorant move that led to my fasting glucose rising to 126, which is only 2 points from where AMA standards start to diagnose a person with Type II Diabetes. Don't do that.) When that failed miserably, I removed all dairy and then all grains of any kind—not just gluten containing grains. I eventually whittled things down to about four different things I would eat. I now know this is not a great idea either.

To make a "here's where I was dumb" story much shorter, once I fixed digestion, I was able to eat a lot more foods. Looking back now, the foods I continued to avoid (mostly grains and dairy back then) are the same foods that many elimination diets include on their "remove" lists as well. For that reason, I will cut to the chase and give you a breakdown of steps you might want to take for crazy-fast improvement and results. If you can remove troublesome foods while you fix your digestion, you may be able to add many of them back in later. When I show you the list of foods to remove, keep in mind that this is not a standard list of foods everyone should avoid. The goal is to remove the foods that most commonly cause trouble for the largest percentage of people. Once you have experienced improvement by removing these foods, you will listen to your body as you add them back in so you can determine the foods that are right for you.

But I Don't Want To Remove Foods

Many of you will be able to see great results by simply following the steps in the first ten chapters of this book. Many of you, however, will not. The bad news is that many of you will need to do more work. The good news is, those who need to do more work still get to see results if they're willing to do that work. Some say they don't want to put that much effort in, but they then continue to bounce from diet to diet, dealing with disappointment after disappointment for the next ten years. I'm not sure how that turns out to be less work. The main point to understand is that you may not need to follow the advice in this chapter. But if you do, just do it. It will be a month out of your life to find real answers. Most people can do just about anything for a month if they have the right tools and the desire for improvement.

By removing the foods that most commonly cause problems for the highest percentage of people, you can magnify your chance of seeing improvement. If you feel better, you can slowly start to add these foods back in, one at a time, to see if any of them trigger a response. If you can figure out which foods are causing your body to go into emergency mode, you can remove that burden and great results will be that much easier. Remember, just because you can eat a food without keeling over or hurling doesn't mean that it's an okay food for you. That food may still be creating a burden that is restricting your body from handling its everyday tasks. And an overburdened body will often result in any number of symptoms.

I will explain the steps here, and then get into more specific situations where this approach may be the most beneficial so you can figure out if it's the right plan for you. If it's not, you should still be able to see improvements with what you've learned to this point in the book, and you'll have even more options once you know your own body chemistry.

Become a JERFer

To JERF is to Just - Eat - Real - Food. That's it. I'm not sure who coined this phrase, but they coined it up real nice because I like it. JERF means eating nothing processed in any way. It's just food. Like I mentioned in chapter ten, real food grows out of the ground, off of a tree, or comes from an animal. If you go to Google images, you can search for some of these terms to see what real food looks like. Search for words like broccoli, chicken, berries, or eggs. In that way, when you go to the store looking for real food, you will have an idea of what it looks like. It doesn't come in a box or a package and you're probably not going to find a cartoon on the front. You might remember that bowl your grandmother kept on the dining room table that was filled with plastic shapes. Real food looks like those shapes. That's what you want. You'll find real food around the outer perimeter of the grocery store. Very rarely will you find real food in the middle of a grocery store. The middle aisles are filled with packaged garbage.

> *Real food doesn't have ingredients. Real food is ingredients.*
> *- Jamie Oliver*

Eating real food will take more effort. Don't think it won't. However, when you learn how to meal plan, use a cooking day, or find restaurants where you can get real food, it will be easy, worth it, and you won't look back. Most people feel such drastic improvement that they wonder why they haven't always eaten this way. As a health pro, one of your biggest responsibilities may be to teach people how to JERF, eat real food.

Do A Clean Sweep

Mark off a four to eight week period on the calendar and commit yourself to success. During this time period, you're going to remove all processed foods, along with any trouble foods, depending on a few circumstances I describe in this section.

If your digestion is already perfect OR if you're going to be using digestive supplements (like Beet Flow, HCL, and Digesti-Zyme) to improve digestion, four weeks should be long enough for most people.

If you are dealing with any digestive symptoms but supplements don't fit into your budget right now, set up an eight week period, as results may be slower and you may need that long.

Foods To Remove

During this clean sweep, you avoid:

All processed foods
All sweeteners (table sugar, cane syrup, artificial sweeteners, etc.)
All grains in any form
All dairy in any form (except pasture-raised ghee or clarified butter, which could be used)
All legumes (including soy in any form)

All alcohol (yes, I just said that)

It's that simple. These are the foods that cause sensitivities in the highest percentage of people. The fact that so many foods contain one of these items allows this list to stay very simple. Corn syrup comes from a grain and is a processed food and is in just about everything. When you remove junk like that, you remove a lot of harmful foods. Soy is in a lot of products, too, so this process will include the need to read the ingredients on anything you consume.

Removing grains, and the starches found within those grains, is going to remove a lot of insulin spikes. For some people, the trouble is in the insulin spikes. A person may be doing okay with the grains themselves, yet the insulin spikes from those grains are causing a world of hurt. Many of these food sensitivity issues may be the result of stress hormones the body makes when the alarm sounds due to the fact that these foods are viewed as invaders. Insulin can also be considered a stress hormone when blood sugar is high. Therefore, removing grains may not only reduce stress hormones created from these grains appearing as a break-in, the removal of grains may also bring down insulin and reduce that burden as well.

What Do I Eat?

This is not a paleo book, but back when we started to set up expert interviews for our documentary, *Why Am I So Fat?*, I started to look into some of the programs that paleo experts were talking about. My surprise was, "Oh, I pretty much eat paleo and I didn't even know it." It's not that I cared about how our ancestors ate, it just so happened that the research I had done pointed to the same healthy food options that the paleo experts were suggesting.

This doesn't mean that you need to eat a strictly paleo diet in order to see health improvements or to lose weight. In this book, I've already covered many steps that you could take to improve your bottom line without eating paleo. But if removing these trouble foods for four to eight weeks is appropriate for you to figure out some trouble foods, searching for paleo recipes will make the whole process a lot easier for you. Depending on which expert you are talking to, there are many different definitions of paleo or a "primal" way of eating. I'm not very concerned about any of those definitions or following any strict paleo guidelines myself. For many clients and readers, specific forms of dairy or other foods restricted on a paleo diet can be very beneficial for them to include. Everything still needs to go back to the individual. But I have found that using a paleo base and expanding from there is a great way to kick start someone in an effort to remove processed foods and do some JERFing.

The point is, as you begin to search for meals without grains, dairy or legumes, searching for paleo recipes will make this effort much easier. On your first search you will find thousands of websites and thousands of Pinterest boards, each with hundreds of recipes to choose from.

While eliminating grains, dairy, legumes, and processed foods, some excellent choices could be eggs (the whole egg), beef, chicken, spinach, artichokes, cabbage, seafood, butternut squash, onions, asparagus, strawberries, carrots, cauliflower, garlic, sweet potatoes, zucchini, apricots, bison, olives, grapefruit, bok choy, yams, beets, lamb (mmm, lamb), broccoli, coconut oil, macadamia nuts, swiss chard, cucumbers, organ meats, blueberries, pumpkin, arugula, kale, extra virgin olive oil, and even animal fats. This list could go on for some time. I simply want to remind you that there are more options out there beyond toaster pastries and your favorite cereal.

In Appendix E I provide a list of foods that can be appropriate for a clean sweep period of four to eight weeks. Many of you will feel so great after making this change that you will continue to eat this way indefinitely. I know I have. With my improved health, I can now slip in some junk from time to time and still feel great. But changing what I shove down my gullet has certainly changed how I feel and I like it. When you've completed your clean sweep, I hope you tweet at me @kickitinthethenuts, and let me know how it went.

Cravings

You've learned a lot about cravings and how to beat them in earlier chapters. If minerals are low and protein is not being broken down, fixing digestion so you can pull nutrients out of your food and taking steps to lift mineral and protein levels can both be life-changing steps for many. If scientists are trying to create processed foods that taste as if they're packed with nutrients--even though they're not, doesn't it make sense to completely eliminate these frankenfoods while you're taking steps to improve your cravings? By removing these foods that are engineered to trigger your brain to scream for more of this junk, you could make the chore of getting past your cravings that much easier. After you have eliminated these foods for about eight days, your cravings for those foods will start to fade if you're taking steps to give your body real nutrition. Combine this with the other steps you'll be taking to improve digestion and your physiology and you could be in charge of your cravings once and for all.

Why This Will Be Easier Than You Think

Though adjusting to any new way of eating can be a challenge in the beginning, this won't be as impossible as you may be thinking. The hardest part for most people is removing the grains because they have been living on carbs. Remember, most people eat a lot of carbs because they can't process fats and protein very well. However, if you're fixing your digestion so you can better process fats and proteins, you will be able to increase your consumption of these foods while reducing your need for grains or other carbs.

When you can properly process fats, you can add in a lot of delicious foods that will satisfy you and keep you satiated for much longer than most carbs can. Proteins, when you break them down correctly, can also act like a slow burning log on the fire and give you energy that can last. Just keep in mind, there are reasons you have needed all those grains and carbs; but if you take the steps to improve those issues, those underlying causes may no longer be part of the equation. At that point, losing the grains becomes an easier task.

Getting Started

Many of these changes can be drastic, I agree. However, with drastic changes come drastic results. That's why you're here, right? To feel better than you've felt in years. Keep in mind that these drastic changes are necessary only when drastic steps are needed. If you respond well to the much easier steps for digestive enhancement, you may not need to do the clean sweep. However, if a clean sweep could help you, yet the thought of all these changes at once overwhelms you, give yourself some training wheels. Once a day, make a meal that fits into your new guidelines and then build on that one meal. Start searching for paleo recipes to find creations you can make and enjoy. Develop an arsenal of foods that you love. When you're ready to go full-force, you will have already adapted to many new foods and recipes; and the transition will be a breeze. Keep in mind that your four-to-eight week period doesn't start until you have completely removed all the trouble foods.

Now, this is what I don't want you to do: I don't want you to tell yourself that you're going to start on Monday so you might as well eat every bad food on the planet for the next three days. That's not a great move to set yourself up for success; and hammering your body with a full-fledged war is not how you want to start your improvement. And yes, I'm watching you.

Bile Flow Support

In chapter three, when I mentioned options for improving bile flow without supplements, this plan is what I was talking about as a backup option if supplements are not in your budget right now. There are interesting rumblings out in the nutritional world about processed foods and/or grains having the ability to thicken bile and restrict its ability to flow properly. I have seen some anecdotal evidence that suggests removing these foods can improve bile flow for some people. The number of success stories that I have heard are far fewer than the success stories I have heard from people using Beet Flow, but maybe you can change that. If you use this method and see improved bile flow, I'd love to hear about it.

Keep in mind that if your self-tests indicated that you are also dealing with a Catabolic Imbalance, you may also need to correct that imbalance to truly improve bile flow.

Autoimmune Issues

If you are dealing with any issues that the medical world classifies as an autoimmune disorder, you may need to eliminate a few additional foods to see improvement with your clean sweep period. It is said that an autoimmune disorder occurs when the body's immune system attacks and destroys healthy tissues by mistake. I agree that this could be true for some disorders, but the term autoimmune has taken on a life of its own and seems to be used in just about any circumstance where the body is showing a reaction. As described earlier in this chapter, when undigested food particles, ones that are not broken down, make it into the bloodstream and the body views this food as an invader, I don't view that as an autoimmune response. I view that as an appropriate immune response since a peanut butter sandwich should not exist in the bloodstream.

In any case, with many of the issues that are classified as autoimmune, thousands upon thousands of people have found great relief by removing troublesome foods from their diet. If you're dealing with an autoimmune issue, you might want to try removing grains, legumes, dairy, and processed foods, along with the following foods:

Eggs
Nuts & Seeds
Tomatoes
Potatoes
Eggplants
Peppers (Including black pepper)
And any other nightshade vegetables

Some clients have dealt with crazy issues like severe psoriasis for over a decade with no improvement. Then, once they remove these foods, they watched the issue completely disappear. That speaks volumes.

To find recipes that fit within these guidelines, search for "paleo AIP recipes." This stands for paleo autoimmune protocol. Not only will the number of recipes you find make this easier, but also the number of people you see talking about their success following these steps will motivate you to take the plunge.

A Word On Gluten

I don't believe that everyone needs to avoid gluten. However, gluten-free eating has now become even more popular than *Game of Thrones*, and gluten-free diets don't even have dragons. Though there is a lot of new evidence suggesting that gluten itself is not the culprit for most people, it does appear that some cofactor or constituent of most gluten-containing foods is a problem and is much harder for many people to process correctly. In that regard, if you find that you do well avoiding gluten, I would continue down that path. Don't let all this new science stating that gluten is okay steer you away from what is working for you.

The reason they believe gluten is not causing problems is because they are running trials where they give people a gluten supplement. Meaning, it's not a gluten-containing food, it's just a capsule that contains only gluten. Well, who in the real world is going to take a gluten supplement? It's not really possible to suck just the gluten out of a slice a bread. For that reason, supplementing gluten is hardly proof that gluten-containing foods are not causing problems for many people. My opinion is that, though most grains are easy to pull carbohydrates out of so you can use those carbs as fuel, there are structures in most grains that are more difficult for many people to break down completely, and this is where the trouble ensues. With the huge number of people who feel better once they remove gluten-containing foods, it's obvious that these foods are harder for many to process correctly.

Don't Be Confused

Don't let this chapter trick you into thinking that I don't approve of eggs or dairy or tomatoes. That is not true at all. Now that you've looked at your chemistry in chapter seven, and we've looked at foods that can help to improve specific imbalances, eggs, butter, heavy cream (including whipped), tomatoes, and many others can be valuable tools. Again, most foods are good for SOMEBODY, but no single food exists that is good for EVERYBODY.

The clean sweep elimination program is just one tool that can be very effective for many people. If you can figure out foods that are causing a tremendous burden, you can remove them and feel better even before you completely fix digestion or improve any imbalances.

You may see foods listed in this chapter as foods to avoid on a clean sweep and then see those same foods later in the book listed under foods that can improve a specific imbalance. That is okay and don't let that confuse you. Depending on the issues that you're dealing with, you might need to figure out for yourself if it's more important to fix an imbalance or test out removing some possible trouble foods. For example, if you discover that butter or cream could be very beneficial for the imbalances that you're dealing with, understand that those foods can help move chemistry; but if they are creating an immune reaction every time you eat them, they are likely still not beneficial for you. You may need to find other tools to improve that imbalance. Everyone is different. You're probably picking up on that by now.

Don't view this plan as the "diet plan" that goes along with this book. Remember, this book doesn't have a diet plan. This book is about helping you figure out what is going to help your body the most and this is only one possible step you can take. It's not about learning the rules, it's about understanding the principles that apply to your individual biochemistry. The goal with this chapter is to remove common trouble foods long enough so you can figure out if you can add them back in or not. It's not a list of foods that are good or bad for all people, always. Keep your body and your chemistry in mind when putting together your action plan. Any mistakes along the way are all part of learning. You haven't failed, you've simply learned more about yourself.

Don't jump on this clean sweep and forget everything else you have learned in this book so far. Simply removing grains, legumes and dairy does not give you a free pass to eat sweet potatoes all day. You still need to be aware of insulin and blood sugar issues.

Reintroducing Foods

Once you have completed your four to eight week removal period, start introducing foods one at a time. Don't run out and have a cream-cheese-lentil pie with a whole-wheat crust. If you feel lousy afterwards, how will you know which one of those foods caused the problem? Introduce a small amount of one food and then give yourself seventy two hours to see how you feel. Reintroducing only small amounts may deter the defense system from waging war on an overwhelming intruder. If digestion has improved and the body can now see small amounts of this food in a more optimally broken-down state, the body may no longer see it as a threat. If you like how you feel for the next seventy-two hours after reintroducing that food, you can introduce another food. If any foods make you feel lousy, tired, or cause some type of unwanted reaction, you will likely need to avoid that food for a longer period of time. But that doesn't mean you need to go back to avoiding all the foods you were leaving out. You have simply uncovered a food that was giving you a problem and after a few days, once you are feeling great again, you can try reintroducing a different food.

You may find that some foods within a "category" might work better than others. For example, you may find that most foods in the "dairy" category bother you, yet butter and heavy cream do okay (these fats are lower in milk casein and lactose and are better tolerated by many individuals). Different types of proteins and compounds exist in every food. If you confirm that wheat sends you running for the toilet, that might not mean that all grains have the same effect. I do find that most people who cut out grains for at least a month feel so much better that they end up leaving them out indefinitely, for the most part. Journaling what you eat and how you feel is a great way to keep track of what is working and what isn't. The more you can monitor, the more you can learn and implement into real life.

Wha'd He Say?

In this chapter, you learned:

- Many food sensitivity issues could have manifested due to poor digestion and an inability to break down those foods into elemental nutrients.
- Even after digestion has improved, there are foods that could still create an immune response and may need to be avoided for a period of time.
- The foods that most commonly cause trouble are grains, dairy and legumes. By avoiding these foods for four to eight weeks, you can then add them back, one at a time, to see if any of these foods are now okay in your body.
- With many autoimmune-type symptoms, you may need to avoid additional foods like eggs, nuts, seeds, and nightshade vegetables.
- By reintroducing foods one at a time, you can more easily discern if a food creates a reaction. If so, you may want to continue avoiding this food.

CHAPTER TWELVE

Physiological Gold

Here's Where It Gets Fun

Now that you have a base understanding of digestion and how imbalances can affect the way a body functions, I'm excited to share insights into ways you may be able to help clients with this knowledge. In this chapter, I dig into some common health issues and explain the most common underlying causes that seem to have the ability to contribute to these symptoms. Please remember that nearly all symptoms can have a variety of underlying causes, and a person's unique physiology needs to be taken into account. I'm hoping you've figured that out by now; but I like to nag, so I just reminded you once more.

It's common to see clients who have been dealing with health issues for years, or even decades. It's rewarding to help them get relief. As the chapter progresses, if you want more insights into issues like these, subscribe to our free podcast, *Kick It Naturally*, where we cover a different health topic in nearly every episode. Let's begin with calcium in the wrong place and how it can cause all kinds of havoc.

Muscle/Menstrual Cramps And Calcium

Have you ever had a charley horse? Holy frijoles, that hurts! I'm talking about those cramps you get in your calf or feet, especially while you're sleeping. It feels like somebody stuck a car battery to your leg while you were asleep, just to see how high you would fly off the bed. You jump up and immediately start punching your leg to try to make the pain go away. Those are less than fun, so let's try to understand why this happens.

Calcium in the tissues is the mineral that allows your muscles to relax once they have contracted. If your tissues do not contain the proper amount of calcium, once your muscles contract, they can get stuck since you don't have enough calcium to let that muscle relax, annnnnd... cramp. Menstrual cramps, too, are most commonly a problem of a lack of calcium at the tissue level. For both muscle cramps and menstrual cramps, magnesium and iron deficiencies may contribute to the problem, but since it is most commonly a problem where calcium is lacking at the tissue level, we're going to focus on calcium for a bit while we're talking about muscle cramps. Now, don't run out and buy some calcium and think that you're going to fix the problem. You may already have plenty of calcium in the system; the problem may be that your calcium is not in the right place. Misplaced calcium can occur for one reason or another; that's most of what we will cover in this section.

I can't say that the calcium in our tissues is the most important calcium we have. After all, bones are pretty important; without them, we would just be a blob on the floor. If humans were built this way, I fear that whole breakdancing phase in the eighties could have been lost altogether, and who wants a world where *Breakin' 2: Electric Boogaloo* never existed. Outside of our bones, however, I do feel that the calcium in the tissues is the most important calcium we have. As soon as calcium deficiencies start to show up at the tissue level, it can be just like an episode of *Three's Company*, where new trouble seems to show up every day.

Calcium And The Overrated Vitamin D

I'm going to get up on a soapbox for a minute, but it's only because I'm not very tall. Vitamin D may be one of the biggest mistakes ever made by the medical and natural worlds. Yes, vitamin D is the nutrient that allows us to move calcium from the intestines into the bloodstream. We are very grateful for that. Otherwise, we would not be able to pull calcium from our food into the system.

The medical world tells us that we need huge doses of vitamin D to assimilate calcium; that's what their clinical trials came up with. In a clinical trial, they test a person's calcium level in the blood (instead of digging into their bones because who would sign up for that?) and then they give that person vitamin D and test their blood for calcium again. Since the calcium level goes up after they have been using vitamin D, that means the vitamin D helps them assimilate more calcium, right? Nope. It's actually almost the opposite.

If you walk outside in the sun for a few minutes your body makes its own vitamin D—just the right amount for your system to help calcium make the jump from the intestinal tract into the bloodstream. With the current thinking, higher doses are recommended. The higher amount not only pulls the calcium out of the intestines into the bloodstream, as is optimal, but also starts to pull calcium out of the tissues AND BONES, then holds the calcium in the bloodstream. Vitamin D makes the blood calcium-retentive, meaning that now the calcium isn't inclined to leave the bloodstream and go down to the tissue level where it can be utilized. If you think of vitamin D as a DustBuster that sucks calcium out of the intestinal tract, that will give you a good visual. In that scenario, if you increase your levels of vitamin D as high as mainstream medicine is suggesting, that DustBuster would turn into an industrial sized Shop-Vac, sucking up calcium into the bloodstream from every direction.

Yes, vitamin D has some beneficial uses in the body, but when we get it in extra high amounts, it could cause much more trouble than good. In high doses, vitamin D pulls calcium out of where it's supposed to be and holds it in the bloodstream. We've already talked about how calcium leaving the tissues can create cramps; now let's cover what other kinds of fun prizes we can get when the calcium that belongs in the tissues begins to leave those tissues and can be held hostage in the bloodstream.

Dr. Royal Lee founded Standard Process, one of the largest distributors of quality supplements sold through health care practitioners. Dr. Lee was one of the early pioneers who first understood how a lack of calcium at the tissue level can affect our immune system. Mark Anderson is a natural health expert who travels the world educating doctors and health care professionals about nutrition. Mr. Anderson has a great recorded lecture called, *The Triad: Dr. Royal Lee and the Immune System.* It's an excellent explanation of the many purposes of calcium at the tissue level. The most important factor to understand when it comes to calcium and the immune system is this: Calcium in our tissues is what triggers our immune system to attack. Without calcium in the tissues, it's almost like the immune system doesn't even know the problem exists. Sort of like that guy who wears a Speedo at the beach and doesn't even understand how much he looks like a tool. In the same way, the normal "be a reasonable human" signal doesn't get to his Speedo-wearing brain; without calcium at the tissue level, the warning that there are intruders doesn't seem to make it to our immune system.

I have a perfect example. If you get a herpes-caused cold sore, we know it was created by a virus. But as long as you have enough calcium at the tissue level, that virus can't flower and you don't get any cold sores. I've seen this a hundred times. A client had been getting cold sores regularly, and once they took the steps to make calcium available at the tissue level, those cold sores just stop. This is why the amino acid, L-lysine, is such a popular "remedy" for cold sores. L-lysine helps to push calcium back down to the tissue level. You might see similar results with someone who seems to catch every virus that walks by. Once the calcium is in the tissues, so the immune system can be notified to attack intruders, those viruses don't take over anymore. It is incredible to see. On the downside, no, pushing calcium back down to the tissue level doesn't seem to knock any sense into the brain of the Speedo-wearing circus freak.

There is some good news about vitamin D for a person who has low mineral and protein content. When this person takes vitamin D, the calcium that gets pulled out of the tissues can thicken up the blood, raise the blood pressure, and that individual who had low mineral/protein content and low blood pressure will often feel and function better. That's why a lot of girls with low blood pressure love to tan. They feel great afterward. The problem is they're mining their bodies of calcium from where it's needed, in order to get this "feel better" result. Yes, they're taking a mineral and thickening up the blood, but they're doing it by "stealing" that mineral from their tissues and even their bones. That's why, even though "info-ads" tell us how important vitamin D is to fight osteoporosis, osteoporosis has been on the rise ever since they've been telling us that. High doses of vitamin D are actually the perfect recipe for osteoporosis. We know we need calcium to build bones. Since mainstream thinking says that vitamin D helps us assimilate more calcium, why wouldn't that help fight osteoporosis? Sounds reasonable? … maybe? However, with your new understanding of what is really going on with vitamin D, it's easy to understand how high doses of vitamin D are truly the perfect formula to pull calcium out of the bones, make them weaker, which can lead to a diagnosis of osteoporosis.

Empirical Labs makes an advanced supplement called Electrolyte Deficiency. It's only available through health professionals who have graduated from our Bio-individuality Coach Course. It's the most effective secret weapon I use with my electrolyte deficient clients. I believe it is so effective because, not only does it contain nutrients that can supply vitamin and mineral resources to lift blood pressure, it also contains a small dose of vitamin D. This small dose of vitamin D is enough to help pull in some calcium that can thicken the blood and help the person function better, but not so much vitamin D that it starts to pull too much calcium out of the tissues.

Once excess vitamin D pulls calcium out of the tissues and holds it in the bloodstream, the bloodstream has all this calcium floating around and needs to get rid of the excess. Of the calcium that floats around the system, some is bound to protein and some is not bound to protein. If the bloodstream doesn't dump the excess calcium, you could be in big trouble (including kidney issues). One way for the bloodstream to get rid of the excess could be for the body to begin to deposit the excess into your joints (arthritis) and onto bones (bone spurs).

They actually employ vitamin D as a rat poison. It's the calcium that is not bound to protein that causes the trouble. Since rats have low protein, the higher levels of vitamin D will raise their blood calcium (the kind not bound to protein) to dangerous levels that will cause kidney failure. Dead rat. It's true that the dose of vitamin D used to kill rats is much higher when you compare the body weight of a rat to that of a human.

"They" try to tell us that the reason vitamin D is bad for rats is the same reason that it's good for us ... because we have more protein. But what about a person, Beth, whose digestion is not properly breaking down proteins and her protein levels are very low? Wouldn't that make excessive vitamin D levels just like rat poison for Beth? This is not at all a clinical "fact," yet most of the girls I see with real cramp issues are having these problems because their digestion is not working well enough to bring in sufficient mineral. If digestion is not working well enough to bring in needed mineral, it's usually not breaking down protein very well either. Still, with this line of thinking, if you are a female who experiences cramps, I would sooner punch you in the stomach than tell you to take high doses of vitamin D.

Why Did My Blood Tests Tell Me I Had Low Vitamin D?

When a person's blood tests come back saying that vitamin D is low, the medical world just looks at the average numbers and says, "Oh, I see his level is lower, he must need more D."

Stop. Think. Why might the body be restricting vitamin D production? Doesn't it make sense that, if a person already had a high level of calcium in the bloodstream, and lower levels of calcium at the tissue level, then the body may have appropriately reduced the amount of vitamin D being produced? Isn't it reasonable that the body doesn't want to pull MORE calcium out of the tissues and into the bloodstream? Why would the body want to take more calcium out of the tissues, where it belongs, and put it into the blood where levels may already be too high? We don't want to find ourselves at odds with the body's innate intelligence.

We've already discussed how the calcium in our tissues is pretty important. To keep the body from stripping tissues of needed calcium, the body will produce less vitamin D. Of course, we aren't inclined to listen to our bodies and we just cram in more vitamin D; but you can see that the body's intentions were good. How easily we can underestimate the wisdom of the body. Be careful. Stop. Think.

There is something else that helps calcium come into the bloodstream. That is sugar. Calcium seems to follow sugar. So, sometimes the vitamin D production is decreased because the blood sugar level is increased. I jump deeper into this topic soon.

Vitamin D And Heart Health

The conclusion that vitamin D is good for heart health comes from a similar "let's be sure we don't think with our brain" approach. The clinical studies basically show that people with low vitamin D are more likely to have heart disease, a heart attack, or stroke. The conclusion they came up with from this piece of information is, "Since the people with low vitamin D keep having heart attacks, just give them more vitamin D." That's like saying the homeless people who are hooked on crack don't have any money because they spend it all on crack. Therefore, if we give them their crack for free, they'll have plenty of money and they will no longer be homeless. The medical and pharmaceutical worlds seem to base a lot of decisions solely on clinical trial statistics. We will talk about these clinical trials in a moment, but first let's dig deeper into this heart health issue.

To present a very vague overview of a high blood pressure issue, I will say this: High blood pressure is normally a situation where, for one reason or another, an individual is having trouble removing excess minerals or junk from the body. As a result, this "junk" begins to thicken the blood and raises an individual's blood pressure to a level that is seen as "too high." There are obviously many more details that go into looking at each individual and the different causes of high blood pressure (such as elevated blood sugar). This very vague explanation is enough to help us understand why vitamin D is not always such a great idea for people with heart complications.

High blood pressure is commonly a thickening of the blood. So we can see that giving vitamin D to a person with high blood pressure may not be ideal. In spite of the fact that vitamin D acts as a vascular relaxant, the calcium being pulled into the bloodstream is just further thickening the blood, causing the kidneys to be more and more overwhelmed and creating even greater risk for heart problems. You can learn more about high blood pressure by listening to the high blood pressure episode of our *Kick It Naturally* podcast.

A fact frequently overlooked in the medical world is that calcium follows sugar. All of these people who have high heart risks almost always have high sugar and high insulin levels. So, their body would already be pulling calcium out of the tissues and holding it in the bloodstream because of all the high sugars. Of course the body would make less vitamin D in this situation, since pulling even more calcium into the bloodstream would just make the problem worse.

Another factor to consider is that most blockages consist of calcium, not only cholesterol, as many believe. (There actually is no correlation between cholesterol and heart attacks, but that's a whole other book. You can learn more by listening to our Kick It Naturally podcast episode about cholesterol). Calcium is what the body uses as a type of "Spackle" to repair the damages from the high insulin levels. By taking vitamin D for "heart health," we're really just giving our body more tools to clog things up. Seriously, our great grandkids are just going to point and laugh. I know it seems unbelievable that we would make such incredible mistakes. But, keep in mind that in this country people used to think it was a good idea to drown someone who they suspected of being a witch. If the woman didn't drown, she was a witch and they executed her. If she did drown, she wasn't a witch and everything was okay. Oh yeah, now she was dead. Well, at least we knew she wasn't a witch.

Calcium Following Sugar

Since we just mentioned calcium following sugar, let's look at how that can affect us. This alone is rarely the main cause for escalated cramps, but can very often be a contributing factor. For those of you who look at chocolate and sugar like they're crack, and you would sooner give up a foot before you considered reducing your sugar and chocolate intake, don't let this information freak you out.

If you're a woman, you have likely noticed that your cravings for sugar and chocolate can skyrocket around your period. Unfortunately for the cramps, when we eat too much sugar, calcium leaves the tissues and follows that sugar. The result is similar to the way vitamin D pulls calcium out of the tissues; but, with sugar, the calcium is following the sugar. Can you blame the calcium? Are you saying that you've never run down the street chasing the ice cream truck? No matter what the cause, calcium leaving the tissues can still leave those tissues depleted of calcium, and can result in any of the problems we've discussed in this chapter.

As if that wasn't enough bad news about sugar, you will also recall how low tissue calcium relates to viruses. With calcium leaving the tissues, it opens the door for any virus to come in and set up camp. No calcium at the tissue level equates to little or no immune system response. You and I have heard our whole lives that sugar isn't good for us, now you get to understand one of the main reasons why. Sugar shuts off our immune system by pulling calcium out of the tissues. Why do you think cold and flu season starts right after Halloween? People always assume the change to colder weather dictates cold and flu season, but many believe it has more to do with sugar consumption.

If you know how to trick or treat like a pro, your bag of candy will last you through November, just in time for fifteen pies to show up on Thanksgiving. By the time you work through those pies, cookies and candy start to become plentiful for Christmas, champagne and parties for New Year's Eve, and a big box of chocolates for Valentine's Day. How does your body have time to move calcium back to the tissue level with this onslaught of sugar? For many people, it doesn't. Flu season hits them hard. I used to get a cold every three weeks, almost without fail. This went on for years. Now that I understand how to keep calcium where it is intended to be, I no longer live that nightmare.

L.A.'s Finest

I have a client who manages one of the most successful rock bands in the history of music. His son is also a client of mine. Obviously, this family is doing okay financially so they spare no expense when it comes to the health of their children. Before they came to me, the son was having a lot of health issues so they sent him to this spiritual guru just outside of Hollywood. This guru was incredibly expensive and was recommended to them by some of their celebrity friends. The son (we'll call him Tommy, just like the kid who used to work on the docks) told me the story of visiting this guru and it might be one of my favorite stories of all time.

Tommy drove up into the mountains outside of Santa Monica to the address he was given for his "guru appointment." He parked in a small parking lot and followed the signs directing him up a small, unpaved path. The winding path went up the side of a mountain. He said it was exactly like what you would expect if you were climbing a mountain to see an old wise man. When he reached the top, he couldn't believe that an old wise man is exactly what he found. Inside a small cabin on the top of a mountain, overlooking the ocean, sat a small bald man with a long gray beard. The guru asked Tommy to sit on a pillow on the floor in front of him. He told Tommy he was going to ask him a few questions about his troubles, and then they would sit in total silence for over an hour while he reached inside his aura to find the answers he was seeking.

The guru asked his questions and Tommy explained how he was having issues with headaches, nausea, and he couldn't sleep because his legs were always restless. The guru simply said, "I see." Tommy started to explain more, but the guru held up one finger signaling him not to speak and to close his eyes. For the next hour and half they sat in silence. Finally, the guru tapped Tommy on the forehead and Tommy knew he was about to receive an amazing piece of information. The guru looked him square in the eyes and said, "Don't eat sugar. That stuff's not good for you." That was it.

I told Tommy, "Man, this guy is a genius!" He puts on this whole show to get his point across, charges more money than O.J. Simpson's lawyer, and just tells people the one piece of information that could pretty much improve anyone's life: Don't eat sugar. This guy really is a guru.

Joint Pain And Bone Spurs

If you've ever mixed salt into water, you've seen the salt dissolve to the point where it just looks like water. If you add too much salt, however, you find that some of that salt will fall to the bottom of the glass. This is called "salting out." Once the water reaches a certain level of dissolved salt, it can no longer absorb more salt and the excess falls to the bottom. Calcium in the blood acts in a similar way. Dr. Melvin Page taught us that calcium will stay ionized (it will continue floating in suspension) if it stays within the proper ratio to the mineral phosphorus. If we find ten parts calcium to four parts phosphorus, that calcium can stay ionized and continue to stay in the bloodstream. If we find twelve parts calcium to four parts phosphorus, that would result in two parts calcium "salting out." The calcium that fell out of solution must be cared for; and now the body will deposit it somewhere or excrete it. It can be different for every person, but this excess calcium is often deposited in joints, like we see in joint pain or arthritis, or on bones, like a bone spur.

When we see joint pain, we can sometimes be looking at calcium that salted out and accumulated in joints over a period of time. You can see that calcium leaving the tissues can cause a lot more trouble than just severe cramps. It can cause a lot more trouble than just turning off your body's immune system and its ability to attack invaders. When we look at what happens to that calcium if too much leaves the tissues, and there is more in the bloodstream than the bloodstream can hold in solution, we see that we can now experience a whole new kind of agony in the form of osteoarthritic pain or bone spurs. There is more to understand, as far as improving these issues, but just this quick explanation can help you get a fuller picture of how important it can be to keep enough calcium down at the tissue level.

Of course, we can't get our blood calcium levels tested all the time. Dr. Carey Reams taught his students that if urine pH goes over 6.4, stop any vitamin D use. He felt like urine pH higher than 6.4 was a good indication that unbound calcium was at a high enough level that it could start to cause some problems. Self-testing helps us again.

Mining Your Own Body

The machine that we call a human body needs resources to function correctly. Resources in the form of vitamins, minerals, amino acids, fats, etc., are needed to allow the body to complete the functions it handles from day to day, or even minute to minute. If digestion is not working properly, and food is not being fully broken down into these primary elements of nutrition, the needed resources are not coming into the system. Fortunately, the body comes equipped with backup plan on top of backup plan when things don't go the way they should. These backup plans know what is needed at the moment to satisfy a crucial lack. Yet, the backup plans can sometimes cause trouble over the long-term; but when you think about it, some of these long-term problems are better choices than the short-term situation that would stop all functions by next week.

There is one specific backup plan that can greatly contribute to cramps, frequent colds, and any other issues that can result from a lack of calcium at the tissue level. When your body is not getting the resources it needs from the food coming in, it still needs those resources and it will usually just go and find them. This is a problem because the 24-hour supermarket that your body is shopping from is YOU. Your body will mine the minerals and nutrients that it is looking for from your own muscles and bones. Your body will literally break down your body in order to give your body the minute-to-minute resources your body needs to operate the systems of your body. (I just wanted to see how many times I could say "your body" in one sentence and still be accurate.)

While the body is mining for nutrients, calcium tends to be among the minerals that are stripped from the soft tissue and hard tissue - muscles and bones. We already know that a variety of health issues are going to become more severe with a lack of calcium at the tissue level. But what happens to our bones if calcium is stripped from them as well? Ever heard of osteoporosis? The medical world describes osteoporosis as if the body is "attacking" its own bones. This is a nice story for those who enjoy a good Braveheart-like epic tale. But doesn't it make more sense that the bones would become weak due to the fact that the body has no choice other than to break down this bone and use those minerals to keep the body functioning? There is much more to understand about osteoporosis, but this brief description is an excellent way to help you understand how the body will stop at nothing to get the resources it needs. Therefore, if digestion is not working properly, digestion becomes a top priority if a client is showing signs of low tissue-calcium. Otherwise, if the body can't get what it needs through digestion, it's going to continue looking elsewhere... and elsewhere is in your muscles and bones.

Resilience Of The Body

When I talk about resilience of the body, I'm describing the body's willingness and ability to return to the ideal state once presented with stresses from the environment. These stresses can emanate from within the body, but they can also originate from external sources. Think of it as your body's ability to adapt to its environment and the current circumstances. When you lose your resilience, you are in essence losing your health. Do you find that you are overly sensitive to some things? If you can't stand the atmospheric pressure, if you can't stand the heat, if you can't stand the cold, if you can't stand the sunlight, if chemical smells are hard to deal with—you're losing your ability to adapt to the environment. I have also heard people refer to this as adaptive capacity.

When looking at individuality, increasing people's resilience can do a lot for their well-being and how they move through life. However, I don't view resilience as something to work on. Improving imbalances, digestive issues, and the other things I cover in this book will often allow the resilience of the body to become stronger naturally. I include this here because it's an excellent way to better understand how the body works. Understanding the resilience of the body and its importance can give you insight as to why the body might do something like pull minerals out of the tissues, even if this can cause a tissue mineral deficiency and result in a variety of problems. The body has great backup mechanisms when it loses its ability to adapt to environmental factors. The part that sucks is that some of these backup mechanisms can result in symptoms that are not so fun. The body does not have a long-term view. It adapts to its environment and stresses on a minute-to-minute basis. If the body needs calcium NOW, it will take it from the bones without accounting for the long-term consequences. The body is more interested in current functionality rather than osteoporosis in fifteen years.

The anabolic/catabolic paradigm requires resilience to oscillate from one state to the other. Early in the morning, a person begins to transition from the anabolic (sleep time) state to a catabolic state, continuing in that direction until the late afternoon or evening hours. In the afternoon hours, the resilience of a person starts to push him back toward the anabolic state; because now the body's environmental tide of life, approaching the sunset of the day, has already begun its push in this anabolic direction. This swing from anabolic to catabolic, and back to anabolic again, can be thought of much like a pendulum.

The problem is, some individuals have very little resilience in their system. Stated another way, they have very little "reserve energy." The result is that their pendulum begins to have less and less swing. This helps us understand one variable that could allow people to get stuck in one state or the other. If there isn't enough "umph" to make a switch from the anabolic state to the catabolic state, or vice-versa, these people just might live most of their lives in the state they are stuck in. Another possibility is they may switch states every two weeks or so instead of back and forth each day, depending on how low their reserve energy is.

When I'm picking a piece of fruit to eat, like an apple or a peach, it's nice if that fruit is not too hard. On the other hand, it is easy for fruit to become very mushy. I don't want mushy fruit anymore than I want a mushy handshake. Shake my hand, for goodness sake. Whether looking at the hard fruit or the mushy fruit, both indicate a loss of resilience and that the fruit is not ideal for consumption. Trees are meant to bend in the wind; it's their resilience that lets them go back to their original shape. Deadwood breaks off in the wind because it has no resilience.

When a person climbs the stairs, blood pressure will normally increase to accept the "load" of climbing the stairs. Resilience allows for blood pressure to return to its proper state when the person is no longer stressed by climbing the stairs. If the blood pressure stays up all the time, this person is unable to return to an ideal rest state.

Are you starting to get the idea? Most of the time, trouble that shows up in the human body stems from no longer having the ability to adapt to environmental factors—a loss of resilience.

Insomnia

Insomnia is one of my favorite topics to cover when talking about the body's ability to adapt. When you can help clients improve insomnia, you often help them improve every aspect of their lives. Trying to get through your day without sleeping is like trying to swim through molasses. I was an extreme insomniac before I understood this situation, and during that time, I was a less-than-pleasant human being. Once I learned how to look at my physiology, and corrected the imbalance that was causing my insomnia, a lot of other health issues started to turn around as well. I can still remember the first time I slept through the night. I woke up and it wasn't dark out anymore. I was like, "what the hell happened? Oh, I slept… Wow!" It truly felt like Christmas every morning for the next three months.

The reason so many suffer from insomnia for so long is that the underlying cause from person to person can vary in an extremely dramatic way. Once I explain this, you will see that the steps that could help one person sleep, would literally make another person sleep less. That is why so many popular "remedies" for insomnia fail for such a large percentage of the population. Once you start to see how imbalances can exist, layered one on top of the other, you will see that a wide variety of issues can create insomnia. But there are really only three imbalances (or a combination of these imbalances) that are most commonly at play when a person can't sleep.

Major Insomnia Cause #1

It is very common to see an insomniac suffering from a Catabolic Imbalance. The catabolic state is the active, break down tissues, create energy, go, go, go state of the body. At night, when we sleep, we should

190

move into that anabolic, rest and repair state. So, if an individual, Jason, is stuck in the catabolic state most of the time, at the cellular level, he is in that awake state. When his body is in the awake state, Jason tends to stay in the awake state too.

Insomniacs often tell you, "My mind is just so active. I can't stop thinking about things long enough to go to sleep. Maybe it's because my brain is so powerful." Yeah, that's not it. When we're awake, our brain is always active. That's what your brain does, it thinks. When a person is stuck in the active, create energy state, the brain will stay active as well. Once you can help the body move into the anabolic, rest and repair state, the person is able to sleep; then the brain does all the things it does while the individual is sleeping.

The biggest mistake I see insomniacs make with this imbalance is magnesium. We're told that 'magnesium is very relaxing and will help you sleep so take it before you go to bed.' The problem here is that magnesium is one of the strongest pro-catabolic minerals available. Therefore, when folks can't sleep because they are too catabolic, how do you think that's going to go when they take something that forces them further into that catabolic state? Not so great. I explain more about magnesium under cause #2.

Major Insomnia Cause #2

Almost as common as a Catabolic Imbalance, you also see insomniacs who appear to be dealing with an Electrolyte Deficiency Imbalance. In chapter six I mentioned that, when minerals and blood sugar both go low at the same time, the body can go into a bit of a panic due to the lack of resources. I also talked about how this is often the main cause for cravings. This same scenario can also cause a lot of insomnia. When resources go too low in the middle of the night, the person may wake up, almost like the body is saying, "Hey, we're in a bit of an emergency down here. Now get out of bed and go do something about it!"

These clients often have low blood pressure, indicating that mineral levels may be low; and there is one more imbalance that is common in this scenario. When insomnia is caused by low resources, these clients often also appear to be dealing with an Anabolic Imbalance. You might be wondering how a person, Thelma, could deal with insomnia if her body is pushed so far into the sleep and rebuild state. If Thelma is severely anabolic, shouldn't she sleep better than anyone? Yes, in some cases, overly anabolic folks not only sleep very well, they also have a hard time getting out of bed in the morning since the body is still in sleep mode. However, you'll remember that one of the markers for an Anabolic Imbalance is urine pH and saliva pH that are close together. That means urine pH often leans on the high side.

When urine pH is high, the insulin response seems to have the ability to be more effective than it needs to be, almost in an overpowering way. I'm not saying that high urine pH MEANS an overpowering insulin response will be present, it's just common to see those two things together. What that means is: When this person with high urine pH eats starches or sugars, the elevated insulin response can sometimes sweep too much glucose out of the bloodstream and into the cells. It's almost like the insulin is working too efficiently. When this happens, glucose levels can drop too low, and the person can experience any number of hypoglycemic-like symptoms. One of those symptoms, when it occurs at night, happens to be insomnia. This makes a lot of sense since the severe drop in glucose can bring about the release of stress hormones for some individuals.

To improve this client's insomnia, it seems beneficial to take steps to lift mineral levels. The higher mineral levels give the body a better buffering system when glucose goes too low. You'll remember that the body can buffer low glucose by raising mineral levels, and buffer low mineral levels by raising glucose. On top of increasing minerals, the client may also benefit from taking steps to allow urine pH to come down a little (if indeed the self-test urine pH measurement is high). If lowering urine pH reduces the overpowering nature of the client's insulin response, she may not experience such a strong drop in glucose when insulin is called into action. The best way to see fast results in this scenario is to help the client consume fewer starches and sugars in the evening. (She could try the 3 p.m. carb cut off or other methods described in chapter 5.) If you can keep blood sugar on a more even keel, instead of creating spikes and crashes, the blood sugar tends to avoid that big crash that can sound the alarms (so to speak) and wake her up.

This is why so many have success using magnesium. It is true that tissues use magnesium in the process of relaxing, and a lack of magnesium can result in a person feeling tense all the time. But the reasons magnesium often helps these folks sleep is because: (A) The magnesium is lifting their mineral levels, and (B) If the magnesium is helping to make them less anabolic, and lowering their urine pH, the insulin response may not be as out-of-control, causing blood glucose levels to crash so hard.

Still, if this individual, Todd, uses too much magnesium, for too long, it could push him too catabolic at night and reduce the quality of his sleep. This is common since most people are told to take magnesium at night. Instead, if Todd took his magnesium in the morning, it could still lift mineral levels, improve an Anabolic Imbalance, and do those things during the day, when he is intended to be more catabolic.

If a low blood pressure client, Cathy, is taking steps to improve digestion, she may also benefit by including more protein with dinner. Protein can act like a slow burning log on the fire, and sustain her through the night. As you look deeper into Cathy's physiology, you may even determine that more fats or specific types of protein could be beneficial as well.

On a similar note, if a client, Martin, has a fast breath rate, say over eighteen, he may be oxidizing too quickly and ripping through protein at a rapid pace. If so, taking steps to reduce breath rate could help, but introducing more foods that are high in purine proteins could create amazing results (as long as he can digest the proteins).

Major Insomnia Cause #3

In appendix C I talk about the Sympathetic and Parasympathetic Imbalances. In an extreme sympathetic state, the body can be stuck in the fight or flight state too long. As you can imagine, if you were in the middle of trying to figure out if it was time to fight or run away, taking a nap probably wouldn't go over too well. Folks stuck in the fight or flight state often have insomnia-type issues. Something could be pushing them too far into the sympathetic state. In those cases, improving what is pushing them sympathetic could help improve the fight or flight tendencies as well—and let them get some sleep. -

You can see that there are a wide variety of problems that can cause insomnia. However, if you understand how to look at clients' physiology, you can help them determine the likely underlying cause of their insomnia.

I enjoy breaking down common symptoms and explaining the most frequent underlying causes like this. We do this on nearly every episode of our *Kick It Naturally* podcast. I'm also creating an extension to this chapter as a free download on my website. In this free chapter 12 extension, I cover the inside scoop on issues like anxiety and panic attacks, female hair loss, acne, and more. Simply go to SixFigureHeathPro.com/extension to download it for free.

Knowledge

Knowledge is power. Knowledge can help more than just about anything when it comes to improving health issues. However, as important as it is to gain knowledge, it is also important to avoid knowledge that may not be so accurate. Clinical trials can be a very misleading source of information.

A new clinical trial reported recently that high blood pressure rates would drop 68% if they would put *Alf* back on the air. I'm pretty sure I'm the only person who has ever written that statement, but it makes my point that we will believe just about anything that was discovered by a clinical trial. It's my opinion that these clinical trials are often the origin of bad information. You understand that every individual is different. No two people have the same chemistry, nor do any two people process foods, emotions or pollutants the exact same way. So, we begin to see that giving a room full of people the same supplement, drug, or forcing them all to wear a Fonzie jacket, really doesn't prove anything.

When we look at results from a clinical trial, the only consistency we know across the board is that all participants were human. We really don't know any of the important factors about these clinical trial participants. We don't know if they are digesting their food correctly. We don't know if they even have the ability to assimilate whatever substance they are testing. It's all a crapshoot. When the numbers turn out that 59% of headache sufferers improved when they ate a peanut butter and jelly sandwich at 5:30 PM every day, suddenly the world comes to a halt at 5:30 to spread a little Jif on some bread. What about the other 41% of the participants? Even if they experienced an increase in symptom severity, the trial still says PBJs help the majority of headache sufferers. Could we rather look at a person's individual chemistry, and then take stock of how a substance moves that chemistry while it creates changes to his well-being? When we don't look at individual measurements, we're just cramming a hundred people in a dark closet, throwing in a Freddy Krueger mask, and then counting the number of people who pee their pants. How is this science?

The only thing we do know about a clinical trial is that it was bought and paid for by somebody. Some company (most often a pharmaceutical manufacturer) put up the money to fund this trial (and trials are not cheap). Could they be hoping to create a specific result that would help them sell a drug, procedure or substance?

The lesson here about clinical trials is this: Even a Fonzie jacket can't make everybody look cool, and don't make decisions about your health based on the results of a group of people whose chemistry was unknown before the trial and remains unknown after the trial. Without a clear, chemistry-driven baseline to start from, how can you come to any conclusions about whatever it was they were testing?

Wha'd He Say?

In this chapter, you learned:
- Calcium is crucial for many functions, and simply supplementing with calcium is not enough. The calcium needs to be available at the tissue level.
- For many people, the common cold may be more about sugar pulling too much calcium out of the tissues and less about the cold weather.
- If needed resources are not being properly brought in and assimilated by the body, the body may mine its own tissues for those resources.
- Insomnia can have a wide variety of underlying causes.

CHAPTER THIRTEEN

Foods Specific To You

The search for a diet that works for everyone can stop now. Really. Shut it down. It's not gonna happen. You're better off wasting your time looking for a chocolate fountain of youth. Wasn't it Ponce De Leon himself who once said, "This diet is pissing me off and I have yet to lose a single pound." Look at it realistically—if one diet worked for everybody, why are there so many diets?

The biggest mistake I see health pros make is that they assume that the diet that works well for them is going to work great for their clients too. As soon as you adopt a new base understanding that there is no diet that is right for every person, and there is no supplement that is right for every person, the results you start to see with your clients will begin to take on a whole new look. If you've been working with clients at all, I'm sure you've seen that there are foods and supplements that can bring about changes in your body that will make you feel as if they have a magical effect, but they don't always bring about the same results for your clients. Since these foods and supplements don't work for everyone, they're really not magic, are they? They are just a more ideal choice for you and your chemistry.

Diet Is Determined By Strength Of Digestion

Your clients may have spent their life bouncing from diet to diet, looking for anything that works. Even as health pros, we tend to read something that interests us and make changes to our diet, looking for any edge we can find. Instead of selecting your diet from the last magazine article you read, you might want to try eating according to what your digestion can handle. Yes, the goal is to correct digestive issues so you can broaden your selection. However, while you're improving your digestion, try adjusting your food selection according to your ability to digest. If you find that this works well for you, imagine what it could do for your clients who come to you with extremely weak digestive systems.

If your HCL production appears to be low, proteins may be harder to digest. If your bile is not flowing properly, fats can be difficult to emulsify and process. If you've become insulin resistant or have a strong Fat Burner Imbalance, you can have a hard time correctly processing carbohydrates and you may want to reduce the amount of starches you are eating. Understanding your current situation can help you better gauge what type of foods you should avoid and what foods you should eat.

Foods That Could Help

I really like the idea of using food choices to improve imbalances. Hippocrates said, "Let your food be your medicine and your medicine be your food." Seeing how Hippocrates is considered to be the "father of western medicine," I'm pretty sure western medicine stopped listening to Daddy at some point. It seems you would have a real hard time finding a medical doctor who would give you any advice about food at all. It's true some doctors are given a poster of a food pyramid and you can even look at it on the wall while your doctor fills out your prescriptions. I have clients with Type II Diabetes who tell me that their doctors never mentioned food to them. Even with Type II Diabetes our doctors don't seem to be teaching their patients that sugars and starches have the ability to quickly raise blood sugar levels (and with diabetics, that sugar level is likely already too high). (By the way, I love that the Hippocratic Oath is to "do no harm." Do you really want someone working on you who's trying to "do no harm?" How about someone who's trying to "do some good"?)

Food (or nonfood in many cases) is what fuels our bodies. If you don't think the type of fuel you eat matters, try putting anything in the gas tank of your car other than what was intended to go there: Gas. If you really don't believe me, fill your car's gas tank with Gatorade or soda or Oreo cookies and then drive back to the bookstore so you can return this book. If you make it to the store, you're right. If not, you can read the rest of this book while you wait for AAA to pick you up. Just don't get upset if the tow truck driver wants to take a picture of you so he can show all his friends the person who crammed cookies into the gas tank. We really are smarter than this as a civilization. When we think about it, it's obvious: The type of food we eat matters. It's just very hard for us to see this concept when we have been taught so many misleading theories our whole lives. After all, most of us were taught that health decisions are beyond our understanding. At least we now have the ability to open our eyes, if only a little.

Below I list food choices that can affect specific imbalances. For each imbalance, I list foods that seem to commonly improve that imbalance and other foods that appear to most frequently push a person further into that imbalance. Keep in mind that you are still an individual and foods that commonly push an imbalance one direction for most people may have an opposite reaction with you. That is why it is so important for you to monitor what you're doing and how your chemistry is moving. Because different individuals have different digestive predispositions and capacities, the same food can have a different effect on similar imbalances from person to person. If you find a food that appears to be beneficial for you, yet you are avoiding that food during a clean sweep, it may be a good idea to continue with your clean sweep. You can always reintroduce that food first once you begin reintroducing foods.

It's a lot of fun finding specific foods that can make you feel better, but most people cannot count on food alone. In nearly every case of a severe imbalance, those people's chemistries have been moving further out of balance for years or even decades. They have likely been making less than ideal choices for a long, long time. To push that chemistry back into balance, it's reasonable to think that they would have to make the right food choices for just as long, if their goal was to become balanced. That is not a scientific formula so don't put too much weight in what I just said. It's just an analogy. So calm down and don't pull out a calendar to try to figure out the exact day in your life when you began to eat poorly. The point I'm trying to get across is that sometimes it will take more than food alone to straighten out a severe imbalance. But in most cases, eating foods that benefit an imbalance can reduce the required effort in other areas (like supplementation) so that you can reach your goals faster.

Supplements are a much more concentrated form of specific nutrients than what can be found in most foods. Some supplements are even made of what are called "complete foods" or "whole foods." No, not from the store, Whole Foods. These phrases just mean that these supplements are made from food instead of from a synthetic, fractionated form of that nutrient. I talk more about these supplements in chapter fourteen. I like to see people use supplements along with the correct food choices in order to get results faster (with less digestive distress) and then gradually reduce the amount of supplements they need until they can keep their body balanced with food choices alone. With that goal in mind, I spend this chapter digging into the foods that can be beneficial for each imbalance.

My final note about this chapter goes like this: If you have a severe imbalance that may be contributing to a specific symptom or issue, and you see a food listed under an "avoid" column for that imbalance, that doesn't mean you can never eat that food again. You can eat that food tomorrow if you want—you just may be slowing down the improvements you hope to see. For example, soft-boiled eggs normally have the ability to push a person more anabolic. If you have a severe Anabolic Imbalance, the best plan is to avoid soft-boiled eggs until you become more balanced. But maybe you have a requirement in your life that makes it impossible to avoid soft-boiled eggs. Maybe you are part of a very specific religion that prays only to chickens and you feel that cooking the egg too much will bring a thunderstorm that would wipe out your crops... or something like that. (I'm pretty sure I'm not supposed to make fun of different religions but I'm going to go ahead and take my chances making fun of the "chanting to chickens, leaving the egg yolk runny" religion.) If you are a card-carrying member of the "chicken people" and still need to eat soft-boiled eggs, you can try to increase your anti-anabolic protocol in other areas to allow you to eat a food that is going to push you the wrong direction (more anabolic). Maybe you need to increase your food intake that will push you less anabolic. Maybe you can add another supplement to make up for it.

It is optimal to avoid the foods that will make a severe imbalance worse, but you do have options. You can get creative if you feel as though removing a food is not an option for you. You will learn that even the time of day that a food or supplement is implemented matters. This may allow you to keep some of your favorite foods in the mix by simply adjusting what time of the day you eat them.

Contradictions From Imbalance To Imbalance

You may notice that if you are dealing with more than one imbalance, "foods to implement" and "foods to avoid" may contradict each other from imbalance to imbalance. For example, foods that are recommended to help an Anabolic Imbalance may also be recommended to avoid for an Electrolyte Deficiency Imbalance. If you come across a similar circumstance, you may need to see what works best for you by watching your self-test numbers when you eat these foods.

Some of you are going to take the suggestions below and turn them into "rules" rather than suggestions based on principles. Please do not allow me to be more than a friend offering suggestions to think about.

I am hoping that you've already performed your self-tests and know which imbalances you are dealing with so you can at least understand which imbalances to focus on the most. If you have not run your self-tests, is it because you hate me? Run your self-tests already. Remember, the best way to be able to teach this information to your clients is to experience it first hand.

Imbalance - Electrolyte Deficiency

Avoid

- Avoid drinking too much water or being unconscious about water intake

> This doesn't mean you don't need more water, you may. However, you need to qualify to drink more water. If you have a low amount of minerals in the system, drinking a lot of water could just wash away the small amount you do have. Work on correcting digestion and increasing your unrefined salt intake and then you can increase your water as your blood pressure comes up.

- Avoid drinking distilled water or tap water

> Since distilled water contains no minerals, drinking it can wash minerals out without replenishing them. Chlorine and fluoride

in tap water can also reduce minerals in the body since the body needs to use its mineral reserves to help safely remove the chlorine and fluoride from the body.

- Avoid eating too many sugars and especially starchy carbohydrates

Implement

- Correctly digesting your food

- Eating food

This means eating breakfast. Often, because digestion is not functioning properly, understandably, many people skip breakfast. After all, why eat protein for breakfast when it's going to make you feel miserable for the next six hours? But if the mineral level is low because of poor digestion, as digestion is repaired, something needs to be given to the body to digest. Once the body sees that it has the ability to pull nutrients out of the food you're eating, the body is going to want more of that. The goal should be to have digestion working well enough for you to have the ability to eat protein for breakfast and feel good.

- Tomatoes and/or tomato sauce

Tomatoes have the ability to thicken your blood, thereby raising your blood pressure. If you like tomato sauce, using it is a great way to make just about any meal beneficial for an Electrolyte Deficiency Imbalance.

- Using an unrefined salt with your food

In my opinion, when it comes to food, unrefined salt can be the most important component to implement for an Electrolyte Deficiency Imbalance. Yes, it is true that correcting any digestive issues takes center stage for this imbalance. However, if you're not getting enough chloride into your system, your body can't begin to make its own HCL in the stomach. This is often one of the missing factors when a person has digestive issues.

When I have clients with extremely low blood pressure and all the numbers are pointing to a severe Electrolyte Deficiency Imbalance, I like to see them load up the unrefined salt at every meal as much as they can. I tell them that if they are eating lunch with a friend, the goal should be to use so much salt that their friend cries out, "What the hell is wrong with you?"

Obviously, you don't want to make your food gross. Don't add so much salt that you can't get through your meal without gagging. But if you can add salt to your meal, take a bite and it still tastes okay, you might want to add a little more. Just stop before it begins to taste like a salt lick. If you don't know what a salt lick is, Google "salt lick" or "mineral lick." You will be intrigued by what you find. People use salt licks with horses a lot. It's kind of funny to see that many horse owners don't really understand why they give it to their horses. They just hear that it's beneficial so they do it. Nature photographers use a salt lick to attract wildlife. Animals come from far and wide to load up on needed minerals. Yet, we humans still view salt as if it's a bad thing. Oops.

The word salary even comes from "salt." In Roman times, soldiers were paid in salt. Would you go to work every day and fight for your life if you were being paid in salt? Maybe you should. Maybe your life would be better since you would probably use some of that salt.

I'm not positive, but I believe it was Mother Teresa who once said, "Salt 'em if ya got 'em."

Imbalance - Electrolyte Excess

Avoid

- Avoid drinking tap water that is loaded with chlorine and/or fluoride

You may notice that I recommend avoiding some of the same things for opposite imbalances. For example, I've listed avoiding tap water under Electrolyte Deficiency as well as Electrolyte Excess. Logic might tell you that if an item is bad for one imbalance, it should be good for the opposite imbalance. However, that is not always the case. It can sometimes be beneficial to avoid a specific item from imbalance to imbalance, and for totally different reasons.

For an Electrolyte Deficiency Imbalance, it was recommended to avoid tap water containing chlorine or fluoride because drinking this water can strip the body of needed minerals. With an Electrolyte Excess Imbalance, tap water should also be avoided but for different reasons. If the body's waste removal systems are not working optimally, chemicals from the tap water can build up, making the bloodstream thicker and harder to keep clean. Remember, with an Electrolyte Excess Imbalance, the blood is often too thick so it doesn't help to bring in more filth and muddy up the system. Drinking adequate water is fundamental in helping the kidneys. In this regard, intake of clean water can equate to changing the bag in the vacuum cleaners of the blood.

- Avoid eating too many sugars or starchy carbohydrates

Sugars and carbohydrates can thicken the blood; therefore, excessive consumption is not recommended with an Electrolyte Excess Imbalance. Measuring blood sugar with a glucometer can be helpful.

- Avoid taking antacids

Antacids restrict proper digestion. Undigested foods become a waste product that the body has to deal with. On top of that, some antacids contain aluminum, which can quickly exacerbate an Electrolyte Excess Imbalance.

- Avoid eating polyunsaturated oils

This can include margarine, mayonnaise, foods fried or cooked in vegetables oil, and some salad dressings. (Coconut oil and real butter are great. Unheated virgin olive oil is okay.)

Implement

- Using an unrefined salt with your food

The initial thought for someone with an Electrolyte Excess Imbalance would be to avoid salt. It is true that if you add salt with this imbalance, you will want to monitor your blood pressure and make sure it does not go up. However, if adding unrefined salt can provide the body with the chloride needed to improve HCL production, then higher HCL production can improve digestion, therefore, reducing the junk in the system that was created as a result of improper digestion. Now, the body has one less burden and can focus on removing waste. This can help the body reduce blood pressure. So, monitoring blood pressure can be important in this scenario.

- Correcting any digestive issues so you can properly break down your food

- Drinking more water

- Eating a lot of low-starch green vegetables

Imbalance – Anabolic

<u>Avoid</u>

- Avoid foods made with hydrogenated and polyunsaturated fatty acids: Canola, corn and soy oils (or what is referred as seed oils)

- Avoid ice cream

- Avoid butter

- Avoid cream

- Avoid cheese

- Avoid juices

- Avoid foods made with sugar

- Avoid coffee

- Avoid tea

- Avoid soda

- Avoid excessive fruit

- Avoid excessive carbohydrate intake

- Avoid vinegar

- Avoid poached or soft-boiled eggs

<u>Implement</u>

- Non-starchy vegetables

- Unheated virgin olive oil (avoid excessive use)

- Lemon juice

- Citrus fruit

- Sardines

- Fried or omelet-style eggs in the morning (not Egg-Beaters or egg whites)

Even in a time crunch, if you make hard-boiled eggs, you can keep them in the fridge and grab one on the run in the morning. When your digestion is working correctly, a hard-boiled or hard-cooked egg can be a powerful anti-anabolic meal and can even reduce your need for anti-anabolic supplements.

Imbalance – Catabolic

Avoid

- Avoid flax seed oil

- Avoid fish oils

- Avoid DHEA (a popular supplement)

- Avoid fried foods

- Avoid canned or processed meats and fish

- Avoid foods made with hydrogenated and polyunsaturated fatty acids: Canola, corn and soy, and other seed oils

- If you eat fried or hard-boiled eggs, eat them only in the morning and limit them

Implement

- Poached or soft-boiled eggs, especially at night

- Non-starchy vegetables

- Real butter/cream/whipped cream (especially in the evening)

- Fresh cheeses such as cottage, mozzarella, and cream cheese (these are not aged cheeses)

- Coconut oil

Imbalance - Carb Burner

Avoid

- Avoid sugar and similar items like corn syrup and honey

- Avoid fruit juices and large quantities of fruit

- Avoid coffee, tea, and alcohol

- Avoid eating polyunsaturated oils

This can include margarine, mayonnaise, foods fried or cooked in vegetables oil, and some salad dressings. (Coconut oil and real butter are great. Unheated virgin olive oil is okay.)

- Avoid meals consisting predominantly of sugars or starches

It could be beneficial for you to include at least a small serving of protein and appropriate fats in each meal.

Implement

- Eating non-starch vegetables

Vegetables like zucchini, squash, broccoli and asparagus may be beneficial because they can provide carbs without such a high level of carbs that the meal spikes your insulin levels.

- Eating some low glycemic carbs early in the day

But try to avoid meals made up predominantly of carbs.

- Being mindful of cravings

Sugar or carb cravings can be a sign that blood sugar may be going too low.

Imbalance - Fat Burner

While you are improving this imbalance, it is important to reduce your starch and sugar intake. (Keep in mind that if you experience drops in your blood sugar and you need starches or sugars from time to time in order to continue functioning, small amounts of sugar will often bring a better result than starches will. But for most people with this imbalance, limiting intake of both starches and sugars will be beneficial.) When you reduce one type of nutrient, another type must be increased to fill in the gaps. I like to increase fat intake with this imbalance since the body appears to be burning fat well. However, it is important that bile is flowing properly so you can emulsify those fats. If you increase fat intake, while bile is not flowing well, it could result in weight gain or breakouts caused by the body trying to push fats that have not been emulsified out of the body through the skin.

Avoid

- Avoid starches, sugar and similar items like corn syrup and honey
- Avoid fruit juices and large quantities of fruit

- Avoid drinking alcohol and soda

- Avoid eating polyunsaturated oils

> This can include margarine, mayonnaise, foods fried or cooked in vegetables oil, and some salad dressings. (Coconut oil and real butter are great. Unheated virgin olive oil is okay.)

- Avoid meals consisting predominantly of sugars or starches

> It could be beneficial for you to include at least a small serving of protein and appropriate fats in each meal.

Implement

- Consuming appropriate fats

> These can include coconut oil, real butter, unheated virgin olive oil, and those found in eggs (the whole egg) or animal proteins.

- Watching your fasting blood glucose

> If your before breakfast fasting glucose is over 95, look for this number to move into a better range and continue making improvements until your fasting glucose is under 95.

Wha'd He Say?

In this chapter, you learned:

- The diet that is right for you should be determined by your ability to digest and process different types of nutrients.
- The lists in this chapter do not provide you with the only foods you are allowed to eat. If you are experiencing a specific imbalance, eating the foods in the "Implement" list more often, may improve that imbalance. Including other foods in your diet, however, can be appropriate and beneficial.

- If your favorite food is listed under "Avoid" for an imbalance you are experiencing, that does not mean you can never eat that food again. Once you take the steps to improve that imbalance, you should be able to enjoy that food again in moderation.

CHAPTER FOURTEEN

Supplements That Could Help

It seems we are always hearing something good or bad about supplements in the news or in health magazines. The truth is that the media is correct in some way or another—all the good and all the bad. Since every person is different and is experiencing different imbalances, specific supplements can either correct that person's imbalance or exacerbate it. Beyond the fact that we need to use the right supplements that will benefit our biological individuality, we also need to use supplements that the body can assimilate. Many supplements on the market today are not worth the bottle they're sold in. I'll teach you what to look for and where to get quality supplements that are right for you. Since many of you and your clients will need the aid of supplements in order to improve digestion or imbalances that could be magnifying other health issues, don't take this information lightly. Proper supplement use can be the foundation of your clients' results; and you don't want your clients wasting money on supplements that are not effective.

Finding Effective Supplements

Many supplements that you can buy in the store are junk. What's worse is it appears that some products may even be made that way intentionally. Most vitamins, minerals and herbs have the ability to move body chemistry. The problem is that most consumers don't know anything about body chemistry and what vitamins will move that chemistry which direction. Some individuals go to the supplement casino (health food store or website) just gambling their money away hoping something will work. In many cases, these gamblers don't win. Wouldn't it make sense that if the vitamin manufacturers didn't want to deal with lawsuits all day long, they could just add binders that would make the supplements very hard to assimilate?

Binders, lubricants and fillers are often added to supplements to hold tablets together, to improve the speed and ease of the supplements' run through the processing machinery, or to make the supplements cheaper to manufacture. Any number of these added ingredients can reduce your body's ability to assimilate the nutrients found in those supplements. It is said that, with most consumer-based supplements, you can assimilate only between 4% and 12% of what's in them. That being the case, it's difficult for people to push their chemistry the wrong way and there's no lawsuit. Whether companies are adding these binders to save money or to avoid lawsuits really doesn't matter. Either way, you still get neither an effective product nor the result you're hoping to find.

There are companies that make high-quality supplements without harmful binders in them. The catch is that most of these companies sell their products only to qualified health care practitioners. In that way, if there's a lawsuit, it falls on the practitioner and not on the company. Dicalcium phosphate is a binder I like to avoid when buying supplements because it can restrict your ability to assimilate nutrients—not only from the supplement, but also from the food you're eating.

Most people choose a supplement because they read that it is good for a specific symptom. Little do they understand that a chemical imbalance is normally causing that symptom. If the supplement they choose can help correct that imbalance, they may see good results. If it doesn't, they will see bad results. Remember, one symptom can have many different underlying causes, so it is very common that two different people with the same symptom can experience very different results using the same supplement. Have I mentioned that it's not a good idea to treat your symptoms? If you don't wake up at least once in the middle of the night hearing me say, "Don't treat your symptoms," I will have failed in my efforts to teach you to look at your underlying causes measured using chemistry instead of looking at your symptoms. Since you now have a better idea of where your body chemistry is because of your self-test results, your food journal and the other online tools, you have an edge that most people never get to experience. Welcome to where all the cool kids hang out. This practice alone will put you miles and miles ahead of most health pros.

Understand this: You're not going to be able to pop a few supplements and correct everything that's been going wrong for the past fifteen years. Supplements are not witchcraft. You're going to have to find a way to eliminate some of the things that are making these imbalances worse and add in new choices that will help you correct them. Any supplement usage is just a boost to help it happen quicker. None of the supplements I talk about in this book are intended to be used indefinitely like an over-the-counter drug often can be. These supplements are meant to correct deficiency or excess issues, and then a person should reduce the supplements they're using until they don't need them anymore. Again, when people start to work on their bodies, they may need to use a lot of supplements in the beginning to get things going in the right direction; then they will be able to reduce supplements as imbalances get corrected. Of course, as we get older, generally speaking, time passes, things change. The things that got us here may not continue to work as well. We need to remain adaptable and continue to figure out what is best for the current state of our body.

What If I Hate Taking Supplements?

No problem. You always have the option to continue being miserable (yes, I understand I'm a jackass). The truth is, many people will be able to greatly improve their situation with food choices alone, or maybe just adding a good unrefined salt. I see that happen all the time. I also see people who are so screwed up, not only do they need the help of good supplements, they often need the help of a lot of them in the beginning.

Once you get in the habit of using supplements, it can be as easy as washing your hair. Yet, it's very interesting how averse some people are to using supplements at all. I have talked with people who have been suffering for years or even decades from issues like insomnia, constipation or diarrhea. They tell me that they don't like to put anything unknown in their body. That's okay. I can understand wanting to keep bad stuff out of your body. But with chronic issues like those mentioned, your body is screaming at you that things are not going as planned and it could really use some help. Take the time to learn more about supplements that could help you so you can feel good about using them.

I've already gone over why we hear so many good and bad stories about supplements. Yet, if you know which supplements are appropriate for you, and how to find the good ones, you're miles ahead of most people. Beyond all that, don't you think it's a little silly to avoid supplements because you're not sure what they're going to do to your body, yet you feel great about keeping candy bars in your desk that contain chemicals and artificial sweeteners that you *know* are harmful? It's up to you to make your own decisions. All I can do is point out how ridiculous some decisions are.

Don't view taking a lot of supplements as popping a bunch of pills. Many natural supplements are concentrated forms of specific nutrients, many made directly from food itself. So, you can view these supplements as part of your food. It's a much more convenient way to get the specific nutrients your body is looking for, rather than needing to shop at fifteen different farmer's markets to find a specific type of organic beet green. Who has time for that? If you view the supplements as the bane of your existence, you're obviously not going to feel good about taking them. A hatred for taking supplements could certainly reduce the benefits that those supplements could bring. However, if you view them as a convenient way to cheat and reach your goals faster, supplements can make your life a whole lot easier. Most health pros understand the benefits of supplements, but it's important to understand, too, that you will come across clients who dislike using supplements. By educating those clients, you can help them benefit from supplement use.

I can't recommend specific supplements to you, so don't waste your time emailing me questions about what you should be using. There are legal ramifications that don't allow me to help in that regard. But in this book, I can show you which supplements appear to help correct certain imbalances and I can even tell you what supplements I may take if I were trying to correct my own system imbalance. After you have that information you can decide for yourself if you want to try anything. Before I get into the supplements that can help improve specific imbalances, let me review the digestive supplements that seem to be beneficial for those who need to improve their digestion.

Digestive Supplement Review

www.NaturalReference.com
Brand: Empirical Labs

Betaine HCL (See the HCL warning under *Improving Your Stomach Acid* in chapter three.)
1-5 per meal (In the middle of the meal.)

Beet Flow
2-3 per meal (Some clients may need more if a low saliva pH indicates the need.)

Digesti-zyme
1-2 per meal

Common Imbalance All Stars

Later in this chapter I talk in more depth about a handful of supplements that seem to be utilized by practitioners more often than others. Remember, generally speaking, there is a hierarchy that often dictates which imbalances are a priority over other imbalances. Since the Electrolyte Imbalances and the Anabolic/Catabolic Imbalances often sit as a top priority for many clients, the advanced, specialized supplements that can benefit these imbalances become the all stars for many health coaches.

Improving Imbalances Through Supplementation

As I go through the imbalances, I list supplements that seem to be beneficial for each imbalance. Just be sure to understand that you are responsible for your own health and you have to decide what dosage is best for you. After you begin using a supplement, don't forget how important it is to continue to run your self-tests and monitor your numbers. Monitoring your numbers can help guide you in the dose you are using for many supplements, once you understand how a supplement can affect your body chemistry.

If you are currently working with health-care professionals (not including yourself), you should always let them know what you are considering using just to make sure it is not contradicting anything they have you using already. In the supplement lists below, I'm not making any suggestions to you because I don't know you. You do remember that you only bought my book and we're not really talking, right? So, I couldn't possibly have a clue what your chemistry is or how much of each supplement you should take and when. I'm sure you see that would be a ridiculous assumption. I'm just listing supplements that I have seen some people use with success. We all know it is recommended to consult your doctor about your decisions, and ask your clients to do the same.

I also list supplements that are contraindicated for each imbalance. This is very important because you don't want to try to fix one imbalance and simultaneously worsen another imbalance that showed up on your *Imbalance Guide*. For example, you may see that Vitamin E can help an Electrolyte Excess Imbalance so you decide to use it since your Electrolyte Excess Imbalance was so strong. But Vitamin E is contraindicated for an Anabolic Imbalance, so if you also showed an Anabolic Imbalance, Vitamin E could actually exacerbate the Anabolic Imbalance issue. Pay attention to what you're doing; and before you use a supplement to improve one imbalance, make sure it is not listed under the "avoid" section of another imbalance that showed up on your *Imbalance Guide*. This is one of the reasons why it can be so beneficial to employ the help of professional health coaches who understand these principles. Not only have they studied these principles extensively, but also they have seen these fundamentals work, first hand and through their clients' experiences. So they can help you eliminate time-wasting moves.

For those of you working with a health coach, or those of you who graduate from our online Bio-individuality Coach Course, there will be a wider variety of more effective supplements available to you. Many of the higher quality supplements that are geared toward correcting the imbalances I talk about in this book are sold only through professionals. You'll need to find a health coach in your area if you feel you need to take your efforts to the next level. I cover some of these supplements that are available only through a qualified health coach in the Common Imbalance All Stars section later in this chapter.

The biggest mistake I see consumers make when it comes to supplements is that they buy a supplement because their friend tells them it is good for a specific symptom—they start to use it and they feel better. "Yay! I found something that works," they tell themselves. They then continue to use this supplement FOREVER! No matter what. Even if the symptom comes back or gets worse, they continue to use that supplement because they think, "Well, this helped me before so it must be something else that is causing the problem or the problem must just be escalating and now I need to add something else too." Don't do that. I've smacked people in the head for less than that. **Watch your numbers, see the patterns, and adjust what you're doing accordingly.** I can't emphasize that enough.

It's also crucial to remember that it is more important to stop doing something wrong than it is to try to find another supplement to try and overpower whatever it is that you're doing wrong. Coming to terms with bad habits and putting an end to those habits will always be more powerful than adding one more thing right.

Before I get to the imbalances, my final point is this: Under some imbalances I list quite a few supplements that may help that imbalance. That does not mean that you should use all of those supplements just because that imbalance showed up on your *Imbalance Guide*. Unless your imbalance appears to be very strong, you might want to start with just one or two of the supplements listed under a given imbalance and then see if your self-testing numbers improve, indicating the imbalance is improving. If you don't see improvement, it might be time to add another supplement that is listed as beneficial under that imbalance.

Just pay attention to what you're doing. Start slow and easy instead of throwing fifteen new supplements into your body at once.

My only exception to this slow-and-easy rule is if you are looking at digestive issues that need attention. When there are digestive issues, and it's likely there will be for most people dealing with significant health issues, you need to address all aspects of digestion. Don't start by using just HCL and think you can add Beet Flow later. You need to address the lack of acid and use the Beet Flow to help bile flow correctly. You also need to make sure you are using some type of digestive enzyme to fully improve digestive issues. With this understanding, it's simple to see that the "start off slowly" approach does not apply to digestion. You still want to start off slowly with your *quantities* and build your way up;

but when it comes to digestion, you really want to hit all the angles from the beginning.

Imbalance - Electrolyte Deficiency

The most important factors with an Electrolyte Deficiency Imbalance are correcting digestion and adding more unrefined salt. Try to make these your priorities and add other supplements from below as secondary tools.

<u>Often Used With This Imbalance</u>

- **L-Tyrosine** An amino acid - Avoid with a Catabolic Imbalance. (Avoid at night.)
- **Zinc** Keep the dose low with an Anabolic Imbalance.
- **Blackstrap Molasses** Keep the dose low with an Anabolic Imbalance. (Blackstrap molasses contains many minerals, including iron. It also contains sugar and should be used in very small amounts.)
- **Concentrace Trace Mineral Drops** (Described below.)

<u>Avoid With This Imbalance</u>

- **Vitamin E**
- **L-Arginine** An amino acid.

Imbalance - Electrolyte Excess

Use water as a supplement. If you have an Electrolyte Excess Imbalance, odds are great that you are not drinking enough water. The lack of water is also likely contributing to your constipation. If you also have a Catabolic Imbalance, and if drinking more water gives you diarrhea, first improve your Catabolic Imbalance; and then you may be able to increase your water intake without inducing a loose stool. But I doubt this is the case for anyone reading this book.

<u>Often Used With This Imbalance</u>

- **L-Taurine** An amino acid - Avoid with a Catabolic Imbalance. (Best taken in the morning, and near lunch.)
- **Vitamin E** Avoid with an Anabolic or Carb Burner Imbalance. (Best taken with dinner.)

- **Vitamin D3**
- **L-Glutamine** An amino acid.
  Allergy medication Of course, I'm not telling you to stop taking a drug that was prescribed to you by your doctor. However, with this imbalance, it is important to understand that (depending on the mechanism of how the drug works) some allergy medications can constrict the vascular system.

Imbalance – Anabolic

You will likely see a lot of clients dealing with chronic constipation. For those individuals, the Anabolic Imbalance and the Electrolyte Deficiency Imbalance will show up more often than the other imbalances I list here. That doesn't mean those clients are going to have one or both of those imbalances if they're dealing with constipation. It will simply be common for those who seem to be a little plugged up to be dealing with an Anabolic or Electrolyte Deficiency Imbalance, or both.

Often Used With This Imbalance

- **Vitamin B12** Can also help the body burn fat. (Best taken with breakfast and/or lunch. Avoid at night.)
- **Magnesium** Magnesium is a strong anti-anabolic mineral. That is why so many people use it successfully to improve constipation issues. [They don't understand why it works, but now you do. Also, remember, magnesium comes bound to other minerals. Each person can check for the correct combination for his own biologic identity.] (Best taken with breakfast and/or lunch. Avoid at night.)
- **Vitamin A** (Best taken with breakfast and/or lunch. Avoid at night.)
- **L-Tyrosine** An amino acid. (Avoid at night.)
- **Vitamin C in the form of Ascorbic Acid** Often used as a gentle way to lower urine pH or acidify a stool that appears to be too alkaline.
- **Epsom Salt** If a client is very constipated and uncomfortable, epsom salt can sometimes bring some relief. It is simply magnesium sulfate. Magnesium and sulfates are both very pro-catabolic and can send more water to the bowels. Stirring a half to a full teaspoon into 16 ounces of water and drinking it in the morning can help loosen a severely plugged-up bowel. This is

not something I would do on a regular basis, but epsom salt can be effective when attempting to relieve severe constipation. It's not, however, something I use as an anti-anabolic supplement unless the person is dealing with major constipation.

Avoid With This Imbalance

- **L-Glutamine** An amino acid.
- **L-Arginine** An amino acid.
- **Vitamin E**
- **Potassium Citrate**

Imbalance – Catabolic

Don't forget about poached or soft-boiled eggs with this imbalance. Any type of egg where the yolk is still runny can benefit a Catabolic Imbalance. Be sure to use hormone-free eggs. Real butter and coconut oil can also be considered to create supplement-like, beneficial results for some people with a Catabolic Imbalance. **Removing** the use of any omega-3, omega-6, or polyunsaturated fatty acids is even more important.

Often Used With This Imbalance

- **Vitamin E** Avoid with an Electrolyte Deficiency or Carb Burner Imbalance. (Best taken with dinner or before bed.)
- **Potassium Citrate**
- **Collagen and/or Gelatin**
- **HMB** (Best taken with dinner.)
- **Glucosamine Sulfate** Great for joint pain when dealing with a Catabolic Imbalance. (Best taken with dinner.)
- **Apple Cider Vinegar** A tablespoon with meals can aid digestion. Even adding some apple cider vinegar to water that you drink throughout the day can be beneficial to a catabolic. Be cautious using apple cider vinegar as it can create loose stool issues if your bile is not flowing properly.

Avoid With This Imbalance

- **Fatty Acids like Fish or Flax Seed Oils**
- **L-Tyrosine** An amino acid.
- **Magnesium** (Including Magnesium Malate)

- **L-Taurine** An amino acid.
- **Vitamin B12**

Imbalance - Carb Burner

<u>Often Used With This Imbalance</u>

- **Vitamin B12** Avoid with a Catabolic Imbalance. Can help move fat into the mitochondria to be burned for fuel. (Best taken with breakfast and/or lunch. Avoid at night.)
- **Vitamin B5** Also great for breakouts if the person is not processing fats correctly. Limit use with an Anabolic Imbalance. (Best taken at night.)

<u>Avoid With This Imbalance</u>

- **Vitamin D3**
- **L-Histidine** An amino acid.
- **Vitamin E**

Imbalance - Fat Burner

<u>Often Used With This Imbalance</u>

- **Magnesium Malate** Avoid with a Catabolic Imbalance. (Best taken with breakfast. Avoid at night.)
- **Vitamin A** Limit with a Catabolic Imbalance.
- **L-Taurine** An amino acid. Avoid with Electrolyte Deficiency or Catabolic Imbalances.
- **Folic Acid** Limit with an Anabolic Imbalance.
- **L-Tyrosine** An amino acid. Avoid with a Catabolic Imbalance. (Avoid at night.)

<u>Avoid With This Imbalance</u>

- **Vitamin B5**

Common Digestive / Imbalance Supplement All Stars

Don't be confused by the heading. Of course I'm not saying that every client should use all of the supplements on this short list. These are simply some of the supplements that will likely become major players in your arsenal. Since it is very common to see clients dealing with digestive issues, Electrolyte Imbalances, and Anabolic / Catabolic Imbalances, I want to go into a little more depth with the all stars.

HCL/Beet Flow/Digesti-zyme Combo

This is the baseline for anyone dealing with digestive issues. Not everyone will need to supplement with HCL, but even if a client appears to need only to improve HCL production, I will still have him take Beet Flow was well. I do this to ensure bile is flowing properly and to ensure that the increased HCL level is not going to go unneutralized as it leaves the stomach. Unneutralized stomach acid can irritate the intestinal lining, create loose stool issues, and in the worse cases, create or contribute to a duodenal ulcer. For those reasons, I require any client using HCL to also use Beet Flow.

For those reasons, a large majority of my clients use these supplements in the beginning. Remember, when new clients come to you, it's usually because they are looking to improve some type of health issue. Not every health issue is caused by digestive issues, but digestive malfunction is very often at least a contributing factor to whatever issue is going wrong. Most of the supplements I discuss in this section are used to help improve imbalances and have little to do with digestion. But if folks can't digest their food correctly and assimilate the nutrients coming in, they will have similar trouble assimilating the nutrients found in many supplements. If a supplement contains minerals, those minerals need digestive action to be properly assimilated. In that regard, to make most supplements effective, it's a good idea to make sure digestion is being attended to, if needed.

Xeneplex Coffee Suppositories

Beet Flow is the big player when it comes to improving bile flow, but in more severe cases, coffee suppositories can be extremely helpful. A coffee enema can work just as well, but I find that most clients are more willing to use a suppository than going through the trouble and mess of performing a coffee enema.

Beet Flow works to thin the bile so it can flow better, but a coffee suppository works to dilate the biliary pathway so that bile can flow with more ease. Most people will see great results by simply using Beet Flow to thin the bile. Yet you will see a significant percentage of clients who need more help getting bile flowing. For these cases, adding in coffee suppositories seems to be effective.

The combo I've seen work better than anything else is to do a Beet Flow flush on one day and a coffee suppository on the following day. (Remember, a Beet Flow flush is 4 Beet Flow capsules every thirty minutes for two hours.) The combination of thinning the bile and dilating the biliary pathway seems to be the most effective way to move bile that may have been backed up for years.

Note: While this combination is usually an effective strategy, it won't work if a person is not drinking adequate water. In some cases, the reason the bile is thick, sticky and not moving is that the person has been dehydrated for perhaps decades. Clients need to accept the importance of hydration and realize that coffee is not a substitute for water. If clients are not drinking enough water, and if they qualify to increase their water intake, this could be another valuable step to improve bile flow.

Vitamin C as Ascorbic Acid

Vitamin C in the form of ascorbic acid can be used, on a temporary basis, for relief of constipation or to help lower urine pH. Vitamin C as ascorbic acid can be found at most health food stores and is affordable, in most cases. The straight ascorbic acid capsules we use from Douglas Labs run around $15 for 100 capsules and can be found on www.NaturalReference.com. The trick is to find a Vitamin C capsule (not a tablet) that is truly ascorbic acid. Many Vitamin C supplements sold today include rose hips, Ester-C, sodium ascorbate, or other forms of Vitamin C that don't seem to be beneficial or acidic enough for the purposes outlined here.

Ascorbic acid can lower urine pH; it can also slightly acidify the stool. We hear from folks who see great results taking one 1000mg capsule when they wake up and again between breakfast and lunch; others take it just before breakfast and just before lunch. Since ascorbic acid can lower urine pH, someone with a urine pH of 5.5 or lower would want to use ascorbic acid sparingly. But for those who do take ascorbic acid, the body will normally pee out any excess water-based ascorbic acid that cannot be used.

We need to clarify the difference of Vitamin C as ascorbic acid compared to whole Vitamin C. Taking ascorbic acid is not the same thing as taking whole Vitamin C. Ascorbic acid is just a fraction of the whole Vitamin C molecule. When ascorbic acid enters the body, other Vitamin C cofactors are pulled from your reserves and combined with the ascorbic acid so it can be used in the wide variety of ways that Vitamin C is useful to the body. For most individuals, those cofactors will run out in about two weeks. To get more whole Vitamin C into the body, we use Bio-C from Empirical Labs; Bio-C is a more complete form of Vitamin C. However, on a short-term basis, ascorbic acid can be very effective at lowering urine pH and for acidifying the stool so it will move more easily. That's what we're doing here.

Additional Ascorbic Acid Benefits and Uses

By taking ascorbic acid closer to your meal (for example, before breakfast or lunch), you may find it helpful in acidifying the stomach. Ascorbic acid is not very effective at acidifying and breaking down your food, so I don't want you to think you can replace HCL with ascorbic acid. Ascorbic acid may, however, improve the acidification ability of the HCL you are currently making or the HCL supplementation you are adding. For example, by adding 1000mg of ascorbic acid before you eat breakfast, you may need to use only three HCL capsules instead of five to get the same acidification. If ascorbic acid is appropriate for you, test this out and see if it allows you to reduce the HCL dose you are using. Just know that ascorbic acid is not the same as the acid in HCL. HCL is more easily neutralized than ascorbic acid; and when HCL is neutralized, its elemental parts are more acceptable to the system.

It is common for those experiencing constipation, acid reflux, and/or bloating to be experiencing a severe bacterial overgrowth in their stomach. The waste from this bacteria is often alkaline and can further alkalize the stomach, making that environment more hospitable for the bacteria to thrive. The alkaline environment may also reduce the effectiveness of HCL your body is producing or HCL capsules you are supplementing with at meals. When this occurs, issues like constipation, reflux or bloating can be magnified. Adding ascorbic acid before your meal can help improve the acidification of the stomach, in some cases.

Below, I talk about using d-limonene when suspecting a severe bacterial overgrowth in the stomach. However, d-limonene is a very aggressive and pro-catabolic supplement. Many of your clients may benefit from first trying the more gentle approach of using ascorbic acid before meals. In many cases, by combining the ascorbic acid with the HCL capsules you or your clients are supplementing, it will be enough to properly acidify the stomach and make the environment less hospitable for the bacteria.

Tip: If you've moved up to an appropriate dose of HCL and still experience bloating or discomfort after a meal, a dill pickle or two may be enough to do the trick. The acetic acid (vinegar) in that form of pickle may be enough to increase the acid concentration of your stomach. Of course, the goal is to concentrate on the use of HCL because that is what your stomach ordinarily uses to acidify your food. However, if your stomach is still not acidic enough, augmenting with ascorbic acid or enlisting the help of the occasional dill pickle after a meal, may be great tricks to have up your sleeve.

...and sometimes d-limonene

This is not a supplement that most coaches use as frequently as the others listed in this section. However, in extreme cases, it can be enough to help pull a person out of a difficult situation. If a bacterial infection in the stomach is reducing your ability to acidify the food you're eating, using d-limonene can be helpful, in some cases. (Remember, many of you will prefer to try ascorbic acid before breakfast and lunch since this option is considered to be a lot more gentle. Many of you may also choose to eat a dill pickle or two after meals that leave you feeling bloated. If the dill pickle move or ascorbic acid is not enough, taking a more aggressive approach, like d-limonene, may prove effective). If an individual is using an appropriate dose of HCL, yet still experiencing symptoms that indicate the stomach is too alkaline, odds are great that some type of freaky bacteria has set up camp in the stomach. Using d-limonene is a great way to wipe out at least a good layer of the bacteria. Some strains of bacteria can be very difficult to completely eradicate. Learn more about h. Pylóri infections in Appendix A.

It appears that d-limonene can be effective at seeping into the mucous layer in the stomach and wiping out bacteria. However, it is very pro-catabolic and should be used with caution. Most people do well if they skip a day between doses and use it only once that day, first thing in the morning, when we are intended to be more catabolic. Though d-limonene is a natural orange peel extract, to give you an idea of its effectiveness, it is also commonly used as a solvent in paint thinners. For this reason, I don't like to see people use d-limonene for the long term. I'd rather see them use it in short cycles, like the medical world might use an antibiotic. It seems that after four or five doses, most people appear to have reduced their bacterial load enough to experience success with therapies that can be less aggressive.

While taking d-limonene, you may burp up an orange taste from time to time. Since d-limonene is made from orange peel extracts, that makes sense. Since d-limonene is so pro-catabolic, an individual who already appears to be leaning too catabolic may want to spread their doses out even further. Taking one capsule first thing in the morning, every three or four days, may be more appropriate in these cases.

For those who have a severe bacterial overgrowth, the die-off of bacteria in your first dose may be strong enough to cause some nausea or a feeling of stomach distress. If that is the case for you, you might want to wait an extra day before taking your second dose. Reports from those who do feel any discomfort often say that the discomfort was greatly reduced in their second dose, and gone by their third.

Advanced Supplement Formulas

The following supplements are available only to qualified health professionals. And not just any health professionals. You would need to graduate from our online Bio-individuality Coach Course to gain access to the following supplements. Since they are not available to the public, I never mention them in my books. But these formulas are truly my secret weapons and can bring about amazing results. Since you're a health pro, I want to share them with you here.

Electrolyte Deficiency Supplement

The type of clients who tend to gravitate your way can vary greatly from practitioner to practitioner. For me, I tend to see a lot of females who are electrolyte deficient. For this reason, I tend to use a lot of the Electrolyte Deficiency formula from Empirical Labs. It contains not only minerals and nutrients that can help raise blood pressure, it also contains a low dose of vitamin D. The fact that the dose is low is very important. As I discussed in chapter twelve, vitamin D can help pull calcium out of the intestinal tract into the bloodstream. Vitamin D can also make the blood calcium retentive, therefore thickening the blood, raising blood pressure, and allowing those electrolyte deficient individuals to function a little better. Since we don't want to see all those problems that high doses of vitamin D can cause, the low dose in this formula seems to be reasonable.

Of course, with an Electrolyte Deficiency Imbalance, the goal should be to improve digestion so the body can pull more minerals out of the food the client is eating. However, since that can take time for some individuals, the Electrolyte Deficiency supplement often allows me to help clients see great initial results. They now have the confidence to do the work that can create lasting results.

Electrolyte Excess Supplement

Many coaches I talk to seem to attract a lot more of the high blood pressure, Electrolyte Excess Imbalance-type clients. After all, high blood pressure is one of the most common health concerns in the US population today.

Though there are a variety of underlying causes for Electrolyte Excess Imbalance, poor bile flow seems to be a very common contributing factor. Therefore, improving bile flow can be job-one with this imbalance (Have I mentioned fixing digestion first?). But the Electrolyte Excess supplement from Empirical Labs can help bring down an elevated blood pressure much faster, giving you more time to work on the bile.

I find this supplement can be so effective that I make sure clients understand how important it is to monitor their blood pressure while using it. If blood pressure goes too low, the client can start to feel tired, dizzy, depressed, or any other symptom that commonly goes along with low blood pressure. This is especially important for clients to understand if they are on blood pressure lowering meds or products. The meds are not designed to balance blood pressure. They are designed to lower blood pressure. So, if clients are taking steps to lower blood pressure naturally, yet they are still on the same dose of blood pressure lowering meds, those meds can push the blood pressure lower than what might be an optimal reading. In no way am I suggesting that you tell clients to lower their blood pressure meds. That's between the clients and their doctors. Your job is simply to educate your clients what to watch for, allowing them to have a better understanding of why they may feel the way they feel if their blood pressure goes too low. It's also important for you to help them understand why they will need to be more diligent about measuring their blood pressure. At that point, they can talk to their doctors about lowering the dose of their medication. Again, they don't talk to you or to me about that, they talk to their medical doctor.

Anabolic And Catabolic Supplement Formulas

Next on the hierarchy of imbalances comes the Anabolic and Catabolic Imbalances. With these imbalances, we use two different formulas from Empirical Labs to give the body nutrients that can allow it to move out of each imbalance. The Catabolic formula is meant to be used by those who appear to be dealing with a Catabolic Imbalance. The Anabolic Formula is meant to be used by those who appear to be dealing with an Anabolic Imbalance. Improving a severe Catabolic or Anabolic Imbalance can be life-changing for many individuals. For that reason, these formulas can assist to achieve results using fewer tools and possibly fewer dietary changes.

Finding A Qualified Health Coach In Your Area

If you would like to find a qualified health coach who can help you with some of these supplement choices, go to www.OurCoalition.org and fill out the "Find a Health Coach" form. The Coalition will locate a health coach in your area who will contact you directly. If there are no professionals in your area, the Coalition can help you find a coach who works with clients through email. These "distance coaches" can help you better understand the simple tests you run on your own chemistry. Remember, working with a coach may also give you more insights into effective methods that can be used when you start to work with clients using this information.

Wha'd He Say?

In this chapter, you learned:

- Supplements are beneficial only if you use quality products that can be assimilated by the body. Supplements improve one's health only if the supplement is appropriate for that person and his or her individual chemistry.

- Don't forget to handle digestive needs when choosing supplements.
- Once you begin using supplements, be sure to monitor your self-test numbers. When your chemistry becomes more balanced, adjust the supplements you are using.
- If you need supplements more intensely geared to specific imbalances, find a professional health coach in your area who has access to high-quality supplements designed to improve the imbalances discussed here (or graduate from our online health coach course so you can gain access to these advanced formulas for yourself and your clients).

CHAPTER FIFTEEN

The World Of Weight Loss

Weight loss is often part of a health pro's business. Even when clients come to you for help with totally different health issues, when you can help them fix the underlying cause of those issues, a body running more optimally can often result in a body that is holding onto less body fat.

If you do specialize in helping clients lose weight, this chapter will provide some of the insights that have allowed me to help clients lose lots of pounds; one safely 235 pounds in a year.

What's Behind Body Fat?

Be mindful that just because an issue *can* create weight gain doesn't mean that it is the cause behind *every client's* weight gain. I feel that it is important for you to be able to help your clients understand the causes behind the causes. Understanding will make it easier and more motivating for your clients to do the work to improve those underlying causes. Answers to a client's "whys" can also reduce anxiety and remove that "why does this happen to me?" feeling.

Stored body fat is often the result of a combination of circumstances and that combination can be different for each person. For example, digestive malfunction is the most common underlying cause for weight gain—especially obesity. However, the reasons that a person may be having digestive issues and how those issues are altering behaviors or manifesting trouble in the body can be different for each of us.

You have already heard some of the topics I cover here. Some of the points you may have instinctively believed to be true. And some will fully freak you out. In any case, know that you may have to re-learn concepts you believed to be true in the past. My question will be, did those concepts work for every client? My guess is that that they didn't. I know. I've been there.

Why Am I Getting Fat? My Friend Never Gets Fat.

People who come to you for help often feel like they are just stuck in an overweight body. Your job is to help them understand why they're dealing with that weight and steps they can take to see results. They need help understanding that weight gain is not socially selective. "If your friends jumped off a cliff, would you jump too?" (If I had a nickel for every time my mom asked me that, the employees at my favorite stores would say, "Great, here comes the guy that pays with all nickels.") Each individual has unique chemistry that is likely different from every other person in the world—much like a fingerprint. But when we look at the chemistry of an individual, we can begin to get an idea of what issues may be causing weight gain in that individual. That explains how two friends can literally eat identical foods, yet one friend gains no weight while the other friend is thinking about buying stock in Spanx.

One person has a body chemistry or functionality that is predisposed to create an environment where fat storage increases readily, while the other friend's body is operating in a manner that prevents that from happening. In my opinion, this is not a curse that an individual is just stuck with. You can get stuck with a brother that constantly hits on all your friends even though he has no shot—there's not much you can do about that. It is much easier to control body chemistry than it is a schmuck brother.

Body Fat May Be Saving Some People's Lives

I don't mean that body fat may be saving some people's lives if it helps them bounce off of oncoming traffic. It is more scientific than that. This topic will be an extension of the *I Love Lucy* example I made in chapter one under *How Medications Work*. As I said, when the liver is overwhelmed and can't remove enough toxicity from the body, the body can store junk in fat cells. This is sort of an emergency back-up plan to take a substance that is harmful and could wreak havoc on the body, and

228

make that substance inert by shoving the toxic stuff into a fat cell. If it is stored in a fat cell, it won't pose any immediate threat. If the body didn't store this junk in fat cells, these toxins could upset the delicate balance of the bloodstream and we could literally die. In that regard, thank you, fat. Thank you for helping me avoid death today.

This is a major source of weight gain for a big percentage of the population. When looking at toxic substances that may need to be stored in fat cells within the body, medication is only one of the possibilities. The list of substances that may be considered toxic to the body could go on for the rest of this book. Things like pollutants in our air and water; chemicals in our cleaning products; and additives, pesticides and hormones found in our food. Even organic, natural foods that would normally be considered healthy can become toxic in the body as they rot and ferment, if not properly digested. What about the alcohol we drink, cigarettes we smoke, or second-hand smoke we walk by? What about the plastics that seep from the bottle into the water we drink? How about the soda we pour into our faces, or the artificial sweeteners we ingest while we're trying to eat "low-fat?" Are you forgetting about the chemicals we make in our bodies while we're stressed or even just irritated because we can't believe that Jerry Springer is still on the air? Our bodies are well equipped to handle trouble from nearly every angle, but sometimes all the trouble combined is just too much. When the load is more than the body can handle, hello back-fat. This doesn't mean that every toxin has the ability to be stored in fat. However, anything that is adding to the toxic load has the ability to trigger the body to store more junk in fat cells.

Obesity & Starvation

I believe that starvation is one of the leading causes of obesity, especially extreme obesity. When I say this to a crowd I always get looks that say, "We paid money to see this guy?" You may say to me, "Look, the guy is standing right there, he's four hundred pounds, he has a bucket of fried chicken in his hand right now... he's clearly not starving."

What I mean is this: He may be eating, but his body is not receiving the nutrition it needs. We've talked a lot about the ins and outs of digestion; and for many overweight clients, your ability to help them improve their digestion will be your secret weapon for weight loss. Think about it: If a guy can break down and assimilate only ten percent of the nutrients in the food he is eating, doesn't it make sense that he would need to eat ten times as much food in order to get the nutrients required for his body to function?

Have you ever found yourself looking at people who are extremely overweight and thinking, "Why don't they do something about that? Don't they have any dignity?" You are allowing your ignorance of the subject to judge someone inappropriately. There is an abundance of fat kids out there who get teased day and night about their weight. By reading this book, you will become part of the army of health pros who can help these kids, and the adults they become. Obesity is not about a lack of willpower or an individual who has no self respect. Obesity is about science and malfunctions in the body that are creating the excess weight.

While filming the upcoming documentary, *Why Am I So Fat?*, I talked to some of the most well respected celebrity trainers and nutritionists on the planet. Some of *them* don't even understand the truth behind weight loss; so, of course, the public view on the topic is going to be skewed. A few "experts" told me that if people just make a decision, they can change their habits. Sorry guys, there can be more to it than that. By the time you finish this book, and you understand the issues that can create obesity, you will know that no amount of willpower can overcome a body that knows how to get what it needs to survive and function. When you come across obese clients, you will help them understand that it's not their fault and you will teach them the steps they need to take to turn things around.

Shut Up About The Calories Already

Yes, I understand that I'm about to rock your whole belief system. I understand that your nutrition certification program supplied you with fourteen calorie counting books, you have a poster that hangs on your office wall listing the calorie content of every food on the planet, and you just downloaded a new app called *Calorie Genie*. (I apologize if there really is a *Calorie Genie* and I just made fun of you. I honestly just made that up. But if that is your product and it's real, please consider getting a better name.)

"But nearly every diet I have ever asked my clients to follow had them count their calories. Every nutritional expert in our government has told us to burn more calories than we eat." Yes, I know. There is a reason your clients don't see results with those diets, and that most of those government officials are big fat guys. Counting your calories is about as effective as painting your car with Crayons. It's very time consuming, you don't get the result you were hoping for, and the little sharpener always falls out of the back of the box... Maybe that last part happens only with the Crayons scenario. But counting calories still sucks.

Do you know how they determine calories? Scientists burn the food in a bomb calorimeter, which is a box (or in some cases, a big fancy oven-looking device) with two chambers, one inside the other. The researchers weigh a sample of the food, put the sample on a dish, and put the dish into the inner chamber of the calorimeter. Inside the inner chamber, they burn the food, either with extra high temperatures or with a flame. Then they measure the rise in temperature of water kept in the outside chamber. Each degree the water temperature rises equates to one calorie, generally speaking. Tell me this, where in the human body is there a high-temperature oven? Or a flame? There's not. Some people are very flamboyant, but even these folks don't have an actual flame. This two-chamber heating method is so far from human physiology, it's a joke.

Calorie experts tell us that a calorie is a calorie is a calorie. They tell us that the unit of energy measured by a calorie in broccoli is the same as a calorie found in banana cream pie. Yes, that may be true when looking at a petri dish found in a lab. The problem is, humans are not petri dishes and we all process those calories differently. Therefore, it's not about the calories that you consume. It's about your body's ability to turn those calories into fuel. If your body has a problem processing carbohydrates or fats or properly digesting protein, those foods are not converted to energy according to the number of calories they contain. If we all processed foods the same way, this calories-in/calories-out formula would be a beautiful thing. Unfortunately, we all process food differently; and this calorie counting method is just one more idea that confuses and frustrates those who can't lose weight.

The real benefit to counting calories, and why some people succeed when they start cranking out the math, is simply that this calorie counting process makes you conscious of what you're eating. It lets you see exactly what you are shoving down your gullet. That's more valuable than just about anything else you can do. When I bring on new obese clients, I tell them that I won't even train them unless they're willing to journal everything they eat. Getting a true visual of what you consume in a day is an amazing tool.

Calories are okay to sort of get an idea of what you're eating, but the whole system is actually fictional. Treating the measurement of your food like you require the accuracy of a NASA mission is a waste of time and effort. If you don't believe me, try eating 2200 calories per day of just chicken, eggs and green vegetables for two weeks. For the following two weeks, try eating 2200 calories per day of Twix bars and let me know which two week period you had better weight loss results.

What you eat is much more important than the total number of calories. I know that you have heard over and over again that if you burn more calories than you eat, weight loss will occur. That doesn't work out for every client, does it? An individual can use calories for a benchmark, but what they're eating is far more important. I don't have any of my clients count calories at all.

It's more important to get digestion working properly and implement eating real food that the body can process than to know the precise caloric identity of a food. A 100-calorie piece of processed snack food will almost always create more fat storage than 200 calories of real food that is optimal for an individual's specific chemistry. (Please don't turn this ratio into some type of modified calorie counting rule.)

Later in this chapter I talk about the benefits of coconut oil with weight loss, how to use it, who qualifies to use it, etc. But to make my point about calories, coconut oil has 120 calories per tablespoon. It also has fourteen grams of fat (thirteen grams of saturated fat). I consume four to six tablespoons of coconut oil every day ... basically five hundred calories before I even add in any of my meals and I still eat four to six meals every day. Meaning, for many calorie counters, I consume a third of your daily calorie intake in just coconut oil. (Note: These high levels of fat and extra calories don't scare my six-pack away like many would believe.) Most of my clients who qualify to use coconut oil consume similar amounts to aid in weight loss.

It's not about the calories. It's about the choices. This topic will make even more sense when I cover how to help clients avoid becoming nut-jobs while they're losing weight. But, if the calorie game is so deeply burned into your brain that you're having a hard time moving past this right now, just know that one of us is right. Either I'm right and there is hope for your obese clients, or all those calorie counting idiots are right and your obese clients are destined to be overweight. I can't wait to find out which one it is. I'm rooting for my team because I don't think anyone is destined to be overweight if that person has the proper knowledge and is willing to turn that knowledge into understanding and implementation.

"Your body keeps an accurate journal regardless of what you write down."

- Unknown

Fat Is The Symptom, Not The Cause

There are countless conditions that are now associated with being overweight: Hypertension, Type II Diabetes, high cholesterol, etc. It seems like every doctor will tell you that if you just lose weight, many of those conditions may improve. Countless studies have shown that if you lose just X% of body weight, you can greatly increase the chance of improving Type II Diabetes, or high blood pressure, etc. But this is backward thinking, in my opinion. I'm not saying that my opinion matters the most, but in this book it does.

This is how I explain my view to clients: The fat is not causing your hypertension. The fat has not given you Type II Diabetes. You don't need cholesterol medication because you are fat. (1) The foods you are eating and (2) the way your body is processing those foods are the two causes behind those issues. These are the same causes that are making you fat. If you understand what I'm saying, you can see that, yes, if you made the changes that allowed you to drop some weight, those changes could also improve any number of these conditions. But to view this scenario the way it is explained to us by the medical world will only confuse you and may point you in the wrong direction.

If you understand that the direct cause of all these issues is either the choices that you're making or the way that your body is processing those choices, then you can do something about it. But, if you go along with what you hear in the media, from your doctor, or in pharmaceutical advertisements, and if you believe that you have a "fat gene" or slow metabolism or thick bones, you may feel like there's nothing you can do about it.

If you think your fat is causing all the problems and you're genetically predisposed to own that fat forever, what choice do you have? You may as well have another slice of chocolate cake and enjoy what little time you have left, right? Are you starting to see why so many people feel like they have no other choice but to use medications, have surgery, or take other drastic measures? The outlook is hopeless out there. The good news is, that outlook is fiction. It's not true. It's entertaining and it sells products, but it's not true. Take the movie *The Avengers* for example. This was a work of fiction. It was funny, exciting, and very entertaining, but that stuff didn't really happen. It was all made up. Weird, huh?

The exciting part for you is that you get to teach people that they do have choices. Options are available, and this book gives you the tools you need to teach your clients how to make those options work for them. It's going to take effort. Don't think it will be easy. But your clients no longer need to go on thinking that they're hopeless or that they are to blame. Some clients may still choose to do nothing about their weight. Some people aren't interested in putting effort toward their goals. That's okay. Sometimes effort is not that fun. Your job is to teach them there are steps they can take to figure out what will work for them; and they will know those options will be there for them when the time is right.

"You may be born with a genetic map, but that does not mean you have to take the trip."

-Me

Fat Does Not Come From Fat

Most avid dieters understand this principle by now and, for most health pros, this will not be groundbreaking information. But for those of you who are still living in the eighties, when every nutrition expert told us to cut the fat and stop eating eggs, I want to cover this here. Please step away from your arcade-size Ms. Pacman and prepare to be enlightened.

Your body fat is not merely a result of fat that you consumed. This has been common knowledge for so long now, and yet I still have clients tell me all time, "I made sure I only ate low-fat stuff." If the label says "low-fat," it usually means that product will make you fat. When manufacturers take fats out of food, they often replace those fats with chemicals, sugars and artificial sweeteners to give it flavor. These replacements cause the body to store fat more than most fats do.

There are fats that are not healthy, like trans fats and that stuff that drips off the french fry cage of the deep fryer. However, our bodies require nutritional fats in order to function properly. By consuming fats appropriate for your body, you can actually accelerate weight loss. There are bodily processes that could not be completed without adequate fats. If you're not consuming enough healthy fats in your diet, your body will hold on to stored fat like it's money in the bank.

Believing a low-fat diet is the best weight-loss plan is a thing of the past. Now that we understand the science behind consuming fats, we realize that entire low-fat train of thought was a huge screw-up. Just remember how easy it was for our culture to believe this myth for nearly a decade. When false information spreads through the public for so long, it can take quite some time for the truth to reach everyone, if it ever does. This understanding may make it easier for you to believe some of the other common mistakes being made in the world of nutrition and elsewhere. You have no doubt encountered evidence of this phenomenon when you saw some idiot still wearing his collar popped up like it's 1983.

"A lie gets halfway around the world before the truth has a chance to get its pants on."
- Winston Churchill

The Saturated Fat Conspiracy

This might bug the crap out of you. Not because I'm going to tell you something else that you shouldn't eat, but because you may come to the conclusion that you've been avoiding great foods in the name of bad science. Long ago, a bunch of scientists discovered a correlation between high levels of saturated fats (particularly a type of saturated fat called palmitic acid) and cardiovascular disease. They concluded that, because so many heart attack victims had high levels of these saturated fats, we should avoid consuming saturated fats. Due to the fact that egg yolks and red meat both contain higher levels of saturated fats, these foods became the red-headed stepchild of the nutrition world.

Newsflash: Those high levels of the saturated fat palmitic acid don't come from consuming saturated fats. Here's how it works: The body stores glucose from carbohydrates in the liver and muscle tissues in the form of glycogen. Once these stores are full, many excess sugars get converted into palmitic acid and stored as a saturated fat. Excess sugars and carbs are the cause of elevated levels of saturated fats for most of those suffering from cardiovascular disease. It's excess carb and sugar consumption; consuming saturated fats has little to do with that equation at all. These fats can also group with glycerol to form triglycerides. High triglyceride levels are said to be a common risk factor for cardiovascular disease.

Cholesterol

The same misguided thinking that had us shy away from saturated fats also had us running in horror from cholesterol. It's time you know the truth. Approximately 85% of our cholesterol stores are made by our liver. Only about 15% comes from our diet. Since cholesterol has so many important functions, when we decrease our dietary intake of cholesterol to lower our cholesterol numbers, our bodies just make more cholesterol to make up for the deficit. Cholesterol is used to repair damage done by high amounts of insulin in the bloodstream, so it would make sense that when insulin goes high, cholesterol would go high too. To lower your cholesterol, lower your carbohydrate and sugar intake, or whatever is causing too much free radical activity—not your cholesterol intake.

Genetics can play a role in how the body is predisposed to operate, but we can normally control the outcome with nutrition and lifestyle changes. Usually a whole family will have high cholesterol because they all grew up eating in a similar fashion, not necessarily because it is in their genes. If it is our family genes, we must all be related since half the nation is going diabetic or pre-diabetic. Most people feel they are powerless because they have been taught that the family genes are the problem so it has nothing to do with environment or diet. Really? Half the nation and it's a genetic problem? We must be evolving incredibly fast, and nobody likes where this evolution is taking us.

There is rarely a malfunction in the body that makes one person make more cholesterol than another for no reason. Your body is making a high amount of cholesterol to fix a problem. With a high portion of the American public being predisposed to insulin resistance, the problem, most commonly, is that the insulin levels are too high. Your body makes more cholesterol to patch up the damage that the high insulin is causing. Yes, as the body patches up more and more damage, the passages can get smaller and smaller and eventually clog up with "excess cholesterol." However, blaming the problem on the cholesterol would be like blaming firemen for fires... "Well, every time I see a fire there are all these guys in yellow jackets and red trucks all over the place. If we get rid of them, there would be no more fires." Why not just lower the insulin levels so your body won't need to make so much cholesterol? Hmmm.

For decades the medical world told us that 220 was the optimal number for total cholesterol in the bloodstream. A few years ago, the medical world came out with "new findings" stating that our cholesterol truly should be below 200. Well, let's say that 35% of the population has a total cholesterol number that falls between 200 - 220, the range that was considered to be healthy for decades. What happens to that 35% of the population when medical authorities lower the suggested blood cholesterol range to below 200? That 35% all become prescription-buying customers, that's what. Wouldn't that give the cholesterol medication manufacturers a 35% increase in sales overnight? Is that the most brilliant marketing you've ever heard? I don't even think Justin Bieber could top that.

Again, good, free-range eggs (including the yolk) and good meat can be excellent dietary choices. Don't be afraid of the saturated fat or the cholesterol, and don't let some Barney tell you otherwise.

Coconut Oil

Don't forget, it is my opinion that there is no food or supplement that is right for everyone when it comes to weight loss, or even improving health. But if anything could come close to fitting those criteria, coconut oil would be the winner.

Before I explain the benefits of coconut oil, let me first explain the circumstances in which coconut oil might not be a helpful tool for weight loss. If you fall into any of these categories, I suggest fixing the described issue so that you *can* use coconut oil.

1. If your bile is not flowing properly, it may be difficult for you to emulsify the fats in coconut oil and digest those fats correctly. If fats are not correctly processed, they can become a problem the body has to deal with. If enough undigested fats accumulate in the body, they can be stored as body fat or the body may attempt to push the fats out through the skin. This can create breakouts or make you the zit captain. If you need to improve your bile flow, use Beet Flow described in chapter three.
2. If a strong Anabolic Imbalance shows up when you run your self-tests in chapter seven, you may want to take steps toward improving that imbalance before you begin to use coconut oil. For some people, coconut oil can have a slight pro-anabolic effect so if you're already too anabolic, you don't want to use something that could push you more anabolic until you have introduced foods or supplements that can help correct that imbalance.
3. If you are constipated or have a hard stool, you may want to do the work to improve your constipation before introducing coconut oil. Moving a constipated person more anabolic can exacerbate constipation. But once you have corrected your Anabolic Imbalance or your constipation, you should be able to use coconut oil moderately and experience its amazing weight-loss benefits.

But It Contains So Much Fat!

I know!!! That's the point. Coconut oil contains healthy fats that your body needs desperately to function properly. Coconut oil is one of the easiest ways to supply your body with those fats every day. Once your body starts to see these healthy fats coming into the system day after day, there won't be that need to be so stingy, holding on to all of your stored fat. If the body is receiving healthy fats every day, it feels better about burning off stored fat and you can lose weight.

As I explained earlier, I consume four to six tablespoons of coconut oil per day. That means I'm taking in up to seventy eight grams of saturated fat per day, just in coconut oil. That doesn't include any eggs, meats or other foods I eat. That doesn't mean that you need to consume that much, or that coconut oil is even right for you. If you're not processing fats well, it won't be. I have just found it to work well for me. Just be sure to use an extra virgin variety of coconut oil if you want to try it for yourself.

Here are some great ways to include coconut oil in your diet every day:

1. Cook with it - Many oils that are okay to use, like extra virgin olive oil, have the ability to become toxic once the oil is heated. Coconut oil holds up to heat better than just about any other oil. At first, coconut oil may taste a little different with certain foods, like eggs. However, sooner or later your body will realize it can really utilize coconut oil, your taste buds will change, and you will end up enjoying it much more than any other oil. All that being said, cooking with it alone is usually not enough to get crazy weight-loss results.

   I add half to a full tablespoon of coconut oil to the skillet anytime I'm making a stir fry or eggs, etc. I have met people who don't like the smell of coconut oil once it has been cooked. For those individuals, Aunt Patty's brand makes a coconut oil that is odorless when cooked.

2. Add a tablespoon to a shake - When coconut oil gets cool, it hardens. Therefore, if you don't have anything else of substance in your shake, like kale, the coconut oil can get a little clumpy in the liquid when it gets cold. But if you use a good blender and add something else for the coconut oil to mix with, you won't really notice it and it will add a nice flavor.

3. Just eat it - Yes, just eat the coconut oil right out of the jar. I have a lot of clients who eat a teaspoon of coconut oil after every meal that they consume at home. It can be a little hard to carry coconut oil around in your pocket; so if you eat the oil only while you're home, that's still better than none. Although... Artisana brand now makes organic raw coconut oil in little ketchup-sized packets. Just don't get the coconut butter because that contains more sugars. The packets of coconut oil contain a little over one ounce, which would equate to just over two tablespoons.

   Keep in mind that coconut oil should always be consumed with a meal. You want that digestive action going on to help you properly emulsify the fats.

4. My Coconut Yummies recipe - This is the greatest trick ever for sneaking healthy fats into your diet and relieving the desire for something sweet after every meal. Below I share my recipe for a great after-dinner mint that can make you feel more satiated,

dramatically aid weight loss, and allow you to have a little treat at the end of each meal.

Coconut Yummies

Melt a cup of coconut oil in the oven or a toaster oven. You can also melt your coconut oil by placing the container in hot water in the sink. Either method can take a few minutes, but do not use a microwave just because it may be quicker! Next, I stir in half a packet of stevia and about 10-30 drops of flavored stevia. Optionally, you can open up four or five capsules of Pau D' Arco and mix them in too. Pau D' Arco is an herb commonly used for its anti-microbial properties; it can add an almost chocolate-like taste to the coconut oil. As an alternative, you can add cinnamon or mint if you prefer those flavors.

To mold the coconut oil into little treats, I use silicone mini-muffin baking dishes. You can see the type I use under BOOK TOOLS > HELPFUL LINKS at www.SixFigureHealthPro.com

I put about a tablespoon or a tablespoon and a half in each mini-muffin hole and put the batch in the fridge to harden.

Enjoy The Fats

Enjoying appropriate fats in your diet can make a world of difference to any weight-loss effort, as long as you correct any digestive issues so you have the ability to process those fats. Many who don't feel well after eating fats have poor bile flow and can't process the fats correctly. Once bile flow is corrected, these individuals will usually enjoy fats once again. Most low-calorie diets eventually fail because they leave the person feeling hungry all the time. Fats can make you feel more satisfied and sustain energy longer. I go over more sources for good dietary fats in chapter thirteen. I even give you food options containing fats that can help to improve specific imbalances.

Wha'd He Say?

In this chapter, you learned:
- An individual may be storing fat for a combination of reasons, and these reasons vary from person to person.

- Excess fat can be more than just "too much of the wrong foods." Body fat is a way the body can store toxins, like medications, chemicals from our food or environment, or even food that did not get properly digested.
- Fixing common digestive issues is a major priority when it comes to weight loss.
- You can count your calories or you can smash yourself in the face with a brick. Both options are not very fun and rarely bring a long-term positive result.

CHAPTER SIXTEEN

Mental & Emotional Issues

Helping Clients Avoid The Psycho Factor

Issues like anxiety, bipolar-type behavior, depression and eating disorders can be exacerbated by the "burn more calories than you consume" weight-loss plan that so many health professionals use with their clients. Emotional stability often relies on the body's ability to function correctly. This chapter will explain many of the mental and emotional problems your clients deal with, and steps you can teach them how to take to see improvement. We also have shows revolving around most of these topics on our *Kick It Naturally* podcast.

In chapter nine, under *Electrolyte Deficiency Imbalance*, I talked about mental and emotional problems that can develop from the body dealing with a lack of resources. You'll remember my talking about how, when your toaster doesn't work, you first look to see if it's plugged in. Many issues that people consider strictly psychological are frequently circumstances where the brain is not getting the resources it needs to function correctly. If physiological circumstances, poor lifestyle choices, or environmental factors are restricting the amount of resources that could make it to a person's brain, what do you think is going to happen when this poor bastard tries to create a caloric deficit in order to lose some weight? Yes, you guessed it... The Psycho Factor kicks in.

Promise me you won't dig into your four-year psychology degree and write me letters explaining that some girls have eating disorders because they were traumatized by their Uncle Biff who locked them in a closet and forced them to eat a case of Twinkies. I know people deal with legitimate issues in their lives and I go over that later in this chapter. However, you'll also remember that, in chapter six, I explained how these same people who are dealing with an issue they consider to be a ten, on a scale of one to ten, can bring that down to a three or four, once the brain is getting the fuel it needs to function optimally. So, even though the problem may have other underlying circumstances attached, in most cases, these problems become a lot easier to deal with when the person is working with a full deck. Most problems have more than one cause. In this book, I'm looking at the biological or physiological issues. Often times, lifting these burdens can make the emotional side easier to work with.

Some of these issues can be a lot more complicated than what I'm explaining here, and we dissect them further in the podcast episodes I mentioned at the beginning of the chapter. I bring this up here only to further explain how creating a calorie deficit is not the optimal idea that many present. I use these points also to emphasize how using more medium-carb meals can help clients avoid any Psycho Factor moments if they see them creeping in due to a decrease in carb or sugar consumption.

There are a wide variety of health issues that could make you want to help clients reduce the amount of processed junk they are consuming. Remember, many clients have gravitated toward eating this junk because processed carbs are much easier to break down, digest, than real food. When digestion is operating poorly, the processed junk may be the only way these clients can access any fuel. It's pretty common for people to go a little crazy while they're trying to lose weight, so it's important to understand that the same result can occur if these folks are removing this junk to create other health benefits as well. A popular candy bar ad campaign that runs constantly on television right now is all about how people turn into someone else when they're hungry. This chapter is about teaching clients how to avoid those moments of insanity, no matter how little or big those insanity fits can sometimes be. The point is: There is no point in changing a client's diet if the new diet makes that client miserable or emotionally unstable. How is your client going to sustain that in a manner that would allow him to either lose weight or create other health benefits? The trick is to help your clients see improvements while making sure their brains get all the fuel they need.

Why Do Pregnant Women Gain Fat And Go Nuts?

I like to use the weight gain that can accompany pregnancy as an example because it's such an extreme situation. It clearly illustrates how a lack of resources can not only lead to weight gain, it can also lead to those moments of "unreasonableness," a.k.a. The Psycho Factor. It doesn't matter how sweet, caring, generous or mentally stable a woman is, at some point while she's pregnant, we all know she's going to snap and we all know none of us will hold it against her. It's common knowledge and we all accept it. Now you're going to get to understand why it happens.

To make a baby takes a lot of minerals and other types of nutrients. Believe it or not, babies aren't just delivered by a stork; it takes resources to build a baby just like it takes resources to build anything. Would you try to build a house without any building materials? Would you start construction without any wood, nails, bricks, concrete or whatever else you were going to build your house out of? Of course not. Your housewarming party would just be a bunch of people standing in your yard eating egg salad while they talk about how you've lost your marbles. Just as when building a house, you need resources if you want to make a cute little human.

When a woman has horribly low nutritional resources, Mother Nature often protects the would-be mother from troublesome issues by turning off the woman's ability to have a baby… and the menstrual cycle stops until her resources come back up. But we often punch Mother Nature in the face and work around her by using pharmaceutical hormones that keep the cycle regular. One of the most common underlying causes for a woman to experience irregular periods, or to go months at a time without a period, is a lack of resources due to improper digestion. That probably makes sense to you now that you've learned how digestion is what allows us to take the food we consume and turn it into life-sustaining resources. Once a woman can fully break down her food and pull the needed minerals out of what she's eating, the abundance of resources often allows her period to come back.

We are taught that menopause is all about these crazy hormonal changes that take place in a woman's body when she reaches a certain point in her life, as if there is this clock in her body that's been waiting fifty years to go off; and once it does, all hell breaks loose. Hormones run amok, the menstrual cycle begins to go haywire, and "Why does my face feel like I'm on fire for forty seconds at a time?" Many women are advised to start cramming hormones into their bodies in order to "correct" this hormonal imbalance that comes with age. Why don't we ever stop to think that there might be a reason that these hormone levels are going crazy? Doesn't it make sense that, if the body is no longer receiving enough minerals and other nutrients it needs to function correctly, it might try to fix things on its own by raising hormone levels in a last-ditch effort to keep the body in a reproductive state? Once the body has tried every trick it has, the cycle will shut down and that individual will no longer have the ability to produce a child. This can be why many women enter menopause earlier than expected.

This also explains why pregnant women can have so many "loony" fits. We hear that this is due to all the crazy hormones flying around. I believe that is true for some cases. However, couldn't these crazy hormonal changes be similar to those that come when the body is trying to figure out what to do about a lack of resources? In this regard, couldn't a lack of resources and hormonal changes be affecting those who are not pregnant as well? What if some people are creating mental issues by creating a nutrient deficiency with their extreme dieting techniques? Many may be creating these issues by just ignoring the task of taking care of the human body they live in. I have clients come to me all the time who have been up since dawn, will finally get around to eating a bag of corn chips around 2:30 pm, and won't eat again until dinner or they skip dinner altogether. Do you really expect your body (much less your brain) to function on so little fuel and/or inappropriate sources of fuel?

If you have children and you send them to school without lunch money and no breakfast, and they are gone from 7am to 2 o'clock in the afternoon without eating, that could be 18 hours without food, depending on when they ate the night before. Child welfare will come and take your children away from you because that's flat out neglect. You wouldn't expect a child to excel with that type of neglect. So why would you expect a different outcome from your own body? In most cases, people who live this way don't really need therapy or a new direction in life; they need breakfast. Yes, digestion is important and that's always a priority, but how are you going to digest anything if you don't first insert it into your gullet?

So, Maybe I'm Not Fat Or Crazy, I'm Just Pregnant?

No. That's not what I said. But the circumstance of having a little human grow inside you is an extreme that can show us how cravings increase as requirements escalate or as supply decreases. I'm hoping this illustrates how behavior can be affected by the nutrients you're supplying your body. It makes perfect sense to us when a pregnant woman says, "BRING ME CUCUMBERS WITH PEANUT BUTTER BEFORE I STOMP ON YOUR FACE!" We get it. Yet, her circumstances are just an exaggerated extreme of the same issues that can make you want to ball up on the floor and cry to old George Michael ballads.

If emotions seem to be elevated, use the same steps you took to get rid of cravings:

- Ensure digestion is working properly.
- Increase any supplements you are using to lift mineral content if you have an Electrolyte Deficiency Imbalance.
- Increase use of unrefined salt.
- Increase medium-carb foods.
- Consume appropriate fats and protein at every meal.

That Time Of The Month

While I'm on the topic of bodily situations that can arise for females, l want to mention the menstrual cycle. If cramps or horrible emotional roller coasters are part of your world every month, be sure to read my book, *Kick Menstrual Cramps in the Nuts*. For now, like we talked about in chapter twelve, understand that your menstrual cycle requires an enormous amount of resources to complete the entire process. Therefore, when your period is approaching, expect resources to be low and the issues that can accompany low resources to be high. Take proper steps to ensure resources won't go too low during this time of the month.

Emotional Issues

The ability of your body chemistry to magnify many emotional issues does not mean that emotional issues do not exist—they do. Remember, improving chemistry doesn't fix all your problems, it can just make those problems easier for you to deal with. However, you still have to deal with them. I don't want to spend too much time on the subject because I don't want this to sound like a therapy session. I simply want you to know this... you can do it. Whatever it is, you can get past it. Why couldn't you? That doesn't mean it will be easy, it may not be easy at all. But the more difficult it is to get past, the bigger the reward will be on the other side, and the more of an inspiration you will be to your clients.

I also want you to keep in mind that, no matter what you are dealing with, there is someone out there who would gladly trade problems with you. Appreciate where you are in your life because everything you're experiencing now is part of *your* journey and nobody can take that away from you. Be grateful for the life you're in and take responsibility for how it has turned out. That may be hard to do at first; but if you can take responsibility for your life, that can be enough to help you understand that you have the ability to change it.

> *"When you have exhausted all possibilities, remember this:*
> *You haven't."*
> *- Thomas Edison*

Get Support

Nobody said you need to get over emotional issues by yourself. What fun is that? Who are you going to high-five when you get there? Find support and don't be afraid to lean on that support. It's likely that your supporter may need to help you as much as you need the help. If your emotional issues have to do with your weight, find a buddy who would like to lose weight too and take this journey together. If everyone in your neighborhood is a skinny bitch, find people or communities online. We have a free and private Facebook support group at www.Facebook.com/groups/kickyourfatsupport. This weight-loss support group has turned into more of a health support group, and we talk about a lot more than just weight loss. The group is filled with both health pros and consumers. It's the perfect place to ask questions while you're learning how to look at your own physiology in this book. Simply click "join" and we will approve you into the group. We have an amazing community there and you can find friends, ask questions and share your successes with others. It can be a huge difference maker and it's totally free.

When Should Your Clients Weigh?

This is the best advice I can give people who deal with emotional issues connected to their weight. Most people will usually not listen to it and say I'll just do it my way, but the people who really follow this rule almost always do well.

Here's the advice: Don't weigh yourself... EVER!

"So, I tell my clients not to count their calories and not to weigh themselves? Are you sure you're not just some moron that decided he wanted to write a book?" No, I'm not sure. But I do know weighing themselves constantly is one of the biggest mistakes I see new clients make.

Your clients don't need to know what they weigh because they're not on a reality show where they win a million dollars for losing the most weight. The number on a scale is very misleading and it will really screw with your clients' heads. The thing that matters is how your clients' clothes are fitting, especially their pants. Use that as the judge.

After all, how many times do you think your clients have been in the middle of a weight loss program and gone without weighing themselves? And how many times have they succeeded to remove all the weight that they wanted to take off and keep it off? Exactly. Probably never on both accounts. Teach your clients to do something different. Just go by how they feel and how their clothes are fitting.

If a client, Judy, wants to be more precise, have her measure her stomach right at her belly button first thing in the morning and mark that on the calendar. Then, have Judy measure her stomach again every two or three weeks. You don't want her to do it more often than that because the body does not respond to what you did in the past day or two. That is not how weight loss works. Weight loss seems to work in cycles of seven to ten days. So, Judy could be doing everything perfectly for seven days, measure herself and see no results and think that she needs to change her approach. Had Judy just stuck with it for a few more days, the accumulative effect of that approach could have shown in another few days and she would have seen results. You don't want Judy to screw with her own head by measuring in the middle of her progress.

As far as actual weight goes, just have Judy weigh herself when she starts, mark it on the calendar, and weigh herself every few months so she can tell her friends, "I lost thirty pounds, Dawg." Make sure Judy takes muscle into account for her weight. If she is working out and she is correcting any digestive issues and maybe she's adding more mineral and protein to her intake, Judy may now have the ability to build more muscle tissue. Muscle weighs more than fat, so Judy's weight can actually go up on the scale, but she still looks and feels better. The measurement around Judy's stomach will never lie, but the scale will lie/mislead/deceive over and over again.

Again, some people don't take this advice seriously; but the ones who do, reach their goals more frequently and experience much less frustration along the way.

Low Potassium Issues

As you learn through experience by working on your own physiology, on top of emotional issues, if you start to feel a little loopy, clumsy or forgetful, this is great information to have. Potassium in the body is a mineral that allows the cells to communicate back to the brain. It's what closes the control loop. The brain says, "Okay, let's do this" and then everybody down in the body communicates back to the brain, "Okay, this is what happened." Without enough potassium, the "this is what happened" doesn't make it back to the brain. Beyond the lack of coordination with your muscle/brain communication, low potassium issues can also cause a lack of coordination in the endocrine system.

When there is a low-potassium issue, it's almost as if the body doesn't know what is going on since signals can't be properly transmitted. This can result in a variety of whacked-out testing numbers. pHs can be all over the board and your test results might not make much sense at all.

Low potassium issues can be easier to detect with equipment and techniques used by those who have graduated from our Bio-individuality Coach Course. However, here are some signs you can look for that commonly coincide with low potassium issues:

- Food seen in your stool

- Burping or bloating
- Significant digestive issues
- Clumsiness
- Absent-minded or forgetful

If these issues sound familiar, you may want to be skeptical of your testing results. That doesn't mean that you should supplement potassium. The next step I would take would be to work on any digestive issues. Once you improve digestion and add protein to every meal, potassium can come into the system through your food. Good sources of extra potassium could be small green bananas, figs, or orange juice. Just keep in mind that these are higher-carb foods, higher-carb foods are not always the best idea, so consuming them in smaller quantities might be appropriate for some people.

Be Patient

Results make it easy to be optimistic and keep emotions positive. However, it's important to understand that, when taking steps to move chemistry, most results will not show up immediately. That's not how the body works. You can't take a supplement or eat a specific food and expect your chemistry to be different an hour later, or even the next day. In that same line of thinking, you can't see a major change in your numbers and look at what you just did and think that was responsible. You can't say to yourself, "Well, I just watched an old episode of *Bewitched* and now my blood pressure is better." That's not how it works. You want the changes to your body to move slowly, just like agriculture does. Let me tell you a story to illustrate what I mean.

I was living in Florida and touring professionally as a comic. I was on a three-month trip all over the West Coast and still had a girlfriend on the East Coast. While I was working a week in Vegas, she flew out to see me. We were sitting at the buffet when we heard over the intercom, "Phone call for Mr. Knievel, Mr. Evel Knievel." We laughed at how someone must have gotten a hold of the intercom and was playing a joke. But that night, Evel Knievel came to my show and sat in the back of the room with my girlfriend. This part has nothing to do with my illustration, I just like to talk about Evel Knievel. The point of the story is that my girlfriend and I broke up on that trip. Not because she wanted me to be dreamier like Evel Knievel, but because with the long time away, we had just grown apart. The split was amicable but as I dropped her off at the airport, she couldn't stop crying. I was sad that we were splitting up, but I just wasn't emotional about it.

I returned to the airport the next morning for my flight back home, as my West Coast tour had ended and I missed all my rednecks in Florida. I got on the plane and sat in the middle seat between two very large men. Normally, when you sit down on a plane, you might share a few pleasantries or at least say, "Hi." For one reason or another, none of us said a word. I may have been silent just because both guys were a lot taller than me and I could tell I was going to lose the armrest battle. About an hour into the flight, the cart started moving down the aisle to serve breakfast.

The stewardess, or sky frolicker, or whatever the current politically correct name is, set my breakfast on my fold-out tray. I looked down to see two pieces of french toast, cut in half, with a sliced-up pear in the middle. Pears were my girlfriend's favorite food. I looked down at the plate for about 30 seconds before tears started running down my face. By the time the air waitress had moved the cart down the aisle, I was sobbing like an eight-year-old girl who just accidentally smashed the cassette for her *Annie* soundtrack. It was full-on uncontrollable sobbing. Not cool. It lasted for more than a few minutes before the guy sitting to my right finally looked over and asked, "Are you okay?" I paused for a moment, collected myself, looked straight ahead and said to him with a trembling voice, "I just really like french toast." The guy to my left looked over to the guy to my right for a brief second, they both looked straight ahead just long enough to let what I said soak in, then we all went back to eating our breakfast and nobody said another word for the rest of the flight.

Do you see my point? I'm thinking that maybe you don't, but it's still a good story. My sobbing was not a result of the pears I just saw. There were layers upon layers of events, emotions and circumstances that led to my making a complete jackass of myself on the plane that morning. That's how your body works. Just because you're trying to improve one imbalance doesn't mean that many layers of imbalances, emotions and chemistry are not being affected in many ways. With that in mind, try not to view a piece of information merely as cause and effect. It is often much more intricate than that and results will often take longer than you want them to take. Be patient. Your health is not an episode of *Miami Vice*. Everything will not be resolved in forty-five minutes.

Calling In A Professional

I've already gone on and on about how tricky this process can be. It's also tricky to rock a rhyme, to rock a rhyme that's right on time... it's tricky. But that's neither here nor there. The point I'm trying to impress upon you is to always remember that you are educating yourself about your body, so you can educate others about their bodies. The human body is just about the most amazing mechanism out there. (Other than a slinky. I just don't see how it does that thing down the stairs.) While you're working to better understand your body, keep in mind that *nobody* totally understands the human body. It's way too complicated. Remember that understanding these imbalances is complex enough, but when you start to realize that one imbalance on top of another can begin to change how the whole system is running, it can be a lot to sort through.

Yes, I know there are people who will totally change their life, or lose an incredible amount of weight, by simply improving their digestion or a slight imbalance here or there. Yet a percentage of you reading this book and a percentage of your clients will really need help beyond what can be covered in this book. The best part about plugging yourself into *The Coalition* and using their tracking tools is that you will be laying the groundwork in case you need to bring in a health coach to help you. When you contact *The Coalition* to find a professional in your area, and you begin to work with that person, *The Coalition* can attach your account to that health coach. This will allow you to share your progress charts with that coach in a secure environment. The coach will then be able to see all of your progress charts and how your chemistry has been moving with the efforts you have been putting in.

Presenting a new health coach with data that you have already been tracking can be a tremendous jump-start—not to mention the fact that you will understand your body enough now to have an intelligent conversation with the person who is guiding you in your education about your body. Unlike a doctor visit where you might not have a clue what he's talking about or why he's suggesting the things he is suggesting, if you've read this book and you've been monitoring your chemistry on *The Coalition*, you will be miles ahead of the game. It will be so much easier for you to be a participant in your own health, allowing you to make your own health decisions with someone to bounce ideas off. If you decide to become a Coalition coach, and receive referrals from the organization, you'll also be miles ahead in your understanding of how to use the system to help your clients.

If you would rather simply dig into our online Bio-individuality Coach Course, and learn the advanced information yourself, go to HealthProCourse.com to learn more.

Wha'd He Say?

In this chapter, you learned:
- A lack of nutrients can create emotional roller coaster issues.
- Many people don't need therapy, they need breakfast.
- Tell your clients not to weigh themselves too frequently. Use measurements or how their clothes are fitting to monitor their progress.
- If you're feeling loopy, clumsy or forgetful, you may be dealing with low potassium issues.
- Be patient.
- If you need help from a professional who has graduated from our Bio-individuality Coach Course, get it. You don't need to do this alone.

CHAPTER SEVENTEEN

Will The Diets Ever Stop?!

Why Popular Diets Don't Work For Everyone

This is my favorite part of the whole book (outside of that time when I was really funny). I love it when my clients learn enough about physiology to understand why the diets they tried before didn't work for them. They usually cuss a little bit, thinking back to all the time they wasted counting calories, or juicing a turkey sandwich, or scouring the countryside looking for some hoggelwart herb that was going to make the fat fall off. It's okay for clients who come to you to be annoyed about the bad advice they received in the past, as long as you understand that it's your job to teach these clients that their failures probably make sense—and they were probably not at fault. Even better, now you're going to get to help your clients understand what to do to either make that diet work for them or put together a plan that is right for each client's body and biological makeup.

Here I break down popular diets and explain why they work for some people and not for others. In each section I group a few diets together. I understand there are variations between the diets I am grouping together, but the major function is the same—so this will save time. My explanations do not mean that these are all bad diets. You get that by now, right? It just means that they are not right for everyone, as the creators of these diets often indicate. I may repeat a few nuggets I have already explained in this book because I want to freak you out when you realize how much you understand now.

Low-Fat Diets

<u>When Do These Diets Work?</u>

The low-fat diet craze hit in the eighties and we're still paying the price today. The fact that we were all walking around in parachute pants carrying giant boom boxes on our shoulders should have clued us in to the fact that we didn't know what the hell we were doing. Alas, Members Only jackets were everywhere, Molly Ringwald still rose to fame and so did the low-fat diet.

You've had a hard time getting me to shut up about bile flow in this book; but if people have reduced or restricted bile flow, they have a hard time emulsifying and processing dietary fats. If those fats can't be processed correctly, they can turn toxic in the body. These toxic fats can be pushed out of the body through the skin, creating horrible acne issues; or the body can store these undigested fats in fat cells, and these people become round.

By removing fats from the diet, these individuals with poor bile flow can remove a burden from the body. Now, those fats don't have to be stored in fat cells and these people can lose weight.

<u>When Do These Diets Fail?</u>

When fats are reduced, something else must be increased. We calculate food by looking at fats, carbs and proteins. If we reduce fats, carbs or proteins must increase. You already learned how higher levels of carbs can spike insulin levels and signal the body to store fat. You also learned that the body needs appropriate fats to perform specific functions in the body. If your diet doesn't include fats that are appropriate for you, your body will be less likely to let go of stored fat.

This is my least favorite diet for many reasons that I've already discussed in this book. Most diet books written in the past ten years agree with me so I won't beat this one into the ground anymore.

Low-Calorie Diets

When Do These Diets Work?

These diets work when you have horrible goals. If your goal is to lose weight on the scale, yet you have no concern for long-term weight gain or long-term health in any way, this is the diet for you (keep in mind that I'm talking like a jackass and at no point will these diets ever be good). When you starve yourself with a low-calorie diet, you're not losing only body fat. In most cases, you're losing muscle as well. In this regard, the scale may tell you that you've lost weight, yet you still feel as mushy as you did before the diet. The loss of muscle will also slow your metabolism and set you up for drastic weight gain the minute you snap and decide you can't live your life eating only four bowls of cabbage soup each day.

The main reason a low-calorie diet can be successful is because it makes you conscious of what you're eating. If you need to track everything you eat in order to gauge if you stayed within your calorie limit, this forces you to look at what you eat each day. It's amazing to see people start journaling their food only to realize, "Wow, I never noticed I drink eleven sodas each day." Also, a lot of processed junk food has higher calories than real food. So, to stay within the limits, dieters will start eating more real food. This will almost always lead to weight loss.

A low-calorie diet can create weight loss only if a person can access stored fat and burn it for fuel. However, remember that it can be difficult for some people to burn stored fat for fuel because their bodies are predisposed to burn glucose. This is normally dependent on the type of calories being consumed, not the number of calories. Most low-calorie diets simply have you count the calories. There is a big difference between 800 calories of chicken and spinach and 800 calories of chocolate chip cookies.

Wow, I really didn't have many positive things to say about these diets in the *When Do These Diets Work?* section. I hate to see what happens when I begin to explain the bad sides of the low-calorie diets.

When Do These Diets Fail?

Almost always. Many people can lose weight initially, but the weight often returns. When you starve the body and fail to provide the nutrients that it needs, the body will steal those nutrients from tissues and bones. If you want to freak out a woman today, just mention osteoporosis. Osteoporosis should not be considered a disease in which the body "attacks" its own bones. The body is breaking down bone to access needed minerals that are not coming into the system. This is most commonly due to digestive issues, yet starving yourself can create the same result.

You can break down not only muscles, tissues, or bones while you're on a low calorie diet, you may break down organ tissues as well. It is very common for the body to pull protein out of our lungs when enough protein is not coming into the system. Here's a hint: You need your lungs.

Starving yourself will set you up for immediate and drastic weight gain the moment you start to eat regularly. It's not a fun game.

Low-Carb Diets

When Do These Diets Work?

Low-carb diets allow people to keep insulin levels low, giving their bodies an opportunity to burn stored fat for fuel. That is the idea I've been pushing through this whole book. However, not all low-carb diets are created equal. Before I examine the differences, let's first look at when low-carb diets don't work.

When Do These Diets Fail?

If you reduce carbs, you need to increase fats and/or proteins. If you have digestive issues, this will be a problem. If you have poor bile flow and can't process fats correctly, the increase in fat intake could lead to weight gain. If you can't fully break down proteins, rotting and fermented foods are going to lead to weight gain. So, even if you're keeping your insulin levels low, but unprocessed fats or proteins are junking up the system, you could have a hard time losing weight. You may even gain weight.

Don't forget The Psycho Factor. If people using a low-carb diet have low mineral and protein levels and low blood pressure, they need to include appropriate carbs or sugars to buffer those low mineral levels. These people would first need to lift their mineral and protein levels or correct any digestive issues before they could use a low-carb diet without becoming miserable.

Variations In Low-Carb Diets

Processed junk food can be a big factor in low-carb diets. Many of these diets promote the use of low-carb snack foods, processed meals, and protein powders that have less than ideal amino acid profiles. Many contain artificial sweeteners that are toxic to the body (and we know that means those toxins can be stored as fat). I always prefer to see people eat real food over a processed food, even if it is low-carb.

Eating Paleo

The Paleo Diet is currently the fastest growing diet in popularity. There are variations within the paleo world; but, generally speaking, if a caveman ate it, you can eat it on a paleo diet. Do me a favor and avoid picturing your plate with a big hunk of meat and a handful of twigs. That's not what a Paleo Diet is all about. It's about eating real food and avoiding processed foods like grains, processed dairy and things you might find in a vending machine.

When it comes to what I personally eat, a Paleo Diet is closer than anything else out there. However, I eat that way because it's the right choice for me, not because it's the right choice for everyone. I also add variations that are beneficial to my chemistry. I tend to lean more catabolic so I consume a lot of butter and heavy cream to help push myself more anabolic. This is okay with some paleo experts, but a big no-no with others. Again, I do what's right for my digestive strength and my body chemistry, not because I'm following a popular diet.

Though I feel a Paleo Diet is the most optimal diet plan out there for me, it still has the same troubles most low-carb diet plans have. I don't really view paleo as a low-carb diet, because that is not the focus; but it does turn out to be very low in carbs since grains are removed.

If a person has digestive issues and can't handle the proteins or the fats included in a Paleo Diet, this diet will also be unsuccessful for him. You still need to look at yourself and how your body is processing foods to know if you can process the foods that make up any eating plan. Again, the strength of digestion is a key factor when selecting the right diet.

Vegan, Vegetarian, and Meat-Free Diets

<u>When Do These Diets Work?</u>

Vegetarian-based diets are often successful because they contain a lot of green vegetables. Green, non-starch vegetables have tremendous nutritional upside. Therefore, if your diet contains a lot of vegetables, many benefits can follow, including weight loss.

In chapter ten I discussed how animal proteins are harder to digest than vegetables or even grains. If people have poor digestion, they will feel much better once they remove animal protein from their diet. This can be beneficial in the beginning until they run out of their reserve of nutrients that can only be found in animal sources.

<u>When Do These Diets Fail?</u>

These diets fail when a person believes that as long as something is vegan, it must be healthy. When people eliminate meat, they often increase carbohydrates and other processed foods. These people also often eat a lot of processed meat replacement products. Many meat replacement products are made predominantly of soy. I have already discussed how too much soy can affect estrogen levels in the body.

Once an individual has been avoiding animal products for long enough (this can be different for every person), problems can arise from the lack of nutrients that can only be found in animal products. A B12 shot is not enough to remedy these deficiencies.

Juicing Diets

<u>When Do These Diets Work?</u>

Juicing allows people to obtain vitamins and minerals from a variety of foods without the body having to do as much work to break down those foods. If a person is dealing with digestive issues, juicing can bring an immediate lift and help her feel better. It can also remove a portion of the process of breaking down that food. This can aid in weight loss by freeing up the body to handle other issues, like excess toxins that need to be removed.

If an individual has extremely effective insulin and can process the sugars in the juice without too much of an insulin spike, weight loss can occur.

When Do These Diets Fail?

When you juice a food, fruit for example, you remove all the fiber. The fiber is there to decrease how quickly those sugars hit your bloodstream. Without any fiber, the sugars from the fruit hit the bloodstream quickly and spike insulin levels. If you are leaning toward insulin resistance, that can be bad news for weight loss.

If you try to incorporate resistance training with a juicing diet, you may find it difficult to add muscle. Without the protein needed to build muscle, your efforts in the gym could be wasted. Since juicing doesn't do anything to correct digestive issues, most people who do see results from a juicing diet will gain that weight back once they return to eating food.

A lot of diets are like rubber bands; for a time, the participants can stretch things and create some results. But the stress it takes to see those results is usually a good sign that these participants will snap right back to where they started once they go back to a more relaxed state. Fixing digestion, optimizing metabolism, and adequately feeding ourselves with the nutrients and resources needed is a great way to see results without the snapback effect.

Beneficial Therapeutic Diets

Elimination Diets

Elimination diets, like the clean sweep outlined in chapter eleven, a "whole 30," or a paleo AIP-type diet can all be extremely beneficial for some people. When digestion has been restored, and improving imbalances does not bring the result I'm looking for with a client, an elimination diet can often bring about amazing results. These diets are definitely worth having in your toolbox. For you, the edge you will have is that you now understand that digestion needs to be functioning correctly for these diets to bring about a benefit for most people.

Again, I don't use these diets with every client because it can be very challenging for many folks to remove all the foods that need to be removed on these diets. However, if someone is motivated enough to improve a major issue, the results that person can see in a 30-60 day period can be exciting enough to change their eating habits forever. Seeing firsthand the power that food selection can have on the body can be enough to significantly change eating habits.

Ketogenic Diets

These diets are very popular right now, and for good reason. When looking to lose a significant amount of weight (100 pounds or more), nothing will work as fast as a ketogenic diet, FOR THE RIGHT PERSON (you knew I was going to say that). I will explain why that is, but I'm also going to explain the downsides of these diets, because there is more than one downside, and some of the downsides can be significant for some folks.

Benefits of a Ketogenic Diet

A true ketogenic diet is very high fat, low carb, and moderate protein. For some, 60-80% of their food intake could come from fat. Since the diet is extremely low in carbs, this allows insulin to stay low, keeping the individual in a fat-burning mode most of the time. By consuming plenty of fat, the body doesn't feel like it needs to hang on to stored fat and the person can drop weight very quickly. Burning fat at a high rate produces a byproduct called ketones. Extremely high ketones accompanied by extremely high blood sugar can create a possibly fatal condition called ketoacidosis. However, this is normally seen only in type I diabetics (and some type II diabetics who are no longer producing enough insulin). Since high blood sugar raises insulin and turns off the production of ketones, it's almost impossible to have ketones and blood sugar go dangerously high at the same time. I explain this because some people mistake ketosis (being in a state of excessive fat burning) with ketoacidosis. They are very different things. Most dieters don't need to be concerned about ketoacidosis when implementing a ketogenic diet.

261

The problem with extremely low-carb diets for some is that the brain needs glucose to function. That doesn't mean, however, that a person must eat carbs for their brain to function, since the body can turn protein into glucose when needed. But for some folks, their brain will not function as optimally without the carbs. However, we now know that the brain can also function on ketones. This allows an individual to be on a ketogenic diet without going mental, since the brain is receiving a usable fuel source. By pushing your body into a more extreme fat-burning mode, an individual can also go longer between meals, while staying satiated and energized. When the body can access stored fat and burn it for fuel, not only does the person lose weight, but also their energy levels and mental clarity can even increase.

Intermittent Fasting on a Ketogenic Diet

If individuals are burning fat at a high rate, they may see benefits from fasting for part of the day, on some days. For example; a person, Henry, could eat dinner on Monday night, and then not eat again until Tuesday at lunch, or, in extreme cases, even dinner. Now, you'll remember from chapter fifteen how much I hate to see people skip breakfast. However, when someone is efficiently burning stored body fat, there appears to be benefits that can come from intermittent fasting. Again, I want to make it clear that I hate the idea of fasting for many reasons. But in this ketogenic-type situation only, I have seen clients benefit. I will say that I recommend trying this only for those who are in a deeper state of ketosis. Below, I explain how many following my weight-loss suggestions move into a slight or occasional state of slight ketosis. A person can get an idea of the level of their ketosis by checking the urine with ketosis testing strips, much in the way that we use pH strips to see the pH of the urine.

The Downsides of a Ketogenic Diet

It all sounds pretty good, right? When you explain a ketogenic diet in this way, a lot of people will say, "Sign me up and hand me some bacon!" However, there are some roadblocks that will make some individuals completely miserable on a ketogenic diet; and even for those who do well, there are some troubles you need to watch out for. I'll start with the most obvious. Everything you're learning in this book is about creating balance in the body, so the body can create energy and function in an optimal manner. By taking steps to help the body process mostly fats, we're literally creating an imbalance. We even have a name for that imbalance: the Fat Burner Imbalance. Under my personal viewpoint below I will explain how I believe there are circumstances where allowing a client to exist in this imbalance can be beneficial. Thousands of first-hand testimonials from those who have benefitted from this diet would be hard to argue with. Still, it is still important to acknowledge that we are creating a stress, an imbalance, by using this diet. Any imbalance has the ability to create problems in the long-term, if a person doesn't know what to look for.

<u>Mineral Levels on a Ketogenic Diet</u>

It appears that elevated insulin levels send the signal to retain sodium. Beyond the elevated blood sugar that contributes to high blood pressure, this may be part of the reason that we see high blood pressure with many insulin resistant individuals. The elevated insulin is telling the body to hold on to all that mineral. When insulin levels are low, it appears to signal the body to pee out sodium and other minerals. This may be part of the reason that, with hypoglycemic clients, it almost seems like they pee out mineral as fast as they can dump it in. It can be difficult to raise low blood pressure with many clients who fall into this hypoglycemic-type category. Since their insulin appears to be operating in an overly effective manner, these folks don't need to produce very much insulin to get the job done. Since insulin levels stay relatively low (even though they are consuming sugars or starches), the body continues to send the signal to pee out minerals.

If you understand what I'm saying (since a ketogenic diet has the ability to lower insulin levels even further), you could see how a ketogenic diet could be problematic for those with low blood pressure. By removing carbs nearly altogether and lowering insulin levels even further, this individual with low mineral levels could begin to pee out even more mineral. When I first started to learn the ins and outs of a ketogenic diet, my thought was that the body and the brain could run on the elevated ketone levels, and this might actually help those with low blood pressure. But it appears that there are too many processes that require plenty of mineral to be present. I have found very little success using a ketogenic diet with those who are already depleted of mineral. Therefore, if you're using this diet with clients, it can be very important to watch blood pressure, to emphasize using plenty of sea salt, and to take other steps that can lift mineral levels. For those who see blood pressure going too low, it might be a good idea to adjust to a different diet.

Breath Rate on a Ketogenic Diet

In my opinion, this is the most problematic aspect of a ketogenic diet. It seems none of the ketogenic experts are talking about this (except one, because she is a student of mine -- EatingFatIsTheNewSkinny.com). We've already discussed that when breath rate goes too low and the blood becomes too alkaline, oxygen can't be utilized correctly. CO_2 is not the only thing that can acidify the blood, but it is the main acidifier of the blood. CO_2 is a byproduct of processing carbohydrates. So, when we remove or greatly reduce the consumption and processing of carbohydrates, we can reduce our CO_2 levels and the blood becomes too alkaline. That doesn't mean that people should not reduce their carbs. Most humans currently living on this planet absolutely need to reduce their carb intake. However, for someone who's bloodstream may already be leaning too alkaline, removing most of their carbs and reducing CO_2 levels may be enough to push the pH of the blood into a problematic range. Watching breath rate while on a ketogenic diet is crucial.

CO_2 is also required for the thyroid to function correctly. Drinking carbonated water is one way to increase CO_2 levels and can be helpful for those who have a slow breath rate. But it doesn't seem to be as effective as including a few carbs, at least some of the time.

Here is the caveat to that thought. If a person can't process carbohydrates correctly (as we see in a type II diabetic) will increasing carb intake lift their breath rate? In my opinion, it won't. Consuming a few carbs can be beneficial for some folks; yet if an individual can't process carbs correctly, he's just adding another burden for the body to deal with. Again, if you're thinking that a specific diet is right for everyone, you're doing it wrong. But this same thinking is why I'm against condemning a ketogenic diet just because certain aspects can be problematic for some people.

Some say that anytime a person goes too long without consuming carbs the body will produce stress hormones. I absolutely believe this to be true for hypoglycemics and those leaning toward a Carb Burner

Imbalance. This is commonly the case because these individuals are often moving too much glucose out of the bloodstream at once, creating the emergency-type situation (a body that is preferring to run on glucose and has no glucose available). There are processes in the body, at the cellular level, that require glucose, but that does not mean that a person needs to consume carbs all day. Glucose needs to be available, but that does not mean it needs to be constantly consumed. There are pathways the body can use to turn protein into glucose and supply a more steady stream of glucose. It's more about blood sugar staying on an even keel than it is about constantly supplying glucose through consumption. The body is meant to burn both glucose and fat for fuel. When glucose levels are low, the body should be able to switch over to burning more fat for fuel and continue operating in that manner. So when an individual is processing fats well and can efficiently burn fats for fuel, the body is still receiving a fuel source; and the stress hormones are not elevated.

Catabolic Imbalance on a Ketogenic Diet

There are supplements that can be used to improve a catabolic imbalance, as covered in chapter fourteen. However, carbs and sugars can be more pro-anabolic than most supplements. It is important that the individual be able to process those carbs, or the carbs will not have the expected pro-anabolic effect. However, it is important to understand that removing most carbs does have the ability to have a pro-catabolic effect on some people. If clients are already leaning too catabolic, they would need to monitor this imbalance closely if they wanted to utilize a ketogenic diet. For many in this circumstance, they will likely find that the ketogenic diet pushes them too catabolic.

However, for those who are dealing with insulin resistance or issues that are the result of excess carb intake, the benefits that come from removing the burden of excess carbs may outweigh the downside of the overly catabolic state, on a temporary basis. Don't overlook the fact that I just said, "on a temporary basis."

My Personal Viewpoint on Ketogenic Diets

For the right individual who has a lot of weight to lose, I don't think any other approach can drop body fat as quickly and easily as a ketogenic diet. But I think that individual needs to be correcting any digestive issues, needs to already be leaning slightly toward that fat burning pathway, needs to have enough mineral in the system to weather the storm if more minerals start to get peed out, AND needs to keep breath rate in a good range.

I also think that many will benefit from a slightly ketogenic diet or a cyclical ketogenic diet. Cyclical in this instance could be that they may eat in a more ketogenic manner on some days, but not on other days; or one part of a day, but not the other part of that day; or for weeks or months at a time, yet include cycles of carbs from time to time. If an individual follows the suggestions in my book, *Kick Your Fat in the Nuts*, after fixing digestion, readers will likely significantly lower carb intake and raise fat intake. Those with very low blood pressure will continue to include medium carb foods until they can bring mineral and protein levels up. Those following my suggestions will also cycle the low amount of carbs they are eating to leave long stretches of the day where they consume very little carbs. As they advance they may go days at a time when the only carbs they consume would come from green vegetables (so the carb levels would be very low). In many cases, these readers will move into a fat burning state, and many will begin to produce higher levels of ketones. The ketones may not be as high as you might see in an extreme ketogenic diet, but they will still exist.

By using a cyclical ketogenic diet, an individual will not likely move into the extreme state of ketosis and may not experience some of the extreme benefits that can come from that state. But that also means that they would not experience some of the problems that can come from being too deep into that state, for too long. This would allow the body to operate at a more balanced state. I also feel that the "too long" aspect is an important part of this puzzle. I existed on a mostly ketogenic diet for five years, and I thrived on that diet. But many seem to share the opinion that after three to five years, the ketogenic diet can begin to create problems or be less effective. I now know that many of those issues likely come from some of the problems I've explained above. For me, my breath rate went way too low and I was far too catabolic. I still eat what I consider to be a slightly ketogenic diet (I say slightly because I consume more protein than would allow a person to move into deep ketosis) yet cycle in medium carb foods, like sweet potatoes, from time to time.

I feel that a ketogenic diet is most useful in a therapeutic capacity or when extreme weight loss is the goal. The list of issues that can be caused by consuming too many carbs and/or an inability to properly process carbs would be a long list, indeed. Beyond the carbs, the list of health problems (especially autoimmune-type issues) that appear to be exacerbated by consuming grains and other processed foods would be a long list as well. Having the ability to remove carbohydrates and/or grains and processed foods in these circumstances seems to be very beneficial for many.

The work that Dr. Terry Wahls is doing to help reverse MS with a ketogenic paleo diet is hard to ignore. As is the work Dr. David Perlmutter is doing to help those with Alzheimer's and epilepsy using a ketogenic diet. Again, my view is that the ketogenic diet is simply allowing the individual to stay satiated and remove the need for carbs, sugars, grains, etc. A ketogenic diet also introduces better quality saturated fats and decreases the polyunsaturated fatty acids. As I see it, it's the ability to remove the carbs, sugars, grains, and inappropriate fats that is allowing people to improve a wide variety of "incurable" ailments. The ketogenic aspect simply makes it easier for a person to sustain that. So, for me, if the benefits outweigh the possible downsides of the diet, and if the person understands what downsides to look for, a ketogenic diet can be a very beneficial therapeutic diet when used on a temporary basis.

For those who are not experiencing some type of health issue that could benefit from the ketogenic approach or don't have an extraordinary amount of weight to lose, I would prefer to see them use a slightly ketogenic or cyclical ketogenic approach if they wanted to use some type of ketogenic diet. I don't normally put clients on a ketogenic diet, but if they follow the guidelines in my weight-loss book, they will often end up consuming a slightly ketogenic or occasionally slightly ketogenic diet. This seems to magnify weight-loss efforts, without creating any of the downsides I have described here.

Wha'd He Say?

In this chapter, you learned:
- There is no diet that is right for everybody.

CHAPTER EIGHTEEN

Oh Yeah, Working Out

There's a reason that I waited until chapter eighteen to cover working out. I wanted to make the point loud and clear that there are seventeen other chapters that are more important. When it comes to losing weight, it's not about the workout. Working out is part of it, but time after time I see people who believe it's the whole enchilada. The reality is that it's more about the enchilada (as in... stop cramming them in your face and thinking that a good workout is going to make up for the damage you just did).

Don't forget that this is coming from a guy who makes his living by helping people work out in the gym. If this is how I make my living, yet I'm telling you this is not where your clients' weight loss results will come from, you might want to pay attention to that piece of information. That doesn't mean that working out is worthless. Don't be a toolbox. What I'm saying is: When it comes to results, nutrition is 90% of the pie (and it's even more effective if you leave out pie).

Do I want your clients to work out? Yes. I would like that very much, please. Your clients' skinny jeans will get worn much sooner if they workout on a regular basis. What I don't want is for your clients to workout like they're Olympians and neglect their diet or their imbalances altogether. Your clients will not see the changes they envision if they skip the nutrition. As long as you understand what I'm saying, I will share secrets to help your clients get the most out of their workout efforts. After all, when it comes to working out, I belong to the 'work smart' camp and we laugh and point at the 'work hard' camp.

I'm not going to give you a workout routine and tell you about exercises that will target your clients' butts or abs. That's not the information that will help the most. When it comes to types of exercises or types of workouts, those factors matter very little. What matters is the level at which an individual works and when and what they eat in relation to their workouts.

Nutrition According To Your Workout

First the basics:
1. Prior to a resistance workout, it's a good idea to eat at least something.
2. For an easy-to-moderate cardio workout, it's beneficial to perform this workout on an empty stomach.

Pre-Workout Nutrition For Resistance Training

For any type of anaerobic exercise, like weightlifting or high-intensity movements, most people will burn available glucose or glucose sources from glycogen. Glycogen is a form of glucose (fuel) that has been stored in the tissues and in the liver. Most people cannot burn fat for fuel while performing any of these anaerobic movements. Therefore, it's a good idea to eat something prior to a resistance workout. If you run out of glycogen, yet you continue working out, you may break down muscle tissue to use as fuel for that workout. Kind of eliminates the point of the workout, right?

Pre-Workout Nutrition For Cardio Training

Remember, some people have a harder time burning fat for fuel than others. But generally speaking, most people can burn body fat for fuel during easy-to-moderate aerobic exercise, like walking or moving in a manner that is not too strenuous. If the cardio becomes too intense, it can translate more into an anaerobic activity due to the muscular strain being placed on the body. The body can also view this vigorous activity as if you are running from a lion or some other threat. As the body creates glucose to use as fuel in this 'urgent' situation, insulin levels can rise and take you out of the fat-burning mode. This is similar to how the body reacts under day-to-day stresses.

A good rule to follow while attempting a fat-burning workout is this: If you are breathing too hard to carry on a normal conversation, you're working too hard to burn fat. I'm speaking generally here, but it is a nice little trick to check where you are without hooking yourself up to NASA-type body monitoring equipment while you walk around the neighborhood.

The problem is, for most individuals, if there is glucose or glycogen available, the body prefers this fuel source over stored fat. This is why it is best to do your easy-to-moderate cardio workouts on an empty stomach. If your body can quickly burn off any glucose and/or stored glycogen at the beginning of your cardio session, it can easily move into fat-burning mode. Many believe that it takes about twenty-five minutes to burn off all your stored glycogen if you are walking or jogging moderately. If you just ate, you may first need to burn off any glucose from that food before you can dip into those glycogen stores.

The Secret Trick

In the gym, the biggest mistake I see people make is that they walk into the gym and head straight to the treadmill where they run for thirty minutes. Next, they move over to the weights and do their resistance training. They then ask me, "Why did you just smack me in the back of my head?" I go on to explain that they just burned all of their glucose and glycogen on the treadmill. They needed that fuel to perform their resistance training. With no fuel left, the body will likely break down muscle and use that for fuel since the body can't use stored fat for fuel during resistance exercises. The point of their running was to burn fat—of which they burned none—since they only burned their glycogen stores the entire run. At this point, they usually thank me for smacking them in the back of the head.

If you just flip the order, your workout will be much more effective. This is how you work smart instead of working hard. You can warm up on the treadmill for five minutes, that's great. However, then do your resistance training while you still have glycogen stores you can use for fuel. By the time you finish your weight training (45-55 minutes later), glycogen stores will likely be depleted. Now you can hop on the treadmill and your body will be primed for burning fat. I recommend keeping your post weight-training cardio to only easy walking (allowing your body to burn only fat), and limit this to a maximum of twenty-five minutes. I explain why below. You can still do hard or intense cardio on its own on a different day. Slow, easy cardio, however, is much more beneficial for weight loss after a resistance workout.

Post-Workout Nutrition For Resistance Training

After beating on your muscles, it's time to give them fuel that can be used for rebuilding. I like to use some type of protein that is easy to assimilate. A protein shake can be perfect. Please make sure you're not using anything that contains artificial sweeteners. Stevia and xylitol are okay. I prefer just stevia, but I'm okay with xylitol if that is your only option.

However, any type of protein food source is okay too (with soft-cooked eggs being the best since a runny yolk is pro-anabolic and can aid in rebuilding muscle). I normally like to try to eat or have a shake within an hour of a resistance workout. That is why I limit any post workout cardio to only twenty-five minutes.

If your goal is to build muscle, rather than simply losing fat, you may want to have a sweet potato or some type of medium-carb starch after your workout. This can accelerate your ability to build muscle, as long as you are not already leaning toward insulin resistance.

Post-Workout Nutrition For Cardio Training

I view my post workout nutrition for cardio the same as resistance workouts. I do, however, have one little trick. Let's say I want to do an intense cardio workout, like a spin class. I can't burn fat during that class because it is too intense. My body, however, can burn fat at a fast pace for about an hour after that class, even if I just sit on the floor and cuss about how hard that class was. With this in mind, I'll eat something about an hour before the class so I have fuel to complete the class; then I'll wait an hour or so after the class before I eat again. If I wait too long, I know my body will start breaking itself down to access fuel, so I try to eat within an hour and a half after that workout. If I immediately refuel with some type of sugary sports drink, my body will begin to burn the sugar from that drink and will not burn fat for the hour after the class.

Timing Is Everything

I like my clients to understand that timing is everything. Yet, it is also very important to simply get up off your ass and do something. Don't skip a workout because all the stars are not perfectly aligned. You can still get results eating at the wrong time, etc. I'm explaining optimal circumstances when it comes to fueling your body before and after a workout. Even though life can get in the way, don't let that get in the way of your workout. Not every workout needs to be a scientific work of art.

Start Anywhere

Keep in mind what the average individual goes through when they decide to start working out. While trying to keep up with the salesman as Mary tours her local gym, the complicated equipment mocks her as she walks by. "What the hell am I supposed to do with that?" Mary thinks to herself. "I think I saw that one at my gynecologist's office." Mary doesn't want to be that girl who climbs up onto the water fountain because she thinks it's a piece of equipment. So what does Mary do? She does nothing. She walks around the gym for about ten minutes hoping that at least one of the machines will resemble something from her elementary school playground so she'll know what to do with it. Mary eventually finds herself on a stationary bike; she gets bored fifteen minutes later and heads to the locker room. Mary goes home that night, never to return, only to have $49 deducted from her checking account for the next twelve years.

The gym is intimidating and we know that. This is what I tell my clients: If you don't have a friend who can show you the ropes, and if you can't afford a personal trainer, start with something less flashy. Ordering a workout video online can be a great first step. Try doing a pushup on your knees twice a week until you can do ten. Do a few crunches or go for a walk. Just do something. Put yourself in motion and let the possibilities create a momentum that will push you forward. In no time, you'll be at the gym, walking up to someone else on the equipment to say, "Um... your face doesn't go there."

Resistance Training

Rest And Repair

With any type of resistance training, the benefit doesn't occur during the actual training. During the training, you're literally breaking down the body. The benefits of that workout don't show up until your body has time to repair and rebuild those muscle tissues. That is where your results come from. A lot of my clients see better results by reducing the number of days in a week that they work out. Personally, I give my body at least two days off per week and require my clients to take off at least one day.

Don't Repeat Muscle Groups

If you lift weights with the same muscle groups two days in a row, you just negated your efforts from the first day. For example, if you work your chest on Tuesday, the benefit from that workout would come on Wednesday when your body was repairing and rebuilding the tissues in your chest. However, if you work your chest again on Wednesday, those muscles never get the chance to rebuild and Tuesday's efforts are lost.

With resistance training, if you want to work out two days in a row, try focusing on one or two muscle groups per day. The following day, those muscles can repair while you're working other muscle groups. Here's one scenario: On Monday you work your legs, shoulders and abs. On Tuesday, you work your back and biceps. (Note: Abs and calves are the only muscle groups that some believe are okay to work two days in a row because of how those muscle fibers are structured. I still like to see a day of rest for any muscle you worked the day before. I normally work each muscle group only one time each week.) If you work your legs on Monday, it is still okay to do cardio the next day since that is not a resistance-type exercise.

Find Some Intensity

An individual's first workout is not the time to shoot for any type of intensity. You want to be smart and build up to any intense workout. If you injure yourself, the lack of working out while you heal could delay results. Still, as your stamina increases, you need to give your body a reason to improve.

"Pushing your body beyond its comfort zone is the trigger that creates upgrades in your physique and in your health."
- I just made that up

Picture doing an exercise that is very difficult for you to complete. Maybe you are doing biceps curls with a weight that is too heavy for you to complete ten reps. At that moment, your body is saying, "Okay, we can't do what this jackass is trying to get us to do. We need to increase muscle fibers in his biceps so we can accomplish this task." And your body can respond by adding more muscle. If you consistently lift weights that are easy for you, your body has no reason to step it up a notch.

You still need to use good form and avoid jerking around weights that are way too heavy for you. If fitness is not part of your health pro offerings, take the time to watch videos or learn from a professional so you understand how to use good form in your own workouts. Bad form or weights that are too heavy will often result in injury. Our 12-Week Fat Loss Course has workout videos for each week. As a health professional, you can get that $129 course for free here: KickItNaturally.com/affiliate-reviews-open

Mixing quick and intense cardio exercises into your resistance training can also be a great way to raise intensity. Between resistance exercises, throw in a little rope jumping or sprinting on the treadmill for a minute. This is a great way to add variety to your workout. Try to keep these quick bursts to only a minute or so at a time.

Lifting Heavy Weights

A common misconception among women is that they fear lifting weights because they don't want to look like a man. Most women do not have the chemical makeup to look like Arnold Schwarzenegger, pre-governor duties. When you see a woman who looks like Joe Piscopo just before he snapped, that woman has likely used chemical enhancements to achieve that. You're not going to lift heavy weights and have your biceps exceed the size of the Pomeranian hanging out of your purse (IT'S SO FLUFFY!). The female body is not designed to build muscle of that size, yet lifting weights heavier than those found on the sissy rack can greatly speed up weight loss. (By the way, did anyone get the fluffy reference? Anyone? Am I the only adult who watches animated movies?)

If you are a woman who adds muscle easily or maybe your thighs get bigger and more muscular than you'd like, look at your chemistry. If you have an Anabolic Imbalance, you may be stuck in the muscle-building mode most of the time. Correcting this imbalance might allow your body to move into the breaking-down mode on a daily basis and your body won't build as much muscle.

If you're looking to add more muscle, you can also use this knowledge to watch your chemistry and implement pro-anabolic food and supplement choices to turbo charge your efforts. However, monitor your chemistry to make sure you're not pushing yourself too anabolic. You don't want to create an imbalance while you attempt to add muscle.

Interval Training

Interval training is popular and can be effective for burning fat. Intervals consist of short bursts of intense activity, followed by longer periods of very easy activity. Moving immediately back into easy activity allows the body to access stored fat for fuel, in many cases. The goal here is to burn fat during the easy activity.

Simply walk slowly for two to three minutes, then run as fast as you can for one minute. Alternate back and forth between these paces for 25-45 minutes.

Sprints

Once you've graduated from long walks and you're experimenting with some jogging, sprints can be very effective and take the least amount of time. I'm not going to get into a lot of the science here, but many believe that short sprints are a much better choice for your body than long runs. When I do sprints, I try to do four sprints, each for one minute, running as fast as I can. I rest for a few minutes between each sprint. This can allow you to perform an effective cardio session in about twelve minutes. That's the whole workout. Be sure you are warmed up and stretched before you sprint. The goal here is to strengthen your heart, increase your body's metabolism and reduce the amount of fat your body stores throughout the day. Like I said, the science behind this one is a whole other book. In any case, it is still very simple to execute.

Don't Starve Yourself After A Workout

If your body is repairing and rebuilding muscle tissue the day following your workout, what do you think happens if you skip breakfast? If you're not bringing in the nutrients needed to build tissue, not only are you missing out on increasing muscle fibers, you're likely going to lose muscle. When the body needs more resources, it will break down muscle tissues (among other necessary parts) to get what it needs. How effective does that make the previous day's workout? Not so much. Unless Oprah was playing on the gym TV and you used that time to soak in her beauty (I think if you mention in your book how pretty Oprah is, she invites you to be a guest on her show... Dr. Oz, you're pretty too).

The only caveat to this rule is if individuals have an extreme Fat Burner Imbalance, or if they are purposefully using a ketogenic diet successfully. These individuals can often practice intermittent fasting successfully since their body has adapted to using a higher level of fat for fuel. This process can have its downsides, as covered under Ketogenic Diets in chapter seventeen.

"When you work your body, give your body what it needs to rebuild your body."
- Guy who overuses the word "body"

Imbalances And Working Out

A strong imbalance can also affect the level at which you should be working out.

Electrolyte Deficiency Imbalance

With an Electrolyte Deficiency Imbalance, your resources are likely already low. View your nutrient and mineral reserves as money in the bank and every workout is costing you money. It's still okay to work out, in most cases. Simply be aware that working out too much could leave you depleted and allow The Psycho Factor to show up. However, if you limit your workouts to what your body can handle, and if you make an attempt to further increase minerals and nutrients on the days you workout, you can successfully incorporate exercise into your life. Increasing medium-carb foods on your workout day is a good idea in these cases.

Catabolic Imbalance

Any form of working out is pro-catabolic, at least a little bit. If a strong Catabolic Imbalance showed on your *Imbalance Guide*, working out too often might cause you to exacerbate that imbalance and fall apart. The right thing to do when dealing with a strong Catabolic Imbalance is to reduce your workout load or increase your pro-anabolic food choices or supplement protocol.

People with a Catabolic Imbalance should also try to work out in the morning, or at least before 3PM when possible. With this plan, they will at least be pushing themselves more catabolic during the day, when they are intended to be catabolic.

Anabolic Imbalance

If you have an Anabolic Imbalance, increasing your number of workouts per week may help you correct that imbalance. I still like to see a person take at least one entire day off per week. However, due to your body being stuck in the rebuilding mode, the breakdown that comes with working out won't be as detrimental to you as it can be to someone dealing with a Catabolic Imbalance.

Sweating

Yes. Do some sweating. There is a reason your body sweats. While working out, there is an increase in lactic acid production and all sorts of other craziness going on. We sweat so the body has a way to remove these acids so they don't accumulate and create havoc. When you work out in front of a fan or cold air conditioner, you're restricting your body's ability to sweat out this junk. Don't do that.

Sweating is another strategy your body uses to remove junk. By allowing your body to sweat, you can speed up weight loss by reducing the load of acids and other chemical reactions that the body has to deal with. There is a point where a person can overheat. That's not what I want you to do. However, allowing your body to sweat during a workout can have many benefits.

If you're someone who never sweats, your pores may be clogged up and that could be contributing to weight gain. Go to a dry or steam sauna to see if you can pop the corks, so to speak, in those pores and allow you to start sweating. If you have an Electrolyte Deficiency Imbalance, keep in mind that the body sweats out minerals while it is sweating out junk. Therefore, don't spend too much time in any type of sauna until you raise your mineral levels.

Wha'd He Say?

In this chapter, you learned:
- For most people, working out will equate to only 10% of weight-loss results. 90% of weight-loss results will likely come from what you eat and how your body processes those foods.
- Prior to a resistance workout, it's a good idea to eat something.
- For an easy-to-moderate, fat-burning, cardio workout, it's beneficial to perform this workout on an empty stomach.
- After warming up, start your workout with resistance training and do any easy cardio afterward.
- Women should not be afraid of lifting heavy weights. The muscles created will help you burn fat faster and create that lean look.
  Starving yourself after a workout can eliminate the benefits of that workout.

CHAPTER NINETEEN

Case Studies & FAQs

Before I dive into this chapter, let's pause and reflect on a few things:

1. Don't treat your symptoms and don't use symptoms to label yourself with an imbalance.
2. Get help. This work can get very complicated. If you run into trouble, find a health coach in your area who can help you, or work with one through email until you can complete our Bio-Individuality Coach Course.
3. I just want to point out that I've completed more than eighteen chapters of this book without once making fun of Paris Hilton or Snookie. Sometimes, I amaze even myself.

When we share case studies in webinars or on podcast episodes, I often hear back from individuals about how eye-opening it was to hear details of other's experiences. For that reason, I want to share a few case studies here and share a variety of frequently asked questions. What I don't want you to do is read a case study or the answer to a common question below, and apply that to your life simply because it worked for someone else. If you were to do that, I would make you go back to chapter one and start the book over. Remember, we are all different and it's crucial to look at our own chemistry and our own circumstances before we implement any health strategy. The benefit here is to look at real life experiences and see the principles from this book in action. I want you to see how other people looked at their numbers and their circumstances and used that information to come up with a plan that was specific to them. This could help you understand your own health issues, and could help you begin to put the puzzle pieces together so you can help your clients see improvements as well.

Equally important, I want you to take note of how the individuals in these case studies continued to monitor their numbers and make adjustments to their actions accordingly. For example, one of the case studies below is for an individual dealing with chronic constipation. I've discussed in this book how something as simple as Vitamin C in the form of ascorbic acid can be a very helpful piece to include in the constipation puzzle for some individuals. When supplementation with ascorbic acid successfully helps a constipated individual have a daily bowel movement, the improvements to that person's health and wellbeing can be astounding. However, if that same individual continued to take a large dose of ascorbic acid indefinitely, without occasionally monitoring their self-tests , the results in a negative direction could be just as extreme. You don't want to be the guy whose appropriate use of ascorbic acid becomes so much of a good thing that he pushes his urine pH below 5.0 or creates a chronic diarrhea issue. Chronic diarrhea can be just as problematic, if not more problematic, than chronic constipation. By monitoring your numbers (particularly urine pH in this case), and continuing to be a stoolgazer, you can make adjustments to your plan just like the people in the case studies below.

This section will also reinforce this fact: When something works well for one person, that doesn't mean it's right for everyone. I once met this guy, Frank, who used his blood pressure monitor to discover that by greatly increasing his water intake he could bring his high blood pressure into a good range. Through his excitement he then insisted that everyone in his family drink the same amount of water that he found to be so helpful to him. After all, it was good for him, it should be good for everyone else. Of course his daughter, who had extremely low blood pressure and hated drinking water for very good reason, didn't do well under her father's water regime. To make matters worse, Frank's daughter didn't even have the option of accessing a salt shaker because the medical advice was to keep salt out of the house. Think how much better things would have been if Frank had taught his family that they needed to figure out what would benefit each one's biological individuality.

Case Study: Stacy Peters (Her name was actually Karen Brown, but I changed it for this book so nobody would know who I was really talking about.)

Stacy was constipated to the point where, if she was pooping once a week, she reasoned things were going well. She was also bloated and experiencing occasional acid reflux. Once she understood that all three of these issues can be strong indications of a lack of stomach acid, she started using HCL with each meal. She started Beet Flow at the same time to ensure her bile would flow properly and be able to neutralize the acidic food product that would be moving from her stomach into her duodenum.

Once Stacy reached her desired dose of HCL capsules per meal, her bloating and acid reflux disappeared completely. This was great news, but Stacy's constipation had only slightly improved. She was still pooping only once, maybe twice, a week at best. She was excited to improve symptoms she had dealt with for so long, but found herself falling right back into her own thought patterns of, "This must be a genetic thing. Maybe I'm just not built to have a bowel movement every day." Stacy enlisted the help of a health coach who asked to see her most recent self-test numbers. Her numbers were:

Saliva pH: 6.5
Urine pH: 6.4
Blood Pressure: 97/69
Pulse: 80
Breath Rate: 17
Breath Hold: 29

With urine pH so high and so close to her saliva pH, this could be considered an anabolic indication. Her high pulse could also suggest an Anabolic Imbalance and she was waking up two or three times a night to pee. All of these factors, along with her severe constipation, led her coach to the conclusion that taking steps to improve an Anabolic Imbalance may help Stacy with her constipation issues.

As Stacy and her coach looked over Stacy's food journals, they noticed that she was eating well for breakfast and lunch (typically meals consisting of a protein and low-starch vegetables or salad); but by the time 3 pm rolled around, Stacy was giving in to major cravings. Stacy would end up splurging on cookies, chips or cupcakes as a snack, and was then eating some type of starchy dinner, like pasta, bread or rice.

With a blood pressure reading as low as Stacy's (97/69), it is common for severe cravings to be a problem, especially when lowering carb intake. Because carbs and sugars can push an individual more anabolic, Stacy's uncontrollable cravings appeared to be exacerbating her severe constipation. Below I list the steps Stacy implemented, with the confidence she gained by communicating with her coach, and why these steps appeared to help in her scenario. Remember, just because these steps helped Stacy doesn't mean they will work for you. However, if you understand why one of the following steps helped to improve a specific imbalance or issue, you can use that information to see with better clarity one more piece of this global picture.

1. Stacy continued supplementing with HCL and Beet Flow. Since the HCL appeared to be improving her bloating and acid reflux, it seemed apparent that she was benefitting from further acidifying the food in her stomach. Because her constipation improved slightly after starting the HCL, her coach suggested that continuing to acidify her stool would likely help.

2. Since Vitamin C (as ascorbic acid) has the ability to further acidify the stool, even between meals, Stacy added 1000mg before breakfast and another 1000mg before lunch. Ascorbic acid seems to help acidify the stomach and to help lower urine pH.

3. To reduce her afternoon and evening cravings, Stacy started including a snack of berries between breakfast and lunch. She also had half a sweet potato with her lunch each day. Since Stacy's mineral levels still appeared to be low (indicated by her low blood pressure), she was trying to include more medium-carb foods earlier in the day. Medium-carb foods (like sweet potatoes, butternut squash and berries), were used to provide Stacy with carbs that could buffer her low mineral levels and help her function throughout the day. Because her body was getting more of what it needed, her late afternoon cravings simply vanished. By reducing her high carb and sugar splurges, her pHs started moving into better ranges (her urine pH went down [perhaps aided by the ascorbic acid she was taking], and her saliva pH slightly elevated), indicating she could be moving out of her Anabolic Imbalance.

4. Concentrace Trace Mineral Drops were also added to each glass of water Stacy was drinking throughout the day. These drops contain a lot of magnesium chloride. Magnesium and chloride can be used to help move a person less anabolic. The variety of other minerals contained in the drops could also help lift Stacy's mineral levels and reduce her cravings.

5. Since Stacy was working with a health coach who had graduated from our Bio-individuality Coach Course and had access to more advanced supplements, Stacy was able to use the Electrolyte

Deficiency supplement from Empirical Labs. Stacy took 2 capsules with breakfast, lunch and dinner to help lift mineral levels.

Within about a week, Stacy was having a bowel movement every other day. After two weeks, Stacy was pooping every day. At this point, you will notice a few changes in Stacy's self-testing numbers:

Saliva pH: 6.7 (Previously 6.5)
Urine pH: 5.8 (Previously 6.4)
Blood Pressure: 107/72 (Previously 97/69)
Pulse: 74 (Previously 80)
Breath Rate: 17 (Previously 17)
Breath Hold: 37 (Previously 29)

Because Stacy was now having a daily bowel movement, and because her urine pH had dropped into a more balanced range, she reduced her ascorbic acid dose down from two 1000mg capsules per day to only one. She was able to continue her daily bowel movements with this lower dose. You'll also notice that Stacy's blood pressure came up a little bit. This rise was enough to help control her cravings, yet is a reading considered to be in the Electrolyte Deficient range (her systolic number was still below 112). For this reason, Stacy continued using her digestive supplements, the Electrolyte Deficiency supplement, adding the concentrated mineral drops to her water, and adding unrefined salt to her meals. It's very common for urine pH to show major changes faster than might be seen with blood pressure.

Remember, this is simply one person's experience. You may see improvement faster, or you may still be sitting on the toilet cursing my name a month later. I'm sure you can see by now the wide assortment of variations that could dictate the speed at which any individual could see results. Continue to monitor your numbers so you can adjust and correct along the way. If you're not working with a health coach, and if you haven't graduated from our Bio-individuality Coach Course, be sure to post your numbers in the progress charts of the Coalition website. In that way, if you decide to get help later, the history you have posted will help guide your coach toward steps that could be appropriate for you. The choices made by Stacy were the result of her conversations with her coach and his assessment of her numbers. Since no two people have identical biological chemistry, it is important to track your own numbers after a clinical decision is applied. Tracking the trends of her numbers allows Stacy to evaluate if her health choices are appropriate and bringing the desired results. The numbers from her self-tests also allow her, with input from her practitioner, to adjust the dosage of her supplements, which can be as important as selecting which supplements to use. This is a great illustration of how important it will be for you to coach clients as they monitor their progress and as they make adjustments when needed.

Case Study: Karen

Anxiety and Panic Attacks

Karen was reading my book, *Kick Your Fat in the Nuts,* in hopes of losing forty pounds. However, once she came across our *Kick It Naturally* podcast episode about anxiety and panic attacks, she changed her focus. Karen had been experiencing severe anxiety and panic attacks for nearly a decade and was excited for the possibility of improving this debilitating issue in her life. While assessing her self-test numbers, Karen also knew she would need to work on digestion since she experienced a lot of bloating and would occasionally go a day or two without a bowel movement. Overwhelmed by all the new information (and obviously feeling a little anxious about everything), Karen enlisted the help of one of our coaches through email. Karen's initial testing numbers were:

Saliva pH: 6.2
Urine pH: 6.7
Blood Pressure: 92/58
Pulse: 85
Breath Rate: 9
Breath Hold: 62

On our podcast, Karen learned that elevated anxiety and panic attacks can have a wide variety of causes; but the two most common underlying causes seem to be an Anabolic Imbalance or an Electrolyte Deficiency Imbalance. Keep in mind that anxiety is a psychiatric term. A panic attack is a physiological event. That doesn't mean that if you suffer from what most call anxiety that it's all in your head. For most who deal with severe anxiety, there are physiological issues magnifying the person's experience. Events and circumstances in life create the feeling of anxiety;

yet if the human body that you're living in is not functioning optimally, those feelings of anxiety can be greatly magnified. Using Karen as an example, she may be able to improve physiological issues, but the circumstances in her life that are causing her anxiety would still be there. The difference would be, the episodes in her life that seemed like a "ten" (on a scale from one to ten) might seem more like a two or three, once her body and her brain were functioning more optimally. To better understand the experience of magnified anxiety, let's first look at the physiology behind a panic attack.

To induce a panic attack, you could inject someone with high levels of lactic acid. In a severe anabolic state, the body makes a lot of its energy through fermentation. Lactic acid is a byproduct of creating energy in this manner. Therefore, while experiencing an Anabolic Imbalance, lactic acid levels can accumulate; and that individual can experience elevated anxiety, or even panic attacks, due to the high levels of lactic acid in the system.

Low blood pressure can be an indication of inefficient minerals, protein, and other nutritional resources. When the system does not have enough resources to accomplish all the tasks it needs to accomplish, doesn't it make sense that the system (and even the person) might not function optimally? When we think of it like trying to pay $800 worth of bills with twelve bucks, it makes sense that a lack of resources could be a major stress on the body and that some systems might not perform optimally. We all know somebody who loses the ability to cope with circumstances when he goes too long without eating. When there aren't enough resources for the body (or the brain) to function correctly, every little problem can seem like a disaster. We accept this to be true with some individuals. Therefore, if Karen had low resources most of the time, it should make sense that the anxiety experienced through life events could be magnified. With this understanding and by looking at Karen's numbers, we can see that she actually may be dealing with more than one underlying cause for her magnified anxiety and panic attacks. Karen's high urine pH, low saliva pH, high pulse, and occasional constipation are all anabolic markers; and her blood pressure is low enough to barely be considered human (though I've seen lower).

With panic attacks, we also often see a bloodstream that is leaning too alkaline. The alkaline pH restricts the ability for oxygen to leave the blood and go down to the tissues where it belongs. At extremes, this can create a panic attack. This is why breathing into a paper bag can sometimes ease a panic attack. By re-inhaling the acidic CO_2 that has been exhaled, the person can quickly acidify the blood enough to allow some oxygen to make it down to the tissues and ease the panic. I also find that, in a pinch, a Pepsi Cola can bring about a similar result. Carbonated water or other sodas could help, but Pepsi seems to be a little more acidic. Am I suggesting that anyone with anxiety drink Pepsi all day? I think you know by now that I'm not. But in a dire situation, the Pepsi could be a quick fix for some people and can be more socially acceptable than a paper bag over your face.

The first thing Karen's coach pointed out to her was that her urine pH was higher than her saliva pH. We call this an inversion in her pHs. You always want to see urine pH lower than saliva pH. When the pHs are inverted, it appears that the body can be running in an almost backward, upside down manner. When you see this inversion with a client, you should also be skeptical of the rest of the client's test numbers. While the body is operating in this haphazard manner, test results can be skewed. Therefore, when I see this inversion, I like to take steps to correct the inversion and then have the client re-test their self-tests to see if the picture has changed.

Since Karen's saliva pH was below 6.5, Karen's coach felt that doing a Beet Flow flush was appropriate. If bile flow is not moving correctly, and if the system is becoming toxic due to an inability to take out the trash, we will often see a saliva pH below 6.5. If performing a Beet Flow flush can help get the bile moving again, you will often see the client's saliva pH come up a little bit the next day. Since it appears that Karen's stomach was not acidifying her food properly (indicated by her bloating and occasional constipation), the improved bile flow that resulted from her Beet Flow flush ended up making her stool even more alkaline, causing her to be more constipated for a couple days. Since Karen had also started including Digesti-zyme and HCL with each meal, her constipation began to improve once her ability to acidify the food in her stomach improved. Karen's bloating was also completely gone within a week.

During this process, Karen also started taking vitamin C as ascorbic acid before breakfast and lunch to help bring down her urine pH. (The ascorbic acid likely contributed to her stool moving with more ease and her reduction in bloat as well.)

Because Karen's breath rate was low, her coach also suggested she use Concentrace mineral drops. These drops contain a lot of magnesium chloride, which can help acidify the blood and raise breath rate; the magnesium chloride can also have almost a laxative effect in many cases. Her coach also suggested Karen drink more carbonated water to help acidify the blood. Remember, by acidifying an alkaline bloodstream, we can allow more oxygen to get down to the tissue level where it needs to be.

After a little more than a week, Karen's coach asked her to retest her numbers to see if the pH inversion had been corrected. Her results were:

Saliva pH: 6.4 (Previously 6.2)
Urine pH: 6.3 (Previously 6.7)
Blood Pressure: 97/64 (Previously 92/58)
Pulse: 82 (Previously 85)
Breath Rate: 10 (Previously 9)
Breath Hold: 59 (Previously 62)

Karen's new plan was able to correct her pH inversion, yet the same imbalances still seemed to show up. This is a good indication that her pH inversion was not creating any misleading test results. With this information, Karen and her coach now felt more confident in taking additional steps to improve the imbalances that seemed to be causing Karen's anxiety. She had not had any panic attacks since she started her new plan, but the magnified anxiety was still present. Karen's coach also gave her access to three advanced supplements from Empirical labs that are listed below (these advanced supplements are available only to coaches who have graduated from our Bio-individuality Coach Course).

Karen added the following steps to help increase mineral levels:
1. Using a quality unrefined salt.
2. Drinking a cup of bone broth each morning.
3. Continued working to improve digestion.
4. Adding 2 capsules of the Electrolyte Deficiency supplement from Empirical Labs (an advanced supplement available only through graduates of our Bio-individuality Coach Course).

Karen added the following steps to help improve her Anabolic Imbalance:

1. Taking Empirical Labs Anabolic (available only through Bio-individuality Coach Course grads) with breakfast and lunch.
2. Taking Empirical Labs Flow A (available only through Bio-individuality Coach Course grads) before breakfast.
3. Using 10-15 drops of Concentrace mineral drops in her water early in the day.
4. Removing most liquid sugars like juice in higher quantities and all alcohol.
5. Reducing her sugar and starch intake and including more medium carb foods, like butternut squash and berries.

With low blood pressure and an Anabolic Imbalance (where higher urine pH can often result in a hypoglycemic episode), problems often occur when blood sugar and insulin spike, and then result in a major blood sugar crash. Since there are not enough minerals or protein to buffer sugars going so low, trouble, like magnified anxiety, can show up for some of these individuals. Others may see this same pattern result in issues like depression, insomnia, or bipolar-type behavior. However, if these individuals can keep blood sugar on a more even keel and remove the spikes and crashes, these troubles can often be reduced or removed. Of course, the goal is to lift mineral levels so there is a buffer when blood sugar goes too low, but that can often take time. Keeping blood sugar on a more even keel can bring about relief much faster for many. Using very small amounts of sugar (like eating two wedges of a cutie orange from time to time throughout the day) could have been another option for Karen as well.

Because Karen's blood pressure was so low, her coach explained how removing all carbs could cause her blood pressure to go even lower and magnify many of her symptoms. But by including medium carb foods (that could supply her with enough carbs to lift her blood pressure, but not so many as to cause a spike of insulin followed by a crash in blood sugar) Karen was able to keep the system on a more even keel. Since starches and sugars, and especially liquid sugars, can be very pro-anabolic, this reduction in carb intake was also able to help her improve her Anabolic Imbalance. Because Karen continued using ascorbic acid, Empirical Labs Anabolic, and Flow A, the reduction in carbs was enough to help Karen see apparent improvement with her Anabolic Imbalance relatively quickly. I say "relatively quickly" because many clients are so accustomed to medications creating a reaction in a couple hours that they look for the same result while making nutritional changes. In most cases, however, nutritional changes are working to improve the cause of the symptom and can take longer. Still, after suffering from magnified anxiety and panic attacks for more than a decade, seeing significant improvement after three or four weeks should be considered "relatively quick" improvement indeed.

After a total of four weeks, Karen's self-test numbers were:

Saliva pH: 6.6 (Previously 6.4; Originally 6.2)
Urine pH: 5.9 (Previously 6.3; Originally 6.7)
Blood Pressure: 108/68 (Previously 97/64; Originally 92/64)
Pulse: 77 (Previously 82; Originally 85)
Breath Rate: 12 (Previously 10; Originally 9)
Breath Hold: 51 (Previously 59; Originally 62)

At this four week mark, all of Karen's imbalances were showing great improvement. Her stool had become regular; her magnified anxiety was showing up only about once a week, and extremely mild; and her pants were starting to feel loose. Three months later, Karen's magnified anxiety was totally gone and she had also lost twenty five pounds. She never made weight loss a focus; yet, since she improved digestion, which allowed her to successfully reduce her carbs and balance her blood sugar and insulin levels, weight loss was a natural side-effect. To this I say, "Good job, Karen!" Karen was actually my client so I know her coach was totally awesome, and probably very humble as well.

Case Study: Donnie

Chronic Diarrhea and Insomnia

Donnie was working with one of our coaches to improve a chronic diarrhea issue he had been dealing with for more than five years. Donnie's loose and urgent stool sent him running to the bathroom three to four times on most days, usually after every meal. He was also dealing with elevated blood pressure and occasional insomnia (usually on a weekly basis). Donnie's initial numbers were:

Saliva pH: 7.1
Urine pH: 5.5
Blood Pressure: 151/86
Pulse: 60
Breath Rate: 11
Breath Hold: 50

Fasting Blood Glucose: 107

Note: Donnie's coach also had him test with an 11-parameter urine test strip (discussed more in the intermediate testing procedures discussed in appendix B). This strip showed bilirubin, which can be a strong indication that bile may not be flowing well. This test strip also showed a specific gravity of 30, which can be a catabolic marker.

When Donnie's stool was formed, it was lighter than the color of cardboard. This stool color, bilirubin on his 11-parameter dipstick, the fact that consuming fats made him nauseous, and his loose stools are all good indications that his bile was likely not flowing well. Donnie's high saliva pH, low urine pH, low pulse, and high specific gravity are a strong indication of a Catabolic Imbalance. Donnie's loose stool and insomnia issues could be used as a confirmation of a likely Catabolic Imbalance, in this scenario. Remember, both loose stool and insomnia can be caused by other issues or other imbalances; yet, when viewed with numbers that strongly indicate a Catabolic Imbalance, these symptoms now become likely confirmations of that imbalance. Since a Catabolic Imbalance has the ability to thicken the bile and restrict the bile's ability to flow correctly, Donnie's apparent imbalance is lining up nicely with the symptoms he is experiencing. This does not mean that Donnie's loose stool and insomnia issues are definitely caused by a Catabolic Imbalance, but it's a nice starting point to work from.

Donnie started with the basics and began to use three Beet Flow capsules with each meal. After a few days, Donnie performed a Beet Flow flush and on the following day used a Xeneplex coffee suppository. The day after the suppository, Donnie's stool started to slow down. It was still loose, but there was a noticeable enough change to help motivate Donnie to do more work.

When it appears that a Catabolic Imbalance can be contributing to chronic diarrhea, the amino acid, L-glutamine, can be very effective at helping the body send more water to the kidneys and less to the bowels. However, glutamine can also raise blood pressure. Since Donnie's blood pressure was already elevated, Donnie's coach suggested that a vitamin E supplement may be more appropriate, since vitamin E is pro-anabolic and has the ability to lower blood pressure.

Five or six days after performing the combination of a Beet Flow flush on one day and a coffee suppository on the next, Donnie did this combo again. The days following this second Beet Flow flush/coffee suppository combo showed great improvement to Donnie's stool, and his blood pressure started to come down. When poor bile flow is junking up the system and raising blood pressure, that blood pressure will often come down once bile is moving again and the body can remove more filth.

Though Donnie's catabolic markers were showing slight improvement and his diarrhea was also improving, his stool was still leaning on the loose side and his insomnia was still present. Now that Donnie's bile flow appeared to be improving, Donnie's coach suggested that including some pro-anabolic fats may be better tolerated than when bile was not available to help emulsify those fats properly. Donnie began introducing butter, coconut oil, and, at night, began to eat poached eggs. All of these foods can have a pro-anabolic effect. These steps, along with the vitamin E he was taking at night, started to speed up his improvement. Donnie's ability to properly process fats also reduced his need to consume as many carbs, allowing his fasting glucose to fall into a better range. As he moved less catabolic, his stool became firm and his insomnia was no longer an issue. After six weeks, Donnie's numbers were:

Saliva pH: 6.9 (Previously 7.1)
Urine pH: 6.0 (Previously 5.5)
Blood Pressure: 130/84 (Previously 151/86)
Pulse: 67 (Previously 60)
Breath Rate: 13 (Previously 11)
Breath Hold: 49 (Previously 50)
Fasting Blood Glucose: 95 (Previously 107)
Note: Donnie's 11-parameter urine test strip no longer showed bilirubin, and his specific gravity came down to 21.

You can see that it would be possible to view Donnie's new numbers as still leaning toward the catabolic side. Those numbers will likely improve as he continues, yet he was able to improve the imbalance enough in only six weeks to see the results he was looking for. If he were to stop all his efforts, Donnie may revert right back to where he was before, since the imbalance still appears to be present. For this reason, it's important to help clients understand that six weeks is rarely enough time to fully improve the cause of a severe imbalance. Continuing to monitor his numbers is crucial for Donnie's success.

Case Study: George Clooney (Keep in mind this is not the dreamy, Academy Award winning actor, George Clooney. This is a totally different George Clooney.)

Elevated Blood Pressure, Chronic Constipation and Excessive Vitamin D Use

George had taken our almost-free, 4-week digestion course and was following the steps to improve his chronic constipation and elevated blood pressure. Before he started, he was having a hard and difficult-to-pass bowel movement every four to five days. He posted in our free Facebook support group that he had been using a dose of five HCL per meal for three weeks. He noted that he had not seen any improvement with his constipation, and listed his self-test numbers in hopes that someone could help him figure out why. George's numbers were:

Saliva pH: 6.8
Urine pH: 6.4
Blood Pressure: 148/88
Pulse: 83
Breath Rate: 12
Breath Hold: 50

When asked if he was using any other supplements, George reported that he was taking vitamin D, since his blood tests indicated that his vitamin D levels were low. Remember, vitamin D is necessary to pull calcium from our intestinal tract into the bloodstream. However, at the high doses that are often suggested by mainstream health professionals, vitamin D can also pull calcium out of the tissues and out of all kinds of other places, and hold that calcium in the bloodstream. This can thicken the blood (note that George's systolic blood pressure is higher than what most would consider to be a balanced blood pressure reading). Holding calcium in the blood can also raise urine pH as the body attempts to remove some of that excess calcium through the urine. [Notice his urine pH of 6.4 and saliva pH of 6.8. This could be considered a possible marker for an Anabolic Imbalance. However, with the understanding that his urine pH may have been higher simply because he was taking too much vitamin D, maybe he wasn't too anabolic at all.]

I talk a lot in this book about how an Anabolic Imbalance can send too much of the body's water to the kidneys and not enough water to the bowels. However, whether or not an individual is even drinking enough water has to be considered as well. When asked how much water he was drinking in a day, George suggested that he usually has a cup of coffee in the morning and another small bottle of water throughout the day. With chronic constipation, it is very common for the individual to be drinking less than enough water. Remember that it's important to look at blood pressure before dramatically increasing water intake. Since George's systolic blood pressure number is higher than what might be considered in a balanced range, it would appear that George could tolerate drinking more water without risking a scenario where he would be washing too much mineral out of his body.

Another member of the support group explained that if reducing his Vitamin D intake doesn't bring his urine pH into a better range, he might want to try adding 1000mg of ascorbic acid before breakfast and lunch. This would likely help reduce his urine pH and further acidify the stool.

After gathering input from a few support group members, George decided upon the following steps:

1. Yes, correcting an Anabolic Imbalance can be very helpful when it comes to helping the body send more water to the bowels and loosen up a hard stool. However, it's even more important to drink enough water in the first place. Once George understood that coffee is not the same thing as water, and that one small bottle of water per day was not enough, he was able to find places in his day to increase his water intake. One member suggested drinking a large glass (20 ounces) of water right when he wakes up each day. In that way, instead of being utilized to help with digestion and other processes, his initial water intake could go toward helping the body wash out more junk and possibly contribute to lowering his elevated blood pressure reading. George took that step each morning and also implemented drinking five or six additional 8-ounce glasses of water each day.
2. George reduced his vitamin D intake in an attempt to allow his blood pressure and urine pH to both come into better ranges.
3. To help acidify his stool and bring down his urine pH (since reducing his Vitamin D intake brought down his urine pH only a little bit), George used 1000mg of Vitamin C as ascorbic acid before breakfast and lunch.

George continued taking Beet Flow and HCL as he implemented these changes. He also added Digesti-zyme to further improve his digestion. He added the Digesti-zyme because he wanted to supply his body with cofactors that can be used to make more HCL naturally. By improving their ability to make more of their own HCL, many individuals can decrease their need to supplement with HCL at a faster pace.

About a week into his changes, George started having a bowel movement every two or three days, instead of every four or five. The week after that he was having a bowel movement every day. His self-test numbers indicated continued improvement. Since he was using the ascorbic acid before meals, he was able to reduce his HCL dose to 3 per meal and continue having a normal bowel movement every day. Here are George's new numbers after following this plan for three weeks:

Saliva pH: 6.8 (Previously 6.8)
Urine pH: 5.7 (Previously 6.4)
Blood Pressure: 128/81 (Previously 148/88)
Pulse: 76 (Previously 83)
Breath Rate: 13 (Previously 12)
Breath Hold: 48 (Previously 50)

Seeing his systolic blood pressure come down to a more balanced reading, George felt that much of his success came from simply drinking enough water. His now lower urine pH of 5.7 helped him come to the assumption that he may have also reduced a slight Anabolic Imbalance and helped the body send more of that water to the colon so the stool could move with more ease.

George continued to drink more water throughout the day, but found that he was able to reduce the large amount he was drinking first thing in the morning and still keep his blood pressure down and his stool moving properly. George was also able to reduce his ascorbic acid use and simply increased it again any time he saw his urine pH go over 6.1.

By continuing to monitor his self-test numbers on his Coalition progress charts and to pay attention to his stool, he will be able to adjust what he's doing in a way that could make his constipation a thing of the past. Good job, George. Even if you're not as dreamy as Danny Ocean.

Note: The increase in water intake was appropriate for George because his elevated blood pressure reading was a strong indication of a greater need for water. However, if his blood pressure had been very low, he would have needed to take steps to lift his mineral levels before he qualified to increase his water intake so drastically.

Case Study: Marcy (Not the Marcy from the Peanuts cartoons.)

Cravings and Binge Eating

Marcy dealt with serious binge eating for more than a decade. She had been seeing a therapist for this specific issue for most of this time. She would eat well for most of the day, but at least one or two nights a week, Marcy would find herself elbow deep in a box of cupcakes or scraping the bottom of a tub or rocky road ice cream. She came across our Cravings and Binge Eating episode of _Kick It Naturally_ on iTunes when she was searching for solutions. Not only was her ten years of therapy not bringing the results she had hoped, but also the treatment was costing her a luxury car payment every month.

After listening to the podcast episode, Marcy immediately signed up for our almost free digestion course so she could learn how to run her self-tests and learn more about her digestive symptoms. Marcy experienced bloating on most days, and nausea more often than not. She had never before correlated her digestive symptoms to her cravings. She had other family members with similar digestive symptoms so she just assumed they were in her genes. Marcy's initial numbers were:

Saliva pH: 6.3
Urine pH: 6.3
Blood Pressure: 98/62
Pulse: 79
Breath Rate: 12
Breath Hold: 44
Fasting Blood Glucose: 68

There's nothing shocking about Marcy's numbers here. Not all binge-eating cases look like this; but with cravings and binge eating, a combination of Anabolic and Electrolyte Deficiency Imbalances are very common to see. Uncontrollable cravings often occur when mineral levels and blood sugar both go low at the same time. A lack of properly processed protein in the system is often at play as well. Urine pH is often higher with an Anabolic Imbalance, and we often see hypoglycemic issues in this scenario. This doesn't mean that the Anabolic Imbalance is causing the hypoglycemia or the cravings, I'm simply stating why these issues are often seen together. Because mineral and protein levels are low with an Electrolyte Deficiency Imbalance, you can see how easy it would be for someone to experience cravings while dealing with both of these imbalances.

Since Marcy's stool was lighter than the color of cardboard, her understanding was that improving bile flow would be important. She started using Beet Flow with each meal for a few days, followed by a Beet Flow flush on one day and a coffee suppository on the next. Marcy started adding one HCL capsule per meal and her nausea and bloating actually got much worse. A member of our Facebook support group explained that if the stomach is overly alkaline (due to waste product from a bacterial overgrowth), mixing a small amount of acid with that alkaline waste can create a fizzy mess. Once the stomach is acidic enough to wipe out the majority of that bacteria and overpower the alkalinity, that discomfort will normally stop. For this reason, those who need HCL the most will sometimes have the hardest time getting started with it. I find that those dealing with a severe bacterial overgrowth can speed this up by using d-limonene, but Marcy didn't need to go that far. She simply used a little ascorbic acid before breakfast to help acidify the stomach, while ramping up her HCL dose to five capsules per meal. Once she reached five HCL capsules per meal, her bloating improved dramatically.

About a week after her initial Beet Flow flush/coffee suppository combo, she performed those same steps again. The next day she noticed that her saliva pH was now up to 6.5 and her stool was darker. As the week progressed, she experienced less and less bloating and less and less nausea. Marcy also noticed that she was able to eat dietary fats without magnifying her nausea. That was definitely new for Marcy. This makes sense since bile flow is required to emulsify the fats we consume. When fats can not be properly broken down, they can turn toxic and magnify nausea issues. Since Marcy's bile flow seemed to improve, as evident by her darker stool, that likely reduced the burden that was contributing to the nausea. With the ability to now remove filth through the bile, it's no wonder Marcy saw the rapid improvement to her nausea.

While improving digestion, Marcy also took steps to increase her mineral levels. She started drinking bone broth each morning and using unrefined salt with her meals. To reduce her blood sugar spikes and crashes, Marcy reduced all the starchy foods she was eating, and replaced those items with more medium-carb foods. Marcy was trying to include things like sweet potatoes, yam, butternut squash and berries every day. Some of those choices are still starches, but they are medium-carb foods with a lower glycemic effect. These foods can supply Marcy with carbs that she needs to buffer her low mineral and protein levels, without supplying such a huge load of starch. These choices helped keep Marcy's blood sugar on a more even keel. For Marcy, it was that huge load of starch that created a sugar/insulin spike followed by a sugar crash, resulting in the overwhelming need to binge. As Marcy increased her mineral levels AND kept her blood sugar on a more even keel, she was seeing pleasant results.

Three weeks into her plan, Marcy suddenly realized she hadn't binged in a week. She was still experiencing light cravings from time to time, but not the uncontrollable urges she had grown accustomed to. She was quite shocked. After six weeks, Marcy's numbers were:

Saliva pH: 6.6 (Previously 6.3)
Urine pH: 5.9 (Previously 6.3)
Blood Pressure: 106/67 (Previously 98/62)
Pulse: 76 (Previously 79)
Breath Rate: 13 (Previously 12)
Breath Hold: 42 (Previously 44)
Fasting Blood Glucose: 74 (Previously 68)

My favorite part is that, when Marcy told her therapist that she hadn't binged in weeks, her therapist was helpful enough to point out, "See, sometimes it just takes 10 years of good therapy to turn things around." Though Marcy knew she didn't need the therapy any longer for her cravings, her Mother still drove her crazy; so Marcy decided to continue seeing her therapist once a month. A significant reduction from her previous three times a week schedule. With the money she saved, she put a down payment on a townhouse.

This wasn't even the first time I had heard of a case like this. A personal client of mine had also been seeing a therapist for over a decade for her cravings. That client quit her therapy three weeks after starting with me. This is not to say that therapy can't be beneficial in many situations, I think it can. But it's also nice to see how many mental health professionals have emailed us to let us know they are now using nutrition and the information we teach to help their clients get better results from their therapy.

Case Study: Jan

Alternation Between Diarrhea and Constipation

Jan was flipping back and forth between constipation and diarrhea. She found that her normal pattern was to experience constipation for four or five days before she switched to having diarrhea a few times per day, often for two or three days at a time. Jan hated both of these options and just wished she could have a normal, formed bowel movement, once or twice a day, like all the cool kids.

Jan heard us talking about this constipation/diarrhea combo extravaganza on one of our *Kick It Naturally* podcast episodes. In this episode we described what seems to be two of the most common causes for a person to experience both constipation and diarrhea. The underlying causes we described seemed to match Jan's circumstances and her self-test results.

In this episode, Jan learned that one possible cause can be a lack of resources restricting your ability to move back and forth between the anabolic and catabolic states. To move back and forth between the anabolic state at night and the catabolic state during the day takes adequate nutritional resources. If an individual has low resources, the body can get stuck in one state for days at a time. If you're stuck in a catabolic state, and the body is sending too much water to the bowels, diarrhea can be the result. If you're stuck in an anabolic state, and the body is sending too much of your water to the kidneys, constipation can show up.

If a low blood pressure measurement indicates a lack of resources, taking steps to lift nutritional resources can often help the body move back and forth between these two states each day. This natural oscillation can direct an appropriate amount of water to the bowels, creating a normal bowel movement.

Another possibility is undigested food rotting and fermenting in your intestinal tract. Depending on where that food is in its rotting and

298

fermenting process, it could move slower through the system, or the toxicity could result in the body's urgency to push it out of the system quickly. Conversely, for some individuals, excessive toxins have the ability to accumulate and slow down the whole system. Working on both ends of digestion (bile flow and stomach acid levels) can often bring about improvement to the back and forth issue between constipation and diarrhea. From the previously discussed viewpoint, improving digestion also allows more nutritional resources to be absorbed from what we eat, facilitating a proper anabolic/catabolic cycle. For this reason, improving your ability to properly digest food could improve this constipation/diarrhea combo in more than one way.

Since it is very common for episodes of diarrhea to be caused by a lack of bile flow and an inability to neutralize acids leaving the stomach, Jan decided to focus on improving bile flow first. After all, if some are experiencing diarrhea and they increase levels of stomach acid without first improving bile flow, that could exacerbate their diarrhea. Jan's numbers also indicated that she might benefit from thinning bile so it could flow better. Her self-test numbers were:

Saliva pH: 6.2
Urine pH: 6.1
Blood Pressure: 100/70
Pulse: 80
Breath Rate: 14
Breath Hold: 47
Note: Jan also used an 11-parameter urine test strip that showed bilirubin and urobilinogen. Both of these markers are strong indications that bile may not be flowing well.

Both Jan's 11-parameter test strip results and her low saliva pH (below 6.5), were strong indications that thinning bile to help it flow better was an appropriate step. Jan was already using 3 Beet Flow per meal, so she did a Beet Flow flush on a Monday and a Xeneplex coffee suppository on Tuesday. The order of these two steps doesn't seem to be as important as doing them one day after the other. As an alternative to the coffee suppository, performing a coffee enema would likely be just as effective. Not everyone needs to perform a Beet Flow flush/coffee suppository combo to get bile moving, but if your bile has been backed up for some time, taking these two steps together seems to be the most effective route.

Jan watched her saliva pH the day after she completed the second step (the coffee suppository). Her saliva pH rose to 6.4 on Wednesday and 6.5 by Friday. This is a great indication that her bile is starting to flow better. Because Jan showed signs of improved bile flow, she felt it was time to work on the other side of digestion: her stomach acid.

As Jan started supplementing HCL capsules with each meal, she could feel that something was changing with her digestion. She didn't feel as lousy after most meals and the diarrhea stopped. She was having formed bowel movements, but still tending toward constipation and having a bowel movement only every two or three days. Her self-test numbers were slowly improving. Jan then started adding 1000mg of ascorbic acid before breakfast and lunch. In about two weeks, Jan was having a formed bowel movement every day, just like all the cool kids. Here are Jan's numbers three weeks after she started this plan:

Saliva pH: 6.5 (Previously 6.2)
Urine pH: 5.9 (Previously 6.1)
Blood Pressure: 109/72 (Previously 100/70)
Pulse: 73 (Previously 80)
Breath Rate: 16 (Previously 14)
Breath Hold: 45 (Previously 47)
Note: Jan's 11-parameter urine test strip no longer showed bilirubin and urobilinogen.

Jan's urine pH came down two tenths of a point; her saliva pH came up three tenths; these are reasonable improvements showing Jan's health going in the right direction. The new, broader separation between those pH numbers was a good sign that she had improved a possible Anabolic Imbalance. The raised saliva pH along with the lack of bilirubin and urobilinogen were also strong indications that bile was flowing better. Jan continued to use Beet Flow with each meal since she was still using HCL, but no longer needed to do any coffee suppositories or Beet Flow flushes. Jan continued to use the ascorbic acid before breakfast and lunch, as she found that her urine pH would go right back up when she reduced her dose. However, while using the ascorbic acid before meals, she was able to reduce her HCL dose to two capsules per meal.

If Jan's diarrhea had continued, she could have tried a Clean Sweep for thirty days, as outlined in chapter eleven. I've posted this entire chapter on my site for free. Simply go to KickItNaturally.com and search for "Clean Sweep" in the search box if you'd like to share this chapter with a friend.

FAQs

Odds are great that at least one of these questions will pop up for you or one of your clients. I highly recommend not only reading through these, but also coming back to this page and reviewing these FAQs if you or one of your clients end up not seeing the results you'd like to see.

I've never had acid reflux or heartburn before. Why am I having it now that I've started taking HCL?

This is actually common and may lead you to believe that supplementing with HCL must cause reflux. Since we're taught to turn off stomach acid when we have heartburn, it makes sense to us that adding more acid could cause heartburn, especially if we've never before experienced any reflux issues.

Remember the LES valve. When the LES valve closes properly, food and stomach acid cannot go back up the esophagus and cause reflux issues. One of the jobs of our stomach acid is to signal the LES valve to close properly. Lack of stomach acid allows the LES valve to remain open.

If you often experience burping, bloating, indigestion, constipation, or feeling like your food just sits in your stomach like a rock for hours, odds are great that your stomach is not acidic enough. Therefore, when you start to use HCL (starting with the low dose of only one capsule per meal), it's possible to experience heartburn symptoms. This is because you have now added enough HCL to feel that acid when it refluxes back up, but not enough HCL to trigger the LES valve to close properly. Those who continue to increase their HCL dosage until they reach an appropriate dose will often see these heartburn symptoms disappear once the stomach becomes acidic enough to trigger the valve to close. When the LES valve closes, it blocks the reflux from coming back up.

The truth is, if you're experiencing any of the symptoms that would lead you to believe that you need to improve your HCL levels, odds are great that you've been having reflux for quite some time. The reflux may have been there, however, since stomach acid was so low (or even non-existent), there was no acid coming up with the reflux. No acid to burn you means no heartburn symptoms. The problem is, our stomachs also contain digestive enzymes that are made to break down protein. Well, guess what your esophagus is made of: protein. In this regard, even if you never feel heartburn, or even if you're taking a medication that has turned off your stomach acid, you could still be damaging your esophagus if enzymes are refluxing back up your esophagus and breaking down those tissues. Certainly, enzymes would not damage the esophagus as quickly as stomach acid could. But over time, those enzymes could be very problematic. Especially if we feel like we've handled the problem by taking our PPI medication religiously.

Some individuals find faster relief by implementing one or more of the following methods;
1. Eating a dill pickle or two at the end of each meal is often enough to acidify the stomach to a level that will trigger the valve to close.
2. Taking 1000mg of Vitamin C as ascorbic acid before each meal may be enough to boost the HCL you are currently using. (If an individual is experiencing a loose stool, ascorbic acid could exacerbate that issue. Therefore, the loose stool should be corrected before implementing the ascorbic acid.)
3. In severe cases, taking a few doses of d-limonene before continuing with the HCL protocol may be an effective step for some individuals. Gasses can cause our food to push back up the esophagus. By wiping out a good layer of bacteria in your stomach, you can reduce the amount of gasses being created by that bacteria, therefore reducing the amount of pressure those gasses can create. (Pyloricin is a supplement I use as part of an H. Pylori protocol. If d-limonene is not appropriate for a client, Pyloricin may be suitable in this scenario.)

Any of these three steps may also allow you to reduce the number of HCL capsules that are required each meal. The d-limonene is a much more aggressive step, so if the dill pickles or ascorbic acid capsules are enough to cease any reflux symptoms, I prefer to see someone go the more gentle route.

When first starting HCL, it is also important to make sure you are not eating starches or sugars with any meal when you will be supplementing HCL capsules. Those carbs can activate the bacteria in your stomach and create more gasses. Once you get up to a full dose of HCL or are able to acidify the stomach enough to trigger the LES valve to close, you should be able to re-introduce higher carb foods while using HCL.

I just started HCL and it makes me nauseous or creates stomach discomfort. Does that mean I don't need to supplement HCL?

It seems that those who need HCL the most, are the same folks who experience some type of discomfort when starting HCL supplementation. In most cases when an individual is making plenty of their own HCL, adding HCL will either create a loose stool issue, or a warming-type of discomfort in the stomach. Unfortunately, when people read this and then experience discomfort when starting HCL, they often assume they must not need additional HCL since it created such discomfort. Most commonly this seems to occur because these individuals have a bacterial overgrowth in the stomach. The waste from this bacteria creates an alkaline environment in the stomach. When you add HCL to an overly alkaline environment, the reaction of the acid meeting the alkaline waste can create a fizzy mess.

Think about that science fair project volcano where the "lava" starts to bubble and expand and rise out of the top of the volcano. This reaction is caused by acid (vinegar) meeting alkaline (baking soda). This is similar to the reaction that is going on in your stomach if you add HCL to an alkaline environment. That discomfort doesn't mean you don't need HCL. It simply means that you might need to wipe out a good layer of that bacteria before you can use HCL comfortably.

Further acidifying the stomach with dill pickles or ascorbic acid, or taking steps to reduce a bacterial infection in the stomach (like using d-limonene cautiously for a week or two), will often allow individuals to start their HCL use without the discomfort from the bubbling mess that was taking place in their stomachs.

My client started the digestive supplements and has gained weight instead of losing weight. What gives?

This is actually common, so it's important that you and your clients are monitoring the right measurements. Because muscle weighs more than fat, weight on the scale can be very misleading. Remember that your body needs resources to build muscle and to rebuild tissues. If you have been digesting your food ineffectively for years, the body likely did not have the resources it needed to rebuild in the manner it was designed to. When digestion improves and the body now has more resources to rebuild muscles and other tissues, weight can go up due to an increase in muscle fibers. This can occur even if an individual is not lifting weights in an effort to build muscle. When this is the case, individuals are likely reducing body fat, even when the scale shows they have gained weight. That's why it's important to measure the waist at the belly button, first thing in the morning, and mark that on the calendar. You can then monitor that measurement every month or so and see a more accurate indication of whether you are losing or gaining fat.

What if I am even more constipated after starting Beet Flow and HCL?

For some, Beet Flow can thin the bile pretty quickly and improve bile flow. Remember, bile is the alkaline side of digestion; and, in most cases, the more alkaline the stool, the slower it will move. Therefore, if you've improved bile flow, but you have not yet ramped up to an appropriate dose of HCL, you could become constipated; or constipation could be temporarily exacerbated.

Keep in mind that even if you've ramped up to an appropriate dose of HCL, but your stomach is too alkaline from a bacterial overgrowth, it could still take more time to improve the acidification side of the digestive process. It's not that the supplements "made you more constipated." It's just that you have improved the alkaline side faster than the acid side so your stool has slowed down, creating constipation. Once the acidification process improves as much as your bile flow has, the constipation will likely improve. Individuals are often looking for a "magic bullet" supplement that will fix their problems. The truth is, it's the correct application of knowledge that primarily fixes problems. Success with supplements comes after and because of the knowledge.

Since I started drinking more water, I'm very tired and/or depressed.

Check your blood pressure at least two hours after a meal. Low blood pressure can indicate low mineral levels in your system. If your mineral levels are low, by drinking more water, you may be washing out some minerals and dropping your blood pressure even lower. A lack of minerals is a common contributor to depression.

As a general rule, drinking more water is needed and can be beneficial for many individuals. You may need to work more on improving digestion and taking steps to lift your mineral resources before you can increase your water intake.

I've been taking HCL but I'm still bloated and/or constipated.

If you've been at an appropriate dose of HCL for a few weeks and you're still not seeing any improvement to bloating or constipation, you may be dealing with a bacterial infection in your stomach (like George Clooney in our case study earlier in this chapter). Waste from bacteria is alkaline and can make the stomach environment more suitable for the bacteria to thrive. If your stomach is very alkaline and neutralizing the HCL that you are supplementing, five HCL capsules may be only as effective as one or two. This does not mean that you should take fifteen HCL capsules to make up for the alkaline environment. That is not advised.

We do see people improve this situation by taking a wider variety of steps to acidify the stomach. Some take steps to wipe out a good layer of stomach bacteria, making it easier to acidify the stomach properly. If you're not already eating a dill pickle or two at the end of each meal, and/or taking 1000mg of ascorbic acid before each meal, these steps may be best to try first. If those more gentle steps have no effect for you, d-limonene or Pyloricin seem to work well for many when there is a bacterial overgrowth in the stomach. One dose every other morning for seven to fourteen days has been shown to bring improvement for many.

I don't recommend taking d-limonene over a long period of time. It can be very pro-catabolic, and seems to be used best in short intervals.

Referencing These FAQs

Don't forget to come back to this chapter and review these case studies and FAQs if you run into any trouble or don't see the results you want to see. Please keep in mind that these are simply real-world examples of steps that have worked for people in specific situations. You still need to monitor your chemistry and apply the steps that are appropriate for you and your biological individuality. By now you understand that just because something worked for one person, that doesn't mean it's going to work for you or for anyone else. Following numbers and digestive clues brings in an analytical component and can guide you down the path that should bring the best results.

If any questions come up that were not covered in this book, don't forget to ask them in our free and private Facebook support group. You can join for free here:
https://www.facebook.com/groups/kickyourfatsupport/

Wha'd He Say?

In this chapter, you learned:
- There's more than one George Clooney.
- Eating too many starches or sugars can exacerbate an Anabolic Imbalance and magnify a chronic constipation issue.
- Drinking more water can often be beneficial, but not every person needs to drink more water. Some individuals simply need to help their body adjust where that water is being sent. Others still may not qualify to increase water intake until they have taken steps to lift their mineral levels.
- Taking Vitamin C as ascorbic acid before meals may help boost the acidifying effects of HCL supplementation and allow an individual to reduce the number of HCL capsules needed to properly acidify the stomach at mealtime.
- If you feel bloated after a meal (maybe you forgot to take your HCL), eating a dill pickle or two is often enough to help acidify the stomach and sooth that distress.

CHAPTER TWENTY

Helping Clients Succeed

You can learn a tremendous amount about nutrition and how the human body works. You can even pass along a lot of that information to your clients. But if your clients don't take the needed actions, or if they don't understand what actions are needed, those clients aren't going to see any results. You remember that succeeding as a health pro is all about helping your clients see great results, right?

Now that you've crammed a whole bunch of physiology into your head, and now that your brain feels just a little bit mushy, let's look at some other insights that can help you see the best results with your clients. This chapter focuses more on what we consider to be the client management side of working one-on-one with clients.

Working With Clients

Each health professional is going to have different preferences when it comes to working with clients. Some of you will prefer to answer all client questions through email, others will want to use the phone. Some of you might want to do a phone consultation before you meet with a client, while others will want to provide information about what to expect through a website or a preconfigured email you send to prospective clients. Through trial and error, you will figure out what works best for you. However, in this chapter I provide insights into why I do things the way I do and give you other options to consider. Maybe I can help you avoid some of the mistakes that I made early in my health pro career.

Clients Paying Out-Of-Pocket

When individuals have been unable to achieve any health improvement in the medical system, they will often begin looking for more natural solutions. One hurdle many of these individuals need to get over is the understanding of why they are required to pay out-of-pocket for natural services. When I first started down this path and began to look outside of the medical community for my own answers, I didn't understand why some practitioners didn't accept insurance. I was already paying for health insurance, shouldn't that cover health-related expenses?

The reality is, many of you will not have the medical credentials required to accept insurance from your clients. The health insurance world is tied directly to the medical world; and a large percentage of natural health practitioners do not fit into that model. For that reason, clients working with these practitioners pay out-of-pocket instead of going through their health insurance company for any type of reimbursement.

This is common in today's world, yet you will still run into clients who may be experiencing this for the first time with you. This is another reason why seeing great results with your clients is so important. When your clients tell their friends about the amazing results they saw with you, their friends will be more willing to pay out-of-pocket.

Helping Clients Understand What To Expect

People don't like surprises when it comes to their health. For that reason, I like to make sure I help future clients understand what to expect when it comes to working with me. Not only will I let them know the fee I charge, I also let them know that most of my clients end up using some type of supplements, at least temporarily. In that regard, they should factor that expense into what they'll be spending while working with me. I'll explain how I use the Coalition For Health Education, the private organization detailed in the next chapter, and that I require all of my clients to become a member of this private club before working with me. Membership has an annual fee of $20 so I explain how that works before clients come to see me.-

If clients are going to come see you at your clinic, it's a good idea to let them know how long the appointment will likely take and what will be involved. If you're going to work with clients through email, you'll likely want to let them know about any testing tools they will need to acquire before you can get started, much in the manner that I explained it to you in the first chapter of this book.

Checking In – Following Up With Clients

This may be one of the most important points in the whole book. If you simply provide your client with new insights and steps that could help, many of them will disappear, never to be heard from again. You've figured out by now that creating real results can be a little more complicated—complicated enough to easily overwhelm some individuals. To help clients succeed in this process, it's crucial to follow up with them and see how things are going. When I first started doing this work, I assumed that when I didn't hear back from a new client, everything was going as planned. If not, the client would have certainly contacted me, right? Wrong. So very wrong. In some cases, the new client was so overwhelmed with the possibility of improving a life-long health issue, they didn't even know where to start. Keep in mind that I likely explained exactly where to start. Still, some clients experience a hiccup in the process, or may not see the result they want to see within four hours—and drop the whole thing. For these reasons, it's important to check in and see if new clients have any questions or concerns.

It's also important for you to initiate the follow-up. You don't need to chase your clients down every week. I certainly don't recommend doing that. However, when new clients start adjusting their diet, or using new supplements, it's important to check in after the first week or so and see how things are going. It's good to casually ask if their self-test numbers have changed at all. It is very common for a client to need to make adjustments and they won't know when to do that if they are too intimidated to ask. Some folks refuse to ask questions because they feel like it makes them look foolish. I try to explain to my clients that I expect and encourage questions. Questions are an excellent way to acquire knowledge. Knowledge is how you create results.

The Importance Of Monitoring

You know by now how hard it is to get me to shut up about monitoring. Your clients should get the same from you. Without monitoring, especially when starting any new supplements or dietary changes, how will you know when to make adjustments? Remember that the self-tests are the "you are here" red dot on the mall map of health. Since individuals need to look at their chemistry to get an idea of where to start, doesn't it make sense that they need to continue to look at their chemistry as they make any nutritional adjustments in their life? By monitoring, we can help them watch to see if the adjustments they made were appropriate and are creating the results they want to see.

Credibility Through The Client's Experience

Testimonials, prior accomplishments, or a referral from a good friend can all go a long way in creating credibility. You can also increase your credibility through your client's experience of working with you. This is another area where self-test monitoring becomes invaluable. When you can tell clients what to expect, or when you help them understand why they might feel a specific way when one of their self-tests shows up in a certain range—and then that happens—that can be pretty powerful.

The self-test numbers will begin to make sense to your clients. They will see the correlation of the numbers with their physiology and/or the correlation of their numbers with how they feel and/or the correlation of their numbers and their symptoms. This can be very gratifying for your clients. Not only does this cause your client's faith in you to increase, it also causes their faith in themselves to increase. As your clients learn how foods affect their self-test numbers and how they feel, they start to adjust what they're eating. When their self-test numbers are out of range, yet they know what supplements can help move things back in the right direction, they feel more in control of their body, their health, and their life.

Making Adjustments

The reality is, nearly any supplement protocol your clients start is going to require adjustments at some point. Most clients require some type of adjustments even in the first week. This is not the same world where a medical doctor prescribes a drug to patients and tells them to 'come back in three months so we can see how you're doing.'

Using supplements can allow body chemistry and metabolism to move into a more optimal range; the speed of this movement differs from person to person. Not all individuals respond in the same way to supplements—so an adjustment is needed. An individual may have appeared to have a major imbalance, yet that imbalance was not as severe as you thought—so an adjustment is needed. A client may see no results—so an adjustment is needed. A client may notice a new symptom that was not there before—so an adjustment is needed. The self-tests help us know when it's time to adjust.

The good news is that, in many cases, self-test numbers will start to go in the wrong direction before any new symptoms show up. The self-test numbers alone can guide adjustments in some cases. Even when you can help clients improve an imbalance or a symptom that they're dealing with, eventually the supplements or food choices could bring that client into balance. If that is the case, continuing at the same rate could have the ability of creating an imbalance in the other direction. Therefore, clients may not only need help understanding how to use supplements and how to adjust food choices, they may also need help understanding how to reduce these efforts when needed.

Helping Clients Understand Improvements In Their Numbers

For many clients, imbalances and self-test numbers will improve before symptoms show any improvement. By teaching clients which self-test numbers may be out of range, and the changes in those numbers that could indicate progress, you give your clients a goal to shoot for. If your clients' self-test results are all moving in the right direction, yet their symptoms have not improved, they may think 'this process doesn't work' and quit. However, if your clients see improvements in their self-tests, they will be more motivated to continue to do the work that seems to be creating these results. Without those self tests, they wouldn't have known they were moving in the right direction.

When a client sees changes in their tests, and especially when they start to feel better with those changes, an amazing thing happens—they start to realize that they have the ability to change the way their body is operating. As your clients start to realize that they create improvements to their health, they become motivated to take other steps that can create improvement as well.

When Protocols Fail

You're absolutely going to have clients for whom you provide help when they set up a protocol to follow, and that protocol fails. There's really no way around this because the body is complicated and you are not a wizard. But you can help clients use what they learned through that failure; you will together have a better idea of what steps to take next. In many cases, if a supplement or diet adjustment creates a very specific response, that response is now new information. That new information can often guide you to a better choice. The better choice you come up with may not have made sense to you before the initial protocol created the result it created. In this regard, there are no failures. Only information gained that can be used to then move toward a favorable outcome for the client.

Another part of your job becomes teaching the client what to look for. For example, many people will feel increased heartburn when first starting with HCL. Before your clients begin HCL supplementation, you can explain this possibility, explain the physiology involved, and explain that reaching the goal of improved digestion can take some time and some monitoring. You can explain that the increased heartburn occurs because the stomach has not yet become acidic enough to trigger the LES valve to close. Without the explanation, new clients feel the burning, may assume the HCL is not right for them, and quit taking it. They may also assume you don't know what you're talking about since you suggested that increasing HCL could improve their reflux. But if you've explained that the increased heartburn is a possibility at first, and explained steps to take to correct it, they will likely continue the protocol and see great results. This is just one of many examples of how folks can make adjustments to what most would consider a failure, and end up seeing great results.

Knowing When To Say, I Don't Know

Here's a hint: When you don't know something, say "I don't know." Practice it now, "I don't know." You need this phrase in your arsenal when working as a health pro. One of the biggest fears new health professionals have is that they might not know the answer to a client's question. Who cares! Nobody, and I mean nobody knows everything about the human body. Even for those who know a lot, these folks tend to learn something new every week that helps them realize they were totally wrong about three different things.

You don't have to know everything. What you do need is to avoid making up answers. I laugh as I write that, but the truth is, new health pros are often so nervous about looking foolish that they simply start rambling. Two minutes later these rookie health pros realize that they just explained to their client that it is very common to experience bloating if you own a german shepherd. Don't do this. Simply tell your client that you don't know, but you'll see what you can find out for them. Even things I sort of know, I forget a lot of the details and need to reference my books when I get to my office. I may even tell a client, "I'm worthless away from my reference material so let me get the right answer for you and I'll let you know." Nailed it! That even sounds reasonable, don't you think?

Understand that you don't need to be the Jeopardy champion of the health or nutrition world to help your clients. Once this is your default state of mind, it takes a lot of pressure off. It can also help you avoid having a string of clients who have all put their german shepherds up for adoption.

Helping Clients Comply

You will have clients who seem to correct their entire world by simply implementing supplement use. However, you will also see clients who need to do a lot more than take some supplements. These clients will need to make major changes to what they are eating, and/or make major changes to their other lifestyle choices. Many of these clients will be resistant to making these changes. When that's the case, I try not to push too hard. Instead, I try to explain to them the reality of the situation. I explain that it's possible for them to see improvement by simply taking a few easy steps. When I see this approach fail with clients, I normally suggest that they try one step (maybe two) for a couple weeks; then if we don't see any changes, other steps will need to be taken if they want to reach their goals. Always remember that their health is their choice.

By allowing them to make their own decisions, while also explaining that other steps are available if their approach doesn't work, it seems to soften the blow a little bit when it comes time to make major lifestyle changes. Plus, if a client can make small changes and see at least a little improvement, it can be very motivating to get them to implement more changes going forward. In any case, know that your clients have likely been stuck in their ways for years; it may take them a little time to come to the realization that change is possible and necessary. I just try to help my clients understand the benefits that those changes could bring, and then let them come around when they're ready.

I also see clients who aren't ready to make changes. Maybe things in their lives are not set up to allow for major changes at that time. By showing patience with these clients, it appears that I leave the door open for them to come back when they're ready. It will be common for you to hear from clients at a later time (even years later) who are now ready to do the work to see improvements. Try not to beat up people if they're not ready yet. Odds are great that they will ask for your help when they are ready.

Our 3-Part Video Series For Health Pros

We put together a free, in-depth video training that goes over some of these ideas in more detail. It was created to help people figure out if a career as a health coach is right for them, and to help them get past some of the common roadblocks a little faster. Each video is about twenty minutes, so there is a significant amount of great information included.

You can sign up to receive this 3-part series for free here: http://healthprocourse.com/video-series-opt-in

Wha'd He Say?

In this chapter, you learned:
- It can be beneficial to help clients understand what to expect before they begin working with you.
- After a client's initial appointment, it's best for you to initiate the follow-up and check in to see how things are going.
- Teaching your clients to monitor their self-tests is crucial for their success.
- With most clients, adjustments to protocols will be necessary. Don't feel like you need to be a know-it-all. When you don't know the answer to a question, tell the client you don't know, but you'll try to find out for them.

Chapter Twenty One

Legalities

It's important to remember that any natural health solution takes money out of the pockets of the pharmaceutical industry. Also remember that those who lobby the loudest (with the most amount of money) often have new laws passed in their favor. For this reason, it seems every year there are new laws popping up somewhere that may not benefit natural health practitioners. For this reason, it's important to understand some legal basics when it comes to protecting yourself.

Keep It Legal – Watching Your Language

One of the most crucial aspects of protecting yourself and keeping your business on the legal up and up, is understanding what you can and CANNOT say. (I'm sorry, I didn't mean to yell at you right there. I just want to make sure you realize that this is an important topic.) Before you say another word to your clients or potential clients, I recommend learning how to watch your language—and I don't mean cuss words. I could give a $&@# if you cuss at your clients, but I do care if you say the types of things that can get a health professional into a whole lot of trouble.

You can be held accountable for anything that you say to your clients, so it's important to first understand what you can't say. This goes for writing as well—not only what you might write in a blog post, etc., but even what you write in an email, text message or tweet. Everything you say counts. This chapter teaches you a few dos and don'ts to keep in mind. It's easy to get excited about the power of nutrition when you see people getting amazing results. It makes you want to tell everyone, "You can take these same steps and put an end to that health condition, too!" But you just can't do that. The reality is, not everyone will see the same amazing results, so you don't want to start your health pro career by making false claims. Instead, you want to help people understand that there is often an opportunity to make enough changes to create improvement to a wide variety of health challenges, and you can guide them through steps that might help them get there faster.

Here is a list of things not to say. By no means is this a full list of phrases or words to avoid, but it's enough to give you a baseline understanding of what could get you into trouble. If you're not sure if you're allowed to say something, play it safe and don't say it. Remember the value of "I don't know."

Things Not To Say

Don't say - "This will cure your disease."

Don't say cure, don't say disease. Cure is a 4-letter word in the world of nutrition and natural health. The word cure has been deemed a medical term and we don't want to step into that medical world if we're not licensed to play in that sandbox. Diseases are labeled in the medical world. Diagnosing an individual with a disease allows medical professionals to prescribe medications that have been approved for that disease. The name of the disease allows an insurance code to be attached to that individual's records so their insurance can pay for the drug. Diagnosing is what allows the money to flow through the system. If you're not licensed to prescribe medications or to diagnose an individual with a disease, avoiding the word altogether is a good idea.

Keep in mind that helping a client get rid of a disease shouldn't even be your intention because that is not what we do as natural health professionals. We simply work to help the body function in a more optimal manner. Is it true that when a body is operating more optimally, many diseases will appear to go away? Sure, that happens all over the world, every day, using a wide variety of modalities. But that doesn't mean you can tell clients you're going to help them fix their disease. That's not your focus; and, in many circumstances, focusing on disease can get you into a world of trouble. Don't do it. Besides, if you're focusing on the disease, you're missing the whole point.

Instead, you can tell clients that others have improved the causes of symptoms that often go along with a specific issue by improving imbalances or other physiological and metabolic disturbances that appear to be limiting the body's ability to function optimally.

Keep in mind that you're also allowed to ask questions. Questions are not statements. Saying, "Has anyone ever asked you if your digestion was operating correctly?" is a great way to start a conversation without using a statement.

Don't say - "Take these supplements" or "use this protocol."

There's a big difference between telling someone to do something and just sharing knowledge that might be available to anyone in books or on the internet. Instead of telling a client to take a specific supplement, you may say something along the lines of "Here's what others have done to see benefits or results." Or, "This is what I might use if I was in a similar situation." So you're not telling someone to do something. You're just sharing experiences of others who have taken steps that created a desired outcome. My health choices are to be made by me. Your health choices are to be made by you. Your client's health choices are to be made by that client. Your family member's health choices are to be made by your family member.

On the Coalition website that our practitioners use to educate their clients, we have a tool where a coach can put together a supplement list for their clients. On the top of the supplement list page that shows up for each client, it states: "Remember, we can't recommend specific supplements to you. However, we can show you supplement choices that other people with similar imbalances have used or what we might use if we were working to improve similar imbalances."

In this regard, your point of view, when speaking to the client, should not be to tell them a protocol that will correct their woes. Instead, you should have the viewpoint of, 'I'm not saying this is your answer, I'm just saying that we've seen other people see success in similar situations so we're putting this out there. Be sure to take self-test measurements so you can determine if something is working for you.'

NEVER say - "Stop taking that medication"

Don't say that. You're gonna go to jail. You know I'm serious since I bolded the all caps on the word **NEVER**. This concept is easy enough to understand. If you're not licensed to prescribe medications, you can't legally tell a client if they should or should not be taking medications. Period.

Yet, in my opinion, it's not enough to simply avoid saying those words. I go beyond cautious on this topic and go on the offensive. I end up telling this to every single client I work with who is on any type of medication: I say or type in an email, "I'm not telling you to come off that medication. I'm not legally allowed to tell you to do that. That has to be between you and your doctor."

Still, you might have clients tell you that they would really love to come off a drug because they hate the side-effects. In those scenarios, I might say something along the lines of, 'If I wanted to come off that medication, I might first work to improve this imbalance or this digestive problem etc. But I wouldn't even consider working with my doctor to reduce that medication until that was handled.' Clients need to understand that there is likely a reason they are on a medication and, in many cases, it could be life-threatening to stop that medication without the doctor's direction. Just because many health issues can be corrected naturally doesn't mean that a person should stop their meds and try to go that route. I prefer to see people work to fix the underlying cause of a problem, and THEN take steps with their doctor to work on reducing the med, after the need for that med has been improved. (This improvement is often evident by tracking the self-test numbers on the Coalition.) But I always make sure clients understand that, when they feel the time has come to reduce or remove a medication, they need to talk to their doctor about that. I explain that coming off of some medications can have adverse withdrawal symptoms or other complications; and it's important to work with their doctor to understand what to expect when reducing or removing any drug.

The main point is to go beyond simply avoiding to tell a client that they should stop their meds. I feel like steering clear of those terms is not enough. I feel like we should also be on the offensive and explain to clients that we are not telling them to go off of their meds. This is crucial because if you explain any negative impacts that a specific drug might

318

have on the body, clients are likely to interpret that as if you said, "Hey, stop taking that drug." Don't let them misinterpret this point. It's important.

Don't say - "Use this meal plan."

In some states, only a registered dietician or nutritionist is allowed to give someone a customized meal plan and tell a client what kinds of foods they should eat. Instead, I say, 'Here are some samples of the types of foods others have eaten with success while dealing with similar issues.' Later in this chapter I show you where to learn more about the specific laws in your state, if you work in the USA. Even in a state that has more leniency, I like to protect myself further and just pretend that I live in a state with greater restrictions.

Don't say - "Doing these steps will fix this problem."

Never say "this will happen" or "this will be the result" because the reality is, <u>you don't know</u>. Have you been paying attention? People are different and have different reactions to supplements, dietary adjustments and changes in their lifestyle. Individuals also vary in their compliance or ability to make better choices for themselves.

Use the language that supports the fact that you're shooting for a specific outcome, but you don't know for sure that the desired outcome will show up. This is the perfect place to teach clients that they need to monitor their chemistry to see what does happen.

Bonus Tip - Avoid Medical terminology as much as you can.

For example, I try not to talk to a client about improving their hypertension because hypertension is a medical classification of a disease or condition. Instead, I might suggest improving an Electrolyte Excess Imbalance because Electrolyte Excess is not a medical term; that's an imbalance that the medical world has not yet addressed.

On the Coalition website, we have a section called Symptoms Interpretation where we can explain to a client some of the more common causes for issues that people deal with. But we never say things like, "this is what causes insomnia." We always explain any health issue in conjunction with an imbalance. For example, when talking about insomnia with a client where an apparent Catabolic Imbalance is present, we might explain how a Catabolic Imbalance could create insomnia. Therefore, when we're talking with a client, we try to relate our discussion to the person's chemistry and not to the symptom, condition, or "disease" that the person is dealing with. Clearly state that we make progress based on the person's individual biologic identity as shown by the self-test numbers.

Obviously, I haven't covered every single thing you should avoid saying, but it's enough to give you an idea of a few guidelines to follow. Just remember that what you say counts. Since you don't know what's going to happen with the client (remember, this is why we monitor), use language that dictates that you don't know what is going to happen. We don't diagnose. We don't treat diseases. We don't prescribe. We don't provide meal plans and protocols. Learning to use the correct language is highly recommended and can add a layer of protection while working with clients.

Know The Laws For Your State

This is a topic that is very difficult to teach in a book because the laws and regulations from state to state vary tremendously. In some states, registered dietitians are the only people who are legally allowed to provide nutritional counseling. The problem with that is that most registered dietitians are all taught the same philosophy, and that philosophy seems to be effective for about 10-15% of the population. That's not great. What this means is for some individuals to find actual answers that will benefit them, they may need to find someone who can teach them ideal principles to follow instead of telling them exactly what to eat.

At the end of the next paragraph is the link to a great website that groups the states in the USA according to how strict their laws and regulations are regarding nutrition counseling. Understanding the laws in your area can help you figure out how you want to work with clients, the language you use, what types of services you offer, and what information you might want to add to a release form that you have your clients sign before working with you. The main goal is to protect yourself legally so you can continue to work with your clients. I'm going to talk about other layers of legal protection in the following section; but understanding the guidelines in your state should be the first step for anyone working in the world of natural health.

This link takes you directly to a map of the USA, broken up by states. The green states are the most lenient when it comes to individualized nutrition counseling and the yellow states are very similar. It is the orange- and red-colored states that have greater restrictions. Check out the map; click on a state to learn more about that state's laws and regulations. If you live outside of the USA, try Googling laws pertaining to individualized nutrition counseling in your area.

http://www.nutritionadvocacy.org/laws-state

Operating In A Private Club Setting

In the next chapter, you'll learn how you can save a ton of time by using the tools on the Coalition website with your clients. For that time-saving aspect, many of you are going to want to use the Coalition. Yet one of the biggest benefits of working in a private club setting is the added layer of protection it provides. Government agencies were put in place to protect the public. That is why so many states are so heavily regulated. The government's goal is to protect the public, even though these regulations may turn out to be harmful for many individuals by almost forcing them to learn from a system that doesn't work. That's not the point I want to get across here. What's important is to understand how you can remove yourself from that formula by working in a private club setting.

The Coalition for Health Education is a legal, nonprofit, private membership organization. This organization is comprised of like-minded individuals who join so they can share ideas about improving health. To work in a private club setting, I require anyone who wants to work with me to also become a member of this private club. In that way, I am offering my services only to other members of this private club. I do not offer my services to the public at all. Since government agencies were put in place to protect the public, I remove myself from that public sector and out of that formula, so-to-speak. Now that I have experienced the added benefits that can come from working privately, I absolutely would not work any other way.

To make the membership legal and binding, there is a $20 annual fee for all general members to join. They can cancel at anytime. I've never once had a client tell me that they're not willing to pay an annual fee to join this private organization. I just explain to them in a very matter-of-fact way that this is how I operate. Since I don't offer my services to the public, I work only with other club members; that's how I do things. People understand that you need to protect yourself as a professional. Since I use the site to educate my clients and help them track their self-test numbers, it makes sense to them that they would need to register on the site to accomplish that.

This DOES NOT mean that you can do whatever you want as long as you're working in a private club setting. You still need to follow the rules for your state. The Coalition is not this huge group of lawyers that will swoop in and save you if you get yourself into trouble. It's just a private club for people to share ideas. You still need to conduct yourself appropriately according to your state's regulations. You still need to use the correct verbiage. This private club is a way of doing things that adds a layer of protection.

Qualifying As A Coalition Coach

Not only do you gain access to all of the monitoring and educating tools on the site if you become a Coalition Coach, you can also receive client referrals. People around the world read our books, listen to our podcasts, and take our courses. When any of those individuals decide they want the help of a coach, they contact the Coalition to see if a coach is available in their area. If you like, you can also be added to the pool of coaches who are willing to work with clients through email when a coach is not available in their area.

Currently, the only way to qualify as a coach for the Coalition is to graduate from our Bio-individuality Coach Course. We have talked about doing some live workshops in the Los Angeles area, so that is a future possibility.

This book covers a lot of what you need to know to succeed as a health pro using bio-individuality. You can find more information in our health pro Bio-individuality Coach Course. We also require folks to complete that course if they want access to the advanced supplements and if they want to qualify to become a coach with the Coalition. The course contains tests in each section; passing the tests is your way of proving that you've learned enough to be responsible with this knowledge. Unfortunately, we're not in the eighth grade anymore and simply doing a book report on what you've learned here is not enough to be granted access. I will explain more about our course and becoming a Coalition Coach in the next chapter.

Wha'd He Say?

In this chapter, you learned:

- It's crucial to understand what you can and cannot say with your clients. Being mindful of your language is a great way to protect yourself.
- If you're not licensed in the medical world, it's best to avoid using terminology from that world when possible.
- In regard to individualized nutritional counseling, laws vary greatly from state to state in the USA.
  Working in a private club setting can create additional benefits and legal protection for your business.

CHAPTER TWENTY TWO

Taking Your Business To The Next Level

With the knowledge you've acquired in this book, you already have some tools that can take your business to the next level. This chapter covers a few techniques and tools you can use to maximize your new knowledge and to leverage your time in a way that can lead to business growth. All of these ideas may not fit your business model, goals, or personality, but it's likely that at least one of the topics I describe in this chapter will be a key factor in the success you experience.

Finding A Niche

This has happened to me, more than once, by accident. When you use what you learn in this book to help clients improve issues they have been dealing with for a long time, those clients will tell their friends, especially those friends who are dealing with the same problem. Clients with insomnia were the first group of people who started showing up at my door. Next, came weight loss and then menstrual cramps. Those who suffer from a specific issue will often form friendships with others dealing with the same affliction, and they talk about it frequently. So it makes sense that, if one were to find a solution, they would rush to share that information with their friends. That's how one referral can lead to another and all of the sudden you have fifteen new clients asking you to help them with their restless leg syndrome.

There are a variety of benefits that can come with finding a niche like this. The biggest benefit may be all the experience you acquire working with a wide variety of clients all dealing with the same issue. This is how many health professionals become a specialist in a particular field. By seeing, first hand, how different imbalances or malfunctions in the body can cause the same symptom for different reasons in different people, you can learn a lot about what might bring the best result in each situation.

As indicated above, referrals that come from friends of your clients is another plus. When your client, Clive, successfully improves a health issue, his friend, Ted, will want to know how Clive did it, especially if Ted is dealing with the same problem. Since you will have taught Clive that there is more than one possible cause for this symptom and it's important to look at physiology to get an idea of the underlying cause for each person, Clive will know better than to tell Ted to simply try the same changes that worked for Clive. Clive and all your other clients will know to send their friends to you so you can help their friends determine what steps may be best for them.

All of that is great, but my favorite part about finding a niche is that it can make it much easier to market your product or services directly to the individuals who need it most. If I want to market the idea of "improving your health" or even "losing weight," that is a very broad market. The competition in a market like that is significant, and the cost of advertising to that market can be extremely high. When marketing is not cost-effective, it usually leads to failure. However, if I've found a niche in something like bloating, not only can I target my marketing efforts to those who have shown interest in improving their bloating, I can also become known as the go-to guy for improving bloating.

It's not required to find any type of specific niche. If you help people improve their health, referrals will come. But if you happen to have more interest or passion about a specific topic, or if you find a lot of your clients are showing up with the same symptom they are hoping to improve, you may be able to take advantage of some of these benefits.

Teaching With Our Free Content

In chapter nine I talked about using our *Kick It Naturally* podcast to attract new clients. By sharing an episode on a specific topic with a potential client who is dealing with that issue, you can help that person understand that solutions are possible for many issues. This process allows you to provide hope to a potential client and let him or her know you can provide coaching through the process toward improvement step-by-step. You can also use these episodes and other content we have created to educate clients who are already working with you. Likely you already know that it's common for clients to forget everything you've told them by the time they leave your office and get back into their car. You can provide a new client, Joel, with everything he needs to improve a life-long struggle and by the time he gets home, if you're lucky Joel will recall, "I think she said something about squeezing a lemon in my eye? I'm not sure."

Providing your clients with content we've created is a great way to reinforce what you've told them. I try to send new clients a link to a podcast episode or a blog post on a topic that they're dealing with if one is available. We've created so much content, sometimes I don't remember all the topics, so you can do what I do. Go to KickItNaturally.com and type the word you're searching for into the search box in the right-hand column. If you find content, you can share that with your client so he/she can be reminded of what you explained in your appointment. Sometimes when clients ask me questions, I'll simply send them a link and tell them that this particular podcast episode explains it in detail. Sharing a podcast episode saves me from having to type out a 2-page explanation; many people learn better by listening anyway, so it helps my clients better understand their situation.

Using Our Books To Attract New Clients

We hear from a lot of coaches who are having success by giving a copy of one of our books to their clients or prospective clients. It's almost like handing someone an in-depth brochure that can introduce the possibilities available to improve health. Some coaches even tape their business card inside the cover. Telling prospective clients that they can call you if they need help implementing any information in the book is a great way to bring on new clients.

There is a special offer on NaturalReference.com so health pros can buy 10-packs of our books at a wholesale price. Our books cover a variety of topics, and our next book, *Bio-individuality*, was written specifically to be used as a tool for health pros. Since this book, soon to be released, is written in a more general manner and walks the reader through steps to improve digestion and better understand their own unique body chemistry, it's the perfect resource to attract new clients and to help educate current clients.

About Our Bio-individuality Coach Course

This *Results* book covers a lot of what you need to know to succeed as a health pro using bio-individuality. You will find even more information in our health pro Bio-individuality Coach course. Anyone who completes the course can choose to access the advanced supplements and can qualify to become a coach with the Coalition. Passing the tests in each section is your way of proving that you've learned enough to be responsible with this knowledge. Since we're not in the eighth grade anymore; simply doing a book report on what you've learned here is not enough to be granted access.

We hear from graduates of the Bio-individuality Coach Course. Some explain that they were excited about this information after reading one of our books, but didn't really have everything start to click until they took the Bio-individuality Coach Course. Comments come both from health professionals and from consumers who simply wanted to learn more about how to improve their own health and the health of their families. It seems that all of the videos, visualizations and additional audio content makes it easier to fully grasp many of the concepts we teach. Here are a few of the popular features that seem to help health pros in their business the most:

The Course Workbook/Reference Tool

This is an amazing Microsoft Word document that functions like a workbook while you go through the course, and becomes your unbelievable reference tool after you graduate. There is a different tab for each module of the course, and a search box so you can find any terms or topics quickly.

When you start working with a new client who is dealing with a specific issue, you can search for that word in the workbook and find the exact location it was discussed in the course. You can click links in the workbook to take you right to the video in the course that talks about that topic. You can even add your own notes to the workbook so you can search and reference your own input at a later time.

The Coaches-Only Podcast Episodes

Personally, I learn faster through audio and video than I do by reading. Everyone is different, which is why this course contains written, audio and video content. But these coaches-only podcast episodes are my favorite part of the course.

When talking about health topics on our Kick It Naturally podcast, we try to speak in terms of what will make the most sense to the general public. We're trying to educate consumers who want to learn more about how their body works. But in these coaches-only podcast episodes, we add a lot of content that can be valuable to health pros; things like more insights into advanced supplements and case-specific insights we've gained by working with clients, etc. It's a great way to dig deeper into the topics that you may have learned by listening to our show.

The Coaches-Only Private Facebook Support Group

This is worth the price of admission all by itself. Once you start the course, you'll be given instructions on sending in the release form that grants you access to this private support group. Here, you can ask questions, get feedback from other coaches and me, and you can even post Imbalance Guides from difficult cases. By posting the numbers from your clients' testing results (be sure to remove clients' full names), other coaches can share insights and steps that worked well with their clients in similar situations.

This is an amazing resource. Remember that the human body is complicated. It can be very helpful to gain insights from the experiences of other coaches from around the world. It's also easy to overlook an imbalance that might be contributing to a problem and another coach might point that out. With all of us working together, we can usually brainstorm a variety of steps that could be helpful.

Nearly 300 Teaching Videos

Did I mention that this course is packed with content? This is not a course you're going to whip through on a weekend. There is substantial content and a lot to learn and absorb. Most people seem to work through the course at their own pace in one to three months.

What Other Health Pros Are Saying

We've had students who were starting from scratch as a coach; they have made enough money to pay for both our Bio-individuality Coach Course and our Health Pro Marketing Course before they even finished the marketing course.

Here's what some of our graduates are saying:

"Though I have been working as a health coach for some time, this course finally helped me to connect the dots and allowed me to get the full understanding of this work. I wish we had material like this to learn from a few years back. It's finally here! So for anybody interested in this work, this course is a big shortcut. An AMAZING shortcut and a reference I can go back and review anytime I need."   - Darek from Shaumburg, IL

"The course was truly great. I learned so much, particularly regarding the importance of understanding each person's specific biochemistry. I loved being able to do the course at my own pace, enjoyed the humor and the animated videos. Keep up the great work."
  • Katherine from Dublin, Ireland

"I had already been studying this material and working with a health coach for a couple years before I took this course. This course not only rounded out my knowledge but supplied me with great reference material and ongoing support as I continue to learn."
  • Roxann from Kalamazoo, MI

See more testimonials from around the world here:
http://healthprocourse.com/testimonials/

Learn more and register for the course
here: http://healthprocourse.com/siteregistration

You even have the option of making monthly payments so you can learn and start earning more income while you're still paying off the course.

Saving Time With The Coalition Website

Beyond the benefits of working in a private club setting, the Coalition also provides you with a plug and play system for educating, monitoring, and communicating with your clients. Understand that many of your clients will have the same questions, and many of those clients will ask those same questions twelve different times. By adding the answers to these questions to your client's Coalition account, when they forget information, they can simply go back to their account to find the answers. You can even add new pre-created content to your client's account by simply checking off the right box. Guess what? It takes a lot less time to check off a box than to write out a five paragraph email. This Coalition website is a HUGE timesaver.

Pre-created Content

You can see that years of work went into putting together the content in the book and presenting it in a manner that can be understood by most people. Knowing that you'll need to teach every client at least some of the information in this book, the Coalition has done all the heavy lifting for you. Since I'm on the board of directors, I've helped put together a lot of the content and helped in creating many of the systems used on the site. That makes me sound like a grown-up.

For each imbalance, you will find a pre-written explanation of that imbalance. For each client, you simply check off the boxes that are appropriate for that client and that content will appear in their account. There is also a section filled with a variety of symptom interpretations. As I explained earlier, each interpretation explains how a specific imbalance may be creating a specific symptom. If an individual is experiencing insomnia and appears to have a Catabolic Imbalance, you can simply check off the box that explains how a Catabolic Imbalance might create insomnia issues.

Under the "Where Should I Start Section" you will find a variety of pre-written explanations for steps that could benefit specific imbalances and other lifestyle changes that could be beneficial under certain circumstances. Some of these sections even include video explanations you can share with clients when appropriate. And all of these explanations can be edited for each client. For much of the pre-created content, if you need to add more info to an explanation or totally customize something for just one client, the Coalition website allows you to do all of that.

Tracking Clients' Progress

For the health pros who have used this system with clients, they tell you that this is where the magic happens. The progress charts allow your clients to input their self-test numbers into the Coalition website and watch their progress in visual graphs. There is even a mobile app where they can input their numbers on their phones. It's this visual representation of changes that can help you and your clients see if an individual is moving in the right direction or not. This can also be a huge motivating factor for clients, as they like to see their numbers moving in the right direction. These progress charts also connect to a pH balancing chart that shows the zone for their optimal pHs (according to their breath rate) and lists foods or supplements that could help move things in the right direction.

Communicating Through Interactive Food Journals

In the Food/Daily Journals section of the site, your clients can input everything they are eating and how they are feeling. Not all clients are willing to do this every day; but when a client is dealing with a major symptom or trying to lose a lot of weight, this step often speeds up results more than any other step.

As they input numbers from their self-tests into their progress charts, those numbers automatically appear in the food journals next to the appropriate time. Now a person can start to watch the foods that they eat, how those foods affect their self-test numbers, and how all of that can affect how they feel or the symptoms they're experiencing. This is real power. This is putting individuals in the driver's seat and teaching them how to be real participants in their own health.

These journals also allow you to add notes for the client under any entry. This saves time compared to sending an email explaining suggestions about each food. Instead of typing out all those foods, under a specific meal, you can just write things like, "Did you eat this because you hate me?" You'll probably end up saying things that will be more helpful than that. But it is very nice to be able to leave a quick note that shows up on the journal in a different color so your clients can easily distinguish your notes from their entries.

Health Pro Coalition Fees

You can receive client referrals and use all of these tools in an active coaching account on the Coalition website for only $15 per month. There is normally a $495 one-time activation fee; but if you graduate from our Bio-individuality Coach Course, the activation fee is only $195 and goes to the nonprofit.

Just as we require all of our clients to join the private organization, we require all of our students to become club members as well. In that way, we're protecting ourselves as instructors, just as we protect ourselves when working with clients. When you register for our coaching course, you must also register for a special coaching student account on the Coalition. This membership level is only $20 per year, like a general membership. (If you already have an active Coalition membership, this $20 fee will be refunded. You still need the special coaching account to complete the course). The difference is this student coaching account includes all the same tools and content as the coaching accounts. You can't add new clients under you with this account until you graduate the coaching course and then activate your coaching account. However, you can test out all the tools on yourself and see how everything works. Once you activate the coaching account, the $20 annual fee goes away and the $15 monthly fee kicks in.

Wha'd He Say?

In this chapter, you learned:
- Finding a niche is a great way to grow your business quickly.
- Our Bio-individuality Coach Course can help clarify a lot of the concepts taught in this book.
- Using the Coalition website can save you time and help you create better results through monitoring your clients' progress.

CHAPTER TWENTY THREE

Marketing And Income Generation

You'll notice that in a book about succeeding as a health pro, it took me twenty two chapters to get to any type of marketing information. This is because I believe your success will come from your knowledge and your ability to help your clients see amazing results. Your reputation and the incredible amount of referrals that come your way are the best ways to create success. Don't get me wrong, the right marketing can be a piece of the puzzle and can be especially helpful in the beginning when you don't yet have a lot of clients. But no marketing in the world is going to help you if you can't help your clients reach their goals. If none of your clients see any good results, that word can spread just as fast and send people running from your door.

For this reason, I like to see health pros lay down a foundation of knowledge and a better understanding of how to succeed with each client before they start to work with piles of clients. Since you were a good kid and made it through twenty two chapters of laying that foundation, I'm now giving you a few great insights into the types of marketing that seem to be working best for health professionals in today's marketplace. Some of this information is going to be very exciting. Just promise you won't jump headfirst into this rabbit hole and forget that you still need to solidify what you've learned in this book so far. Continue to read more, listen to our Kick It Naturally podcast, or take our Bio-individuality Coach Course to continue to increase your understanding of how to get the best results with your clients. That is the skill set that will turn these marketing secrets into steady cash flow for you and your business.

Remember, word of mouth is still king. People talking about the good results they experienced with you is still the best marketing out there. But with technological advances today, there are some new methods that can take the principles from word-of-mouth marketing and turbo charge them on a grander scale.

Intro To Marketing

The days are gone of putting your business in the phone book and then sitting back and waiting for new clients to call. Have you seen the phone book lately? It's about the size of that PMS pamphlet that they handed out to all the girls when I was in middle school. People don't look in the phone book anymore. They look online. They look to their friends. More often than not, they look to their friends online.

When looking for any type of service, people want to hear about the experiences of their friends when using similar service providers. I want to know why my friend likes his barber. Why does my sister trust the roofer that worked on her house? Do my friends know anyone who can teach me how to play the piano? We look to the people we know, like and trust. We want to know who they know, like and trust. More often than not, that is where we take our business. This is why referrals are so powerful. New clients who are referred to you by their trusted friends walk in the door already feeling like they know you. These new clients have already witnessed living testimonials; and they will be much more likely to follow any suggestions you may have. They already believe you know what you're talking about since you were able to help their friends.

Social media has taken this approach to a whole new level. Now, when you're looking for a plumber, you can simply put up a post asking your friends, "Hey, does anyone have a good plumber in Orange Park?" Not only can you get input from your closest friends, it's also possible to see recommendations from that lady you met while you were waiting in line at the DMV six months ago. You thought it was strange that she wanted to add you as a Facebook friend while you were both waiting for your names to be called, but now she's given you the name of a plumber with excellent rates. Even though we hardly know the slightly stalker-esque DMV lady, it doesn't seem to hamper our enthusiasm for this referral. We feel like another human liked this plumber, so this plumber must be okay.

This is why Yelp.com is so popular. When you're out of town, and looking for a good restaurant, Yelp can show you reviews from hundreds of people. It's like asking hundreds of your friends what they thought of this place and getting an immediate response from all of them. It's social proof that this particular restaurant was enjoyed by a large number of people. It's the same reason we read product reviews on Amazon. (By the way, if you want to leave this book a review on Amazon, you will be my new favorite person.) We want that social proof. When we feel like others have enjoyed a product or service provider, we will likely enjoy the experience as well. This is why testimonials are so beneficial in our business.

Testimonials

As a health professional, people want to know how your clients feel about their experience working with you. Testimonials are another form of social proof. Here's the technique: You have to ask them. Most people won't know that a testimonial is going to help you grow your business; nor will writing a testimonial be top on their to-do list. People are busy and they have enough to worry about. You have to ask. When it's possible to include a photo, that seems to greatly magnify the effectiveness of a testimonial. When prospective clients can see a face that goes with the praise, it seems to solidify its validity.

I try to tell clients that I don't need an essay; just a paragraph will work great. Make it as easy as possible for them. If you helped them improve their lives, clients will be more than happy to provide good testimonials.

The Power Of Influential People

Another ace up your sleeve can be the understanding that the power of testimonials can be magnified when applied to well-known or influential people. This is one perk I have experienced by working with celebrities. It doesn't matter that my potential clients have never met any of the celebrities who work with me. The fact that potential clients know who the celebrities are and have seen them in movies or on TV makes those potential clients *feel* like they know those celebrities. The potential clients feel like 'since this celebrity who I like on TV' works with that health pro, he must be okay.' It's a strange thing, but it seems to be pretty close to universal.

Even if you live in a town with no movie stars, there's a way for you to capitalize on this. Even if you don't run into Mr. T at the grocery store on a weekly basis, there are still people in your community who are well-known. Every community has local news anchors, real estate agents who plaster their faces on every park bench, or even Crazy Eddie from the Discount Mattress Factory. These can all be recognizable names and faces that allow prospective clients to feel like they have a connection with you. People are simply more willing to pay you for your products or services when they feel there is some type of connection. It almost feels like a referral from a friend. Something that makes them feel like they can know, like and trust you.

When I was first starting out, I put effort into seeking out well-known people and offering them some type of barter, discount, or even a free trial—anything I could do to start working with them as a client. What's great is, when you can gain one influential client, that will often attract more.

Effective Marketing Strategies Today

Some of the most effective marketing strategies used today take advantage of this basic human tendency to spend money where we feel most comfortable. Word-of-mouth referrals allow prospective clients to instantly feel as if they know, like and trust you; therefore, greatly increasing the chances of doing business with you. If we want to capitalize on this foundational principle of marketing, our goal should be to simply increase the number of people who know, like and trust us. How do we do that? By providing free information that will be beneficial for your target customers.

To accomplish this goal, there are basic strategies and there are advanced strategies. Basic strategies could include simply creating valuable content, attracting potential clients to that content, and leading them to your website where they can take advantage of your products or services. This can be enough if you have the ability to create a lot of traffic coming to your site and consuming your content. However, I want to share some techniques that will take you to the next level. The goal should be to create a system that will attract new leads, build a relationship with those leads, and turn those leads into paying customers—and do all of this on autopilot. After all, you want to spend your time learning about health and helping people. You don't want to spend the majority of your hours working on marketing for your business.

What Type Of Content Should I Create?

The easiest way to get started is to set up a website with a blog and write short articles on topics that would be beneficial to the audience you want to attract as new customers. If you've never written before, start by searching for other blogs that cover topics you would like to cover, and start soaking in how they are written. It's easier than many think. If you've never set up a website or blog before, I will point you to our free Intro to Marketing Course later in this chapter. That course walks you, step-by-step, through the simple process.

If you're not a fan of the idea of writing, there are other ways to create content. You can make videos, audio content, like a radio show or podcast, or even hold live workshops on a webinar. We talk about all of these options in more depth in our Health Pro Marketing Course, but know that you are not restricted to writing articles if that is not attractive to you.

Simply choose the form of media that appeals to you, soak up how others have created similar content, and try it out for yourself. Getting over the fear of starting is often the hardest part, so just make a decision and do it at least once, before you have time to think about it. Once you've started, you might find you have a knack for sharing the information you have with others.

By sharing what you know via free content that you create, you're giving potential customers an opportunity to get to know you better. You're allowing those who consume your content to see how you think and gain insights into information you have that might help them improve their lives. If you can share information that somehow improves the lives of the individuals who are consuming your content, you have a better chance of turning those people into paying customers. Even without a referral from a friend, you can increase the number of people who know, like and trust you, simply by providing valuable content that improves the lives of your audience in some way.

The Automated System

Sharing what you know through content is actually the easy part. The tricky part is getting anyone to read, watch, or listen to that content. This is where the automated system comes in. There are a variety of ways to attract people to your material through word-of-mouth, social media, and paid advertising. Yet the real magic comes from building an email list of people who are interested in the topics you want to cover.

You can build a huge following on social media, but you never know if that platform is going to change or fade away. You may have learned this the hard way by putting all your effort into building your MySpace following. We put an extraordinary amount of effort into building our Facebook following to over 200,000 fans. We were literally reaching millions of people every week with our posts. Then, out of the blue, Facebook changed the algorithm that determines the number of people reached by each post. Overnight, we went from reaching millions to reaching hardly anyone at all. Uncool.

With an email list, however, you own that list. You're in charge of when you email those on your list, the information you share, when and how you present offers to that list, it's all up to you. And the best part? You can use software that will email those on your list automatically, so you don't have to manage the process on a daily basis. Having a daily, weekly, or monthly newsletter could be beneficial for some people, but then you have to constantly create new content to mail to your email list. Not to mention, if someone joined your newsletter in May, they would have missed all that brilliant content you created in March and April. That was your best stuff!

Instead, I want to show you how to create a sequence of emails, that provide information on a specific topic, and then take the reader through a journey. That journey will not only provide your subscribers with great value in their lives, it will also build a relationship between you and those subscribers, and increase the chances of turning them into paying customers. All of this can be done with a CRM (customer relationship manager). A CRM is an online tool that allows you to collect, categorize, and manage subscribers' emails and automate systems so you can reach out to potential customers without having to manually send thousands of emails.

Wide varieties of systems are available today, ranging from almost free to thousands of dollars per month. Price can depend on the current size of your email list and the functions you're looking for. I go over a few of the most popular options and give you a tour of the system I use (which happens to be the most cost-effective system out there) in our free Intro to Marketing Course at Healthprocourse.com/intro. I'll walk you through a quick overview of how to use a CRM effectively; but, if I lose you with any of this, that free intro course walks you through all of this with videos that make it make it easier to understand. I just want to give you a quick outline of the automation possibilities, if this is new to you.

Step 1 - Create a lead magnet.

A lead magnet is a free piece of content that you give away as incentive for someone to opt-in to your email list. This could be a short e-book, some type of checklist or cheat sheet, or even a free course or an educational series of videos. You just want to create something that will be valuable to those who fit your target audience. You can offer this for free and set up a form on your website for visitors to sign up to receive this free gift and be added to your email list. While visitors are signing up for my lead magnets, I like to tell them that I'll send them an email soon with a free bonus to make sure they get the most out of the free gift. In that way, they're not surprised when I email them; and they may even be looking forward to it.

Step 2 - Add these subscribers to an automated email sequence.

You can set up your CRM to automatically add subscribers to a specific list, according to which web form they used to opt-in for your free lead magnet. For example, if I'm giving away a cheat sheet for "The Top 5 Weight Loss Tricks Most People Ignore," I would want to make sure these subscribers were attached to an email sequence that would help them get the most out of that cheat sheet. I would likely provide more information about weight loss since these individuals signed up to receive weight loss tips. You can set up the sequence of emails ahead of time, and even designate how many days should pass before the subscriber receives the next email.

Step 3 - Build a relationship by sharing insights, quality content, and life-experiences.

In this sequence of emails, not only do you want to continue to educate your subscribers based on the topic of interest they signed up for, you also want to let them get to know you better as well. I like to show my personality any time I can. I want subscribers to feel like they know me. I don't want to simply provide information; I want to share information as if I were sharing it with an old friend in a coffee shop. The information in this sequence should also take things to the next level. My lead magnet should be enough to open the door; but when I'm teaching subscribers in an email sequence, I want to expand on what they learned in that lead magnet and share more in-depth content that should help your subscribers improve their lives. It's also beneficial for this email sequence to lead to some type of offer. Remember, this book is about turning your passion into a lucrative business, so you can't leave out the lucrative part.

Step 4 - Pitch your offer.

After anywhere from three to eight emails (three or four seems to be the sweet spot), it's time to offer these subscribers an opportunity to become paying customers. If you've set up your sequences effectively, and if you've prepared the content effectively, the next logical step for your subscribers would be to sign up for whatever it is you're offering. If the information you provided in the lead-up sequence helped your subscribers, they will be able to see that signing up for your offer could help improve their lives even more. For example, if a subscriber was able to learn how to improve cravings through your email sequence, doesn't it make sense that working with you one-on-one might help this person improve other aspects of his/her health and reach goals faster? Of course it does.

Step 5 - Create a sense of urgency.

If you're new to any type of marketing, here's your biggest piece of information: People procrastinate. And we're real good at it too. When making an offer, put a deadline on that offer. If you don't, people will put it off FOREVER! That's how humans work. We're busy. We have a lot going on. If we can put off something to tomorrow, that's exactly what most of us will do. Let's say that your product or service is exactly what Sally needs, and she will truly benefit in a way that could change her life for the better. Sally even believes that your product or service is exactly what she needs. But if Sally never signs up, you can't help her, can you? Have you ever been shopping for something online, got distracted by a crying baby, or maybe by a video of a cat, and then never got around to placing your order? We've all done that. By placing a deadline on your offer and creating that sense of urgency, you can help those who truly want your product to take action and sign up.

A sense of urgency can also help those who are sitting on the fence, by pushing them off in either direction. If they're not going to buy, that's okay. You just don't want people sitting on the fence; they may never get off. When I send a subscriber an offer, I'll normally follow up with two to three more emails leading up to the deadline. Not only do I want to remind them of the deadline, I also want to answer the most common concerns or objections about signing up. Many won't buy the first offer you make them, that is okay. Your offer may not have been right for some subscribers in their life at this time. You're still building that relationship; you're still helping them improve their lives; and, down the road, a new offer might line up with what those subscribers need the most.

Step 6 - Rinse and Repeat

If someone buys my product or service, I generally have my system set up to then add them to a new email sequence designed for those who register for that offer. The intention of this new sequence is to provide more content and help those who buy get the most out of what they signed up for. If a subscriber does not buy, they might be added to a different sequence that could provide them with more valuable content and then pitch another offer down the road. Once you have this automation in place, the goal is to simply add more new subscribers to the top of the sales funnel (as these systems are often called). Another goal could be to create new offers and new sequences to send new and existing subscribers through.

If this description was hard to follow, don't worry. Our free Intro to Marketing Course can walk you through this whole process with videos, and even show you how to select and set up your CRM.

Our Free Intro To Marketing Course

If you don't already have a CRM and don't already have email sequence systems already in place, or even a website for that matter, definitely register for our free Intro to Marketing Course found here: http://healthprocourse.com/intro

Not only does this course walk you through how to setup the automated email systems described above, it also shows you how to set up social media pages and techniques to attract new leads. Once your system is set up and you know how to attract new leads, you can then turn your attention to simply attracting new leads. The automated system can take care of the rest.

Our Marketing Podcast

To gain more insights into marketing, be sure to subscribe to our free podcast, *Six Figure Health Pro*. On this show, I either teach some type of marketing or business growth strategy (almost like a mini-training), or I interview a health professional or marketing expert who will share insights, inspire ideas you can use in your business, or motivate you to reach your goals. Many of our guests have taught methods you can use to grow your business, while others have shared stories of how they carved out an amazing career in the health and fitness industries—possibly careers that you didn't know were available. Go to SixFigureHealthPro.com to check out the show.

Creating New Income Streams

As a health pro, you have a lot of opportunities to add new income streams. Supplement sales can be a major income stream for health professionals. If you can learn how to guide clients through improving digestion with the supplements we talk about in this book, not only will your clients see better results, you can also turn that into a new stream of income. On NaturalReference.com, you can register as a health professional. You will then have a code your clients can use to order supplements and you will receive a commission (currently 28%). Again, you would need to graduate from our Bio-individuality Coach Course in order for you and your clients to gain access to the more advanced supplements. However, qualified health professionals can submit their certification or license to gain access to an account on which commissions can be earned for sales of the standard supplements that are available to the public.

Affiliate sales can be another great source of income. Since many health pros talk about products they recommend anyway, why not earn a commission on sales that come from your website. Amazon has a great affiliate program where you can earn small commissions on just about anything they sell. Just make sure your website has valuable content in place for your visitors before you apply or they may turn you down. We go over a wide variety of income streams in our more advanced Health Pro Marketing Course. If you complete the free intro course and like what you learn, you can continue learning in our more advanced marketing course. For now, I want to tell you about how you can create a new income as an affiliate for our courses.

Make Money With Our Courses

We now have students in more than forty countries who are teaching their clients and their followers how to use bio-individuality to improve health. By signing up for our affiliate program, these health pros are making money by promoting our online courses. Many of our students were promoting our courses simply because the courses were helping their clients see better results. The videos in the courses seem to make it a whole lot easier to understand. These videos walk people, step-by-step, through how to run their self-tests, fill out their imbalance guides, and much more. Since so many professionals were promoting our courses, we put together an affiliate program so they could make money in the process.

It would be nice for you to be able to receive a 20% commission on any of our courses that you sell. However, since I was drunk when I set the system up, all affiliates currently receive a crazy 50% commission. I know, right? We're flat-out splitting the profits with you. If you use the information in this book to improve any health issues for yourself, this process could become even more profitable for you. It seems that the coaches who are seeing the best results as affiliates are those who are able to promote our courses as "This course contains the info that helped me fix _____."

To learn more and register, go to Kickitnaturally.com/affiliateprogram

Join Our Free Facebook Marketing Support Group

If you have any questions about marketing or if you just want to see what's working and not working for other health pros from around the world, join our free Health Pro Profit Squad. This is a private Facebook support group where you can ask questions, get suggestions and receive feedback from other pros on marketing systems you're trying. I even jump into this group and provide feedback as well. Just click 'join group' and we'll approve you into the Profit Squad. Join us here: Facebook.com/groups/healthproprofitsquad/

Wha'd He Say?

In this chapter, you learned:

- Testimonials are an excellent way to attract new clients.
- Allowing potential clients to opt-in to an email sequence is a great way for these subscribers to get to know you better.
  You can get started in your marketing efforts by registering for our Free Intro to Marketing Course found here:
  http://healthprocourse.com/intro

CHAPTER TWENTY FOUR (THE SUM UP)

Review & Make Your Plan

Now What?

Let's take a moment to lay out the important points that I've covered so you have an easy reference you can use to put your plan together. I know this was a lot of information and you may feel a little overwhelmed and excited at the same time. Just take a deep breath and I'll cover the important points that you don't want to forget and a few that will help you move forward and avoid pitfalls.

You're likely excited about the possibilities and all the information you know is going to help your clients see great results. But don't forget that the best way to better understand these principles is to experience them. Therefore, this sum up is going to be about looking at the steps you can take to better understand your body chemistry, and possibly even create some improvements in your health and in your life.

You've learned an incredible amount of information so this section is where I pull a Mr. Miyagi and help you put it all together in a usable format. By the end of this wrap-up, you should be saying, "Ah, that's why that bastard had me painting his fence."

Bring It All Together

Achieving lasting weight loss or improved health is most commonly about the foods you are eating and how your body is processing those foods. Remember, you can be eating foods that many view as healthy;

but if your body is not processing those foods correctly, what you're eating is creating a burden your body has to deal with. Correcting any digestive issues or imbalances will greatly speed up your results.

Here are major points to remember:

1. Correct any digestive issues so you can pull needed resources out of the food you're eating. DON'T SKIP THIS.
2. Ensure you are pooping it up real nice. A stool that is too hard and leaning toward constipation or too loose and leaning toward diarrhea needs to be corrected. Both constipation and diarrhea can lead to a wide variety of problems for a wide variety of reasons.
3. Reduce any types of starch and sugar intake that might be causing major spikes and crashes in blood sugar. Eating in a manner that allows insulin levels to stay on an even keel can allow your body to burn stored fat as fuel. Beyond this benefit, keeping blood sugar steady can also reduce crazy hormonal fluctuations that can result from both sugar spikes and sugar crashes.
4. Don't let cravings derail your efforts. Instead, listen to them and learn. Watch your self-test numbers and take the necessary steps if cravings are calling your name.
5. If mineral levels, protein levels and blood pressure are low, use medium-carb foods to fight off cravings while you bring up your resource levels (either by correcting digestion or by adding unrefined salt and other mineral-lifting supplements).
6. Work toward correcting any imbalances that may be contributing to symptoms.
7. Don't be afraid of fats in your diet. Be sure, however, that your bile is flowing well enough to process those fats. If you're not sure, use a beet greens product (like Beet Flow) to get your bile flowing (or supply supplemental bile if needed).
8. Eat real food! Most processed foods are packed with chemicals, sugars, and carbohydrates that can exacerbate a wide variety of imbalances and symptoms. Your body may be able to deal with a lot of these downsides, but many of your clients will not have the resilience to overcome the onslaught of chemicals and carbs. Remove these trouble foods for at least thirty days, just to see how you look and feel. If you can experience this for yourself, it will be easier to talk your clients into doing the same.

These are some of the most important steps for many individuals. Since you have read this book, measured where your chemistry is, and understand how to monitor yourself, you know which of the foregoing factors apply to you the most. Since everyone is different, some of the points may not be as important or even apply to you. Remember, this book is about figuring out your specific body chemistry. It isn't about reading a bunch of stuff and then just following the summary list at the end. It's about responding to measurements. You can't manage what you don't measure. Pay attention to your progress and make adjustments accordingly. Once you see the value in monitoring and taking stock of changes, you'll be more likely to teach your clients to do the same.

Fix Digestive Issues

By reviewing your *Digestive Issue Validators* on your *Imbalance Guide*, you know if you need to put some attention toward improving digestion. Odds are great that if you're dealing with any type of health-related symptoms, you do. **Don't skip this step. You will not get the results you want if you don't improve digestion through supplementation.** I have seen people improve imbalances using only food and lifestyle choices; but very few will correct digestive issues without the aid of supplements, at least temporarily. If you're not digesting food successfully, and if your body is not getting the resources it needs, imbalances and malfunctions will be common, in most cases. Digestion is huge. Don't skip it.

Correct Your Imbalances

Taking steps toward correcting an imbalance and *actually* correcting an imbalance are not the same thing. To Improve symptoms requires correcting the imbalance that is causing those symptoms. If you take steps to correct an Electrolyte Deficiency Imbalance, but your blood pressure is still incredibly low and all your numbers are still pointing to an Electrolyte Deficiency Imbalance, then more needs to be done to correct the imbalance.

You don't want to be the guy who says, "I did what you told me to do and I'm still an emotional wreck." Put more stock in your numbers than in what you are doing to correct them. If your self-test numbers still show an imbalance, the symptoms will often still be there to go right along with that imbalance. Just because you did some work to correct the imbalance doesn't mean that you did ENOUGH work to correct YOUR imbalance. For some, it will take more effort and more time to see the results and to move the body closer to balance. If you are experiencing a stubborn imbalance, get help from a professional who can guide you or see if anyone in our free health-related support group has any suggestions. You're probably just missing a key point or doing things to work against yourself as you try to create improvements.

Monitor Your Numbers

Monitoring is a crucial step. When a person starts feeling better, it becomes easy to forget why this improvement came to be. I see a lot of clients who do the work to see improvement and then they stop doing the right things, go back to their old habits, and wonder why all of their symptoms are making their lives miserable again. You wouldn't workout for one month, lose a little weight and expect that weight to continue to stay off if you stopped working out. You have to continue to be aware of how your body is operating if you want to continue to see results. Yes, the amount of monitoring you'll need to do may drastically decrease once the body is in balance. Monitoring less frequently will certainly be appropriate once you're feeling great. But you still need to check your numbers from time to time and make sure everything is going as planned. This will allow you to steer clear of many problems.

Don't Work Against Yourself

Taking steps in the right direction is absolutely the most important way to get started. However, the steps you take in the wrong direction still count. For example, if you're dealing with an Anabolic Imbalance and implementing anti-anabolic supplements, you may not see any results if you're still eating a lot of pro-anabolic foods. Eating a lot of sugar or starches can exacerbate an Anabolic Imbalance, and could be more powerful than your anti-anabolic supplementation.

The good news for this example is that you now have the tools to correct the cravings that cause you to eat all that junk. By correcting those cravings, reducing starches and sugars becomes a lot easier. Your own experience with cravings should turn into understanding as well as patience. Exercising patience with yourself will help you exercise it with your client base.

Try to remember that there is already a lot working against you, and it is likely not your fault that you are dealing with these issues. I feel like some of the despicable farming methods used in this country have to be responsible for a lot of our deficiencies. You may feel people shouldn't have to work this hard at living, and you're right; but profiteering in the farming industry is a reality. Keep this in the back of your mind in case your issues return, so you can become vigilant again about taking the right steps. In the same way that it can be fun to grow a nice plant, it can also be enjoyable to continue feeling better and having more vitality.

Make Your Plan

If you fail to plan, you plan to fail. Is it a little annoying that I said that? Yes, it is. But if it gets you to put together a course of action, I'm okay with being annoying. It doesn't take much for life to get in the way. Writing up a plan in a notebook can help you fit this into your life, instead of allowing life to keep you from your goals.

Since what you eat counts, know what you're going to eat before it's time to eat. If you wait until you're starving to decide what you're going to eat that day, you're going to end up with a scoop of Golden Grahams in a taco shell. Once major hunger strikes, all proper judgment can go out the window. Plan what you're going to eat ahead of time and you will make better choices.

In a similar vein, grocery stores have a magic threshold that erases your brain as you walk in the sliding glass doors. Know what you're going to buy before you get to the store.

If you find that you need to use supplements to improve digestion or an imbalance, plan that as well. Most of us live our lives on the go. Burger King doesn't carry the supplements you need, so you can't just drive through and grab them while you're out. Success will take making some new habits; yet when you plan ahead, everything gets easier.

You're not going to make just one plan and stick with that forever. Remember that your plan will be adjusted as the measurements change on your *Data Tracking Sheet*.

Avoid Screwing Yourself Over

There really is no such thing as a "side effect"—only direct effects. When you use a supplement, change your diet, or increase or decrease water intake... all these things have the ability to change your body chemistry, and that change can create an effect. It's not a side effect; you did something and things changed. It's a direct effect.

I have heard "side effect" described as choosing to put up with poisonous or negative effects in order to have a particular benefit. Don't you think the better choice is to have only benefit? Let's choose the positive without the price of a negative.

Avoid looking at any changes like, "This doesn't work for me," and therefore quit trying to balance your body. Whatever change you are creating is just more information. If something creates the opposite reaction than what you're looking for, then you can use that information to steer in the right direction. If you understand how to look at the clues, you don't have to jump ship just because a bird crapped on the deck of the boat.

If you choose a course of action, and your measurements show things going in the opposite direction, try to remember that a change in measurement that goes in the opposite direction is still wonderful information. You're finding your way. If a supplement or food choice doesn't work, that information can go a long way in determining what WILL work for you. Why did a choice push you in the opposite direction? Use that information to look for an answer. Find a practitioner to help you decipher why anything might push you in the wrong direction. Going in the wrong direction is not a problem if you turn it into a clue to guide you in the right direction. If you need help but can't afford it, join the free community described below, and post questions to see if other community members have experience with similar situations.

Here are two examples. A young man by the name of Soupy was having stomach pains. (Good thing I changed his name for this book. That would have been very unfortunate if his name was really Soupy.) Soupy's body was not creating enough stomach acid to break down the food he was eating. As his food would rot and ferment, gases were created that would expand his stomach and cause pain and bloating. He started using HCL supplements and immediately his pain began to reduce. But he also started experiencing painful heartburn.

Remember, the LES (Lower Esophageal Sphincter) valve at the top of the stomach is triggered to close when stomach acid levels rise due to digestion kicking in. Without enough stomach acid, that valve doesn't close and you can have reflux. If there is no stomach acid, you won't even feel that reflux because there is no acid coming up to burn you (you can learn more about this in Appendix A, or by listening to our *Kick It Naturally* episode, *Understanding Acid Reflux, Heartburn and GERD*). If you begin to add HCL supplementation, now you have some acid in your stomach. But if you haven't reached a high enough dose to trigger that valve to close, now you have reflux that contains acid and you get burned. This can happen even if you are avoiding starches while you initially begin increasing HCL intake (as explained in chapter three.)

Soupy thought that since he had never experienced heartburn before, it must be the HCL that was giving him heartburn so he stopped using it. If he had just increased his dosage according to instructions, his acid levels would have triggered the valve to close, reflux would have stopped and he could have continued receiving the relief from his stomach pains that follow every meal for him. By misunderstanding what his body was telling him, he missed an opportunity to improve his health and eliminate a horrible discomfort he lives with every day.

Another example is what happened to Sugarplum. Yes, her name really is Sugarplum. Sugarplum wanted to correct her Electrolyte Deficiency Imbalance and also lose weight. She began using supplements to improve her imbalance and correct her digestion. She lowered her carb intake so her insulin would not spike as often and cause her body to store fat. This helped her to drop weight.

But her cravings for sugar also began to skyrocket. She had never had uncontrollable cravings before so she assumed that the supplements she was using had messed up her body in some way and caused her to be a sugar freak so she stopped taking supplements. This is a fun deduction; but, as an option, we could also use science and logic to figure out what happened to Sugarplum.

You learned earlier that cravings are mostly created from low minerals and/or low blood sugar. Sugarplum was taking the right steps to improve her Electrolyte Deficiency Imbalance; but her imbalance was strong and her blood pressure was still extremely low, indicating that she still had a low level of minerals and protein in her system. Once she lowered her carb and sugar intake to lose weight, there was now nothing left to buffer the system—not enough minerals, not enough sugars, and she was not successfully digesting protein. Cravings almost always skyrocket when sugars, minerals, and amino acids are all low.

Before she started attempting to raise her mineral levels with supplements, she never had cravings because she was buffering her system with carbs and sugars (which is the reason she had gained weight in the first place). As long as sugars are high, a person won't get those cravings. Weight gain often shows up as a result of keeping those sugars high, but the uncontrollable cravings are kept at bay.

If Sugarplum would have added some medium-carb foods (not starch) to her diet, instead of eliminating all carbs, the sugars from those carbs could have continued to buffer her low mineral content. Her weight loss would have been more gradual, but that's okay since she would also be keeping her cravings away. As her mineral content and blood pressure began to climb, she could have reduced her carbs further at that point if she still needed to lose weight. The important lesson here is not to look at the changes you make as "not working" or "causing crazy side effects." As I said, these were all direct effects—not side effects. These effects just needed to be looked at logically so she could use them to steer her next move.

The moral of both these examples is this: Don't screw yourself. Most people never have an opportunity to correct the issues that are plaguing them. Don't screw yourself out of that opportunity because you decide to ignore how your system works. Listen to the clues that show up. If they don't make sense to you, get help from someone who can help you decipher them. Stay determined and keep in mind why you started this journey. You can improve a wide variety of health issues if you're willing to do the work and stick with it. Do self-tests. Measure your numbers so your situation will make sense to you. Then, you can regulate what is needed.

Finding Supplements

Remember, a lot of the supplements I talk about in this book are not found in stores. Most products that I talk about in this book can be found on www.NaturalReference.com. Don't forget about digestion when ordering supplements. If you're like most individuals who are dealing with health issues or symptoms, digestion will be the priority and you will likely be ordering Betaine HCL, Beet Flow, Digesti-zyme, and pH strips to cover all three aspects of digestion and to monitor your progress. All of these products are available without a health coach. If you are licensed or certified as a health pro, you can go ahead and register for a practitioner account. Once you register, go ahead and email in a copy of your license or certification and that will speed up the process of having your account approved. You can then begin earning a commission on any orders placed with your practitioner code.

Optimal Measurement Ranges

Optimal pHs According To Breath Rate

Breath Rate	Urine pH	Saliva pH
Above 16	5.8 - 6.3	6.5 - 7.0
Below 16	5.5 - 6.0	6.5 - 7.0

Optimal Blood Pressure Reading
120/80
A systolic number between 112 and 130 is considered to be in range.
A diastolic number between 74 and 87 is considered to be in range.

Optimal Breath Rate
Between 14-18 breaths per minute

Optimal Breath Hold Time
Between 41 - 64 seconds

Continue To Learn

Just like anything, the more you learn, the easier it becomes not to suck at it. Continue learning. Visit our website at www.KickItInNaturally.com and soak in piles of free information. Type any keyword in the search box to see if we've covered that topic in a podcast, article or video.

What Else Are You Struggling With?

If you have other health issues you are hoping to improve, I would love to hear from you. Simply go to www.KickItNaturally.com and click on "Contact Us" and send me a message. I can't legally give you one-on-one advice. But when I hear the issues that people need help improving and the things that haven't worked for them, it can help us figure out what type of content we should be working on next or what topics we should be covering on our next show. If we've already made some content that might help you, I'll try to send you a link so you can get your answers much quicker than it took me to find my own. As a health pro, there is nothing quite as powerful as improving your own health issues and becoming your own walking billboard.

Follow Me

Join more than 230,000 fans and follow us on Facebook. Click on "Like" and then hover over that button to click on "Get Notifications." If you don't click "Get Notifications," Facebook may not share page posts with you and you may miss out on big announcements. (Facebook shares page posts with only a fraction of a page's followers; by clicking "Get Notifications" you'll be included.)

Facebook.com/KickItInTheNuts
Facebook.com/KickItNaturally
Twitter - @KickItInTheNuts

For health pro marketing info, follow us at: Facebook.com/sixfigurehealthpro

Our Podcasts

This is fun. Be sure you follow us on Facebook and we will post topics every week for our upcoming shows. You can add your questions to our posts and we'll cover them for you on the show. It's almost like you're there, but I don't need to bring extra chairs into the studio. We have a great time and I think we accidentally teach things.

To browse a wide variety of topics we've covered on previous shows, go to Kickitnaturally.com/full-list-of-show-topics/

Give Yourself A Reminder

Many readers have reported benefiting from subscribing to our free content. When you subscribe to our free podcast on iTunes or Stitcher (for Android) or to our free Youtube channel, you'll get free weekly content. When you swing by Youtube or open the podcast app on your phone, new shows will remind you to check in and learn something new or get a reminder of the things that have helped.

To subscribe on iTunes or Stitcher, download either free app to your phone, search for Kick It Naturally, and click on subscribe. If you also want to listen to our health pro marketing show, search for Six Figure Health Pro and do the same. It's all free. You can also subscribe to our Youtube channel and keep up with our latest videos here: Youtube.com/c/KickItNaturally

Help Us Spread the Word or Become a Coach

How annoyed are you that it has taken this long to find this information? Once I got over being angry, I knew I wanted to share this info with anyone I could. The best ways to help us spread the word are to subscribe to our podcast, leave us a review on iTunes, and leave a review for this book on Amazon. Those steps increase our rankings so more people can find us. If you want to reach more people that you know, follow us on Facebook and share our posts so your friends can happen upon this information just like you did.

If you want to take things to the next level and dig deeper into these principles, check out our online Bio-individuality Coach Course at www.HealthProCourse.com. With nearly 300 videos, we walk you through the process of learning how to look at other people's physiology, start or grow your career as a health coach, or just learn more so you can help your loved ones improve their health.

Register For Our Free Health Pro Intro To Marketing Course

If you haven't already, be sure to sign up for our free marketing course. It's a great introduction to a world that many health pros know nothing about. You can find the course here: HealthProCourse.com/intro

Join The Community And Get Support

Join the free and private Facebook group found here: Facebook.com/groups/kickyourfatsupport

It started as a weight loss support group, but has evolved into a place where people come to ask questions about all sorts of health issues. Just click on "Join Group" in the upper right corner. Make friends, share goals and successes, and find answers to your questions from people who are going through the same journey. Everything posted in the group is visible only to others in the group. Therefore, you can post things like, "I just pooped my pants again. Any suggestions?" and you don't have to worry about broadcasting that to all of Facebook. This is the group where you want to post any health-related questions. To ask your health pro marketing questions, join the Health Pro Profit Squad support group here: Facebook.com/groups/healthproprofitsquad

Be Excited

Right now, in your hand, you are holding answers that some people search for their entire lives and never find. You now have knowledge that can be the "cheat sheet" to helping people improve their health and change their lives. Don't take it for granted.

Final Words

For the final words of this book, I select tweed and spatula.

APPENDIX A

More Digestive Explanations

Reflux, Heartburn And GERD

Now that you understand the benefits of both acid production and bile flow working correctly, let's talk about issues that can pop up when one side is not working optimally. I'm referring to the multi-billion dollar industry of reflux, heartburn, and GERD (gastroesophageal reflux disease). The marketing surrounding these issues may mislead an individual more than just about any other current health information out there. First of all, there are many different causes of reflux; but it appears that very few cases, if any, are actually caused by "too much acid," as advertisers explain when marketing their products.

At the bottom of your esophagus, there is a little valve called an LES, lower esophageal sphincter. This valve opens to let food enter the stomach and then it closes, so that the food doesn't go back up your esophagus and burn you. Sometimes, people have a small hiatal hernia where part of the stomach is pulled up above the diaphragm. This can keep that valve from closing and can result in an acid reflux problem. That is one possibility.

However, the most common cause of reflux problems involves the acid level of the stomach. The LES is HCL activated, meaning that when the stomach makes enough HCL, it activates that valve to close so digesting food doesn't reflux back up. I've already mentioned that some people don't make enough HCL on their own. So doesn't it make sense that, if there isn't enough HCL in the stomach to trigger the valve to shut, the valve would stay open and the person would get reflux? People aren't having reflux because of too much acid; they're having reflux because there is not enough acid.

Pharmaceutical companies sell us drugs that turn off the acid, so when we experience reflux, we can't feel a burning and we assume the originating issue has been dealt with. The problem with that is twofold. First, the stomach also contains digestive enzymes that can come back up with reflux. These digestive enzymes are made to break down protein. What is the esophagus made of? Yes, protein. Therefore, using these drugs stops the burning sensation, but it doesn't stop all the damage that reflux can cause. A reduction in acid coming up could certainly reduce damage. However, it's important to understand that the enzymes coming back up the esophagus still have the ability to cause damage as well. The second problem created by turning off the acid is... you just turned off the acid. I've already covered how important your stomach acid is, how it is the defense barrier for your entire body, how it is a primary step of digestion, and how it's an ignorant idea to turn it off.

When you hear about a drug being a proton pump inhibitor (PPI), this refers to the hydrogen proton pump in the human body. These PPI-type drugs restrict the body from producing hydrogen. Hydrogen is required for the body to make its own HCL. So by turning off the hydrogen, you turn off the acid. Not only are the PPI-type drugs another punch in the mouth to your liver (I already discussed how all drugs work by overwhelming the liver enough to be able to stay in the system and do their job), they also turn off your digestion. Now, any food you eat not only doesn't nourish your body like it is intended to, but also this undigested, rotting, fermenting food becomes another problem for your body to try to remove or to store in fat cells. Pretty good little pill, huh?

To reduce reflux, most reflux sufferers can actually *increase* the amount of stomach acid they have which will trigger the LES to close so they no longer experience reflux. This also allows the body to fully break down its food, pull out the minerals and then use those minerals to make the proper amount of stomach acid. Remember to follow the guidelines in chapter three on implementing HCL supplementation. It's important to start slow and ramp up your dose. In the beginning, It can also be crucial to avoid starches and sugars with any meal where you are supplementing with HCL. Those carbohydrates have the ability to excite bacteria, causing more gasses and more pressure to push food back up the esophagus. Once you have corrected the reflux issue, you may be able to add a few starches and sugars back into meals that include HCL supplementation.

To learn more about how to improve these issues, go to www.KickItNaturally.com and search for reflux in the search box. There, you'll find our podcast episode on Acid Reflux, Heartburn, and GERD.

Crohn's, Colitis, And IBS

What about the other end of digestion? What about the bile side of the action? If bile is not flowing well enough to neutralize the acid product coming from the stomach, now there is acid going through the intestines. And why does the stomach make acid? The primary job of stomach acid is to help digest protein. It's the hydrochloric acid that breaks down food and allows protein to become accessible to the body. Think about it; if you don't neutralize that acid, what do you think it's going to do to your intestines? Your intestines are made of protein, just like your esophagus. How about that? Does anybody you know have symptoms that were diagnosed as IBS, Crohn's, or colitis? Don't you think this could be the acid that has been produced in the stomach, but has not been neutralized sufficiently in the duodenum by the proper amount of alkaline bile? Now this acid product goes through the intestines like "Zingo!" Why? Because the acidity of this product is making the intestines burn and the body is going to respond to this acidity and march that product right through the person in a big damn hurry. With this understanding, doesn't it make sense that it comes shooting out the back door in such a rush?

Beyond that, sodium likes to follow chloride. Water likes to follow sodium. So there's also going to be sodium that is attracted to this chloride in the hydrochloric acid (the HCL that didn't get neutralized). Then more water will go to the bowels since chloride from HCL that has not been neutralized will draw the sodium with its water into the bowel. It would be like the boy band One Direction showing up to your cookout because they wanted hot dogs. Not only would you have five fewer hot dogs, you would also have a yard filled with thousands of screaming little girls. The good news is, the water rushing to this guy's bowels will help dilute this acid product that is burning the intestinal walls. The bad news is, he just crapped his pants. This guy is going to have diarrhea and he is going to wonder why, when he sits on the john, it's like he was shot from rockets. It's because his body is saying, "This acid product is burning the daylights out of my little intestines. Get it out of here!"

Probiotics and gut flora are a hot topic these days. People who experience these diarrhea-type issues need help in this arena because that un-neutralized acid scorching through their intestines just fried their gut flora. The terrain needs to be right for gut flora to flourish. As you can imagine, the towering inferno from hell is not the right terrain. This is a very incomplete explanation, but it's a great visualization to help explain the balance that is required in order for digestion to function correctly. Both ends of the process are important. It's clear that trouble arises when one side or the other isn't holding up its end of the bargain. To learn more, go to www.KickItNaturally.com and search for Crohn's, colitis, or IBS.

Other Causes For Chronic Diarrhea

Most of us know a bad bug can cause diarrhea. But with chronic diarrhea that lasts and becomes debilitating, other causes are more common. The lack of proper bile flow seems to be the most common cause; yet there are others to consider, especially when improving bile flow doesn't seem to have the desired effect. Bear in mind that for MANY clients, simply using Beet Flow is not going to be enough to get bile flowing correctly if it's been backed up for a long time. Many will need to do the combo of a Beet Flow flush one day and a Xeneplex coffee suppository the next day. Some clients will need to perform this combo a number of times to get bile moving properly. Also keep in mind that the gallbladder dehydrates bile to give it greater capacity to neutralize stomach acid. If a person is not drinking adequate water, Beet Flow and Xeneplex will not overcome chronic dehydration. So always learn a client's hydration status and build resources as needed to enable this person to drink water without losing a sense of well-being.

When bile flow doesn't seem to be the problem, the next thing to consider is, surprisingly, a lack of stomach acid. It's definitely not very common to see diarrhea caused by a lack of stomach acid; yet approximately one in twenty cases will show this phenomenon. If bile is flowing well enough and if the food product leaving the stomach is not acidic enough, that bolus will now be too alkaline. A substance that is too alkaline can irritate the intestinal lining just like a substance that is too acidic can cause irritation. It's the other end of the spectrum, but it can still create irritation and cause the body to want to rush that product through the intestinal tract and out the back door.

There is a technique a person, Claire, can try if an overly alkaline stool might be the cause of her diarrhea. Claire can simply take 1 or 2 HCL capsules in the middle of one meal. Generally speaking, I always like to try to fix any loose stool issues before a client would start with HCL, but this is a one-time test. Just make sure Claire understands what to expect so she can do this test at home. A person with diarrhea doesn't want to test out HCL while on a long train ride. In any case, adding the HCL should either make the diarrhea much worse or, possibly, slightly better. If the diarrhea gets worse, that can be considered a pretty good confirmation that more work needs to go into improving bile flow or even bile production. But if the diarrhea improves, Claire might try increasing the HCL again at the next meal and see if the stool improves more. If so, that is a good indication that the diarrhea was the result of an overly alkaline stool.

The other cause of diarrhea that I consider when other causes have been ruled out is food sensitivity. If a food is creating a problem, the body may want to rush it out the back door as well. If improving bile flow and testing stomach acid doesn't seem to be creating any improvement, I like to see a client do the AIP [Paleo Autoimmune Protocol] version of the clean sweep in chapter eleven. Removing those foods for thirty days will often show improvement with those tough cases. During the reintroduction phase, if a food causes loose stools to come back, that individual can usually simply avoid that food moving forward and create long-term improvement.

Birth Control Medications

Many birth control medications contain synthetic estrogen. It appears that synthetic estrogen (or even natural estrogen at elevated dosages) has the ability to sludge up bile, therefore restricting proper bile flow. The liver is made to excrete all the estrogen that a woman produces each day. When a liver is overwhelmed and not functioning properly, estrogen excretion may not be optimal and the woman can become estrogen dominant. Therefore, the level at which excess synthetic estrogen may sludge up the bile can vary greatly from woman to woman, depending on her liver function. In any case, bile that is too thick and sticky can't flow correctly; and I've already covered how bad that is.

When bile can't flow correctly, you can't properly digest your food and break it down into its elemental components. You may also get nauseous because bile is the main method that the body uses to remove toxins out the south gate (bowels). If your bile flow reduces because of birth control meds, those toxins can build up and you can experience nausea. It's your body's way of telling you, "Look, we can't handle the food you've put in here, do you really need to keep adding more?"

In addition to turning off the body's main path of junk removal, birth control medications are often a synthetic drug or a natural hormone given in doses that are not typical in humans. In order for the dose to stay in the body long enough to do its job, it has to be a dose high enough to overwhelm the liver. Otherwise, the liver would just remove it from the body before the drug had a chance to perform its intended purpose. So, any drug can't work unless it first punches your liver in the mouth. Now, the drug keeps the liver busy and the liver can't do its normal jobs of removing toxins and properly removing estrogen. As the toxins get backed up, you get nauseous or you can gain weight since your body is forced to store those toxins in fat cells. That's one of the reasons so many women gain weight on the pill. If a birth control drug overwhelms the liver, reducing the ability of the liver to remove extra estrogen that was contained in that drug, that could result in the bile thickening more and more as time passes. The thicker the bile gets, the less it has the ability to flow correctly, the harder it is for the liver to do its job—and this cycle could continue to snowball.

Birth control meds are also believed to kill all, or most of, your intestinal flora. If birth control medication stops a woman's bile from flowing correctly, there is nothing to cool off the acid product coming from the stomach and the intestinal flora can burn up. Without the beneficial bacteria, bad guys start to take over, creating an overgrowth of harmful bacteria and yeast, like candida.

Just in case you didn't catch my drift here, birth control medication can be one of the worst things a woman can do if she wants to have a healthy body. I realize pregnancy has the potential to wreak havoc on the body as well; at least with pregnancy, 10 years later you have someone to take out your trash for you. However, there is a freedom of choice in these matters; there are birth control options available that will allow you to continue digesting your food properly.

Gallbladder Removal / Gallstones / Olive Oil-Lemon Drink

When I see a client with health issue after health issue, one of my first questions is, "Do you still have your gallbladder?" Doctors are taught that the gallbladder really doesn't do anything anyway; so, if there are stones or blockages, why not just yank it out? The problem is that your gallbladder is where your body stores and dehydrates bile; and, without the proper amount of bile, you can't digest your food completely. The gallbladder also concentrates the bile, so that when its alkalinity drops down on the acid product from the stomach, there is a good digestive sizzle. You've already learned that proper digestion is needed to obtain nutrients from your food. Eventually, without proper digestion, all the mineral and nutrient deficiencies will cause problems and imbalances. The majority of health issues lead back to digestion in one way or another. You can digest food correctly only if you have enough acid in your stomach, enough bile from the gallbladder, and bicarb and enzymes from the pancreas dropping down into your duodenum. Without your gallbladder there is no bile storage, so you rarely have enough bile to sufficiently handle the bolus of food coming from the stomach into the small intestine.

The digestive system is a crazy, complex, miraculous machine. With so many bits and pieces at play, the system is vulnerable to problems that would cause it to function below par. Do you really think a system will work the way it is meant to if you take out part of it (i.e. the gallbladder) and chuck it in the garbage? When any part of the digestive process is not functioning, troubles can show up for months, decades, or even a lifetime. You may not even know you're having digestive concerns because you feel okay when you eat (or you've forgotten what it feels like to feel good). But the lack of nutrients coming into the system, which can be created by a lack of digestion, is always going to come back to bite you in the butt. They may even literally bite you in the butt. (That was a parasite joke for those who didn't keep up.)

There is one technique that can simulate bile production from the gallbladder. Many people who have lost their gallbladder use this technique with success to improve their digestion. You can buy ox bile supplements in most health food stores. Remember that bile is alkaline. If you take an ox bile product with your food, you're going to neutralize your stomach acid as long as the ox bile is in your stomach. That's not fun and will likely make you feel very bloated. The optimal time to take the ox bile product is about two hours after a meal or at least an hour before a meal. (I've heard from clients who have experienced good results by setting an egg timer for 90 minutes after they finish their meal to remind them to take their ox bile.) I like the hour before a meal best, but it can be difficult to remember. By moving that bile through your intestines between your meals, you can neutralize the acid product coming from your stomach and almost simulate the sizzle that all the cool kids have in their digestion. This ox bile isn't going to work as well as true digestion, yet without a gallbladder, this ox bile schedule can be one of the most effective options for any type of improvement.

Many people without their gallbladder will eventually end up with some type of loose stool issue. Since there isn't enough bile storage to neutralize the acid coming from the stomach, that acid just keeps trucking through the intestinal tract. The hitch is that this issue usually arises months or even years after gallbladder removal, so they never connect the two events. Using an ox bile product (as I described in the previous paragraph) is the most effective method I know to improve or prevent these loose stool issues, outside of buying a used gallbladder from someone at a garage sale (though I'm not sure how that would work with all the haggling that goes on at garage sales). You might try calling the guy who took it out and ask him to reinstall it.

If you have gallstones and you're thinking about having your gallbladder removed, you might want to try smashing yourself in the face with a hammer instead. You may indeed prefer a nice hammer smashing over some of the troubles I have seen from people who have had their gallbladder removed. There are things you can do to improve your gallbladder function and help soften those gallstones without cutting out the whole package. (If someone told you that your big toe needed to be removed, you would make sure he knew what he was talking about; you would also be careful that you did not get a "second opinion" from some crony of the guy who gave you the first opinion. We know that because of gangrene or something very grievous, some big toes do need to be removed. But if you went into the doctor's office with toenail fungus and the doctor said the answer was to cut off your toe, you would probably find somebody else to help you. It seems a person would value his gallbladder at least as much as his big toe. I think internal organs generally eclipse appendages in value, but that's just me.) Now that you and I know how digestion really works, we work at helping the gallbladder, not removing it. Some doctors view the gallbladder as if it were a disposable Ziploc baggie that can just be dumped in the trash. You and I can continue to work at helping ourselves and our clients.

There is an old-school remedy for a gallbladder attack that still holds true today. Instructions were even printed right on the label of every carton of epsom salt. The label said, "Take 4 tsp of epsom salt mixed in warm water." This will clear most gallbladder attacks because it can squirt the bile through and clear out the blockage. Be warned that this little remedy can give you some crazy diarrhea since epsom salt is magnesium sulfate. Both magnesium products and sulfur products can push more water to the bowels, so a large dose of magnesium sulfate can create a bit of a show shooting out the back door. But an episode of diarrhea beats a lifetime of diarrhea every time. You would still need to do the work to get your bile to flow better so you can soften up those stones and keep more stones from forming (magnesium malate can often be helpful in this effort if a person qualifies to use magnesium), but this is a great little option that has worked for over a hundred years for those suffering from gallbladder attacks.

There are some great recipes on the Internet for olive oil and lemon drinks that can help clear out a gallbladder. However, if you do any cleanses like this that can also clear out a liver, and if your bile isn't flowing well, you're just dumping all these toxins into the body while the body has no way to remove them. This can trigger some crazy rashes as a result of the body trying to push junk out through the skin; or you can really overload and hurt your kidneys as they try to handle the whole load. With this in mind, be sure you learn how to thin your bile and get it flowing better with specific beet leaf products *before* you try any of those liver/gallbladder-type cleanses. You may have some big trouble if you don't. Are you listening to me right now? This is important, so please don't ignore what I'm saying and go straight for a heavy duty liver cleanse without first addressing your bile flow with the beet leaf products described in chapter three.

H. Pylori Infections & Natural Protocols

Approximately 30% of the population over 65 years of age doesn't make enough HCL. In the world of research, it is commonly assumed that this decline in HCL production in later adult life-is a "normal" and common consequence of getting older. However, recent studies indicate that the secretion of HCL does not decrease in the stomach as a person ages; HCL production actually appears to increase, especially in men. Even more evidence shows that the frequently observed reduction or loss of HCL production is generally the result of asymptomatic infections. The most common infection of this type for humans is Helicobacter pylori, or I'll just say H. pylori like all the fancy people say.

It is now a popular opinion that the older you are, the more likely it is that you currently have an H. pylori infection. That percentage goes up with each year of life that you have under your belt. For example, a 40-year-old person would have a 40% chance of having an H. pylori infection. I'm not a fan of treating according to the "at your age you need..." point of view, but these numbers do give a good indication of how common an H. pylori infection can be.

The chances of an H. pylori infection goes up dramatically if you have ever used any type of acid reflux or heartburn medication that turns off stomach acid. Many believe that it is difficult for H. pylori to colonize in a stomach with sufficient stomach acid; but if that level of stomach acid is temporarily reduced, H. pylori can invade and then find ways to survive once the production of stomach acid returns. It appears that H. pylori have the ability to crawl up into the mucous lining of the stomach, escape the acid during digestion, and then come back out once acid levels have dropped again. I believe that is why, if people with an H. pylori infection begin to use HCL supplementation or other products designed to kill H. pylori, those people will experience some improvement in their reflux symptoms. Yet, they won't experience complete eradication unless they take extra measures.

H. pylori can be such a major factor with digestion because this bacteria survives on or eats hydrogen. Hydrogen is what your body uses to mix with chloride to make HCL. If H. pylori is eating all of your hydrogen, your body won't be able to make very much HCL. I discussed earlier how countless people who are not making enough stomach acid likely don't have the minerals needed to make HCL. But you can see how an

H. pylori infection could scarf up enough hydrogen to remove an important factor in HCL production: The hydrogen.

Most of the acid reflux and heartburn medications out there are PPIs, proton pump inhibitors. They work by turning off the proton pump that makes hydrogen. Now the body can't make HCL anymore, so the person doesn't feel the reflux and the symptom is gone, just like I talked about earlier. But these drugs were actually developed to take care of H. pylori. By turning off hydrogen, you can starve H. pylori and they die. It just turned out that scientists realized turning off HCL production (and therefore digestion) could remove the symptoms of any reflux or heartburn, so they began marketing PPI products in that manner.

The compelling detail about these PPI drugs is that they can starve H. pylori, yet your odds of having an H. pylori infection increase if you've ever used one of these drugs. How could that be? Since you asked, I guess I'll tell you. It is widely accepted that most people won't start making hydrogen again for up to three weeks after they have ceased taking any type of PPI medication. This means people are not making HCL as long as they can't make hydrogen. Consequently, even if the lack of hydrogen starved the H. pylori out of existence, the acid-free "window of opportunity" is open for two or three weeks for any little critters to come in and set up camp. You may recall I talked about how H. pylori can exist in an acid stomach as long as they get in while the acid levels are low. Isn't it realistic that H. pylori could make their way back in while people are barely starting to make hydrogen again? Maybe individuals are making enough hydrogen to feed bacteria, but not enough to create the acid barrier that keeps them all out.

This lack of acid barrier can also allow other types of bacteria in the front door—other bacteria that may live on carbohydrates instead of on hydrogen. If these bacteria can flourish in the three-week window of an acid-free environment in the stomach, they can create an alkaline environment which could stay more alkaline even after the body begins making HCL again. The waste product from some bacteria is alkaline, therefore making the environment more inhabitable for them. Do you see how just having the door open can set up the environment for H. pylori to reinfect the body? This isn't even considering the fact that, once you turn some people's digestion off, they have a hard time getting it started again, especially when it wasn't working well to begin with. That's why they took PPI medication in the first place. Seeing that the body can't break down what is being eaten well enough to pull the minerals out of the food, that individual may not have enough minerals needed for the body to make HCL again once the hydrogen turns back on. This shows how easy it can be for people to lose their optimal digestion for weeks, months, or even years. No matter how you chalk it up, you can see the wide variety of circumstances that could allow a bacterial infection to make its way into the body.

You may recall how reflux, or heartburn, is often caused by the activity of bacteria in the stomach. Doctors who deal with this issue a lot tell me that, when they test for an infection in the stomach, they almost always find H. pylori and maybe some other type of pathogen as well. When symptoms of a bacterial infection in the stomach are present, H. pylori is very commonly at least one of the culprits. Other than creating common digestive symptoms like reflux, heartburn, or decreased ability to digest food, an H. pylori infection could exist for years or decades without showing any real symptoms. Therefore, this infection can very often go undiagnosed. The new DNA stool tests that your doctor can order can be expensive if your insurance doesn't cover them; but it can be nice to know if you have an infection or not. Even without lab tests to confirm the presence of H. pylori, I've seen people just use supplemental products as if they have an infection since most products used to fight H. pylori would be acceptable for temporary use whether you had an infection or not.

Before you become too aggressive toward an H. pylori infection you are not certain exists, it might be best to take steps to improve digestion. Since you may be dealing with a number of imbalances at first, the extra supplements it can take to wipe out an H. pylori infection could be overwhelming. I like to see someone first add HCL supplementation; additional HCL is usually all that is needed to increase acid production. If HCL capsules do not correct the problem and you feel like you may be dealing with H. pylori infection, using the information described below may be the best bet for you. You could also enlist the help of a professional health coach, who may be able to better understand some of your self-test numbers and determine if an H. pylori test or supplementation is right for you.

Side note: Some folks are dealing with a Sympathetic Imbalance or maybe they are constantly stressed or living at the speed of light. This stress can also restrict a person's ability to properly produce sufficient

HCL. If this sounds familiar, an excellent option may be to simply calm down before you jump to the conclusion that you must have an H. pylori infection.

Here is the complex supplementation that seems to be most effective at wiping out an H. pylori infection. This infection can be difficult to take care of. It's my experience that a few things need to be used in conjunction with each other to have a successful outcome. When fighting H. pylori, even the medical world will use two different antibiotics and a PPI at the same time. The problems with this method are: Not only are you using antibiotics which kill bacteria but could still lay the foundation for fungal problems later on, you are also turning off the protective acid barrier and opening the door for any bad guys that want to come in while the acid is shut down. I'm not much of a fan for any strategy that lets every annoying little scumbag in the world of bacteria, fungus, and parasites come on in for a party.

Here are the main players in the natural world that seem to get the best results when used together in an attempt to eradicate H. pylori:

Zinc

Zinc has the ability to kill H. pylori, specifically liquid zinc in the form of zinc sulphate. This is a great place to start. A company called BodyBio makes a liquid zinc that I like a lot. I've seen people use 15 drops twice a day with pretty good success. Zinc is also believed to be one of the minerals needed to produce your own HCL, so that can be a nice bonus. If you're using HCL supplementation, including zinc may be a good idea because doing so will give your body an additional tool it can use to make its own HCL. Empirical Labs makes a digestive enzyme called Digesti-zyme that includes a little bit of zinc. This is a great formula to use when you're trying to increase HCL production.

Along with zinc, it is also popular to use an amino acid, L-Carnosine, for this issue. You can even find "zinc carnosine" manufactured by many companies. I still like to use the liquid zinc even if I'm going to use zinc carnosine. If I use plain L-Carnosine capsules with the liquid zinc, one L-Carnosine capsule twice a day seems to be effective.

HCL

Since H. pylori are happier in an alkaline environment, increasing stomach acid is always an important step. Not only can H. pylori scarf up all your hydrogen so the body can't make much HCL, they also pee ammonia. Ammonia is an alkaline substance and can alkalize the stomach even further, totally pimping out their pad to optimize life for H. pylori and many other bacteria that would be eradicated in a more acid stomach pH.

Pyloricin

Pyloricin is an herbal product made by a company called Pharmax. It's available to consumers at many health food stores and online retailers. When you open the bottle and smell the capsules, your reaction will be, "Oh yeah, I wouldn't want to live in a place that smelled like that either, so I imagine this will work nicely." It's not disgusting to take, you're just swallowing capsules. But it does make your pee smell funky so you know it's doing something, right? The word on the street (and the words coming out of my mouth from my experience) is that this product works better than just about anything else out there.

I've seen people take two capsules, three times a day, and work through two bottles and be done. I still use this product in conjunction with other efforts I'm describing here since I don't think any of these supplements would do the job on their own. I will also add that if you are a toxic person, and maybe you get nauseous easily, you will want to start slowly on this product because it is strong and could be a little overwhelming to a sensitive person.

d-Limonene

d-Limonene seems to be very effective at seeping into the mucous layer in the stomach and wiping out bacteria. However, it is very pro-catabolic and should be used with caution. Most people do well if they skip a day between doses and use it only once a day, first thing in the morning, when we are intended to be more catabolic. d-Limonene is a natural orange peel extract.

Pepto-Bismol

What? I know, I know. Pepto-Bismol is not very natural. But it's basically just bismuth. Be sure to use the original and not the cherry flavored or any of the other varieties that have extra junk in them. Bismuth is a heavy metal that is found in our bodies already and can be very effective at wiping out bacteria in the stomach. When H. pylori begin to die from the other supplements you are using, they can often clench on to the side of your stomach and create a cramping feeling. It's really not that fun. If you feel this, you can take Pepto-Bismol which will help finish them off and relieve your cramping faster. (Not to be confused with menstrual cramps, this is not the same thing.) The cramping may still last a while longer, but using the Pepto can reduce the duration of those cramps. Since the active ingredient, bismuth, is a heavy metal, I try not to use Pepto-Bismol for longer than a week to ten days at a time.

So, Pepto-Bismol isn't one that I start off with, but I do recommend having it on hand once you start the rest of this strategy so you can be ready if you experience any stomach cramps.

Bee Propolis or Mastic Gum

I describe bee propolis and mastic gum together because they work in similar fashions and seem to be the most popular choice. I've never seen anyone with H. pylori use one of these products without improvement, but I've also never seen anyone totally eradicate the problem with one of these supplements and nothing else. I'll explain how they work and you'll understand why. I do, however, feel that they are an excellent part of the arsenal I would use to wipe out H. pylori. I just hear a lot of people suggesting that this is enough to take care of the problem and I don't agree with that at all.

When a mouse crawls into a beehive, the bees sting it to death and the mouse invader is neutralized. Now, if you're a bee, you have a dead and rotting mouse in your house. It's not like the bees can just chuck it out the back door. What they do is cover the mouse in what is called propolis. It basically mummifies the mouse so that it doesn't rot in the hive. That's why bee propolis is used as a natural antibiotic. It goes in and essentially mummifies any bacteria so it can be safely removed from the body. Mastic gum works in the same way. The problem is, H. pylori can crawl up into the mucous lining of the stomach and avoid being swept away in a sticky cocoon. I certainly believe that you can wipe out a percentage of the infection with each dose; but at the rate H. pylori replicate, I think other tools need to be used as well to take care of the whole problem. That's why people seem to see improvements when they use bee propolis or mastic gum, but the problem often multiplies again as soon as they discontinue use.

Since bee propolis and mastic gum also have the ability to wipe out good bacteria, using probiotics for a couple weeks after you are done using the bee propolis or mastic gum may be a good idea. It seems like people do well with two or three capsules of bee propolis or mastic gum twice a day on an empty stomach—first thing when waking up and again right before going to bed.

SIBO

We want to quickly cover SIBO (Small Intestinal Bacterial Overgrowth) because this issue seems to be all the rage in the world of natural health and functional medicine. It appears that all the cool kids have SIBO. The small intestine does have the ability to experience an overgrowth of bacteria that you don't want existing there, but we don't normally put our total focus on correcting that problem. It appears that many practitioners treating SIBO forget to put any attention on the actual cause. In most cases of SIBO, the issue exists because the front door was left open and hordes of bad guys found their way in.

Without proper HCL production, the body's initial protective barrier is shut off. If bacteria can ride in on every meal you eat, doesn't it make sense that this bacteria could set up camp in your small intestine, start replicating kids and sending them to college? When people want to improve any type of SIBO issue, it's crucial to first correct all phases of digestion further upstream. Stomach acid, bile flow and pancreatic secretions all need to be functioning correctly in order to create any type of improvement in the small intestine. If an individual uses some type of antibiotic or a natural antimicrobial to wipe out bacteria, but have not done the work to correct any digestive malfunctions upstream, doesn't it make sense that they could start the process all over again with their very next meal?

In most cases, improving HCL production and improving bile flow will improve digestion enough to balance out the intestinal tract and reduce any SIBO issues. Yet, I have seen cases where simply improving the HCL production and bile flow sides of digestion were not enough to bring about full relief. If HCL is able to help reduce a bacterial overgrowth in the stomach, it may not have the same effect in the small intestine since the acid should be neutralized by adequate bile flow as it first enters the small intestine. The acidification/neutralization process is often enough to keep the bad guys out. However, if a severe bacterial overgrowth already exists in the small intestine, additional steps may need to be taken to see full relief. You just don't want to take these steps if you're not first correcting any digestive issues upstream.

I've also heard from practitioners who specialize in SIBO that when a bacterial overgrowth exists in the small intestine, it is often accompanied by a fungal overgrowth. This makes sense to me since the front door was left open. If one bad buy can get in, why not let in everybody? For this reason, some practitioners have seen good results by using a cycle of natural antifungals along with antimicrobials once digestive function is restored. I don't focus on this a lot because I have found more success by simply helping clients improve digestive function. It seems issues in the small intestine have the ability of working themselves out once digestion is restored. However, I included this section since I have also seen a few severe cases that needed more work.

APPENDIX B

Intermediate Testing Procedures

Here I include procedures for intermediate tests that you can run to acquire more information about yourself. You won't need to use all of these procedures with all of your clients; yet for some clients, these measurements could be the difference in seeing real results or not. You should have already read chapters seven and eight before jumping into these intermediate testing procedures.

To get the most from these intermediate testing procedures, you need to include the results from your simple self-tests from chapter seven. Be sure to have your filled-in *Data Tracking Sheet* handy so you can include that data along with any new findings from the intermediate tests discussed here. The simple tests from chapter seven include:

- pH of Urine and pH of Saliva
- Blood Pressure and pulse
- Breath Rate
- Breath Hold Time
- Blood Glucose

Many of the tests explained in this appendix not only provide more information about the physiology discussed in this book, they could also give insight to additional imbalances that were not covered in the main chapters. In Appendix C you will learn about the Sympathetic/Parasympathetic Imbalances and the Acid/Alkaline Imbalances.

To perform one of these intermediate tests, you need to get a pack of 11-parameter testing strips for urine (the 10-parameter versions are also suitable). You can find these urinalysis reagent test strips on Amazon.com. Some brands may sell only 10-parameter testing strips. These varieties will work just as well.

If you have acquired the tools needed to run the intermediate tests, go to www.SixFigureHealthPro.com and click BOOK TOOLS to download an *Intermediate Imbalance Guide* to use for these procedures. You input the information from these procedures onto the *Intermediate Imbalance Guide* instead of the basic version. You will learn how to fill out this guide later in this appendix.

These are great tests that everyone should run initially, if you have the ability to do so. You won't need to run most of these tests as often as the frequently used tests from chapter seven, yet they can provide excellent information as you get started.

Resting to Standing - Blood Pressure Test

To get an indication of how your body is recovering from a given stress, you can perform a "resting to standing" blood pressure reading. You take your blood pressure reading two times in a row during this test.

1. To test your resting blood pressure: Lie down, rest a minute or two, then test on your left arm according to the directions for your blood pressure cuff, just like you did previously in your normal resting blood pressure test in chapter seven.
2. To test your standing blood pressure: Remain in the lying position, push the button to start the inflation again, then stand up and hold your arm still as not to disturb the machine from taking its reading. You may need to have the machine in your other hand so you can hold it as still as possible as you get up. If the tube from the cuff to the machine is long enough, placing the machine on a table next to you is the best option. If the tube is not long enough, try to hold the machine as still as possible (along with holding yourself as still as possible) so the machine will not show an error code and require you to retest. If you do get an error code, you simply lie back down, rest for about 30 seconds to relax, and repeat both steps one and two.

Since you won't likely perform this test very often, a space is not reserved for it on the *Data Tracking Sheet*. Instead, just place both resting and standing readings on each line separated by a slash. For example, your systolic pressure line might look like this: 122/130. The 122 would indicate your systolic (top) number while you were lying down and the 130 would represent your systolic number when you were standing up. Then, you can do the same thing for your diastolic and pulse numbers. If you're inputting these numbers into the Coalition progress charts, you would only enter the resting numbers there. The ideal result is to see your standing systolic reading higher than your resting systolic reading. If the standing number is lower, this can be an indication that your system may be having a hard time recovering from a given stress.

Dermographic Line

To perform this test, run the non-ink end of a pen across the inside of your arm and then wait 20-30 seconds to see if your skin turns red, if your skin turns white, or if the mark just disappears. If the mark disappears, you would be considered balanced in this test.

This is an autonomic nervous system indicator. Typically if a person's vascular system is constricted, the dermographic line stays with a white center and can indicate the individual is leaning too far on the sympathetic side. If the dermographic line stays red, that can indicate a person is leaning toward the parasympathetic side.

Gag Reflex

Gag reflex is another indicator of the autonomic nervous system. High gag reflex is indicating that a person is leaning toward the parasympathetic side. The lack of a gag reflex indicates a leaning toward the sympathetic side. No test is required here. Simply ask yourself, if I'm brushing my teeth and the toothbrush goes a little too far back, do I have a tendency to gag?

Pupil Size

Pupil size is another indicator of the autonomic nervous system. Small pupils indicate parasympathetic; large pupils indicate sympathetic. Looking at the colored area of your eye, if your pupils cover less than 25% of that space, they can be considered small. If your pupils cover more than 50% of the colored area, they can be considered large. If your pupils take up between 25% - 50% of the colored space, this can be considered normal.

11-Parameter Urine Dipstick

On the website, Amazon.com, you can search for Urinalysis Test Strips. You will likely find 10-parameter and 11-parameter versions. Either of these products will work. A canister of 100-125 test strips will run you $10-$25 and very few people will need to order these more than once. These urinalysis test strips (also referred to as a 10-parameter or 11-parameter urine test strip) measure blood, urobilinogen, bilirubin, protein, nitrite, ketones, ascorbic acid, glucose, pH, specific gravity and leukocytes, in urine. Not only can these measurements help you recognize which imbalances may be the most severe for you, but also these measurements could uncover some fairly major issues that could cause all kinds of trouble if undetected. In my opinion, with these test strips, people can uncover information that is very meaningful—all for about ten cents a strip.

When using an 11-parameter urine test strip, all of the measurements can be read right away except the leukocytes reading. You want to start a two-minute timer as soon as you dampen the test strip and read the leukocytes box right at that two minute time. Pee into a cup and then dip the strip all the way into the cup. You may have to bend the strip a little by pushing the strip against the bottom of the cup in order to get all the colored boxes covered in urine. Pull the strip out right away and touch its edge on a paper towel to wick away some of the excess urine. Read the colors against the color chart on the strip container. On the *Data Tracking Sheet,* circle the colored boxes that match the ranges on your dipstick for each reading.

This dipstick is a great, inexpensive way to look at some more in-depth numbers. I recommend using this 11-parameter dipstick at least once to get a bigger picture of what is going on with your body. Of course, you'll want to perform repeat tests if the dipstick test indicates a problem that you need to track. As I explain each parameter, understand that some of the words are all big and fancy. I just want to let you know what's available on these dipsticks. In this section, I give you a quick blurb about some of these variables. I don't spend time defining what some of these terms mean. Instead, I just let you know what indications they can provide.

Non-Hemolyzed / Hemolyzed

Blood should not be seen in urine. If it is, that could be an indication of either kidney or bladder distress or trauma. Sometimes non-hemolyzed blood can be seen during a woman's monthly cycle; if that is the case, the test should be administered again at a different time of the month.

Bilirubin

Bilirubin should not be seen in the urine. When bilirubin is seen in the urine, that means it did not go out the biliary pathway, down through the intestines and out the south gate (your butt). It is a validator that the biliary pathway isn't running as nicely as it should. Since bile flow is so important for digestion and waste removal, this is an excellent parameter to have access to.

Urobilinogen

Urobilinogen is not normally seen in urine. Urobilinogen is bilirubin that has been eaten for lunch in the intestines by bacteria. When bacteria eats bilirubin, they poop urobilinogen. This can be common if an individual is constipated.

Protein

Protein should not be seen in the urine. If it is, that can be an indicator that the kidneys may be overwhelmed. Protein in the urine can also be an indicator that the body is breaking down its own tissue.

Nitrite

A positive reading for nitrite is one of the indicators of a UTI (urinary tract infection)—some type of bacteria in the bladder.

Ketones

Ketones are produced by the burning of fat. Typically diabetics show ketones because they are not burning carbohydrates, they are burning fat. People on the Atkins Diet, or a ketogenic diet, were given ketone strips to show that they had reached the goal of ketosis, so that they would burn fat. I'm not saying this is your goal. This parameter can help indicate if your body is predisposed to burn more fat or more glucose.

Ascorbic Acid

Ascorbic acid will alter the readings on the dipstick. So while this reading lets you know how much ascorbic acid might be being excreted in the urine, it also alerts you that some of the reagents may react improperly when there is too much ascorbic acid.

Glucose
The dipstick color chart shows that some glucose in the urine is "normal." I might agree that is "common" however one would not want to conclude that it is "optimal." I don't feel it is correct that glucose should be in people's urine. Typically you see a glucose reading in the negative box, showing no glucose—that is how you want to see it.

pH
I already talked about urine pH in chapter seven. This is just nice to have on the strip so you can conveniently check pH with all the other parameters.

Specific Gravity
Specific gravity can be used to validate whether or not your body is leaning too anabolic or too catabolic. This alone is not an indication, however, it can be a great piece of data when looking for further confirmation.

Leukocytes
If you see both leukocytes and nitrite in the urine, that is a very positive indicator of a urinary tract infection and bacteria in the bladder.

Bonus Test - Hemochromatosis

Hemochromatosis is also known as iron overload. Women who still get their period regularly have a much lower risk of experiencing any iron overload conditions since you bleed out iron every month. All the same, since excessive iron levels can cause so much trouble, it's really smart to know your iron levels before you start to use any iron supplements. You can find out for free by donating blood. When you donate blood to the Red Cross, they will always check your iron levels first to make sure you can afford to give up any iron before they start draining blood out of your arm like a giant mosquito. If your iron is too low, they won't let you donate. They will prick your finger and put a drop of your blood into a little box that will output a number indicating your blood iron levels. Below 12.5, they won't let you donate. It is not likely that your number will exceed 15; but if it does, you may want to have a full iron panel done at a lab. Read on and I will provide you with a website where you can order one through the Internet, without a doctor's prescription, since it is used only for educational purposes.

There is a hereditary DNA malfunction, hemochromatosis, which is very common for men of Irish or Scottish descent. I am both Irish and Scottish, yet 23 doctors never figured out that I have hemochromatosis. Even though my iron levels were through the roof, nobody picked up on it. One doctor even asked me if I eat a lot of spinach. I told him no and he simply said, "Good, don't." That was it. Seeing that there is no reasonable drug or expensive procedure to correct hemochromatosis, it simply isn't in a doctor's ongoing education, since that education is most commonly provided by pharmaceutical companies.

Iron overload issues are not very common, and you may never run into a client dealing with this issue. I simply want to add this information to all of our titles to spread awareness of this problem, especially for males (or females who no longer have a period) who are of Irish or Scottish descent. The medical world has removed the iron panel from most standard blood tests to cut down on costs, but they will add it on your test for free if you ask. You just have to know to ask. This condition is very easily treated if you know it is a problem for you. If you don't know, it can certainly cause a world of trouble and baffle doctor after doctor, run up a six figure medical bill, and flat out be annoying.

In the past, I have used the website www.healthcheckusa.com to order iron panels without a doctor's prescription. You simply buy the test online (it will run you about $60) and they email you a form to take into the lab. You just show up with the form and they draw a blood sample. You'll get your results back in a week or two. You may need a professional to help you interpret them, but the result sheet usually at least indicates if specific numbers are high or low. If your numbers are high, the same website also has a hemochromatosis DNA test you can order to find out if you carry any hemochromatosis genes.

It's all about education. There is now a wide variety of tests that you can order online in this manner. It's very easy to do and most tests are reasonably priced. It really works just like when your doctor sends you to a lab for a test, but in this scenario, the test results are sent to the online company and they send you a copy too (either by mail or email). There is value in consumers having the ability to learn about their own bodies so there are companies that can make this happen without a doctor.

Learn More

To learn more about advanced testing equipment, take our Health Pro Results Bio-individuality Coach Course at www.HealthProCourse.com.

Sorting Out The Data

On the *Intermediate Imbalance Guide*, you see that some items have special symbols next to them. The items with a dagger symbol (†) are measurements that you acquire by using the 11-parameter urine dipsticks. The delta symbol (Δ) indicates measurements acquired with use of a special set of equipment or with help from a professional. You can see that you can gain quite a lot of info with just the basic tests that were outlined in chapter seven, using tools like pH strips, a blood pressure cuff, and a stopwatch or egg timer.

You can follow along as I go through each measurement on the *Intermediate Imbalance Guide*. Many measurements are self-explanatory, but there are a few that I describe in a little more detail because they could use extra clarification. You can then use this as a reference tool as you're filling out your *Intermediate Imbalance Guide*. You don't want to check off an item if you don't really understand what it means. Having blank items is normal and should be expected. You want to check off only the items that are clearly a problem for you. For example, under catabolic, you see "Soft/Loose Stool." Check it off only if that is something you have been experiencing frequently, over the last month or so. Don't just check it off because you went to Mexico once and had some butt soup for two weeks. In that same regard, don't say you're not constipated if you're using two tablespoons of Milk of Magnesia every day in order to see any movement. Check off only the things that are apparent for you regularly so you don't sway your "snapshot" and make yourself look like someone you're not.

Imbalance Guide Content

< less than (i.e. Pulse < 70 means Pulse is less than 70)
> greater than (i.e. Glucose > 100 means Glucose is greater than 100)
† requires an 11-parameter urine dipstick
Δ requires special equipment or a professional

Electrolyte Status

For both of the imbalances under "Electrolyte Status," the numbers are pretty self-explanatory. *Resting Systolic BP* is the top number of your blood pressure while you are lying down or resting in a seated position. *Standing Diastolic BP* is the bottom number of your blood pressure while you are in a standing position. *Pulse* is the number that comes up on the very bottom of most automatic blood pressure cuffs (for this form you want to use the pulse from the lying or seated position). Some individuals have a pulse that skips beats. These individuals should understand that this is unacceptable, even though it is often seen by professionals as "normal." It's best to regard a skipping pulse as far from "ideal." This issue can be time sensitive enough to talk to a health professional.

Imbalance - Electrolyte Deficiency

- Low Blood Pressure (Resting Systolic BP < 112)
- Standing Diastolic BP < 73
- Pulse < 70

Imbalance - Electrolyte Excess

- High Blood Pressure (Resting Systolic BP > 130)
- Standing Diastolic BP > 87

Circadian Rhythm (Cellular Permeability)

Imbalance - Anabolic

- Urine pH > 6.3
- Saliva pH < 6.6
- † Specific Gravity < 1.011
- Low Debris in Urine (This means that if you have your urine in a clear cup, you really won't see much floating around in there. Anabolic people are usually stuck in the rebuilding state, so they're not doing a lot of breaking down of old tissues or cells and the amount of debris found in the urine is much lower. You see the opposite under the catabolic state as a catabolic individual seems to always be peeing out junk the body is throwing away.)
- Hard Stool/Constipation
- Body Temp Trending Higher
- Polyuria (Polyuria means frequent urination.)
- Difficult to Rise (Meaning the snooze button might be your best friend.)
- Δ Adjusted Surface Tension > 69
- Δ Saliva mS < 4.5
- Δ Urine rH2 High

Imbalance - Catabolic

- Urine pH < 6.1
- Saliva pH > 6.9
- † Specific Gravity > 1.020
- Soft/Loose Stool
- Oliguria (Infrequent urination, or frequent but in small amounts.)
- † Protein on Dipstick (This can be a strong catabolic marker because it's an indication that the body is breaking down tissues in the body. The protein that you're seeing here is protein from bodily tissues and usually not protein from a chicken sandwich.)
- Wake Easily
- Body Temp Trending Lower
- High Debris in Urine
- Migraines (A true migraine starts in the back of the head or the neck. The word "migraine" has come to describe any really bad headache, but not all headaches are truly migraines. If your headaches start at the front or top of your head, don't check this item.)

- Δ Adjusted Surface Tension < 67
- Δ Saliva mS > 5.5
- Δ Urine rH2 Low

Energy Production

Imbalance - Carb Burner

- Breath Rate > 18bpm (The "bpm" stands for breaths per minute. Remember, each inhale counts as one. Don't count on both the inhale and the exhale.)
- Breath Hold < 45sec
- Low Blood Pressure (Resting Systolic BP < 112)
- Δ Glucose < 70 (I categorized this in the "need equipment" group, but you could do this test with a glucometer that can be purchased at any pharmacy.)
- Urine pH > 6.3
- Saliva pH < 6.6
- Irritable When Hungry

Imbalance - Fat Burner

- Breath Rate < 14bpm
- Breath Hold > 60sec
- High Blood Pressure (Resting Systolic BP > 133)
- Δ Glucose > 100
- Urine pH < 6.1
- Saliva pH > 6.9
- Type II Diabetes

Autonomic Nervous System

Imbalance - Parasympathetic

- Small Pupils
- Pulse Pressure < 37 (The pulse pressure is a measurement found by subtracting your Resting Diastolic BP number from your Resting Systolic BP number. This number is your pulse pressure. When you register on *The Coalition* and input your blood pressure numbers into the progress charts, the charts will automatically calculate your pulse pressure for you and display it on the graph as well.)

- Gag Reflex Increased (If you brush your teeth and your toothbrush goes a little further back, do you gag? When you go to the dentist, do you gag?)
- Red Dermographic Line (With this test, you run the non-ink, round end of a pen across the inside of your arm and then wait 20-30 seconds to see if your skin turns red, white, or the mark just disappears. If the mark disappears, you don't need to add a check here. If it turns white, you'll place the check under "White Dermographic Line" in the Sympathetic section.)
- Low Body Temp (Below 98.6 degrees Fahrenheit. It should probably be at least a full point below or above before you would check this box or the high body temp box under sympathetic.)
- Warm Dry Hands
- Fingertips Warmer than Triceps (This is too hard to test on yourself since your triceps are the back of your upper arm, but you can have someone grab your fingertips and your triceps at the same time and tell you which is warmer. I recommend not having someone on the subway help you with this. Awkward.)
- Allergies
- Asthma

Imbalance - Sympathetic

- Large Pupils
- Pulse Pressure > 46
- Gag Reflex Decreased (You generally don't have a gag reflex.)
- White Dermographic Line
- High Body Temp
- Cold Hands
- Fingertips Colder than Triceps

Acid/Alkaline Balance

Imbalance - Tending to Acidosis

- Breath Rate > 18bpm
- Breath Hold < 41sec
- Shortness of Breath

Imbalance - Tending to Alkalosis

- Breath Rate < 14bpm

- Breath Hold > 64sec

Digestive Issues

- Low Blood Pressure (Resting Systolic BP < 112)
- Standing Diastolic BP < 73
- Burping or Bloating (Many people don't really understand what bloating means. If you ask a woman, "Do your clothes fit tighter at night than when you put them on in the morning?" and she says, "Yes," she's bloating. As far as burping goes, I'm not talking about a huge belch. But if you have little burps after a meal, that is burping. Many people don't even notice that they burp until you ask them and they'll come back a day later and say, "Ya know, I really do burp.")
- Passing Gas
- Reflux/Heartburn
- Δ Total Ureas < 13
- Light Colored Stool (Either it is lighter than the color of corrugated cardboard, or your stool color will vary from light to dark depending on what you eat.)
- Constipation
- Urgent Diarrhea
- Nausea
- Δ rH2 > 20 or Δ rH2 < 17.5
- † Bilirubin on Dipstick

Okay, I Can Add Check Marks... Now What?

Once you've gone through the *Intermediate Imbalance Guide* and added a check mark next to each piece of information that applies to you, you're ready to begin getting to know yourself. As you look over each imbalance box, the idea is just to see if one side has more check marks than the other side, and by how much. An entire box could have almost no check marks, or the check marks could be evenly distributed to both sides. Either of those options can be an indication of balance in that area. However, if you have more check marks on one side of an imbalance box than you do on the other side, that can be an indication of an area that could use some work. You're going to have to use your judgment here. Having one check mark on one side, and none on the other side, is hardly evidence of an imbalance. I really like to see at least a 30% increase of the check marks on one side compared to the other side before I start to consider there to be any imbalance. Of course, in most cases, I usually consider measurements to be more influential than symptoms.

Don't confirm an imbalance with just symptoms. If you have a few symptoms that are common for an imbalance, but none of your numbers point in that direction, I don't usually view that as enough to point me in any one direction. I really want to let the chemistry guide me and then use symptoms as tools of confirmation that the chemistry is an accurate picture. If an imbalance appears to be strong, go to the bottom of the *Intermediate Imbalance Guide* and circle that imbalance. If it looks like you could be leaning that direction, but it's not so bad, you can just underline the imbalance to indicate that it needs work but may not be your biggest trouble area. While evaluating your numbers, also look at how far out of range your numbers are. For example, if your systolic blood pressure is 89, that's a pretty long way from 112 so you can add more weight to that particular parameter. If your systolic blood pressure is 111, yes, that is still below range, but you may have just caught yourself at a low point and you'll want to test that number a couple more times over the next week or so. This allows you to see how you're trending. Obviously, how your numbers are trending over multiple measurements is a more complete picture than a single measurement. This is why the graphs on the Coalition are so useful. A person can begin to see improvements over a longer period of time. Healing is a slower, agricultural effort compared to symptom relief.

When you test all your numbers, you're really looking at a range. You don't know if the day that you tested is an example of your best day or your worst day. That is why you will continue to check the simple self-tests a couple times a week so you can start to look for patterns in your numbers. If your systolic blood pressure is below 95 every time you test it, you know it's low. Just keep in mind that you're not using NASA equipment. It's just a blood pressure cuff you picked up at the pharmacy, right next to where they sell condoms that are ribbed for her enjoyment. It's probably not high-tech stuff or it wouldn't be sold right next to the contraceptive devices. You may often notice that you can check your blood pressure and see a systolic of 101 and then check it a few minutes later and see a systolic of 92. That's okay. Those are both low and you at least understand the range that you are in. It is the same with pH strips. You're using pH strips that are just indicating a measurement that you're interpreting through a color, you're not using a pH meter that's accurate to the hundredth.

Conclusions

Once you've completed this process, make your conclusions just like you did in chapter eight. The only difference is you now have more data to guide your decision-making process. In Appendix C you can read more details about all of the imbalances covered in this section.

APPENDIX C

Imbalances

I like to include an explanation of all ten imbalances in the appendix of all of my books. This allows you to use this section as a reference source and gives me the chance to cover any imbalances that may not be covered from book to book. With that in mind, some of this material may be review for you. However, since I didn't yet cover four of the imbalances in this book, I include explanations of the Sympathetic and Parasympathetic Imbalances and the Acid and Alkaline Imbalances here.

Electrolyte State

The electrolyte status is defined by blood pressure (although a graduate of our Bio-individuality Coach Course may have equipment that can look at other variables in this equation, like conductivity of urine and saliva). In the world of natural health, where the terrain of the body gives so many insights into how the body is functioning, if an imbalance can exist in one direction, there must be an opposite to that imbalance. Otherwise, there would be no middle ground, no place where the body could be considered "balanced." Seems reasonable, right?

Imbalance - Electrolyte Deficiency

Very few doctors ever complain about your blood pressure being low. Since there is no drug that is labeled for low blood pressure, the ramifications are not in their training. We all know that high blood pressure can cause heart attacks and strokes (blowouts). When they say your blood pressure is great even though it's too low, they're saying that you'll never have a blowout. But is it fun to run around on flat tires all day? An optimal blood pressure reading is said to be 120 over 80. So, if 140 over 90 is considered high blood pressure in the medical world, wouldn't having those numbers off by the same amount in the other direction be regarded as low blood pressure? Shouldn't a reading of 100 over 70 be considered low?

When blood pressure is low, this is often a reflection of low mineral and protein levels in the bloodstream. When blood pressure is low, it can be a reflection of a decrease in your salts or the vascular system being too open (dilated). Our mineral content not only comes from actual salt, but from our food too. If your digestion is not working properly, you can't assimilate the minerals from the food you're eating and the mineral content in your system can decrease. (I went over this in more detail when I talked about digestion in chapter three.) There are a few other possible contributing factors that can result in low blood pressure. In most cases, however, digestion is the most prevalent contributing factor to low blood pressure. When we see low blood pressure, for example, anything lower than a systolic reading (the top number) of 112 and a diastolic reading (the bottom number) lower than 73, we consider that there is likely an Electrolyte Deficiency Imbalance present.

The minerals or salts in the system represent the conductivity, the ability for electricity to flow through the system. When the mineral content is low, there's no spark; and energy can be low. Without this energy, the brain can't function at its full potential, a result created by the lack of minerals required for signals to travel through. Many people with depression and some other manifestations of "mental illness," are often just cases where there is not enough mineral in the system. Low blood pressure often means there's not enough spark to give the brain what it needs to function correctly and/or there is not enough mineral to control blood pH sufficiently.

Possible symptoms that can show up with an Electrolyte Deficiency Imbalance:
- chronic fatigue
- low blood pressure
- menstrual cramps
- poor circulation
- decreased libido
- depression or anxiety
- vertigo or dizziness when standing

- cravings
- insomnia

Imbalance - Electrolyte Excess

If an Electrolyte Deficiency Imbalance normally indicates a lack of electrolytes, the opposite would be a state where too many electrolytes are present. This is called an Electrolyte Excess Imbalance.

In general, high blood pressure can be an expression of insufficient or lousy kidney function. This means that, when excessive electrolytes start concentrating in the bodily fluids, it's usually a result of insufficient hydration (not drinking enough clean water) or impaired excretion of mineral salts through the kidneys. High blood pressure can also result from a constricted vascular system. In any case, electrolyte stress can lead to hypertension (high blood pressure) and other circulatory and cardiovascular problems. A vascular system that is constricted often points to an autonomic nervous system issue or a buildup on the arterial walls. (I talk more about the autonomic nervous system in the section about Sympathetic and Parasympathetic Imbalances later in this appendix.)

Stiffening arterial walls can lift pulse pressure, which is the difference between the systolic and diastolic blood pressure numbers. When the pulse pressure becomes greater and greater as the arterial walls become stiffer and stiffer, the heart becomes weaker and weaker. If you are a person with high blood pressure who is trying to bring it down naturally, watching the pulse pressure correct itself helps to validate that you are doing the right thing. Remember, *The Coalition for Health Education* has a tool that calculates your pulse pressure for you so you can just monitor the changes without worrying about the math.

Possible symptoms that can show up with an Electrolyte Excess Imbalance:
- high blood pressure
- hardening of the arteries
- heart attack
- stroke
- poor circulation
- inability to properly transport oxygen, nutrients, waste products, antibodies and more, throughout your system

Catabolic/Anabolic States

At the cellular level, the body is always in an anabolic state, a catabolic state, or in the process of switching back and forth between the two. During the day, our cell membranes are intended to open up (much like a flower) so nutrients can get in and out more easily. This "more open" state is called a catabolic state. At night, our cell membranes are intended to become more closed (again, like a flower) so nutrients cannot get in and out as easily. This "more closed" state is called an anabolic state. Cells don't actually open and close like a flower, this is just a basic view that allows us to talk about the different states of our cells. Both states are appropriate, and even necessary, for a body to function optimally. Due to many possible factors, some people can get stuck in one state and their body will not switch back and forth as intended.

When the body operates correctly, we oscillate back and forth from the anabolic state at night, while we sleep, and a catabolic state during the day, while we're active. Without this natural oscillation, many problems can occur. When the body shifts from anabolic to catabolic, that's when the endorphins in the brain are released, which can help people from becoming depressed. Though there are many other factors that commonly contribute to depression, you see that this natural oscillation between the anabolic and catabolic states can be important.

Imbalance - Anabolic

First of all, there are many benefits that take place while a body is in an anabolic state. This is the state where the body engages in most of its repairing and rebuilding processes. You've probably heard the word anabolic in reference to steroids. Weightlifters take anabolic steroids in order to be in the tissue building, anabolic state when they are not playing fair with muscle building.

While an anabolic state can have its benefits, any state can cause problems when pushed to an extreme. Although it is very appropriate for the cells to be in an anabolic state at night, some individuals stay in a more anabolic state most of the time. These individuals are said to be experiencing an Anabolic Imbalance.

If you're stuck in an anabolic state most of the time, it can be very hard to get up in the morning because your body, at the cellular level, is actually still in sleep mode. In the same way that many people who suffer from insomnia are stuck in a catabolic state where their body is always awake, anabolic people can have a hard time getting their bodies in motion in the morning. The snooze button can be their best friend. Be sure to understand, however, that everyone who experiences insomnia is not necessarily stuck in a catabolic state. There are aspects to an Anabolic Imbalance that can also cause insomnia for totally different reasons. You can learn more about insomnia by going to www.KickItNaturally.com and searching for our insomnia podcast episode. Please don't think that, if you suffer from insomnia, you must not have an Anabolic Imbalance because a Catabolic Imbalance is only one possible cause for insomnia. There are insomnia cases that exist quite well in an anabolic state too. Also, don't think that if you pop right out of bed in the morning that you can't have an Anabolic Imbalance. Remember, imbalances can show their heads in different ways for different people. There are no "rules" to follow, only guidelines to help you along.

This Anabolic Imbalance can also cause constipation by sending too much of the body's water to the kidneys and not enough to the bowels, making the stool harder and more difficult to move. An Anabolic Imbalance can also cause individuals to pee high volumes of urine frequently throughout the day. They will often have to get up in the middle of the night to tinkle.

Possible symptoms that can show up with an Anabolic Imbalance:
- constipation or hard stool
- tachycardia (rapid heart rate)
- anxiety/panic attacks
- frequent urination
- difficulty waking in the morning
- viral problems

Be sure not to just assume you have an imbalance because you're experiencing some (or even all) of the symptoms that commonly show up with that imbalance. Without looking at your specific chemistry, and without understanding how your body is operating, and without determining what is causing your issues, you're really just throwing darts while blindfolded when you try to treat symptoms without putting them in context of objective numbers.

When it comes to cellular permeability, the catabolic state is the opposite of the anabolic state. It's the other side of the coin. The catabolic state is where the body kind of "breaks down and cleans house," so to speak. In a catabolic state, the body is primed to use oxygen to create energy, so it is appropriate to be in a catabolic state during your waking hours to keep you going all day. This, along with what I just explained about the anabolic state, helps to show how both the anabolic and catabolic states are appropriate during the appropriate (day and night) times. However, in the same way that I talked about people who lean too anabolic, some individuals will stay in a more catabolic state most of the time. These individuals are said to be experiencing a Catabolic Imbalance.

If someone is stuck in a catabolic state, the cell membranes can become too permeable and this individual will often burn up muscle and protein and even membrane fats. Breaking down tissues and muscle so they can be rebuilt is a beneficial aspect of the catabolic state, but when a person is in that state too often and for too long, that "cleaning house" process can turn into a body that is flat out falling apart. The more muscle we lose, the lower our metabolism, and we may burn less fat.

Insomnia is very common with a Catabolic Imbalance because the cell membranes appear to be more permeable, which is a characteristic of the daytime state. These people can't sleep because their bodies are still awake and operating at full speed. Most sleeping aids will knock you out in the head so you can sleep, but your body will still be wide awake all night. As a result, you might either wake up exhausted or you become tired again a few hours after waking.

Possible symptoms that can show up with a Catabolic Imbalance:
- insomnia
- migraines
- chronic diarrhea or loose stool
- hair falling out
- muscle loss
- chronic pain
- loss of connective tissue or difficulty in healing
- aging quickly
- joint and muscle pain; arthritis (especially rheumatoid)

- oliguria (insufficient urination, perhaps often but in small amounts)
- low body temperature
- bacterial problems

Since an overly catabolic state is sometimes described as a lack of sterols at the cellular level, increasing your intake of sterols and saturated fatty acids, such as real butter or coconut oil, can be one method to help improve this imbalance. However, I find that most individuals with this imbalance also need to use more nutrients like specific vitamins, minerals and amino acids in order to see lasting improvement. That being said, increasing your sterol intake while optimizing digestion can be a great place to start.

Energy Production

The next two imbalances I cover are Fat Burner Imbalance and Carb Burner Imbalance. These deal with energy production and how the body uses food for fuel. Before I explain energy production, understand that I will be leaving out complicated methods the body can use to create energy. This is not an exhaustive explanation.

To create energy, simply speaking, our bodies burn either fat or glucose. Your body is designed to burn both types of fuel for different purposes. Despite that, changes can occur in our bodies or in our lives that will train our bodies to prefer one fuel over the other. In time the body may stop burning the other type of fuel almost entirely. This is another reason why there is no such thing as the diet that is right for everyone. It doesn't exist. Some people burn fats much better than glucose and some people are the opposite. This really puts all these arguments into perspective about "low-carb," "low-fat," "high-protein," "the drunk diet," "I only eat things that start with the letter F..." I could go on for days. They're still all going to be wrong for most folks. In order to find the right "diet," you really need to look at a person's digestive capacity and biological individuality, because each person processes foods differently.

Imbalance - Carb Burner

Carb Burners are people who are predisposed to burn off all their glucose and do not seem to burn fat very well. Now, it's not that they won't burn fat, but they will always prefer to burn off all their glucose first. This is commonly referred to as hypoglycemia. Just keep in mind that the hypoglycemic can also be a step away from becoming diabetic. "But if he's hypoglycemic, how can he be a step away from becoming diabetic?" It's because many hypoglycemics have way too much insulin in the system and their system responds as though there are five furnaces in the house. Every time the house gets cold, instead of one furnace coming on and slowly warming up the house and then turning off, FIVE furnaces turn on and the house is hot enough to make you cuss by the time the furnaces shut down.

A Carb Burner's insulin can work like too many furnaces. These individuals have become insulin resistant, but they have not been insulin resistant long enough that the cells have stopped responding to the insulin altogether. They're at that stage where the cells are still responsive enough to the insulin that, when the pancreas produces up to five times the amount of insulin it normally would, the insulin reaches a critical level and all the sugar goes into the cells very quickly. These people can get very severe headaches in the front of their heads. They may also complain that their head feels full or they'll get fuzzy brained; this is due to the blood sugar dropping far too rapidly. Using a blood sugar glucometer periodically through the day can quantify that the blood glucose has gone too low. This low blood sugar can make these folks extremely miserable, and being around them when blood sugar levels drop can be equally miserable. If you live with, or if you are this person, you know exactly what I'm talking about.

Possible symptoms that can show up with a Carb Burner Imbalance:
- lack of energy; physical and mental fatigue
- high or low blood sugar
- shortness of breath
- high cholesterol
- overweight or underweight
- irritable when hungry

Imbalance - Fat Burner

If you find that you show indications of having a Fat Burner Imbalance, you most likely are burning much more fat than glucose. If you also have high cholesterol, high triglycerides and a high fasting glucose, any of these markers can be another indication that you are not processing glucose effectively.

Many individuals who are overweight and have this imbalance will ask, "How is it that I'm burning mostly fat but I'm still so fat?" This is because their bodies are turning almost every carb and sugar that they eat into fat. In order to process sugar or glucose, the body is having to take all sugar or glucose coming in and turn it into fat before it is able to be "burned" for energy.

Possible symptoms that can show up with a Fat Burner Imbalance:
- lack of energy; physical and mental fatigue
- Type II Diabetes
- metabolic syndrome (or insulin resistance)
- high blood pressure or cardiovascular disease
- weight gain
- gallbladder trouble
- high triglycerides

You may have noticed Type II Diabetes on the list above. This doesn't mean that if you have a Fat Burner Imbalance that you're diabetic. It just means that in this fat burning state, the body prefers to burn fat and can often move into a predicament where it will burn very little glucose, if any. In these cases, glucose can accumulate in the bloodstream and, abracadabra, you're insulin resistant and type II diabetic. Remember, I am only describing an imbalance in this section and not a disease. However, a neglected imbalance certainly can manifest itself eventually as a disease, just like neglecting to change the oil in your engine can manifest itself as a blown up engine.

By improving this imbalance and allowing the body to once again process both types of fuel, a person could increase energy and lose some weight, since such a large percentage of glucose would no longer need to be stored as fat.

Autonomic Nervous System

Sympathetic Dominance refers to the autonomic nervous system (ANS). The ANS is a mechanism in the body that happens without having to consciously think about it. You don't have to think about whether your heart is beating, it just does. The other side of the nervous system is the Parasympathetic Dominance.

The sympathetic side is the speed side—the fight-or-flight stress response. The parasympathetic side is the slow side—the rest-and-digest state. These two systems are hard-wired, in a sense, to the heart, to the entire digestive system, and to all the lower level glands, organs and systems.

Imbalance - Parasympathetic

A Parasympathetic Imbalance is often where I find individuals who suffer from allergies or asthma. This can be a tricky imbalance because if an individual has a strong ANS imbalance, especially on the parasympathetic side, that person can often see a response that is opposite of what is expected when working to balance the body. For example, if a specific food or supplement tends to push one measurement, like urine pH, down for most people, that same food or supplement could actually push up that measurement for a parasympathetic dominated person. I've never heard a good explanation as to why this can occur for some, but it seems the defense system and immunological issues affect this anomaly. It is seen frequently enough in parasympathetics that you need to know this anomaly exists. That is why learning to monitor your body is so important. Monitoring your body will also alert you when the time has come to get the help of a professional who understands the wide variety of nuances that can occur when looking at layer upon layer of imbalances and their priorities in the body.

Possible symptoms that can show up with a Parasympathetic Imbalance:
- allergies
- asthma
- small pupil size
- frequent urination
- increased saliva
- muscle cramps at night
- eyes or nose watery
- eyelids swollen
- gag easily
- poor circulation

Imbalance - Sympathetic

The sympathetic side of the ANS is reactive. As a stress situation presents itself, the system turns on, does its job, and in doing so possibly pushes to the outer bounds of homeostasis (perfect balanced health). Because of this action of the ANS, other systems in the body can be deprived and suffer. Not unlike the transmission in your car, systems in the body can "lock up," fail to relax, and become stuck in a gear, thus causing a myriad of symptoms that seem to defy logic. The stress situations that are instigating the reaction of the ANS could be emotional, nutritional, or mineral in origin. If individuals are stuck in a sympathetic state, they can feel stressed and on edge, and can even have trouble sleeping since they are stuck in fight-or-flight mode.

Possible symptoms that can show up with a Sympathetic Imbalance:
- large pupil size
- low levels of urination
- increased temperature
- sweaty hands
- dry mouth/eyes/nose
- get chills often
- cold extremities (like hands or feet)
- unable to relax
- irritated by strong light

pH Balance - Acid/Alkaline Imbalances

Everybody just calm down. This can be a very hot topic in the world of natural health. If this book is your first taste of natural health, this section may open your eyes to some incredible things. Kind of like the series LOST, but this will actually make sense. However, if you have already read, or have been introduced to, information about the pH of the body, I may need to spend time fixing the damage that some other numskulls have created.

The bloodstream has a very narrow pH value that it must stay within in order for our bodies to function properly. If the blood moves too far acid or too far alkaline, we can literally die. The body doesn't want this to happen, so it does whatever it can to keep the bloodstream at a balanced pH level.

In the natural world, when people talk about pH, they frequently talk about how we all need to "alkalize." "Alkalize, alkalize, alkalize." "Alkalize or die a slow, miserable death," they tell us. These pH "gurus" explain how we are all too "acid" and it's killing us one by one. Of course, when someone follows these approaches and tries to alkalize themselves, and they completely fall apart, the guru tells them, "That's okay, you're going through a 'healing crisis'. Just stick to it and you'll be fine." No, what we're going through is a guru crisis. There currently appears to be a crisis where a few gurus need to be punched in the neck so maybe they will stop ruining the well-being of half of their readership.

These readers who started to fall apart after "alkalizing" themselves were likely falling apart because they were pushing an imbalance that already existed even further over the edge. Remember how I talked about the fact that an imbalance can't exist unless there is an equal imbalance in the other direction? If someone told you one pair of glasses will fix everyone's vision, you would question his intelligence or just poke him in the eye. We all know that reading glasses can help farsighted people while nearsighted individuals need the very opposite type of lens. Any author who tells the reader that EVERYONE should do ANYTHING is trying to sell something.

The haphazard confusion starts here: Some individuals truly are too "acidic." I talk about what this means in just a moment. For now, I'm going to continue using the same ignorant terminology that most of the pH gurus use. When individuals have an Acid Imbalance, and they truly can benefit from "alkalizing" themselves, these individuals can follow the instructions laid out by a pH guru and they may see tremendous improvement to their health, or at least to their well-being. In some cases, these results could even be considered miraculous. Still, let's just calm down for a minute. If we know that every imbalance (like an Acid Imbalance) has an opposite imbalance in the other direction, what are these pH gurus doing to the people who have an Alkaline Imbalance (the opposite of an Acid Imbalance)? They're making these individuals miserable and calling it a "healing crisis." That's what they're doing.

To go right along with all of the pH and alkalizing books and experts out there, we also find shelves upon shelves of "alkalizing" products in every health food store. You can't throw a stick down the aisle of a health food store without hitting a product that boasts its ability to improve your health through alkalizing. (By the way, if you do this, the employees will come right up to you and ask you not to throw sticks in their store anymore... like I'm the one doing something wrong here.) It is also likely that these products will increase in popularity since many people will reap benefits from their use... many people with an acidity issue, that is. To understand the tragedy in this, let's go over the Acid and Alkaline Imbalances.

The most important thing to understand is this: When I discuss an Acid or Alkaline Imbalance in any book I write, I am talking about <u>blood pH</u>. Measuring <u>urine pH and saliva pH</u> in a context of breath rate and breath hold can be incredibly insightful and useful, but urine pH or saliva pH are not always an indication of the pH of the blood, as many pH gurus will have you believe. It's a nice story, it just happens to be a fictional one. I already showed you how to measure urine pH and saliva pH. For now, I'm just going to dig into *blood pH* since this *is the crucial parameter when looking at an Acid or Alkaline Imbalance.*

Imbalance - Tending to Alkalosis

Alkalosis is an imbalance where the bloodstream is too alkaline. When the blood leans alkaline, oxygen can't leave the bloodstream and go to the tissue level where it needs to be to help your body create the energy required to run properly. In science, this is known as the Bohr Effect.

If a doctor checked your oxygen levels, he would put a device called a pulse oximeter on you and he might tell you that your oxygen is great... you have plenty of oxygen. But, if the bloodstream is too alkaline, the oxygen cannot be released from the bloodstream and go into the tissues where it can be used. The result: You can feel wiped out. The oxygen is there, it just can't get to the right location in order to be properly utilized. In an effort to correct this, when the bloodstream is too alkaline, the body will slow the rate at which you breathe. Carbon dioxide (CO_2) is acid inducing to the bloodstream so the body tries to reduce the amount that you breathe in order to hold on to more CO_2, allowing it to acidify the bloodstream. Pretty neat trick Mother Nature came up with, don't you think? By using the CO_2 to acidify a bloodstream that is too alkaline, some oxygen can be released from the bloodstream and can make it to the tissue level.

Possible symptoms that can show up with an Alkaline Imbalance:
- chronic fatigue
- sleep apnea
- joint and muscle pain; arthritis

- allergies; asthma
- muscle cramps
- fluid retention

In regard to sleep apnea, many cases are caused by structural issues (such as a flap that doesn't seem to be flapping correctly); yet almost as many are caused by a bloodstream that is too alkaline. The breath rate drops so low due to an overly alkaline bloodstream that eventually the body says, "I'm gonna acidify this bloodstream and get some oxygen down to the tissues where it needs to be even if it kills this guy," and this would show itself as sleep apnea symptoms.

By looking at all the trouble an overly alkaline bloodstream can cause, do you see how important it is to look at people as individuals and measure where they are before you start blabbing about how everyone needs to alkalize? Just because something brings about an amazing result for one person, doesn't mean that it's not going to turn someone else into a zombie. This is another example of how people are different. Why is that so hard for many people to grasp? I've met individuals who can't get enough Maury Povich; yet if you forced me to watch that show, I might not ever talk to you again. We know people are different in their preferences; if they weren't, how would John Tesh have a fan base at all? Since people can have different tastes, doesn't it make sense that they could have different chemistry as well?

Imbalance - Tending to Acidosis

The physiology in a person with Acidosis problems expresses too much acid (or H+) in the bloodstream. One cause can be an imbalance in potassium, or an inability of the kidneys to properly excrete the acid— and balance is lost. The breath rate in these individuals becomes accelerated because the kidneys, being unable to easily control the acid level in the bloodstream, can be helped by the lungs huffing off CO_2, because CO_2 acidifies the bloodstream. These individuals normally have a short breath-holding time and a rapid breathing rate, exposing the fact that the kidneys are not having an easy time controlling the pH of the blood. This can be remedied (depending on the cause) by assisting the system to buffer the acids more effectively and excreting them. This is not just a failure to excrete acids, it's also a failure to buffer them. This helps us to understand why using foods or supplements in an effort to "alkalize" an individual can be so beneficial. This is how a pH guru can hit home runs with some people who will then think he is so brilliant. These people with the overly acid issues can really benefit by increasing the nutrients that can be used to buffer these acids. Even a broken clock is right twice a day.

An inability to properly digest protein can often be an issue in these cases since the biggest buffer of acids in the body is protein. Obviously, it is more profitable for the industry to sell green drinks and alkalizing supplements than it is to help people better digest their protein. Yet, in some cases, simply improving protein digestion can be a great step toward giving the body the tools it needs to buffer those acids on its own.

Possible symptoms that can show up with an Acid Imbalance:
- shortness of breath
- rapid heart rate
- poor retention of important mineral nutrients
- fluid retention
- poor function of your kidneys, lungs, adrenal glands and many other organs and glands
- digestive issues

Alkalizing Water And Water Filters

The first step in digging through this dung is to remember that some individuals have an Acid Imbalance. Their blood is tending toward being too acid. If this is you, one of these alkalizing water filters could certainly help you feel better if it was pushing your blood to a more balanced state. You would know if it was working or not if your breath rate started to come down. In this scenario, you would start to feel better and would tell all of your friends it was because of the "magic water" that was coming out of your water filter and you're so excited because you only have sixty-three more monthly payments before it is paid off.

Let's not stop there. To a lot of my clients, I will hold up a bottle and say, "Have you heard of this? It's called WATER!" because it's so obvious that they're not drinking any. Water is one of the most important components of our health and yet so few people drink enough to help their bodies wash out all the junk. They think that if they're drinking a soda or coffee, that's enough. "It has water in it," they tell me. But soda, coffee, and sport drinks are hardly a replacement for water. None of those beverages have the ability to truly hydrate the cells like water can. Most of those drinks just introduce more junk into the body rather than giving your body what it needs to wash junk out. But tell me this: If a guy pays $3000 for a water filter, do you think he might drink some water? You bet he will! He'll probably go fill up a glass every time he opens his checkbook or checks his bank statement. "Where the hell did all my money go? Oh yeah, I guess I should go get a glass of water."

When you take a person who hasn't been drinking any water, and you start getting H2O down his gullet, that can often be enough to turn his whole world around. You start to hydrate the body, you start to clear out junk. Pounds get dropped, joints become more flexible, all sorts of happy stuff can happen—just by adding some water. Too bad... he could have done the same thing with a ninety-nine cent jug of spring water.

I'll call this water filter mortgaging consumer "Bill." Bill tells his friend Tanya about this filter and talks her into buying too. (Certainly this is just about her health and has nothing to do with the fact that Bill will be making multilevel marketing money off of Tanya's purchase.) But Tanya starts to feel worse. She's exhausted and finds it easier to just sit on the couch all day. If you checked Tanya's breath rate you might see that it's around eight inhalations per minute. With a breath rate that low, it could be that Tanya's blood is leaning too alkaline and this alkalizing water is pushing that imbalance further into the abyss.

Since Tanya hears testimonial after testimonial from people who have improved their health by drinking this water, she thinks it must be something else that is bringing her down. It can't be the water because every multilevel marketing meeting she goes to plays loud music and people dance around because they feel so good. Meanwhile, Tanya's blood is so alkaline that oxygen can't get down to the tissues and she just wants to lay down on the floor until they turn off the Macarena.

When deciding if alkalizing water is right for you, it's crucial to look at breath rate and to understand if your blood could benefit from drinking this water or if it's just going to make you worse. Even if you do have an Acid Imbalance, and if drinking alkaline water could benefit you, be sure to continue to check your breath rate for improvement. You don't want to correct an Acid Imbalance so well that you create an Alkaline Imbalance. Monitoring yourself and your numbers is what this type of health movement is all about. It's not about finding something that makes you feel better and using that product until you die. It's about using something until your body is balanced and then reducing it until you don't need it anymore. It's the knowledge that makes you better, not the product.

As a side note, remember that the first thing that water hits is your stomach. If you're drinking alkaline water with your food, that alkalinity is going to reduce the effectiveness of stomach acid levels that may already be too low.

APPENDIX D

Those Who Paved the Way

Dr. Carey Reams

Dr. Carey Reams was an agrarian. He did soil chemistry and he learned, primarily, how to make things grow in the soil. By people coming to him for help, he was pushed into biology and working with animals and humans. What remained at the root of his mentality was all this knowledge about what made produce grow exceptionally well. What needed to be done in order to bring the proper level of minerals into the produce? What got a result in the crop? There are a lot of stories about how Reams adjusted minerals in the soil to affect the growth of produce. If you wanted to do something in soil, he knew how to do it. That mentality was then brought forward into looking at health from a simple ground-up standpoint. Reams looked at the mineral content in a person, much like he looked at the mineral content in the soil.

Dr. Emanuel Revici

Dr. Emanuel Revici was all about looking at the cell's oil-based membrane and the proteins that are mixed in with it. He explained what was going on with the permeability of the cells. Through learning about cellular permeability, we came to understand that there is a natural tide to life, or a rhythm. This is where the anabolic/catabolic language comes into use. We see that during the daytime it is proper for a person to be in a catabolic state—when he is giving his energy to the day. Conversely, as surely as night falls and the dandelion flower closes, the anabolic state is entered and the person goes to sleep to rebuild and restore himself. Everyone needs to be cycling between these two states. As people lose their vitality or resilience, this tide of life becomes impeded and an individual can get stuck in the anabolic or catabolic state 24 hours a day. Without the necessary vitality to allow the natural oscillation process to continue, it is statistically true that those who become stuck in an anabolic state are more prone to viral issues occurring in their system. Those who have lost their resilience and are stuck in a catabolic state are more prone to bacterial issues. Now comes the reasonableness of the system where if a person is really oscillating every evening from catabolic to anabolic, and every morning from anabolic going back to catabolic, then the viruses don't have a home and the bacteria don't have a home because the system is oscillating. Thus, there is never a time when, for many days, there is a hospitable environment for those issues to take hold.

There is a good book about Dr. Revici, written by William Kelley Eidem, called *The Doctor Who Cures Cancer*. This is a story of Revici's life and work and is an excellent introduction into the intellect he provided us.

Thomas Riddick

Thomas Riddick understood colloidal suspensions. What is the bloodstream? It is a colloidal suspension. This is information that painters understand perfectly; if you can't keep pigment in suspension, then it is going to separate, fall to the bottom of the paint can and harden. If that pigment falls out of suspension then you aren't going to sell much paint. You aren't going to get the pigment to the wall, it's not going to dry correctly and it isn't going to work. With Riddick's research, we came to understand a lot more about the heart and how to make the bloodstream flow easier so that the heart does not work so hard.

Certainly, when half of America is dying from a heart-related problem, we would be curious to know what to do to make things easier for the heart. That used to be understood before profit-driven thinking took over. I don't want that to sound like I'm bitter, I'm not. I do wish that those who put profit over the public's well-being could be locked in a room and forced to listen to old Menudo albums until they promise to change their ways, but I'm not bitter. I don't want you to think that I'm the type of person who would Menudo-style waterboard someone. Still, wouldn't the world be a better place? If this was taken care of, the only issues we would need to get rid of are smoking in public, people who stink, and those who drive slow in the left lane. Order restored.

Dr. Melvin Page

Dr. Melvin Page was a medical doctor whose research showed that proper nutritional balance in the body could improve the health of someone's teeth; the health of the body would coincide with the improvement of dental health. When the patient's calcium-to-phosphorus ratio was in a balanced proportion, he found that the patient would present no cavities. (The actual proportion is ten-to-four in the blood, for those who like it when I say things that make me sound fancy. For those who say, "What the hell is he talking about?" just use the word "balanced.") Moving outside of this ratio would not only enable cavities, but other health issues as well.

Dr. Page was also very interested in, and had a lot of success with, hormones. He found that you couldn't even get a good read on hormones if the blood sugar was elevated. For this reason, he would require avoidance of carbohydrates for at least 72 hours before any hormone testing was done. When we look around us today, with the rate that the population is having trouble with diabetes, hypoglycemia, and blood sugar issues, is it any wonder that there are also a lot of hormonal issues going on? Dr. Page generated a lot of information that we try to implement.

Dr. Page and all these other doctors serve to validate or challenge each other's views. It's as though they were all looking into the same room (human physiology) but through different windows, giving a different perspective on very similar issues.

Recommended Reading

The Doctor Who Cures Cancer - William Kelley Eidem
> The story of Emanuel Revici, M.D. that introduced us to the anabolic/catabolic shifts in the body.

Nutrition and Your Mind - George Watson
> An excellent book that demonstrates how the types of foods we eat can make a difference in our physical health and mental health.

APPENDIX E

Clean Sweep Food Lists

Quick Notes

- Stick to the plan for at least 4 weeks (8 weeks if you have digestive issues but can't use supplements to improve digestion.)
- Don't consume any foods that are not allowed. Not even one bite. Excuses don't count.
- If you're dealing with any autoimmune-type issues, use the AIP Remove List below as well.
- When you begin to reintroduce foods, add one food at a time and wait 72 hours to see if you have a reaction before reintroducing any other foods.
- Keep in mind that some foods listed below may not be optimal for specific imbalances. You may still need to reduce or remove some of these items if you are also working to improve specific imbalances covered elsewhere in this book.
- In rare instances, I have seen some individuals do okay with a small amount of raw nuts during their clean sweep (as long as these folks were not doing the autoimmune version where no nuts are allowed). I never view consuming a lot of nuts as a great idea because many contain a lot of fatty acids that can contribute to an inflammatory response. This clean sweep process can be very restrictive and quite an adjustment from the standard American way of eating. For that reason, it may be okay if you need to include some raw nuts to help you avoid the other foods that are crucial to leave out during a clean sweep. If you need a little more variety to keep you from snapping and eating a loaf of bread, I view adding in a few raw nuts as a strategic maneuver. I would continue to avoid peanuts and almonds. If you do okay on your clean sweep without any nuts, I would leave them out altogether.

Foods To Remove

Grains (corn, wheat, buckwheat, millet, rice, rye, spelt, kamut, oats, etc.)
Dairy products of any kind
All processed foods
All alcohol
Legumes (beans, soy in any form, chickpeas, hummus, etc.)
All sugar and sweeteners of any kind

Foods To Include

Proteins

Organic/ grass fed/ pastured / wild caught varieties are the best, but not required.
Meats (beef, bison, lamb, venison, elk, and other animals that have a rumin)
Poultry (chicken, turkey, pheasant, etc.)
Eggs (no hormones or antibiotics)
Organ meats (I recommend grass fed with organ meats)
Processed meats (turkey or beef sausage or bacon (no sugar added)
Seafood

Vegetables

Artichoke
Arugula
Asparagus
Beets
Beet greens
Bell peppers
Bok choy
Broccoli/Broccolini/Broccoli Rabe
Brussels sprouts
Butternut squash
Cabbage
Carrots
Cauliflower
Celery
Collard greens

Cucumber
Dark leafy greens
Eggplant
Garlic
Green beans
Jicama
Kale
Leeks
Lettuce
Mushrooms
Okra
Onion/shallots
Parsnips
Pumpkin
Radishes
Rutabaga
Rhubarb
Sugar snap peas
Spaghetti squash
Spinach
Sprouts
Squash (all)
Sweet potatoes/yams/white sweet potatoes
Swiss chard
Tomato
Turnip
Watercress
Zucchini

Fats

Animal fats from animals with rumins
Coconut oil
Coconut flakes (unsweetened)
Coconut milk (avoid versions containing xanthan gum, guar gum, or carrageenan)
Ghee/clarified butter
Extra-virgin olive oil
Olives

Fruit

Apples
Apricots
Blackberries
Blueberries
Cherries
Dates/Figs (high in sugar)
Grapefruit (limited)
Grapes
Kiwi
Lemon/Lime
Mango
Melon
Oranges
Papaya
Peaches
pears
Pineapple
Plums
Pomegranate
Raspberries
Strawberries
Tangerines
Watermelon

Vinegars

Apple cider vinegar
Coconut vinegar
Red wine vinegar
Balsamic (with no added sugar)

Any non-seed herbal teas are okay

For Autoimmune Protocol, Also Remove:

All nightshade vegetables (tomatoes, potatoes, peppers (including ground pepper), eggplants, etc.)
All nuts and seeds

Culinary herbs from seeds (mustard, cumin, coriander, cardamom, fennel, fenugreek, nutmeg, dill, fennel)
Eggs
Chocolate (You can do it!)
Stevia
Dried fruits

Remember, search for "Paleo AIP recipes" and you will find plenty of ideas.

You got this!

Appendix F

A Healthy Body In An Unhealthy World

Nobody can avoid everything that is bad for the human body. It's just not possible in the world we live in. Even if you cancel your DirecTV subscription, fire your dog walker, and move out into the woods, you can still have a bird fly over and poop in your mouth while you're sunbathing next to a natural stream. The tactic is not to try to eliminate every toxin, chemical and pollutant from entering your body; but, instead, to put your body in a position where it can have an easier time of removing those problems. That's the whole point in improving the "flow" of the body and balancing the systems that make it all work.

While you're helping your body perform at a higher level, the next goal is merely to learn about the facets of your life that are contributing to your body's toxic load, then get rid of the ones that are the easiest for you to eliminate. Don't feel like you need to run in horror from every environmental or household pollutant within a thirty-mile radius or you're going to be doing some Forrest Gump-type running. However, if there are factors in your life that are easy for you to change, go ahead and change them. Each change will be one less irritant that your body has to deal with—one less task that it needs to take care of before it can move on to more important bodily processes. You may also run into clients who are dealing with severe health issues and can use all the help they can get. For those folks, some of these tips could be a great help.

For most people, however, it's my view that the body is more than capable of handling some of this junk. Worrying about every possible toxin is just going to create more stress, more harmful chemicals that accompany that stress, and more work for your body to do. Criminy Pete! Chill out and enjoy your life.

In this section, I also talk about items that many people feel are healthy solutions. I explain why these people are idiots. They may not truly be idiots—they may just be misled—but I'm going to call them idiots anyway, just because it's faster and easier. Bear in mind that almost every product, method or idea out there could benefit *somebody*. I think there are very few ideas that are completely invalid for the entire population. I just get annoyed when people try to push their products on everyone and market their products as if they are the solution to every human ailment existing today. I feel strongly that there is no such product; a lot of it has to do with what happens to be popular at any given moment. I mean, now it seems popular to watch shows about people getting screamed at in a kitchen. Who saw that coming?

Chemicals In Tap Water

I was at my brother's house in Florida this summer when we decided to use his pool testing kit to look at his tap water. We tested both his pool and the water from the tap in his kitchen. We both sort of freaked when we saw that there was more chlorine in his tap water than in his pool! What the...?! My brother freaked because he thought, "Man, I must really need more chlorine in my pool," and ran out to his shed to add more. But his pool wasn't green with algae; and the issue became clear the next day. As we all played a game of paddle ball in the pool, our eyes were burning. He really didn't need more chlorine in his pool—he needed less in his tap water.

Most city water treatment plants use both chlorine and fluoride to treat the water. Both of these chemicals are harmful to the human body in their own right. An immediate impact these chemicals can have on the body is their ability to "displace" iodine from the body. I say "displace" because that is how most researchers view what chlorine and fluoride are doing to iodine levels in the body. Though iodine levels do normally go down if consuming chlorine- and fluoride-laden water, I view this another way: Iodine acts as a disperser in the body. It disperses toxins so they can be removed from the system. The body views chlorine and fluoride as toxins. (Yes, I know your dentist told you fluoride was good for your teeth, but what he didn't tell you is that it is not good for your body... oops. He will also tell you mercury in your mouth isn't dangerous.) Therefore, iodine is used to help disperse these toxins. In essence, these chemicals are stripping, or displacing, the iodine from the system; but it's easier to view this as the body is using up its iodine to deal with this problem. In any event, an iodine deficiency can be created.

It is widely accepted that iodine is required for proper thyroid function, and thyroid "conditions" have been on the rise in the past decade or so. Although I feel that the rise of this epidemic has more to do with the rise in popularity of prescribing thyroid medications, it could also be partially due to the fact that cities are using more and more chemicals to treat our water. It is also important to consider that iodine is a mineral that can be difficult for some people to absorb. Some minerals are easier to absorb than others and come into the system even if the system is imbalanced. Iodine, on the other hand, requires a more balanced system in order to be absorbed properly. That's why giving iodine to patients with thyroid issues will often bring no result. You can dump all the iodine you want into a person; but if that iodine can't be absorbed, it's not going to help.

The significance of this, in reference to water, is understanding this: If people already have a low level of iodine, you can see how drinking tap water filled with chlorine or fluoride could really do a number on their iodine levels. Crazy to see how just drinking tap water could result in a thyroid issue, right? Yet, understanding the science makes it hard to argue. There are certainly other causes of thyroid problems, but understanding this point could be important for some folks.

Most filter pitchers filter the water through carbon which does very little to remove chlorine and fluoride from your tap water. When it comes to filters, I like the good reverse osmosis filters that can be installed under your sink; but even these filters can remove good minerals while they're removing the bad stuff. If you use a reverse osmosis filter, it's a good idea to add mineral drops back into your water. Adding just three or four drops per glass of water can replenish some of the minerals that may have been stripped during the filtration process. (Of course, if you have high blood pressure, you would cut that dosage in half.) Don't think that mineral drops purchased at a health food store are going to give your body all the minerals that it needs. The best move is to improve digestion so you can pull more minerals out of your food. However, adding minerals to water that has been stripped of many of its minerals can have its benefits for some people.

Spring water is the best option, but it can be costly to buy. I don't really like the idea of distilled water for most people because it is void of any mineral whatsoever, and can wash away more mineral than spring water might. For some people, merely getting any form of water into them is going to be beneficial; so again, I don't want to split hairs with water for some. But since I'm talking about ways to reduce the intake of toxic substances, the type of water can be important.

Shower Filters

Now that you understand the trouble that chlorine can cause, let's hit the showers because most of us don't think about how the water we bathe in can affect our bodies. It's true that most of us don't drink the water coming out of the showerhead while we're washing our hair, but we do continue to breathe while we're showering. When that hot water turns into mist and steam, it still contains all the chemicals that are in that water. As we breathe in this steam, those chemicals come into our lungs then into our bloodstream even faster than if we were drinking the water. In a way, this could make the need to filter our shower water even more important than filtering the water we're drinking. Since this water has a faster path to your bloodstream, doing something to remove or reduce this chlorine can be a good idea.

This is a pretty easy fix and I have had a lot of people tell me they started feeling better after they added a shower filter. I myself was getting extremely tired after my showers and the only thought I could come up with was, "How long was I in there?!" I never considered that the steam in my shower was filling my lungs with chemicals that my body was scrambling to figure out how to remove. You can buy a shower filter for about $30 at most health food stores. You just screw it onto the shower's water source between the pipe coming out of the wall and the shower head itself and you're done. You can even buy replacement filters for less so you don't have to buy a new filter system every time.

These shower filters usually run the water through carbon. We already know how that won't remove enough chlorine and fluoride to make water suitable for drinking. In this regard, we know these shower filters are not likely removing all the chemicals from the water. But with such an easy and inexpensive step, you can at least begin to reduce the amount of chemicals in your showering experience. For a lot of people, this simple step can reduce the load on their bodies and bring some relief. I hope I didn't scare you away from showering and your plan is to simply stink from now on.

Microwaves

Much of this book has been about correcting issues to allow your body to use the food you're eating and to improve its ability to remove junk and toxic substances that your body can't process. That's why microwaves are an important topic. If you're going to correct your digestion so that you can actually pull the nutrients out of the food you eat, the food you eat should be something that your body can use. Too many sources have scared me away from using microwaves. It is believed that the way microwaves heat food is a process that changes the molecular structure of the food in order to create the friction that makes it hot. When you change the molecular structure of a natural food, it can become unrecognizable to the body and the body may not be able to process it correctly.

There are as many studies that show this to be false as there are studies that show this problem to be true. Is it easier to heat something in the microwave? Of course it is. But you need to understand: If anything heated by a microwave not only loses its nutritional value to the body, but also becomes a problem that the body has to deal with, that is not worth the risk to me. It will take you longer to prepare your food without a microwave; but it could be time that you save in the long run by reducing the number of doctor and hospital visits you need to make. I just use my microwave as a very fancy clock.

You may still be skeptical and thinking, "Okay Tony, I'll fix my digestion, but why ya gotta mess with my Hot Pockets?" I'll give you a little experiment. Go down to Home Depot and buy two identical potted plants. Name one plant "Ricky" and the other one "Reject Bastard-Child." I guess you can pick your own names if you want. In any case, take them home and put them in the same light. Water one plant with normal water, and the other plant with water that has been microwaved. Don't pour the hot water in the plant because obviously that won't go well. Just microwave some water and let it cool to room temperature before you water with it.

At the end of your experiment, I think you will find that one plant is happy, while the other plant has earned the name I suggested. Many believe that microwaves can even change the structure of water and turn it into an evil substance.

Many chain restaurants have switched over to cooking all of their food in microwaves. Food is shipped in bags and the "cooks" simply pop the bags in the microwave. The only cooking they do is in the deep fryer. Are ya kiddin' me? If I was in the boardroom when they made that decision, you would have heard a world of cussing.

What Am I Cooking In?

To keep this brief, understand that what you cook with counts. If you're cooking in plastics, aluminum, or typical "non-stick" cookware, some of these poisons are off-gassing into your food and into your body. This creates another toxin that your body has to deal with. Some of these heavy metal toxins don't have an exit strategy from the body and can accumulate and cause all types of trouble. Glass is always safe to cook with or drink out of, stainless steel is rarely suspect (with the idea that magnetic stainless steel is best since it won't deliver significant amounts of nickel into the food). Enamel cookware and titanium cookware are also considered to be safer than most non-stick cookware.

What's In My Mouth?

The medical field is not the only world that practically gives us a "daily allowance" of toxins. We learned in the middle of the 18th century that mercury is poison and nothing has changed since—mercury is still poison. After the dentist finishes putting mercury into someone's teeth, he takes what is left over and puts it in a special container marked "hazardous materials." That container then goes into another container marked "hazardous materials." Next, a little truck that has the special markings and permits required to haul hazardous materials comes and picks up that mercury from the dentist's office. And of course the ADA doctors will still tell you it's safe to put mercury in your mouth and let it seep into your head 24 hours a day. Dental work that is toxic, medications that are toxic—with all this disclosure I feel like I'm breaking the news to Honey Boo Boo that there is no Easter Bunny.

Smoking

Smoking? Seriously? I don't really need to explain this, do I? I think you understand that most people would need to stop smoking to have any chance of improving health. People think that smoking just affects the lungs; but it also puts a lot of tar and chemicals in the body that need to be filtered out by the liver. As I said in an earlier chapter, the two most important factors in health for most people, in my opinion, are digestion and liver function. We aren't what we eat—we are what we can assimilate and what we can't remove. If your liver is overwhelmed, the body is having a hard time removing all the junk that should be removed. If it can't be removed, the junk will be stored in joints, tissues, or fat cells.

Here's the good news: The people who have a difficult time trying to quit smoking are almost always people with a low mineral and protein content. The nicotine and the chemicals constrict the vascular system to raise blood pressure. So, when people with no mineral identity try to quit, it can sometimes be hard for them because smoking was helping to lift their blood pressure. If you are a smoker and your *Imbalance Guide* shows that you may be dealing with an Electrolyte Deficiency Imbalance, losing the smokes might just be a whole lot easier when you improve this imbalance. You're still going to have to want to quit. It's not going to be magic, but it will make it physiologically easier. Understanding how the body works can change the viewpoint of choices that we make in our lives. This new understanding can reveal that a bad habit could actually be a form of self-medication. The exciting part is that the bad habit is easier to get rid of when it no longer represents the main choice for the "medication." To learn more, go to www.KickItNaturally.com and type "How to Quit Smoking" in the search box. You will find the link to our podcast episode on this topic.

Antibiotics

Antibiotics don't just break apart the bad bacteria in your body; they also break apart all the good bacteria that live in your intestines. These good bacteria do these good things: Help with digestion, control infestation from yeast and bad bacteria like candida, make the B vitamins we need,

420

and help clean putrefied fecal matter off colon walls. When we take antibiotics and wipe out all the good bacteria along with the bad, we need to strive to replace the good bacteria with probiotics and eating foods that will help gut flora.

Here's another issue many people, like me, have with antibiotics: Many antibiotics are actually made from fungus. When you use these antibiotics to break apart a bacterial problem or improve a viral problem, you're actually setting up the terrain of the body in a way that allows fungal problems to flourish. Imagine you have a garden and weeds are taking over in a big way. Would you try to eliminate those weeds by planting new weeds that were designed to kill the original weeds? That sentence alone sounds horribly dumb just from the number of times "weeds" showed up. If the sentence sounds stupid, obviously the idea is not that brilliant. If you want to get rid of a problem, it might be a good idea to use a method that isn't going to end up creating another problem.

Flu Shots

No.

Alkalizing Water And Water Filters

In the marketplace today, there is a lot of information about "alkalizing" that is a heaping pile of fiction. I don't cover the Acid and Alkaline Imbalances in this book, but I do include them in Appendix C. However, if you are currently using, or plan to use any alkalizing products or alkalizing water, be sure to read about them in Appendix C. It's very important that you understand if these products are right for you or not.

MORE ABOUT TONY

Like most natural health experts, Tony began his career in stand-up comedy. Touring professionally as a comic for nearly a decade, he never envisioned that he would one day teach the world how to sleep, poop, and even lose weight.

On Valentine's Day, 2004, Tony lost his voice and it didn't came back. After twenty-three doctors couldn't figure out the problem, Tony decided it was time to dig for his own answers. Eight years later, not only did Tony figure out his own issues, he also happened upon hidden information about how to improve countless other health problems.

Though Tony likes to boast about the fact that he holds no legitimate credentials (nor does he believe that we need any more "experts" from the same pool of knowledge already failing so many with health issues), he is greatly respected by his peers in the natural health industry. The biggest manufacturers in the health, fitness and organic products industries send Tony their products every year in hopes of winning one of his GearAwards.

Beyond working with many celebrity clients, Tony is on the executive board of *The Coalition for Health Education*, a nonprofit association that helps professionals and their clients learn about health through nutrition. Additionally, Tony teaches monthly webinars about nutrition to doctors, nutritionists and other health care professionals from more than thirty-five countries.

You can also find Tony producing documentaries like the upcoming, *Why Am I So Fat?* A film that teaches the truth about weight loss while showcasing Tony's client, Gabe Evans, who lost 200 pounds in 9 ½ months by treating Tony's word as gospel.

To learn more about Tony, visit www.KickItNaturally.com

REFERENCES

Chapter 1: Hi

Chimonas S, Evarts SD, Littlehale SK, Rothman DJ. Managing conflicts of interest in clinical care: the "race to the middle" at U.S. medical schools. *Acad Med.* 2013 Oct;88(10):1464-70. doi: 10.1097/ACM.0b013e3182a2e204.

Harrison C. US Patent Office issues guidelines on natural product patent eligibility. *Nat Rev Drug Discov.* 2014 Apr;13(4):250. doi: 10.1038/nrd4303.

Aceto JF. Patent portfolios after myriad, how to fit in those new genes. *ACS Med Chem Lett.* 2013 Jul 12;4(8):681-3.

Sloss A, Kubler P. Prescribing in liver disease. *Aust Presc.* 2009;32:32-5

Wilkinson GR, Shand DG. Commentary: a physiological approach to hepatic drug clearance. *Clin Pharmacol Ther.* 1975 Oct;18(4):377-90.

Mitchell SJ, Hilmer SN. Drug-induced liver injury in older adults. *World J Gastroenterol.* 2007 Jan 21;13(3):329-40.

Andrade RJ, Robles M, Fernández-Castañer A, López-Ortega S, López-Vega MC, Lucena MI. Assessment of drug-induced hepatotoxicity in clinical practice: a challenge for gastroenterologists. *World J Gastroenterol.* 2007 Jan 21;13(3):329-40

Chapter 2: Helping Your Clients See Real Results & Chapter 3: Digestion

Untersmayr E, Jensen-Jarolim E. The role of protein digestibility and antacids on food allergy outcomes. *J Allergy Clin Immunol.* 2008 Jun;121(6):1301-8

Barrett J. POPs vs. Fat: Persistent Organic Pollutant Toxicity Targets and Is Modulated by Adipose Tissue, *Environ Health Perspect.* Feb 2013; 121(2): a61.

Evans D, Pye G, Bramley R, Clark AG, Dyson TJ, Hardcastle JD. Measurement of gastrointestinal pH profiles in normal ambulant human subjects. *Gut.* Aug 1988; 29(8): 1035–1041.

Fallingborg J. Intraluminal pH of the human gastrointestinal tract. *Dan Med Bull.* 1999 Jun;46(3):183-96.

Fallingborg J, Christensen LA, Ingeman-Nielsen M, Jacobsen BA, Abildgaard K, Rasmussen HH, Rasmussen SN. Measurement of gastrointestinal pH and regional transit times in normal children. *J Pediatr Gastroenterol Nutr.* 1990 Aug;11(2):211-4.

Kelly G. Hydrochloric Acid: Physiological Functions and Clinical Implications Alternative Medicine Review. Volume 2, Number 2. 1997, p.117

First Principles of Gastroenterology: The Basis of Disease and an Approach to Management, J.J Freeman & A.B.R. Tomson, p.177

Reshetnyak VI. Physiological and molecular biochemical mechanisms of bile formation. *World J Gastroenterol.* 2013 Nov 14;19(42):7341-60. doi: 10.3748/wjg.v19.i42.7341.

Sjöblom M, Singh AK, Zheng W, Wang J, Tuo B, Krabbenhöft A, Riederer B, Gros G, Seidler U. Duodenal acidity "sensing" but not epithelial HCO_3^- supply is critically dependent on carbonic anhydrase II expression. *Proc Natl Acad Sci U S A.* Aug 4, 2009; 106(31): 13094–13099

Allen A, Flemström G. Gastroduodenal mucus bicarbonate barrier: protection against acid and pepsin. *Amer Jour Phys* January 2005 Vol. 288

First Principles of Gastroenterology: The Basis of Disease and an Approach to Management, Fifth Edition, H.J. Freeman and A.B.R. Thomson, JANSSEN-ORTHO, p.193,197-209

Camilleri M, Parkman H, Shafi M, Abell T, Gerson L. Clinical Guideline: Management of Gastroparesis. *Am J Gastroenterol.* Jan 2013; 108(1): 18–38.

First Principles of Gastroenterology, 5th Edition: The Stomach and duodenum; B.J. Salena and R.H. Hunt, p.144

Cater RE 2nd (1992 Dec) The clinical importance of hypochlorhydria (a consequence of chronic Helicobacter infection): its possible etiological role in mineral and amino acid malabsorption, depression, and other syndromes *Med Hypotheses*; 39(4):375-83 PMID: 1494327.

McCarthy D. Adverse effects of proton pump inhibitor drugs: clues and conclusions. *Current Opinion in Gastroenterology.* November 2010, Volume 26, Issue 6; p 624–631

Prousky J. Is Vitamin B3 Dependency a Causal Factor in the Development of Hypochlorhydria and Achlorhydria? *The Journal of Orthomolecular Medicine Vol. 16, 4th Quarter 2001*

Hwang C, Ross V, Mahadevan U. Micronutrient deficiencies in inflammatory bowel disease: from A to zinc. *Inflamm Bowel Dis.* 2012 Oct;18(10):1961-81.

Recker RR. Calcium absorption and achlorhydria. *N Engl J Med.* 1985 Jul 11;313(2):70-3.

Heizer W. Normal and abnormal intestinal absorption by humans. *Environ Health Perspect.* Dec 1979; 33: 101–106.

Iwai W, Abe Y, Iijima K, Koike T, Uno K, Asano N, Imatani A, Shimosegawa T. Gastric hypochlorhydria is associated with an exacerbation of dyspeptic symptoms in female patients. *J Gastroenterol*. 2013 Feb;48(2):214-21.

Ostrow J, Resnick R. Hyperchlorhydria, duodenitis and duodenal ulcer: A clinical study of their interrelationships. *Ann Intern Med*. 1959;51(6):1303-1328.

Hunt RH. The protective role of gastric acid. *Scand J Gastroenterol Suppl*. 1988;146:34-9.

Marshall BJ, Barrett LJ, Prakash C, McCallum R, Guerrant R, Urea Protects Helicobacter (Campylobacter) pylori From the Bactericial Effect of Acid. *Gasteroenterology*. 1990;99:697-762

Border J R. Multiple systems organ failure. *Ann Surg*. Aug 1992; 216(2): 111–116., p.114

Parsonnet J, Friedman GD. Helicobacter pylori infection and the risk of gastric carcinoma. *New England Journal of Medicine*, Oct. 17, 1991 - Vol 325, No.16; p.1127

Champagne ET. Low gastric hydrochloric acid secretion and mineral bioavailability. *Adv Exp Med Biol*. 1989;249:173-84.

Mackay JD, Bladon PT. Hypomagnesaemia due to proton-pump inhibitor therapy: a clinical case series. *Oxford Journals, QJM: An International Journal of Medicine*, Volume 103, Issue 6, Pp. 387-395

Champagne E. Low Gastric Hydrochloric Acid Secretion and Mineral Bioavailability: Mineral Absorption in the Monogastric GI Tract. *Advances in Experimental Medicine and Biology* Volume 249, 1989, pp 173-184

Davies RE, Roughton FJW. Hydrochloric acid production by isolated gastric mucosa *Biochem J*. 1948; 42(4): 609–621.

Zollner G, Trauner M. Mechanisms of cholestasis. *Clin Liver Dis*. 2008 Feb;12(1):1-26, vii.

Pratt DS. Cholestasis and cholestatic syndromes. *Curr Opin Gastroenterol*. 2005 May;21(3):270-4.

Alrefai WA, Gill RK. Bile acid transporters: structure, function, regulation and pathophysiological implications. *Pharm Res*. 2007 Oct;24(10):1803-23.

Scott-Conner CE, Grogan JB. The pathophysiology of biliary obstruction and its effect on phagocytic and immune function. *J Surg Res*. 1994 Aug;57(2):316-36.

Di Stefano M, Vos R, Vanuytsel T, Janssens J, Tack J. Prolonged duodenal acid perfusion and dyspeptic symptom occurrence in healthy volunteers. *Neurogastroenterology & Motility*. (2009) 21: 712–e40.

Freeman HJ, Thomson ABR. First Principles of Gastroenterology: The Basis of Disease and an Approach to Management, Fifth Edition. *Janssen-ortho*, p.192-209

Mowat A P, Arias, I M. . Liver function and oral contraceptives. (1969) *Journal of Reproduction Medicine*, 3, 19-29.

Boston Collaborative Drug Surveillance Programme (1973). Oral contraceptives and venous thromboembolic disease, surgically confirmed gallbladder disease and breast tumours. *Lancet*, 1,1399-1404.

Forker EL. The effect of estrogen on bile formation in the rat. *J Clin Invest*. 1969 Apr;48(4):654-63.

Somero G. Temperature adaptation of enzymes: biological optimization through structure-function compromises. *Annual Review of Ecology and Systematics* (1978): 1-29.

Thomson A, Keelan M. The aging gut. *Canadian Journal of Physiology and Pharmacology*. 1986, 64(1): 30-38.

Prasad AS. Clinical, endocrinologic, and biochemical effects of zinc deficiency. *Spec Top Endocrinol Metab*. 1985;7:45-76.

Chapter 4: Elimination & Digestion Gone Wild

Tontisirin K, Valyasevi A. Protein Energy Malnutrition Related to Diarrhea in Thai Children. *Journal of Nutritional Science and Vitaminology* Vol. 27 (1981) No. 6 P 513-520

PEM, PROTEIN ENERGY MALNUTRITION. "Protein Energy Malnutrition."
Pediatric Clinics of North America, 2009

Dragstedt L, Dragstedt C, McClintock J, Chase C S. A study of the factors involved in the production and absorption of toxic materials from the intestine. *J Exp Med*. Aug 1, 1919; 30(2): 109–121.

Pathological Physiology of Internal Diseases, By Albion Walter Hewlett, New York And London D. Appleton & Company, 1917, p.146

Nutrition and Diagnosis-related Care, 6th Edition, By Sylvia Escott-Stump, p.471

Layer P, Keller J. Pancreatic enzymes: secretion and luminal nutrient digestion in health and disease. *J Clin Gastroenterol*. 1999 Jan;28(1):3-10.

Rosado JL, Solomons NW, Lisker R, Bourges H. Enzyme replacement therapy for primary adult lactase deficiency. Effective reduction of lactose malabsorption and milk intolerance by direct addition of beta-galactosidase to milk at mealtime. *Gastroenterology*. 1984 Nov;87(5):1072-82.

Faria AM, Gomes-Santos AC, Gonçalves JL, Moreira TG, Medeiros SR, Dourado LP, Cara DC. Food components and the immune system: from tonic agents to allergens. *Front Immunol*. 2013 May 17;4:102.

Chapter 5: Understanding Insulin & Blood Sugar Control & Chapter 6: Cravings

Elliott SS, Keim NL, Stern JS, Teff K, Havel PJ. Fructose, weight gain, and the insulin resistance syndrome. Am J Clin Nutr. 2002 Nov;76(5):911-22.

L C Groop, R C Bonadonna, S DelPrato, K Ratheiser, K Zyck, E Ferrannini, and R A DeFronzo. Glucose and free fatty acid metabolism in non-insulin-dependent diabetes mellitus. Evidence for multiple sites of insulin resistance. J Clin Invest. Jul 1989; 84(1): 205–213.

Sidney A. Portis, M.D. LIFE SITUATIONS, EMOTIONS AND HYPERINSULINISM. *JAMA.* 1950;142(16):1281-1286.

Heller RF, Heller RF. Hyperinsulinemic obesity and carbohydrate addiction: the missing link is the carbohydrate frequency factor. Med Hypotheses. 1994 May;42(5):307-12.

Bolton RP, Heaton KW, Burroughs LF. The role of dietary fiber in satiety, glucose, and insulin: studies with fruit and fruit juice. Am J Clin Nutr. 1981 Feb;34(2):211-7.

B. Hildrum, A. Mykletun, E. Stordal, I. Bjelland, A. Dahl, J. Holmen. Association of low blood pressure with anxiety and depression: the Nord-Trøndelag Health Study. J Epidemiol Community Health 2007;61:53-58

M. Buyzere, D. Clement, D.Duprez. Chronic Low Blood Pressure: A Review. Cardiovascular Drugs and Therapy 1998;12:29–35

A. Zaidi; P. Clough, P. Cooper, MD; B. Scheepers, MD; A. Fitzpatrick, MD. Misdiagnosis of epilepsy: many seizure-like attacks have a cardiovascular cause *J Am Coll Cardiol.* 2000;36(1):181-184.

L. Castilla-Guerra, M. Fernández-Moreno, J. López-Chozas R. Fernández-Bolaños. Electrolytes Disturbances and Seizures Epilepsia Volume 47, Issue 12, pages 1990–1998, December   2006

Anuradha K, Hota D, Pandhi P. Investigation of central mechanism of insulin induced hypoglycemic convulsions in mice. Indian J Exp Biol. 2004 Apr;42(4):368-72.

Tabrez S, Roberts IM. Malabsorption and malnutrition. Prim Care. 2001 Sep;28(3):505-22, v.

Ubesie AC, Kocoshis SA, Mezoff AG, Henderson CJ, Helmrath MA, Cole CR.Multiple micronutrient deficiencies among patients with intestinal failure during and after transition to enteral nutrition. J Pediatr. 2013 Dec;163(6):1692-6.

Martin CK, Rosenbaum D, Han H, Geiselman PJ, Wyatt HR, Hill JO, Brill C, Bailer B, Miller BV 3rd, Stein R, Klein S, Foster GD. Change in food cravings, food preferences, and appetite during a low-carbohydrate and low-fat diet. Obesity (Silver Spring). 2011 Oct;19(10):1963-70.

Pizarro M, Balasubramaniyan N, Solís N, Solar A, Duarte I, Miquel JF, Suchy FJ, Trauner M, Accatino L, Ananthanarayanan M, Arrese M. Bile secretory function in the obese Zucker rat: evidence of cholestasis and altered canalicular transport function. Gut. 2004 Dec;53(12):1837-43.

Astrup A, Dyerberg J, Selleck M, Stender S. Nutrition transition and its relationship to the development of obesity and related chronic diseases. Obes Rev. 2008 Mar;9 Suppl 1:48-52.

El-Sayed H, Hainsworth R. Salt supplementation increases plasma volume and orthostatic tolerance in patients with unexplained syncope. Heart 1996; 75:134–140.

Kane-Gill SL, LeBlanc JM, Dasta JF, Devabhakthuni S. A Multicenter Study of the Point Prevalence of Drug-Induced Hypotension in the ICU. For the Critical Care Pharmacotherapy Trials Network (CCPTN). Crit Care Med. 2014 Jul 10.

E Huskisson, S Maggini, M Ruf. The Role of Vitamins and Minerals in Energy Metabolism and Well-Being. Journal of International Medical Research 2007 35: 277

Micronutrient Availability, Chemistry and Availability of Micronutrients in Soils. J. Agric. Food Chem., 1962, 10 (3), pp 174–178

Mattes RD, Popkin BM. Nonnutritive sweetener consumption in humans: effects on appetite and food intake and their putative mechanisms. Am J Clin Nutr. 2009 Jan;89(1):1-14.

Chapter 7: Simple Self-Testing & Chapter 8: Understanding Your Biological Individuality

Guyton A. Blood Pressure Control-Special Role of the Kidneys and Body Fluids. *Science*252.5014 (Jun 28, 1991): 1813.

Knochel JP. Neuromuscular manifestations of electrolyte disorders. *Am J Med*. 1982 Mar;72(3):521-35.

Riggs JE. Neurologic manifestations of electrolyte disturbances. *Neurol Clin*. 2002 Feb;20(1):227-39, vii.

Weiner M, Epstein FH. Signs and symptoms of electrolyte disorders. *Yale J Biol Med*. 1970 Oct;43(2):76-109.

Mäestu J, Eliakim A, Jürimäe J, Valter I, Jürimäe T. Anabolic and catabolic hormones and energy balance of the male bodybuilders during the preparation for the competition. *J Strength Cond Res*. 2010 Apr;24(4):1074-81.

The Doctor Who Cures Cancer. William Kelley. Be Well Books, 1996

An Analytical System of Clinical Nutrition. Guy Schenker. P. 235

Brooks G, Mercier J. Balance of carbohydrate and lipid utilization during exercise: the "crossover" concept. *Journal of Applied Physiology* June 1994 Vol. 76 no. 6, 2253-2261

Scheutz F, Poulsen S. Determining causation in epidemiology. *Community Dent Oral Epidemiol*. 1999 Jun;27(3):161-70.

Bättig B, Steiner A, Jeck T, Vetter W. Blood pressure self-measurement in normotensive and hypertensive patients. Journal of Hypertension. *Supplement: Official Journal of the International Society of Hypertension* [1989, 7(3):S59-63]

Louie AK, Louie EK, Lannon RA. Systemic hypertension associated with tricyclic antidepressant treatment in patients with panic disorder. *Am J Cardiol.* 1992 Nov 15;70(15):1306-9.

Grodins FS. Respiration and the regulation of acid-base balance. *AMA Arch Intern Med.* 1957 Apr;99(4):569-72.

Chapter 9: How Imbalances Contribute To Health Issues

Mitchell P. Foundations of vectorial metabolism and osmochemistry. *Biosci Rep.* 1991 Dec;11(6):297-344; discussion 345-6.

Oliver W J. Sodium Homeostasis and Low Blood Pressure Populations Epidemiology of Arterial Blood Pressure. *Developments in Cardiovascular Medicine.* Volume 8, 1980, pp 229-241

Gomez T, Molé P, Collins A. Dilution of body fluid electrolytes affects bioelectrical impedance measurements. *Research in Sports Medicine An International Journal* 4(4):291-298 · December 1993

Cravioto J, Delicardie ER. Mental performance in school age children. Findings after recovery from early severe malnutrition. *Am J Dis Child.* 1970 Nov;120(5):404-10.

Sandstead H. Nutrition and Brain Function: Trace Elements. *Nutrition Reviews* Volume 44, Issue Supplement s3, pages 37–41, May 1986

Watson G, Comrey A. Nutritional replacement for mental illness. *Psychol.,* 1954, 38, 25 1-264.

Kellum J A. Determinants of blood pH in health and disease . *Critical Care* 2000, 4:6-14

Electrolytes Disturbances and Seizures. Luis Castilla-Guerra, María del Carmen Fernández-Moreno, José Manuel López-Chozas and Ricardo Fernández-Bolaños

Rhoades J D. Salinity: Electrical Conductivity and Total Dissolved Solids. Methods of Soil Analysis Part 3—Chemical Methods

Brown RT, Polinsky RJ, Lee GK, Deeter JA. Insulin-induced hypotension and neurogenic orthostatic hypotension. *Neurology.* 1986 Oct;36(10):1402-6.

Kobori H, Nangaku M, Navar LG, Nishiyama A. The intrarenal renin-angiotensin system: from physiology to the pathobiology of hypertension and kidney disease. *Pharmacol Rev.* 2007 Sep;59(3):251-87.

Engelmann W, Schrempf M. Membrane Models for Circadian Rhythms. *Photochemical and Photobiological Reviews* 1980, pp 49-86

Revici E. Research in Pathophysiology as Basis for Guided Chemotherapy, with Special Application to Cancer. Princeton, NJ: D. Van Nostrand Company, 1961.

Alenghat FJ, Golan DE. Membrane protein dynamics and functional implications in mammalian cells. *Curr Top Membr*. 2013;72:89-120.

Brinkmann K. Circadian rhythm in the kinetics of acid denaturation of cell membranes of Euglena gracilis. *Planta* (Berlin)1976a, 129:221–227.

Carrasco L. The inhibition of cell functions after viral infection. 1977, *FEBS Lett*. **76**:11–15

Eskin A, Corrent G. Effects of divalent cations and metabolic poisons on the circadian rhythm from the Aplysia eye. *J. Comp. Physiol*. 1977, **117**:1–21.

Cummings F W. A biochemical model of the circadian clock. 1975, *J. Theor. Biol*. 55:455–470.

Aldridge J. Short-range intercellular communication, biochemical oscillations and circadian rhythms. *Handbook of Engineering in Medicine and Biology* (1976): 55-147.

Adam K. Sleep as a restorative process and a theory to explain why. *Prog Brain Res*. 1980;53:289-305.

Papahadjopoulos D. Cholesterol and cell membrane function: A hypothesis concerning the etiology of atherosclerosis. *Journal of Theoretical Biology* Volume 43, Issue 2, February 1974, Pages 329–337

Erecińska M, Wilson D F. Regulation of cellular energy metabolism. *The Journal of Membrane Biology* 1982, Volume 70, Issue 1, pp 1-14

Ginsberg L, Gershfeld N L. Membrane bilayer instability and the pathogenesis of disorders of myelin. *Neurosci Lett*. 1991 Sep 2;130(1):133-6.

Caroli A, Del Favero G, Di Mario F. Lipid pattern and plasma insulin in diabetics with gall stones. *Gut* 32.3 (1991): 339-340.

Ravussin E, Smith SR, Ann N Y. Increased fat intake, impaired fat oxidation, and failure of fat cell proliferation result in ectopic fat storage, insulin resistance, and type 2 diabetes mellitus. *Acad Sci*. 2002 Jun;967:363-78.

Teff KL, Grudziak J, Townsend RR, Dunn TN, Grant RW, Adams SH, Keim NL, Cummings BP, Stanhope KL, Havel PJ. Endocrine and metabolic effects of consuming fructose- and glucose-sweetened beverages with meals in obese men and women: influence of insulin resistance on plasma triglyceride responses. *J Clin Endocrinol Metab*. 2009 May;94(5):1562-9.

Chapter 10: Conflicting Advice Everywhere & Chapter 11: Remove The Trouble & Chapter 12: Physiological Gold

W.J. Parker, L.D. Muller, D.R. Buckmaster. Management and Economic Implications of Intensive Grazing on Dairy Farms in the Northeastern States Journal of Dairy Science Volume 75, Issue 9, September 1992, Pages 2587–2597

Van Den Bogaard AE, Stobberingh EE. Antibiotic usage in animals: impact on bacterial resistance and public health. Drugs. 1999 Oct;58(4):589-607.

Walsh C, Fanning S. Antimicrobial resistance in foodborne pathogens--a cause for concern? Curr Drug Targets. 2008 Sep;9(9):808-15.

Wm. Armstrong. Gastro-Intestinal Toxins: Their Clinical Significance and Therapeutic Indications. Br Med J. Jul 31, 1897; 2(1909): 269–271.

A. McAfee , E. McSorley, G. Cuskelly, B. Moss, J. Wallace, M. Bonham, A. Fearon. Red meat consumption: An overview of the risks and benefits. Meat Science Volume 84, Issue 1, January 2010, Pages 1–13

Gibson RS. Content and bioavailability of trace elements in vegetarian diets. Am J Clin Nutr. 1994 May;59(5 Suppl):1223S-1232S.

J Cook, E Monsen. Food iron absorption in human subjects. III. Comparison of the effect of animal proteins on nonheme iron absorption. Am J Clin Nutr August 1976 vol. 29 no. 8 859-867

Craig WJ. Health effects of vegan diets. Am J Clin Nutr. 2009 May;89(5):1627S-1633S.

Pilis W, Stec K, Zych M, Pilis A. Health benefits and risk associated with adopting a vegetarian diet. Rocz Panstw Zakl Hig. 2014;65(1):9-14.

J. Woo, T. Kwok, S.. Ho, A. Sham, E. Lau. Nutritional status of elderly Chinese vegetarians. Age and Ageing Volume 27, Issue 4 Pp. 455-461

Ritz E, Hahn K, Ketteler M, Kuhlmann MK, Mann J. Phosphate additives in food--a health risk. Dtsch Arztebl Int. 2012 Jan;109(4):49-55.

H. Schroeder,. Losses of vitamins and trace minerals resulting from processing and preservation of foods. *The American journal of clinical nutrition* 24.5 (1971): 562-573.

Worthington V. Effect of agricultural methods on nutritional quality: a comparison of organic with conventional crops. Altern Ther Health Med. 1998 Jan;4(1):58-69

A. Simmons, J. Schlezinger, B. Corkey. What Are We Putting in Our Food That Is Making Us Fat? Food Additives, Contaminants, and Other Putative Contributors to Obesity Current Obesity Reports. Feb 2014

J. Ruzzin, D. Lee, D. Carpenter, D. Jacobs. Reconsidering metabolic diseases: The impacts of persistent organic pollutants Atherosclerosis. Sep 2012, Vol. 224: 1-3

Petrakis NL, Barnes S, King EB, Lowenstein J, Wiencke J, Lee MM, Miike R, Kirk M, Coward L. Stimulatory influence of soy protein isolate on breast secretion in pre- and postmenopausal women. Department of Epidemiology and Biostatistics, University of California, San Francisco 94143-0560, USA. Cancer Epidemiol Biomarkers Prev, 1996 Oct, 5:10, 785-94

Baird DD, Umbach DM, Lansdell L, Hughes CL, Setchell KD, Weinberg CR, Haney AF, Wilcox AJ, Mclachlan JA. Dietary intervention study to assess estrogenicity of dietary soy among postmenopausal women. J Clin Endocrinol Metab 1995 May;80(5):1685-1690

Swagerty DL Jr, Walling AD, Klein RM. Lactose Intolerance Department of Family Medicine, University of Kansas School of Medicine, Kansas City 66160-7370, USA.

Chapter 13: Foods Specific To You & Chapter 14: Supplements That Could Help

Diesendorf M, Colquhoun J, Spittle BJ, Everingham DN, Clutterbuck FW. New evidence on fluoridation. *Aust N Z J Public Health*. 1997 Apr;21(2):187-90.

McDonald TA, Komulainen H. Carcinogenicity of the chlorination disinfection by-product MX. *J Environ Sci Health C Environ Carcinog Ecotoxicol Rev*. 2005;23(2):163-214.

Coplan MJ, Patch SC, Masters RD, Bachman MS. Confirmation of and explanations for elevated blood lead and other disorders in children exposed to water disinfection and fluoridation chemicals. *Neurotoxicology*. 2007 Sep;28(5):1032-42. Epub 2007 Mar 1

Newsholme P, Procopio J, Lima M, Pithon-Curi T C, Curi R. Glutamine and glutamate-their central role on cell metabolism and function. *Cell Bio & Func*. 2002

Chapter 15: The World Of Weight Loss & Chapter 16: Mental & Emotional Issues

Stackelberg PE, Furlong ET, Meyer MT, Zaugg SD, Henderson AK, Reissman DB. Persistence of pharmaceutical compounds and other organic wastewater contaminants in a conventional drinking-water-treatment plant. Sci Total Environ. 2004 Aug 15;329(1-3):99-113

Wittassek M, Angerer J. Phthalates: metabolism and exposure. Int J Androl. 2008 Apr;31(2):131-8. Epub 2007 Dec 7.

Swithers SE. Artificial sweeteners produce the counterintuitive effect of inducing metabolic derangements. Trends Endocrinol Metab. 2013 Sep;24(9):431-41

Björntorp P, Rosmond R. Obesity and cortisol. Nutrition. 2000 Oct;16(10):924-36.

Chen JQ, Brown TR, Russo J. Regulation of energy metabolism pathways by estrogens and estrogenic chemicals and potential implications in obesity associated with increased exposure to endocrine disruptors. *Biochim Biophys Acta*. 2009;1793(7):1128-1143.

Wells JC. Obesity as malnutrition: the dimensions beyond energy balance. Eur J Clin Nutr. 2013 May;67(5):507-12.

J. Painter. How do food manufacturers calculate the calorie count of packaged foods? Scientific American, Jul 31, 2006 Food Science and Human Nutrition, University of Illinois

Hall JE, Brands MW, Henegar JR. Mechanisms of hypertension and kidney disease in obesity. Ann N Y Acad Sci. 1999 Nov 18;892:91-107.

Hall JE[1], Brands MW, Henegar JR, Shek EW. Abnormal kidney function as a cause and a consequence of obesity hypertension. Clin Exp Pharmacol Physiol. 1998 Jan;25(1):58-64.

Simmons AL, Schlezinger JJ, Corkey BE. What Are We Putting in Our Food That Is Making Us Fat? Food Additives, Contaminants, and Other Putative Contributors to Obesity. Curr Obes Rep. 2014 Jun 1;3(2):273-285.

Caramia G. Butter, my love, joy, sorrow and rehabilitation: not simply cholesterol and saturated fatty acids. Pediatr Med Chir. 2014 Mar-Apr;36(2):65-73.

Liu GC, Coulston AM, Reaven GM. Effect of high-carbohydrate-low-fat diets on plasma glucose, insulin and lipid responses in hypertriglyceridemic humans. Metabolism. 1983 Aug;32(8):750-3.

Dashti HM, Mathew TC, Khadada M, Al-Mousawi M, Talib H, Asfar SK, Behbahani AI, Al-Zaid NS. Beneficial effects of ketogenic diet in obese diabetic subjects. Mol Cell Biochem. 2007 Aug;302(1-2):249-56. Epub 2007 Apr 20.

Goedeke L, Fernández-Hernando C. Regulation of cholesterol homeostasis. Cell Mol Life Sci. 2012 Mar;69(6):915-30.

M. Fernandez, Dietary cholesterol provided by eggs and plasma lipoproteins in healthy populations. Current Opinion in Clinical Nutrition & Metabolic Care: January 2006 - Volume 9 - Issue 1 - p 8–12

Quiles JL, Huertas JR, Battino M, Ramírez-Tortosa MC, Cassinello M, Mataix J, Lopez-Frias M, Mañas M. The intake of fried virgin olive or sunflower oils differentially induces oxidative stress in rat liver microsomes. Br J Nutr. 2002 Jul;88(1):57-65.

Chapter 17: Will The Diets Every Stop & Chapter 18: Oh Yeah, Working Out

Dashti HM, Mathew TC, Khadada M, Al-Mousawi M, Talib H, Asfar SK, Behbahani AI, Al-Zaid NS. Beneficial effects of ketogenic diet in obese diabetic subjects. Mol Cell Biochem. 2007 Aug;302(1-2):249-56. Epub 2007 Apr 20.

Romijn, J. A. Regulation of endogenous fat and carbohydrate metabolism in relation to exercise intensity and duration. *American Journal of Physiology* 265 (1993): E380-E380.

G. Brooks, J. Mercier. Balance of carbohydrate and lipid utilization during exercise: the crossover concept. *Journal of Applied Physiology* 76 (1994): 2253-2253.

Barnett C, Carey M, Proietto J, Cerin E, Febbraio MA, Jenkins D. Muscle metabolism during sprint exercise in man: influence of sprint training. J Sci Med Sport. 2004;7:314–322

Rennie MJ, Edwards RH, Krywawych S, Davies CT, Halliday D, Waterlow JC, Millward DJ. Effect of exercise on protein turnover in man. Clin Sci (Lond). 1981 Nov;61(5):627-39

J. A. Romijn, E. F. Coyle , L. S. Sidossis, J. Rosenblatt, R. R. Wolfe. Substrate metabolism during different exercise intensities in endurance-trained women. Journal of Applied Physiology May 2000 Vol. 88no. 5, 1707-1714

D. Pascoe, L. Gladden. Muscle Glycogen Resynthesis after Short Term, High Intensity Exercise and Resistance Exercise Sports Medicine February 1996, Volume 21, Issue 2, pp 98-118

Lillioja S, Bogardus C, Mott DM, Kennedy AL, Knowler WC, Howard BV. Relationship between insulin-mediated glucose disposal and lipid metabolism in man. J Clin Invest. 1985 Apr;75(4):1106-15.

Paul A, Robert E. Johnson. Disclosure by dietary modification of an exercise-induced protein catabolism in man. *Journal of applied physiology* 31.2 (1971): 185-190

Andersen LL, Tufekovic G, Zebis MK, Crameri RM, Verlaan G, Kjaer M, Suetta C, Magnusson P, Aagaard P. The effect of resistance training combined with timed ingestion of protein on muscle fiber size and muscle strength. Metabolism. 2005 Feb;54(2):151-6.

Gibala M. Molecular responses to high-intensity interval exercise. Appl Physiol Nutr Metab. 2009 Jun;34(3):428-32. doi: 10.1139/H09-046.

W. Kraemer,N. Ratamess. Hormonal Responses and Adaptations to Resistance Exercise and Training Sports Medicine. April 2005, Volume 35, Issue 4, pp 339-361

Varrik E[1], Viru A, Oöpik V, Viru M. Exercise-induced catabolic responses in various muscle fibres. Can J Sport Sci. 1992 Jun;17(2):125-8.

Robergs RA, Ghiasvand F, Parker D. Biochemistry of exercise-induced metabolic acidosis. Am J Physiol Regul Integr Comp Physiol. 2004 Sep;287(3):R502-16.

Chapter 19: Case Studies & FAQs

Fallingborg J. Intraluminal pH of the human gastrointestinal tract. *Dan Med Bull.* 1999 Jun;46(3):183-96.

Fallingborg J, Christensen LA, Ingeman-Nielsen M, Jacobsen BA, Abildgaard K, Rasmussen HH, Rasmussen SN. Measurement of gastrointestinal pH and regional transit times in normal children. *J Pediatr Gastroenterol Nutr.* 1990 Aug;11(2):211-4.

Kelly G. Hydrochloric Acid: Physiological Functions and Clinical Implications Alternative Medicine Review. Volume 2, Number 2. 1997, p.117

Davies RE, Roughton FJW. Hydrochloric acid production by isolated gastric mucosa *Biochem J.* 1948; 42(4): 609–621.

Zollner G, Trauner M. Mechanisms of cholestasis. *Clin Liver Dis.* 2008 Feb;12(1):1-26, vii.

Pratt DS. Cholestasis and cholestatic syndromes. *Curr Opin Gastroenterol.* 2005 May;21(3):270-4.

Alrefai WA, Gill RK. Bile acid transporters: structure, function, regulation and pathophysiological implications. *Pharm Res.* 2007 Oct;24(10):1803-23.

Kelly G. Hydrochloric Acid: Physiological Functions and Clinical Implications Alternative Medicine Review. Volume 2, Number 2. 1997, p.117

Davies RE, Roughton FJW. Hydrochloric acid production by isolated gastric mucosa *Biochem J*. 1948; 42(4): 609–621.

Pratt DS. Cholestasis and cholestatic syndromes. *Curr Opin Gastroenterol*. 2005 May;21(3):270-4

That's it. Close the book now.

Printed in Great Britain
by Amazon

49933515R00245